Plate I. *Members of the West Kent Group carrying out a field survey on the line of Ringway 3*

EXCAVATIONS IN WEST KENT
1960-1970

The Discovery and Excavation of Prehistoric, Roman, Saxon and Medieval Sites,
mainly in the Bromley area and in the Darent Valley

BY

BRIAN PHILP

SECOND RESEARCH REPORT IN THE KENT SERIES

Published on behalf of the
West Kent Border Archaeological Group
by the
Kent Archaeological Rescue Unit
CIB Headquarters, Dover Castle, Kent

1973
(Copyright Reserved)

Dedicated to

MRS. N. M. ROBERTS

and the late

ALAN CHRISTOPHER JONES

An octogenarian and a young archaeologist whose hard work, enthusiasm, loyalty and goodwill provide a shining example to part-time and full-time archaeologists of all ages.

The Unit is greatly indebted to the
Department of the Environment
for a substantial grant towards the cost of publication.

Printed in Great Britain by Headley Brothers Ltd 109 Kingsway London WC2B 6PX and Ashford Kent

CONTENTS

LIST OF FIGURES

LIST OF PLATES

FOREWORD

In the last thirty years the whole pattern of archaeological excavation has undergone a radical change. Just as the building of the railways over a century ago led to the discovery of many archaeological sites, so the commercial excavations for new buildings, services, pipelines and deep ploughing since the last war have given tremendous opportunities for new discoveries about the distant past of our land. The nineteenth century finds stimulated the formation of our County archaeological societies and many of these have given a century of wonderful amateur service to local archaeology. The pace of modern excavation, however, is often far too swift for the personalities and resources of many older societies and a new type of organisation consisting mostly of young, mobile and highly trained enthusiasts has come into being as a direct response to the new requirements. No better example of such a dedicated group can be found than the West Kent Border Archaeological Group and it is a very great pleasure and privilege to welcome this publication of thirty sites which they have excavated during eleven years.

The particular value of the work of a group of this kind lies not only in its organisation and ability to provide groups of trained excavators to examine any of the sites which come to light unexpectedly during commerical excavations but also, by concentrating in a definite area, they are able to give an overall picture of the pattern of settlement of the whole of the unrecorded past. One of the rather surprising results of the exploitation of our countryside is to find that the pattern of archaeological sites is astonishingly dense. Many more remains of our past lie buried beneath the soil than seemed possible a few years ago and the sheer size of the problem of their proper record and elucidation would intimidate any but the most enthusiastic, but careful archaeologists.

This volume illustrates admirably the role of the responsible, dedicated amateur when faced with the archaeological problems of the 1960's. Without adequate publication all excavation is simply destruction. This publication, with its promise of more to come, ensures that all the hard work of the members of this Group has not been wasted but has contributed in a unique way to our knowledge of the past history of the County of Kent. As far as this County is concerned there has never before been a comparable single publication which has shed so much new light on its remote past and provided so much basic data for further evaluation by future generations of archaeologists.

No praise could be too high for this splendid and skilful group of people. They have met fully the challenge of the new situation in local archaeology and we of the older generation of archaeologists are proud to welcome this record of their undertakings and to express our admiration for their enthusiasm and capacity for real hard work. Our generation could not have met such a challenge, but they have and all who love the past must indeed be grateful.

NORMAN COOK
RONALD JESSUP

June, 1973

INTRODUCTION

This Report deals with most of the excavations by the West Kent Border Archaeological Group from 1960 until 1970. It covers work on 30 sites, 26 of which were actually discovered by the Group, the majority in West Kent and just three across the border in East Surrey (Figs. 1 and 2). Although this work has substantially increased the number of known sites in the area and radically modified local settlement-patterns no attempt is made here to comment on the wider implications as this forms part of another study. The work does, however, demonstrate the potential of similar areas in South-East England.

THE WEST KENT BORDER ARCHAEOLOGICAL GROUP

The Group was formed by the writer early in 1960 specifically to undertake archaeological work in the Bromley-Westerham area of the West Kent Border. A policy, then formulated and still pursued, includes:

1. Listing and plotting on large-scale maps all known archaeological sites and finds in the area.
2. Surveys of farmland, woodland and any other available areas in an attempt to locate new sites (Plate I).
3. Excavation of all sites threatened with destruction. These sites to be given first priority.
4. Limited excavation of suspected sites to determine their nature, extent and importance.
5. Training in excavation methods and techniques to create a skilled team of excavators for rescue-work in any part of Kent and sometimes beyond.
6. Promotion of archaeology in the Bromley area and where possible throughout the County of Kent.

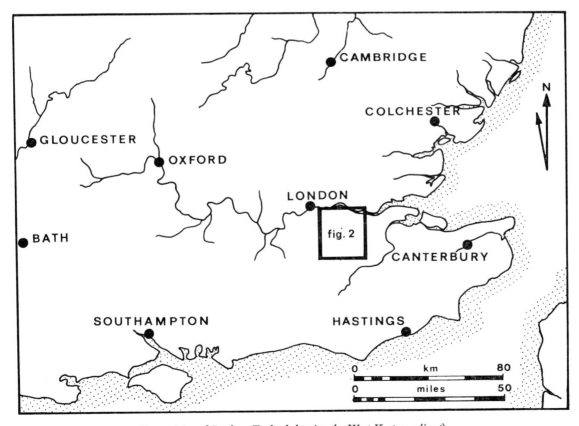

Fig. 1. *Map of Southern England showing the West Kent area (inset).*

I

Local people soon joined the Group and membership, always restricted to those *able to take an active part in archaeological field-work*, remained at a steady 20–30. At first there was no formal membership and the Group only began its regular monthly meetings in 1962. It joined the Council for Kentish Archaeology (then K.A.R.G.C.) in 1964 as a founder-member and has taken an energetic part in all its activities ever since. The Group has also made regular contributions to the *Kent Archaeological Review* and to *Archaeologia Cantiana*. A major advance was the purchase in 1967 of a substantial wooden building which the Group erected in Bromley. This building has been in continual use during the evenings as a work-centre for the processing of finds and for the preparation of reports.

A programme of winter lectures specifically for the public was started in 1967 and is regularly over-subscribed. Another milestone was when the Group launched the Bromley Training School in January, 1968, in conjunction with the Bromley and Beckenham Adult Education Centres, at Lower Warbank, Keston (Plate II). This was the first training-school of its type in Kent and in that and in each subsequent year more than 60 students, of widely differing ages and professions, have taken part. As a direct result membership of the Group has increased and the scope of rescue-work and surveys greatly expanded. In addition the Lower Warbank site provides an ideal setting for annual open-days to which very large numbers of visitors have been attracted and catered for in different ways.

Apart from a Council for British Archaeology grant of £120, made retrospectively towards the cost of the work-centre, the Group has very largely financed its own activities. Subscriptions have always remained nominal and the main sources of income have been jumble-sales, sale of publications and open-days at Keston. In 1970 the Group funds stood at about £450.

The first excavation attempted by the Group was on Hayes Common, the most difficult site in the area, where many enigmatic features had baffled local antiquarians for more than 100 years. Seven years' (1960–66) hard labour during the summer months on this comparatively barren site proved too stiff a test for many would-be members, but it resulted in the discovery of a Bronze Age farmstead and provided some vital training. Other extensive work resulted in the discovery of a Roman bath-building and a Neolithic site, near Baston Manor (1964); in the re-excavation and subsequent consolidation of the Roman tombs at Keston (1967) and the excavation of the Iron Age, Roman and Saxon sites at Lower Warbank, Keston (1968–70) threatened with eventual destruction. The work at Keston will be the subject of a separate report.

Throughout the period covered by this Report the Group undertook detailed field-surveys of selected areas, mostly in the winter months. Hundreds of acres of farmland and woodland were examined and dozens of surface-indications investigated. Trial-holes excavated on suspected sites exceeded 900, of which less than 100 produced archaeological evidence. This work did, however, produce a crop of new sites, several of which are covered by this Report.

First priority was always given to emergency excavations, both local and further afield. Indeed of the 30 sites reported here 26 were actually being destroyed or were in areas threatened with destruction. Of these 16 were located during pipe-line operations (Plate IIIa) by the South Eastern Gas Board, whose ready co-operation is grate-fully acknowledged. 'Operation Gaspipe' produced a total of seven new sites in 1965; 'Operation Gaspipe West' produced three new sites in 1966; 'Operation Gaspipe East' revealed six new sites in 1969 whilst 'Operation Gaspipe South' in 1970 produced none! The Group also undertook the major rescue-excavation of the Saxon cemetery at Polhill (1964 and 1967) and of the Darenth Roman villa (1969), both with the backing of the C.K.A. emergency-scheme.

In addition to these operations the Group was able to assist, sometimes very considerably, with rescue-excavations at Reculver (1963 and 1966); at Springhead (1963); in the City of London (1964 and 1968); at Faversham (1965 and 1967); at Weston Wood, Surrey (1966); at Radfield (1968) and at Dover (1970). Indeed as a direct result of all this work, heavily subsidised by a few individuals, the full-time CIB (Kent) Archaeological Rescue Unit was formed at the end of 1971. Operating from its Government-provided headquarters at Dover Castle its strength mainly depends upon members of the Reculver and West Kent groups.

In the eleven years covered by this Report more than 300 people have worked with the Group at different times. Of these some deserve special mention for their hard and sustained efforts over many years. In the first place the Group was fortunate in having two hard-working secretaries, Miss Elizabeth Warman (now Mrs. Healey) for 1961–5 and Miss Edna Mynott (now Mrs. Philp) for 1965–70. Miss Mynott, Mr. Denis Broadfoot, Mr. Gerald Clewley and Mr. John Willson all made considerable personal contributions to the work as supervisors over long periods.

Of past members Mrs. Stella Brandham, Mrs. Dorothy Witherspoon and Mrs. Muriel Woolven; Misses Pamela George, Marianne Last, Glynis Price, Anne McGarry, Edwina Philpot, Hilary Pugh, Jennifer Teulon, Elizabeth Warman and Janet Weeks; and Messrs. Andrew Appleby, David Bartlett, Bernard Brandham, Gerald Cramp, Ralph Ellis, Nigel Field, Cedric Hart, John Horne, the late Christopher Jones, Michael Kellaway, John Parsons, Henry Robinson, John Swale, Christopher Terry and David Witherspoon all worked for extended periods and are gratefully thanked.

Of present members Mrs. Majorie Broadfoot, Mrs. Thelma Dutton and Mrs. Joy Saynor; Miss Audrey Button; Messrs. Denis Broadfoot, David and Peter Bolton, Peter Couldrey, Ronald Fendt, Richard Garnett, Derek Garrod, Ray Gierth, Maurice Godfrey, Peter Grant, John Halligan, Colin Martin, Edward Tayler and Richard Tedbury continue the excellent working tradition developed over the years.

THIS REPORT

This Report follows the pattern of *Excavations at Faversham 1965* produced by the C.K.A. as its first Research Report in 1968. As with that report footnotes have been largely eliminated and references, numbered progressively throughout the text, are placed at the back.

As it is hoped that the Report will form a useful basis for future archaeological work in West Kent the sites have been discussed in chronological order ranging from the Neolithic to the 17th century. The finds, too, have been numbered progressively through the text (Nos. 1–629) so as to eliminate recurring numbers and thus avoid confusion. More particularly this arrangement should provide a numbered catalogue of dated local material to facilitate reference and study in future years. In any case the system follows the accepted norm save for the Saxon material from Polhill, where the grave-goods are arranged in types rather than by graves. It is hoped that even the most pedantic of specialists will forgive this variation.

For reasons of cost, only the major sites have accompanying location-maps and generally these are set onto the large-scale site-plans. With every site, however, details of location in general terms, the N.G.R., the Ordnance Survey parcel number and physical measurements have been given. Measurements in the text are normally in yards, feet and inches, as taken in the field, but all plans and sections have both Imperial and metric scales. Some of the specialist reports give dimensions in millimetres.

As regards the work on this Report the author has spent more than 2,500 hours in its preparation, almost double that for the Faversham Report. The text has been typed by Mrs. E. Philp and Miss W. Dolphin and checked by Miss A. Button and Mr. D. Broadfoot. Most of the plans, sections and drawings have been prepared at the Group's work-centre at Bromley by members of the Group of whom Mrs. J. Lock, Miss A. Button and Miss P. George; Mr. P. Couldrey, Mr. G. Clewley, Mr. R. Gierth, Mr. M. Godfrey, Mr. R. Tedbury and Mr. T. Woodman deserve a special word of thanks for their efforts in this respect. So, too, do Mrs. P. Crozier and Mrs. J. Newbery for their constant help in the final stages of the Report. Finally, Mr. M. Godfrey has very kindly undertaken extensive survey-work on several of the larger sites so that the site-plans are complete.

The work of particular draughtsmen, illustrators and specialists is acknowledged in the text, but of the latter special thanks are due to : Dr. I. Smith for her report on the prehistoric pottery from Baston Manor; to Mrs. E. Healey for her help with the text on Hayes Common and also the report on the finds; to Mrs. S. C. Hawkes for her report on the Polhill material and its implications and to Mr. D. N. Broadfoot for his report on much of the flint. Mr. G. B. Clewley kindly provided the preliminary descriptions of much of the Romano-British pottery which was sorted and classified into basic types by Mrs. P. Crozier and Mrs. J. Newbery. The terms used by the author in the study of the Romano-British pottery are those coined locally, in the absence of a comprehensive study, to provide rough guide-lines for future local research.

Finally, it is hoped that this Report will stand as a tribute to the many part-time archaeologists of the West Kent Border Archaeological Group in return for their hard work, undertaken often in difficult and even dangerous conditions, always with good humour and great enthusiasm.

BRIAN PHILP,
West Wickham.
1st May, 1973.

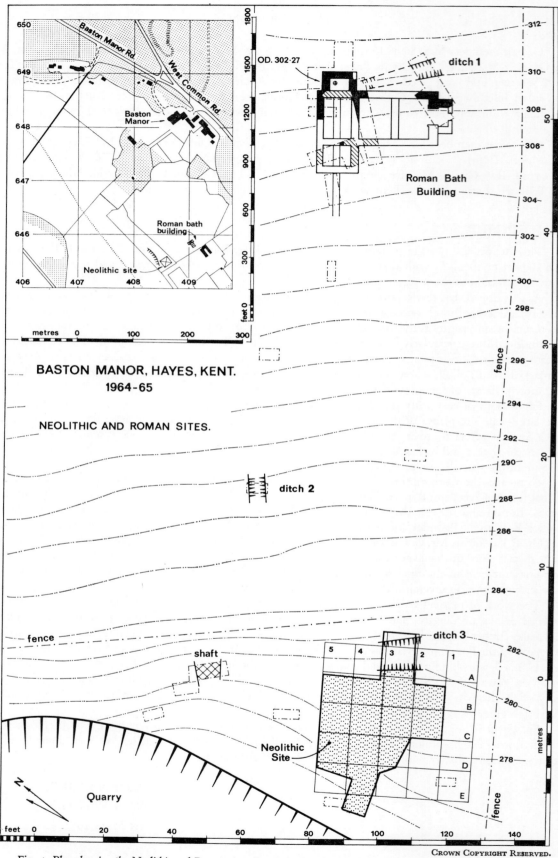

BASTON MANOR, HAYES, KENT.
1964-65

NEOLITHIC AND ROMAN SITES.

Fig. 4. *Plan showing the Neolithic and Roman sites, Baston Manor, Hayes (Sites 1 and 13) with location map (inset)*

SITE 1. A Neolithic Site near Baston Manor, Hayes, Kent

This site (N.G.R. TQ.4088.6456) lies at the southern limit of the parish of Hayes, Kent, roughly a mile south of the parish church (Fig. 4). It occupies part of the eastern end of a narrow strip of woodland (O.S. parcel 8159) halfway up the north-east slope of a wide valley. The centre of the site is about 180 ft. south-west of the Roman bath-building near Baston Manor (Site 13) and lies adjacent to Keston Court Riding School, but in 1964 it formed part of Nash Farm. It lies on brickearth over Upper Chalk and the elevation is about 280 ft. O.D.

The site was discovered (Refs. 1 and 2) on 14th July, 1964 by the Group whilst trial-trenching in search of the Roman building reported in 1854 as being south of Baston Manor. The very first trial-hole in this wood produced the only polished axe (No. 49) from the site, a large Mortlake bowl (No. 6) and several flint flakes. A limited programme of work was undertaken from September, 1964 until February, 1966 with no attempt being made at total excavation. A clearing was made in the wood and a nine-foot grid laid out over a small area. Eight squares were completely excavated, nine more partially excavated and the work concluded with a series of outlying trial-holes. The site was then backfilled and restored. This work produced a large quantity of pottery and flint and established the presence of an important Neolithic occupation site (Plate IIIb). Two Neolithic polished, greenstone axes of Cornish origin are recorded from the next parish of Keston having been found at different times in the past hundred years. The find-spot of one (Ref. 3) is not known, but the other was found in 1952 only about 700 yards south of the Baston site (Ref. 4).

Thanks are due to the then owner of Nash Farm, Mr. P. H. Legge, for kindly consenting to the excavation on his land and to the farm-manager, Mr. P. Hewings, for his interest and encouragement. Of Group members working on the site special mention must be made of Mrs. M. Broadfoot, Misses J. Buckle, M. Last, E. Mynott (now Mrs. Philp), G. Price and E. Warman (now Mrs. Healey); and Messrs. A. Appleby, D. Bartlett, D. Broadfoot, G. Clewley, R. Critchfield, N. Field, R. Gierth, C. Hart, J. Horne, C. Jones and J. Swale for their sustained efforts. Mr. D. Broadfoot supervised the work during January and February, 1965 when most of the team was helping with the rescue-excavations at Faversham Abbey. Dr. I. F. Smith has very kindly supplied a detailed report on the prehistoric pottery and the corresponding drawings, whilst Mr. D. N. Broadfoot has written the report on the flint. Miss R. Chatters and Mrs. M. Luyke-Roskott have kindly drawn the flint and Mr. R. Tedbury the site-plan.

THE EXCAVATION (Fig. 5)

The area excavated within the gridded area was about 1,100 sq. ft. Apart from root and animal disturbance the soil sequence was virtually constant across the whole site, in descending order, as follows:

Layer 1. 7 in. of black sandy loam.
Layer 2. 12 in. of light-brown sandy loam and pebbles.
Layer 3. 5 in. of light-brown sandy loam.
Layer 4. 10 in. of yellow-brown sandy loam.

The thin topsoil layer contained very few finds of any date. The underlying pebble layer, containing more than 120 pieces of Roman tile and pottery and some flint, represents hillwash from the pebble-beds higher up the slope. The third and fourth layers, which produced the great bulk of the Neolithic material (Plate IIIb), appear to represent a mixture of fine silt and disturbed subsoil. The undisturbed natural brickearth was generally encountered at a depth of nearly 3 ft. From this sequence it is clear that the bulk of the pebble hillwash swept across the site in Roman or later times bringing with it Roman debris from the site above. This may have been caused by ploughing or by severe erosion. Clearly several thousand tons of soil have moved down the hillside since about A.D. 100 and effectively buried the Neolithic site under about 1 ft. 6 in. of soil.

1 Numbers prefixed by the letters Ref. in round brackets relate to references given on page 226. Numbers prefixed by the letters No. or Nos., often in round brackets, refer to drawings of individual finds arranged in numerical order throughout the Report.

The two primary layers contained pottery, flint and 'pot-boilers'. The following table lists these under the squares in which they were found.

Square	Potsherds	Pot-boilers	Flint	Totals
A3	4	5	116	125
B2	3	16	44	63
B3	18	114	135	267
B4	19	532	149	700
B5	29	844	138	1,011
C2	—	38	97	135
C3	59	362	248	669
C4	27	414	101	542
C5	22	258	111	391
C6	1	3	31	35
C7	—	32	14	46
D3	2	54	74	130
D4	22	285	155	462
D5	5	152	240	397
E4	13	24	219	256
E5	—	6	48	54
F4	1	57	142	200
Misc.	—	—	147	147
Totals	225	3,196	2,209	5,630

TABLE A.
Distribution of material from the Neolithic site near Baston Manor

From this table it is clear that the central area was densely covered with material and that the concentration falls off in all directions. It also gives a density of five objects per sq. ft. based on the area excavated. The flint tools and waste, the pottery and the 'pot-boilers' were always found in close association with each other, often touching, so that it is difficult to escape the conclusion that they all formed part of a single deposit. A particularly dense area of 'pot-boilers' in square B5 may mark the position of a small hearth. A study of the pottery (see below) suggests a maximum date-range of about 2700–1800 B.C., though it seems likely that the site was actually occupied within one or two centuries of 2000 B.C. (see discussion).

Several features were also encountered during the excavations, but none of these could positively be identified as Neolithic. A broad, shallow ditch was found in square A3 and this contained Romano-British pottery in its primary filling (Site 13, Ditch 3). A small pit, about 3 ft. in diameter, with vertical sides and a cupped base, was found overlapping squares C4 and D4. It was cut about 3 ft. into the natural brickearth and contained no finds. Owing to the presence of a large deep-rooted tree, which had to be felled, it was not possible to determine whether this feature was sealed by the primary layer or by the hillwash.

Two more ditches and a short gulley were also found. The ditch in square D5 was V-shaped in section, about 6 ft. wide at the top and about 5 ft. deep with a flat base about 3 ft. wide. The ditch in square E4 was U-shaped in section, 3 ft. wide and about 2 ft. deep. The gulley in squares D4 and E4 appeared to be about 12 ft. long, 2 ft. 9 in. wide and about 1 ft. 3 in. deep being U-shaped in section. The two ditches and the gulley all contained a fill of light-brown loam in which were several worked flints. Each appeared to be overlaid by the primary layers and fragments of Neolithic pottery were actually found above each feature. Considered with the lack of Romano-British material from the respective fillings it is tempting to suggest that all these features were dug in Neolithic times. It is, however, important to remember that very large quantities of soil have washed across this site and that there is considerable disturbance by large roots. It is equally possible that these three features and

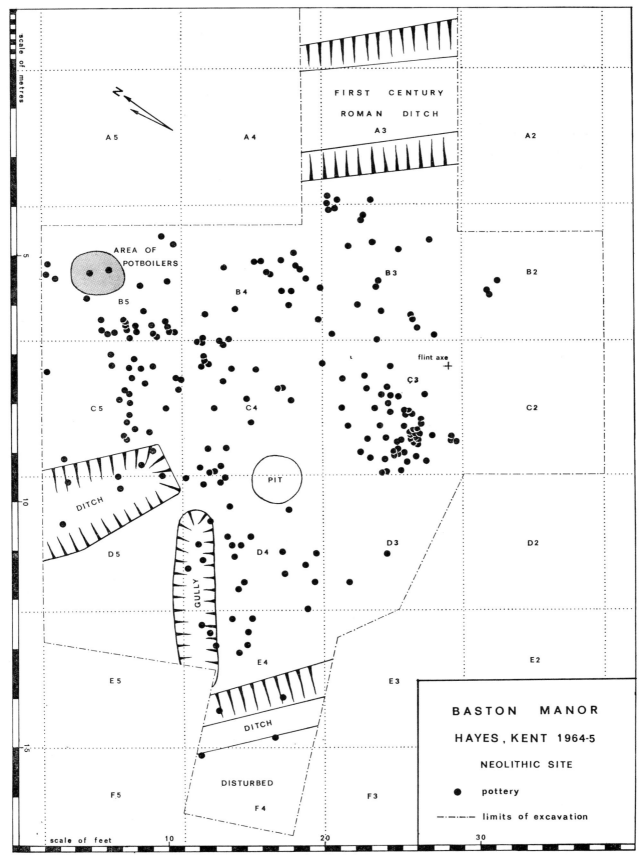

Fig. 5. *Detailed plan showing Neolithic site, Baston Manor, Hayes (Site 1).*

the small pit were all dug in Roman, or later, times before the main bulk of the pebble-hillwash arrived and that the Neolithic material may have been redeposited.

        About 50 ft. north-west of the centre of the main Neolithic area was a shaft, 8 ft. in diameter and 22 ft. deep. This had been cut down into the underlying chalk with almost vertical sides and a roughly flat base. The upper 14 ft. 6 in. of its filling consisted of brown loam and pebble, below which there was only chalk rubble. Several Roman potsherds and tile fragments were found in the upper 8 ft. of the shaft, including a mortarium stamped with the name of Albinus (No. 244). Initially it was hoped that the shaft would prove to be a Neolithic flint-mine, but as the excavation progressed large flints were found protruding from the sides and clearly no attempt had been made to quarry them. The total absence of Neolithic material in the filling of the shaft, so close to a large quantity of Neolithic domestic rubbish, suggests that the shaft was not open in Neolithic times. Even the Roman material may have washed into the shaft with the loam and pebble at any time after the 1st century A.D. and on balance it seems likely that it was no more than a chalk-well dug in post-medieval times. Chalk blocks were, however, used in the construction of the Roman bath-building and it is just possible that the shaft was a Roman quarry. If so, it is remarkable that no Romano-British material was found in the primary filling.

        A trial-hole dug in the adjacent Riding School, about 20 ft. east of square B2 produced about 40 worked flints, a fine leaf-shaped arrowhead and a minute sherd of pottery. Another trial-hole in the Riding School, about 150 ft. east of the main area produced another 45 flints. Those trial-holes dug to the north and west of the site produced almost nothing and it seems from this evidence that the site extends only to the east. Almost immediately to the west of the main area the slope of the hill rapidly increases. This is due to a large chalk quarry, now largely silted and overgrown. A single trial-hole at the bottom of this revealed about 12 ft. 6 in. of filling over a hard chalk base, but no Roman or Neolithic material. On balance it seems likely that this quarry was dug sometime between the 16th and 18th centuries.

DISCUSSION

        It is clear that the site at Baston Manor represents one of the most important Neolithic sites so far found in Kent. The large amount of domestic rubbish points to an occupation-site and it seems likely that huts existed nearby, though no trace of these was found in the small area examined. Large numbers of 'pot-boilers' (fire-cracked flints) suggest the presence of hearths.

        Of the 225 potsherds recovered it has been possible to identify parts of 50 different vessels. The majority of these are Late Neolithic types (Mortlake, Fengate and Beaker wares) though a few typologically earlier styles (Undecorated? Neolithic and Ebbsfleet wares) are present.

        Of the 2,209 flints recovered 93 (4%) can be identified as implements or hammer-stones, the remaining 2,116 (96%) is waste. This compares with 10% and 90%, respectively, at Hurst Fen and 3% and 97%, respectively, at Durrington Walls. The density is about 16 per sq. yd. as against 40 per sq. yd. at Hurst Fen. It is clear that the Baston assemblage represents a flint industry of unknown extent. The flint was probably obtained from the nearby Upper Chalk which outcrops within a few yards of the site.

        The site lies on a small area of brickearth which is light and well-drained. Less than 180 ft. up the slope are deposits of thick clay forming the Thanet Beds and these are in turn capped by the Woolwich and Blackheath pebble-beds above. Springs tend to form at the junction of the clay and pebble and indeed one was found during the excavation of the Roman bath-building. The Neolithic site may well have been chosen with regard to both this spring and the close proximity of the flint-bearing chalk.

        As regards dating the polished axe, the leaf-shaped arrow-head and the Mortlake and Fengate wares, are all Late Neolithic in character. The collection does, however, include several vessels which are typologically several centuries apart from the Fengate and Mortlake wares. Dr. Smith has shown that the few Ebbsfleet sherds are similar to those which elsewhere have a radiocarbon date of about 2700 B.C. and that the Beaker sherds are similar to those which elsewhere have a radiocarbon date of about 1800 B.C.

        The close association of all the sherds at Baston, however, tends to argue against the deposit forming over a period of 800, or more, years. Just how one small site might be occupied (continuously or not) over such a period and the domestic pottery be discarded in the same small area is very difficult to explain. Frankly, the circum-stantial evidence of the finds suggests a much shorter occupation, perhaps by the same community, for a period of no more than about 50 years. It is tempting to ignore the circumstantial evidence, but considering the somewhat fluid state of our knowledge of such early pottery it may be wiser to regard it as the paramount consideration. If the site was only occupied for a short span of time then the bulk of the pottery suggests a date within one or two centuries of 2000 B.C.

The site still has considerable potential in that it is covered by a thick layer of hillwash and that the greater part to the east is as yet still unexplored. On no account should this site be developed without adequate facilities for proper archaeological investigation and indeed worthwhile results will only be achieved by planned, large-scale work and the use of mechanical aids.

The chance discovery of this site in a region not noted for its prehistoric sites does, perhaps, illustrate the potential of the area and of West Kent. It seems likely that dozens of Neolithic occupation-sites await discovery in West Kent alone and that the total number for the whole County should be calculated in hundreds. That barely twenty such sites are at present known (Ref. 5), is an indication of the possible potential and a pointer to those carrying out rescue-work in the County.

THE FINDS

(1) THE PREHISTORIC POTTERY (Figs. 6 and 7)

By Dr. I. F. Smith

Amongst some 225 sherds recovered it has been possible to recognise parts of 50 different vessels, mostly Late Neolithic types (Mortlake, Fengate and beaker wares), with a few examples of typologically earlier styles (Undecorated? Neolithic and Ebbsfleet wares). The assemblage forms a notable addition to the Neolithic pottery of Kent, where Fengate ware in particular has not been recorded hitherto.

The 50 vessels classified and described individually below have been numbered serially within each class. The 21 that are illustrated (Nos. 1–21) are marked by the appropriate number on the left-hand side of the text.

Most of the pottery of all classes exhibits some degree of weathering and the state of preservation of individual fragments seems to be entirely fortuitous, since the surviving parts of a single vessel may vary in condition from fresh and virtually unaltered to severely abraded. Some 40 featureless fragments and crumbs are too weathered to permit classification.

The term 'grog', used in the descriptions below, refers specifically to particles of previously fired clay; these may derive from crushed pot fragments or from clay specially prepared for use as filler.

Description and Catalogue of the Pottery

UNDECORATED? NEOLITHIC (UN)

No. 1. UN-1. Three sherds from rim and body. Black, leathery texture, full of small irregular cavities left by solution of a calcareous or organic filler (corky) (from D5-5).

No. 2. UN-2. Two sherds from rim and body. Pale, red surfaces, grey core. Abundant particles of flint, mostly under 1 mm.; hard, with traces of semi-burnish (from C3-3).
UN-3. Body sherd; black; hard; lacking visible inclusions. Thin wall and curvature suggest a cup.

EBBSFLEET (E)

No. 3. E1. Two sherds from rim, neck and body; buff surfaces, grey core; moderate amount of flint, up to 2 mm.; hard, well finished, but flints protrude. On rim, incised lattice; inside rim and in shoulder zone, rows of jabs made with pointed implement, each set surmounted by row of less distinct impressions; on body, rows of impressions made by solid implement of irregular shape (from B3-4).

EBBSFLEET OR MORTLAKE (E/M)

No. 4. E/M1. Shoulder sherd; ware as E1 but flints somewhat coarser and texture more laminated. Above and below shoulder, rows of indistinct semicircular impressions made with implement (from B4-4).
E/M2. Eight sherds from body and possibly shoulder; brown exterior, dark interior and core; abundant flints up to 4 mm.; hard, gritty. Decorated with rows of complex impressions of 'bird-bone' type.
E/M3. Three small body sherds; ware as E/M2, but less gritty. Indistinct impressions of 'bird-bone' type.

MORTLAKE (M)

No. 5.　M1. Ten sherds from rim, neck and body; surfaces buff to brown with grey tones; sand, sparse flint up to 7 mm. and grog; laminated in section; fairly well finished. Ring-joint visible in all rim sherds. Across rim and in neck, short twisted cord impressions; on body, ridges pinched up and showing concomitant fingernail impressions (from B5-4 and C4-4).

No. 6.　M2. Thirteen sherds from rim, neck, body and possibly base; surfaces buff with orange tinge, black core; moderate amount of flint, up to 5 mm., and some grog; laminated in section; surfaces smoothed but flints protrude. Three ring-joints visible at rim, neck and shoulder. Inside rim, incised lattice; on exterior, rim to shoulder, herring-bone designs executed with plain stamps of various sizes; on upper body, pinched ribs with incidental fingernail impressions; plain zone below. Some thick (15 mm.) undecorated fragments may belong to base (from C3-4, C4-4 and C5-4).

　　　　M3. Sherd from lower part of body, near rounded base; exterior yellow with red tinge, interior and core dark; coarse sand, sparse flint and abundant dark grog; hard, compact ware. Pinched-up ribs above plain area where profile thickens towards base.

　　　　M4. Five body sherds; surfaces buff with orange tinge, core dark; sparse flint. All exhibit ridges as in M1–M3.

　　　　M5. Two body sherds; exterior buff with orange tinge, interior and core dark; abundant fine flint. Vague indications of ridges.

　　　　M6. Body sherd; surfaces buff with orange tinge, core grey; flint and soft dark inclusions, possibly grog. Abraded? 'bird-bone' impressions.

FENGATE (F)

No. 7.　F1. Four collar and body sherds; exterior dark with reddish patches, interior red, core grey; sparse angular flint (? and quartz), up to 7 mm., a few rounded quartz pebbles, up to 2 mm., pellets of haematite, grog, fragments of calcined bone; laminated in section, hard, well finished. On collar, twisted cord in herring-bone; in neck, deep pits made with finger; on body, widely spaced vertical fingernail impressions; on inner rim bevel, oval impressions probably made with tip of fingernail; row of larger fingernail marks inside base of collar (from E4-5).

No. 8.　F2. Eleven collar and body sherds; collar, neck and interior dark, exterior reddish brown below shoulder; sand, flint and grog up to 5 mm.; hard, well finished. Indications of ring-joints. On collar, alternately hatched areas, the lines made by slightly overlapping impressions of fingernail tip; in neck, narrow pits made with cylindrical implement; on body, rows of irregularly shaped fingernail impressions; on rim bevel and inside collar, incised lattice (from D4-3 and C4-3).

No. 9.　F3. Fifteen collar, body and possibly base sherds (upper profile incomplete); exterior patchy, buff to reddish brown, interior dark; angular flints up to 9 mm. and a few small flint pebbles; hard, dense ware, fairly well finished. On collar, alternately hatched areas, made as in F2 but fingernail impressions end-to-end and somewhat broader; in neck, widely spaced pits, probably made with implement; on body, rows of fingernail impressions, jabbed in from left and producing slight rustication; on inner bevel of rim, oblique oval fingernail impressions. A plain sherd, 15 mm. thick, may come from flat base (from C3-4).

No. 10.　F4. Two sherds from collar and neck; exterior black, interior dark brown; abundant angular flint (? and quartz) up to 10 mm., and some grog; hard, leathery texture. Ring-joint at base of collar. On collar, alternately hatched areas, one triangular, executed as on F2 in neck, pits made with finger; on inner rim bevel, herring-bone made with tip of fingernail (from C4-4).

No. 11.　F5. Six sherds from collar, neck and body (none joining); surfaces red, core dark grey; few small flint pebbles and possibly pellets of haematite; a distinctive, soft, homogeneous fabric, perhaps made of brickearth; very well finished. On collar, alternately hatched areas, lines made with fingernail tip, individual impressions tending to be straighter and more widely spaced than in F2–F4, design repeated inside collar; on inner rim bevel, herring-bone made with fingernail; in neck, one large surviving pit made with finger. Body sherds (not illustrated) have paired vertical fingernail impressions (from B4-4).

　　　　F6. Three sherds from collar; now black, with traces of original thin red surface layer; sand and grog; corky through loss of some (?other) inclusions; soft, roughly finished. Incomplete rim profile displays form and decoration identical with F5.

　　　　F7. Fragment from base of collar; surfaces reddish brown, core grey; abundant grog; also somewhat corky; soft. Form and decoration similar to F5–6, but lacks internal ornament.

No. 12.　F8. Seven sherds from collar, neck and body; collar, interior and core dark, exterior below shoulder reddish brown; sand and abundant flint, mostly fine, with few particles up to 7 mm.; hard, laminated in section; fairly well finished, but flints protrude. On collar, vertical and in part, oblique lines made by overlapping impressions of fingernail tip; in neck, narrow cylindrical pits made with implement; on body, widely spaced oblique fingernail impressions; on inner rim bevel oblique nicks made with fingernail (from E4-3 and D4-3).

No. 13.　F9. Two sherds from collar and neck; brown over all with darker patches on collar; abundant angular flint (? and quartz) up to 5 mm., and grog; also corky; hard, fairly well finished. On collar, broad, deep grooves with rounded ends, vertical and oblique; in neck, traces of a pit; on inner rim bevel, small irregular impressions of fingernail tip (from D4-4 and C4-4).

　　　　F10. Sherd from base of collar and part of neck; exterior buff with orange tinge, interior and core grey-brown; grog only; soft, greasy. On collar base, traces of two broad, shallow depressions made with ball of finger.

　　　　F11. Three sherds from upper part of collar; black throughout; sparse flint, up to 4 mm., and grog; hard. On convex collar (profile as F2), deeply incised herring-bone; motif repeated on inner rim bevel.

　　　　F12. Sherd from base of collar; now black, with traces of original thin red surface layer; flint and grog. Faint indications of herring-bone or zigzag motif.

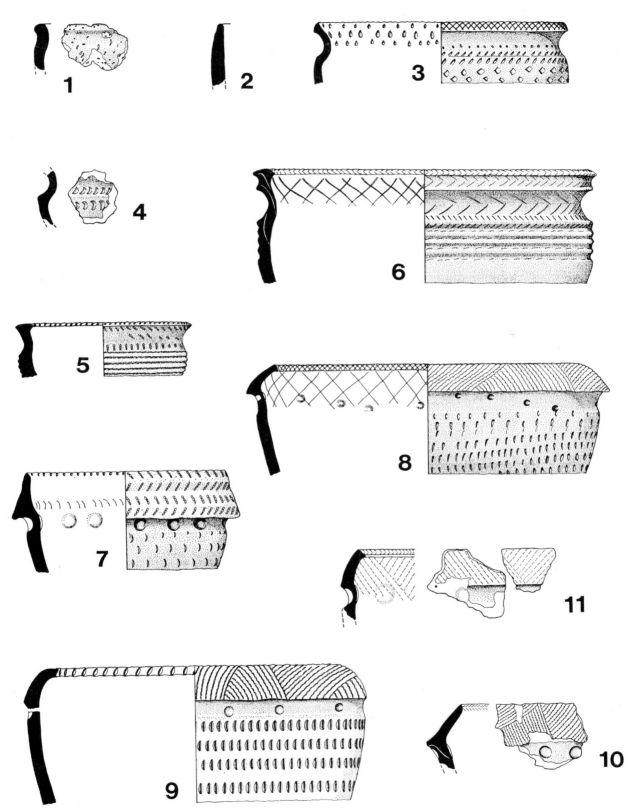

Fig. 6. *Neolithic and Beaker pottery* (⅓), *Baston Manor, Hayes (Site 1).*

F13. Eleven sherds from collar (inner half) and body; surfaces red, core dark brown; no visible inclusions and extremely corky, possibly through loss of shell filler; friable and tending to split. No internal decoration; trace of pit at base of collar; on one body sherd, zones of upright fingernail impressions.

No. 14.   F14. Two joining sherds from neck, shoulder and body; exterior red, interior and core black; grog and a single small flint pebble; brittle, well finished. In neck a pit made with fingertip; over shoulder and on body, herring-bone made with fingernail (from A3-3).

F15. Twelve sherds from neck, body and base (none joining); exterior pale red, interior and core dark; abundant angular flints up to 8 mm.; pellets of haematite, grog; hard, thick ware. In neck, large pits made with finger, closely spaced; on body, neatly executed zones of close-set oblique fingernail impressions aligned from right to left, becoming more diffuse at basal angle. Flat base at least 20 mm. thick.

F16. Two very small sherds, apparently from neck, shoulder and collar or body; exterior and core black, interior brown; angular flints, mostly fine, a few up to 5 mm.; laminated in section, hard, well finished. In neck, trace of shallow pit; other sherd carries two parallel incised lines.

F17. Sherd from slight rounded shoulder; exterior reddish brown, interior red, core grey; sparse coarse sand and angular flints up to 8 mm.; hard, fairly well finished, but flints protrude. Twisted cord impressions, irregularly spaced, both vertical and oblique, over shoulder.

F18. Seven body sherds, some large; exterior light brown with pink tinge and dark patches, interior and core black; angular flints; hard, rough ware. Undecorated; single or grouped parallel striations probably represent summary treatment with pebble. Curvature suggests vessel of sub-conical form with narrow base.

F19. Six sherds from body and base; exterior orange with traces of thin dark red surface layer, interior black with red patches, core black to grey; corky, but also a few particles of flint and some haematite pellets; soft, heavy ware. One body sherd retains traces of a zone of fingernail impressions; the fragment of flat base is 15 mm. thick.

F20-25. Eight body sherds, apparently from six different vessels; exteriors generally reddish; varying amounts of flint. All exhibit traces of fingernail impressions.

No. 15.   F26. Three sherds from lower body and base; exterior dark red, interior brown, core dark; fine sand and grog; also corky; hard, thick ware. On wall, paired fingernail impressions extending nearly to base (from B4-4).

F27. Sherd from basal angle; exterior yellow with traces of original thin red surface layer; core and interior black; corky; laminated in section; greasy. No decoration. Base apparently had protruding foot.

F28. Three sherds, one from thick flat base, the others indeterminate; exterior reddish, interior and core dark brown; may contain grog; soft, homogeneous ware, possibly made of brickearth.

BEAKER (B)

No. 16.   B1. Body sherd; exterior pale red, interior and core dark; sparse grog only; well finished. Incised decoration; irregularly spaced oblique lines divided subsequently into zones by horizontals; a plain zone above (? or below) (from C3-4).

No. 17.   B2. Three sherds from body and base; external half, pale red; internal half, reddish brown; fairly abundant flint, up to 4 mm., coarse sand with pebbles up to 3 mm., dark pellets of uncertain nature, sparse grog; well finished. Decorated body sherd (illustrated) displays zone defined by barbed-wire lines and filled with neat herring-bone executed with a plain oval stamp. Other body sherd and base fragment plain; base has slight protruding foot (from C4-4).

No. 18.   B3. Body sherd; now grey, retaining traces of original red surface layer; sparse flint, up to 2 mm. and grog; well finished. Decorated with irregular paired fingernail impressions; no rustication (from C3-4).

B4. Body sherd; external half pale red, internal half dark grey; sparse flint, under 1 mm., sand, minute angular particles of unidentified dark substance, some grog; well finished. Blurred traces suggest decoration similar to that on B2.

B5. Two body sherds; exterior reddish, interior black; abundant coarse sand and some grog; well finished. Blurred traces of one or two horizontal lines.

B6. Body sherd; pale red surfaces, yellow core; abundant coarse sand and grog; indications of ring-joints. Severely weathered; no surviving decoration.

OTHER FRAGMENTS (OF)

No. 19.   OF1. Body sherd; thin red surface externally over black core and interior; abundant flint, up to 3 mm.; coarse, thick, laminated in section, with flints protruding. Decorated with roughly incised design suggesting lozenges (from C5-4).

No. 20.   OF2. Fragment of dish; refired and now bright red with grey patches; abundant fine sand and some grog; hard. Undecorated. At basal angle part of a perforation (from F4-3).

No. 21.   OF3. Body sherd; now grey, with traces of original red surfaces, core dark; abundant sand and possibly grog; thick, heavy, laminated in section. Ring-joints. An applied band (box-cordon) carries boldly impressed herring-bone (from D5-5).

Comments

The least securely classified fragments are clearly those listed as 'Undecorated? Neolithic'; in view of their restricted numbers and the small size of the surviving pieces, identification must be tentative. The provisional suggestion is made that they belong within the general tradition of plain, round-bottomed bowls in use during the earlier Neolithic in Southern England. The rim forms do not suggest an immediate relationship with the pottery of this class known from East Kent (Refs. 5 and 6), but seem rather to find their nearest analogies in Sussex. UN-2 (No. 2) may be compared with the deep, bag-shaped pots with simple upright rims from the causewayed enclosures at Whitehawk (Ref. 7) and The Trundle (Ref. 8). The cup fragment, UN-3, would also be in place in this context (Ref. 9). UN-1 (No. 1) is less easy to match, but there is some similarity to a few rims from the sites mentioned (Refs. 10 and 11).

The Ebbsfleet bowl, E-1 (No. 3), is typologically indistinguishable from the decorated specimens in the group found in the bed of the Ebbsfleet (Ref. 12), now believed to have been deposited earlier than a block of wood with a conventional radiocarbon date of 2710±150 B.C. (BM-113) (Ref. 13). E/M-1 (No. 4)–E/M-3 cannot be classified with precision since they lack rims and the decoration and flint-filled fabric would be appropriate to either Ebbsfleet or Mortlake ware.

Remarkable features of both the Mortlake and the Fengate pottery from this site are the dominance of ornament executed with fingernails, the relative rarity of cord impressions and the strong preference within each group for one particular decorative motif. Five of the six Mortlake bowls have pinched-up ridges on the body and on M-2 (No. 6) the effect is accentuated by the form of the rim, constructed so as to present two more ridges above the neck. Comparable ridging occurs on Mortlake bowls in the Thames valley: at Weybridge, Surrey (Ref. 14), Iver, Bucks. (Ref. 15), Stanton Harcourt, Oxon. (Ref. 16), and more interestingly, on five vessels associated with other Mortlake ware in Pit II at Heathrow, Middlesex (Ref. 17).

In the Fengate group seven of the twelve collars are ornamented with alternately hatched areas, as F-2 (No. 8), the lines being formed by end-to-end or partly overlapping impressions of the pointed tip of a fingernail. This kind of ornament, often accompanied by nicks or herring-bone designs on the inner rim bevel, is known on Fengate ware from Peterborough (Ref. 18), and Astrop, Northants (Ref. 19), Icklingham, Suffolk (Ref. 20), Cam, Gloucs. (Ref. 21), and the West Kennet Avenue, Avebury, Wilts (Ref. 22). Treatment of necks and bodies is also unusually standardised in the Fengate ware from Baston Manor: a majority, if not all, of the necks have carried a row of pits, and, apart from F-17 and F-18, all the walls have simple fingernail impressions arranged in rows or zones. A slight degree of rustication was produced only on F-3 (No. 9).

The extent to which the later (Mortlake and Fengate) styles of Peterborough ware reflect reaction with intrusive beaker ceramic traditions, in particular with the utility or domestic forms of beaker, was first pointed out by Professor Piggott in his discussion of the Peterborough ware from the West Kennet long barrow (Ref. 23), and the argument has subsequently been elaborated by Dr. D. L. Clarke, who has demonstrated the decisive role of the Barbed-Wire and East Anglian beaker groups in the development of Fengate ware (Ref. 24). Decoration by means of linear finger-nail impressions, as on the Fengate rims in the present assemblage, is but one trait that can be traced to this source and it is therefore especially interesting to find here two sherds of Barbed-Wire beakers (B-2 (No. 17) and B-4). The single or paired fingernail impressions on the bodies of some of the Fengate vessels may be compared with B-3 (No. 18), a sherd representative of the domestic ware common to several beaker groups, including the Barbed-Wire and East Anglian. Charcoal from a pit at Site 114, Lion Point (Jaywick), Essex, which yielded beaker sherds with 'barbed-wire' decoration together with coarser ware ornamented with fingernail impressions variously arranged—paired in vertical columns, end-to-end in horizontal lines, with finger-pinched horizontal ridges (Ref. 25)—has produced a conventional radiocarbon date of 1800 B.C.±150 (BM-172) (Ref. 26).

The finger-pinched ridges on the bodies of the Mortlake bowls from Baston Manor appear also to have been copied from beaker models. The technique, originally introduced by Clarke's Primary Northern British/Dutch beaker group (Ref. 27), was later adopted by the East Anglian and the various Southern groups. The numerical predominance of the Barbed-Wire and East Anglian beakers around the estuary and the lower reaches of the River Thames (Ref. 28), indicates these as the probable inspiration for the ridged bowls here and those from the Thames valley sites mentioned above. It is, however, worth noting that amongst the ridged vessels from Heathrow, Middlesex, there is part of a bowl of simple form, lacking neck and shoulder (Ref. 29), which bears a detailed resemblance to two ridged bowls from Hampshire that Clarke assigns to his Developed Southern beaker group, while noting that the heavy rims are derived from Mortlake Fengate forms (Ref. 30).

Yet another instance of the processes of interaction between ceramic styles can be seen in OF1 (No. 19) from Baston Manor. In the technical sense it should be classed with the beaker fragments because of the style of decoration, but the crude execution of the design and the thick, gritty, laminated fabric, indistinguishable from that of the Mortlake and Fengate pottery at the site, suggest the work of an indigenous potter.

The sherd with box-cordon ornamented with a herring-bone design, OF3 (No. 21) seems to be un-paralleled in the South-East. It must come from a very large container and in the circumstances this seems likely to

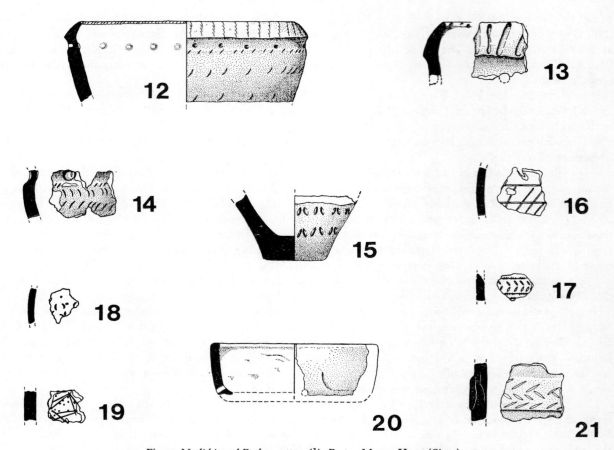

Fig. 7. *Neolithic and Beaker pottery* ($\frac{1}{3}$), *Baston Manor, Hayes (Site 1).*

have been a large storage beaker. Comparison might be made with a giant beaker from Castleshaw, Yorks., which has a pair of cordons of similar proportions (Ref. 31).

The fragmentary dish OF2 (No. 20) with part of a perforation in the basal angle is matched by more complete examples from the West Kennet long barrow (Ref. 32) and from Luce Sands, Wigtownshire (Ref. 33). These dishes have perforations in the bases and in the walls and resemble in turn an 'incense cup' which accompanied a primary cremation in a bowl barrow at Wilsford in South Wiltshire (Ref. 34). 'Incense cups' frequently take the form of miniature versions of other types of vessel, and the implication may be that perforated dishes, perhaps strainers, were common domestic utensils, though few have survived. A rusticated vessel with perforated base from a beaker domestic site at Stainsby, Lincs., points to the probable cultural context of these utensils (Ref. 35).

(2) THE FLINT MATERIAL (Figs. 8 and 9)

By D. N. Broadfoot

A total of 2,209 pieces of worked flint was recovered from this site and this may be divided into three main groups. Group A represents material recovered from the topsoil and hillwash deposits (layers 1 and 2). Group B represents material recovered from the two primary layers (layers 3 and 4), and Group C represents material from outlying test-holes and from other deposits. The assemblage has been classified in Table B below and 34 artefacts are illustrated.

		Group A	Group B	Group C	Totals
Tools	Knives and blades	2	28	3	33
	Scrapers	11	21	4	36
	Axe	—	1	—	1
	Arrowhead	—	—	1	1
	Others	4	6	—	10
Hammerstones		7	4	1	12
Waste	Nodules	12	2	—	14
	Cores	29	71	7	107
	Flakes	252	608	102	962
	Misc.	298	602	133	1,033
Totals		615	1,343	251	2,209

TABLE B.

Classification of the flint material from the Neolithic site near Baston Manor

Of the tools 33 flakes have been classed as blades or knives (No. 22), but it must be said that many of the other flakes could with some justification be placed in this category. Fifteen have cortex, some are clearly broken and all are very sharp.

Of the 36 scrapers (Nos. 23–48) only eight have no cortex. Three are on small cores and six on thermal flakes. Of the remainder 15 are end scrapers, 11 are side scrapers and one small one is both. Twelve are discoid and all but seven are monofacial. Of the 26 illustrated scrapers 12 may be called end scrapers, seven side scrapers and seven are both end and side combined.

The individual tools which are illustrated and described, include a polished axe (No. 49), a leaf-shaped arrowhead (No. 50), a burnisher (No. 51), a polished knife (No. 52) and a saw (No. 53). There is also a backed knife (No. 54) and a notched flake (No. 55). Those not illustrated and described include a broken piercer, about 57 mm. by 22 mm., monofacial and tapering to a blunt point at the bulbar end. The dorsal face is keeled and there is secondary working on two opposite edges, the point also being worked. There is an awl, a keeled 'rejuvenation' flake partly cortexed, 68 mm. by 18 mm. with a multifacial blunt point showing wear. There are also two points, the broken ends of implements similar to the pieces mentioned above.

The hammerstones were all much the same size and type, cortexed, with abrasions at each end. The nodules and miscellaneous pieces amount to 1,047, about half of the total flint finds. They are mostly cortexed, some with bulbs of percussion while others are thermal or the result of shattering.

Of 107 cores 15 had no cortex. Two resemble circular choppers of relatively thin section and each has had three or four large flakes removed. Three cores have beak-like projections which strongly resemble awls, each point having at least four faces.

The cores fall roughly into six groups, excepting the choppers.

(1) 42 are of varied indefinite shapes, most having at least four flake scars. This group includes the awls and there are four more which are either scrapers or roughouts.

(2) A group of 12 have flat single-strike flake surfaces, with cones of percussion and cortex on the top, with several flakes removed from the sides.

(3) A group of 18 is similar to (2), but has little or no cortex. Many are also worked multifacially but are less like the results of tool-making; four are fairly flat.

(4) A group of 13 have half-round sections with flat semi-circular bases and a band of cortex running up to the apex. Several long flakes have been struck from each, giving them a pyramidal appearance.

(5) A group of nine are roughly spherical with flakes removed all round and appear to be the centres of the original nodules. There is little or no cortex.

(6) A final group of 13 resemble group five, but have considerably more cortex.

The flakes and chips total 962. Of these 693 flakes can be classified into five groups. All were distributed proportionately throughout groups A, B and C.

The great majority of the 138 singly-struck cortexed flakes had percussion bulbs. Thirty-seven have sharp edges with fine irregular pittings and serrations indicating wear.

The cortexed flakes with two or more strikes totalled 327, which subdivide as follows:

(1) 145 are sufficiently rough or so struck as to make it very likely that they are no more than waste flakes and were not utilised.

(2) 147 could all have been utilised and many show signs of this and indeed approximate to actual tools, though of no definite type. Several resemble scrapers before the final retouching and might be considered as roughouts.

(3) Another 35 all bear retouching, serrations and other signs of use and could all have been used as knives or scrapers.

Of the non-cortexed flakes five of the 42 singly-struck are possible artifacts. There are 140 multi-struck, which fall into two groups of 90 and 50. The former are a varied collection, some of which could have been and probably were used, but are cruder than the following group. The latter are an extremely interesting group which would repay further study. The majority must surely be artifacts, probably knives—16 of them are razor sharp. Three are remarkably like arrowheads, but with very little retouching. Five are flat and rounded, the flake face being the result of a single strike. The dorsal face is much trimmed with a long flat flake removed along one side to produce a plane-like edge.

There are 46 flakes of the 'core rejuvenation' type, though there is some doubt as to whether this type of flake does in fact arise from core rejuvenation rather than intended blades which have followed a plunging fracture line as a result of a mishit.

Comments

A total of 93 implements and hammerstones can be identified amongst the 2,209 items in the flint assemblage (excluding 'pot-boilers') recovered from the Baston Manor site. These represent about 4% of the total assemblage with the remaining 96% (2,116 items) being waste. This compares with 10% and 90%, respectively at Hurst Fen, Suffolk (Ref. 36a) and 4% and 96%, respectively at Durrington Walls, Wiltshire (Ref. 36b). With 1,958 items coming from the main area of excavation at Baston, which covered 1,100 sq. ft., a density of 16 items per sq. yd. is produced. This compares with 40 per sq. yd. at Hurst Fen.

The flint on the site was found in close association with more than 200 pieces of pottery of Late Neolithic type. Recognisable flint types of this period are certainly present, sometimes only singly as with the white-patinated polished axe, the typically asymmetrical leaf-shaped arrowhead, the polished knife, the saw and the finely serrated keeled flake. Several large convex scrapers point more to the Middle Neolithic, as at Hurst Fen, which was also largely a flake industry.

There is a dissimilarity with the pre-barrow occupation at Arreton Down, Wilts. (Ref. 37), which was considered Late Neolithic, lacking the accepted types but suggesting by the presence of notched flakes and bifacial core tools a continuing Mesolithic tradition which is not evident at Baston, except for the saw.

There is perhaps a greater affinity with the flint from the West Kennet Long Barrow, Wilts. (Ref. 38), which was also found in association with Late Neolithic pottery. It is difficult to draw any further parallels in view of the general scarcity of detailed flint studies elsewhere.

Catalogue of the Illustrated Flint from Baston Manor, Hayes (Figs. 8 and 9)

No. 22. Knife cortexed along steep side. Fine secondary flaking along sharp edge with considerable usage-striations on other side of edge on flake side (from D3-3).

No. 23. End scraper with sharp edges on three sides and central ridge down dorsal face interrupted by hinge fracture. Steep secondary flaking at rounded end in finer and shallower form at one side. The sharp edges show some signs of wear (from C3-4).

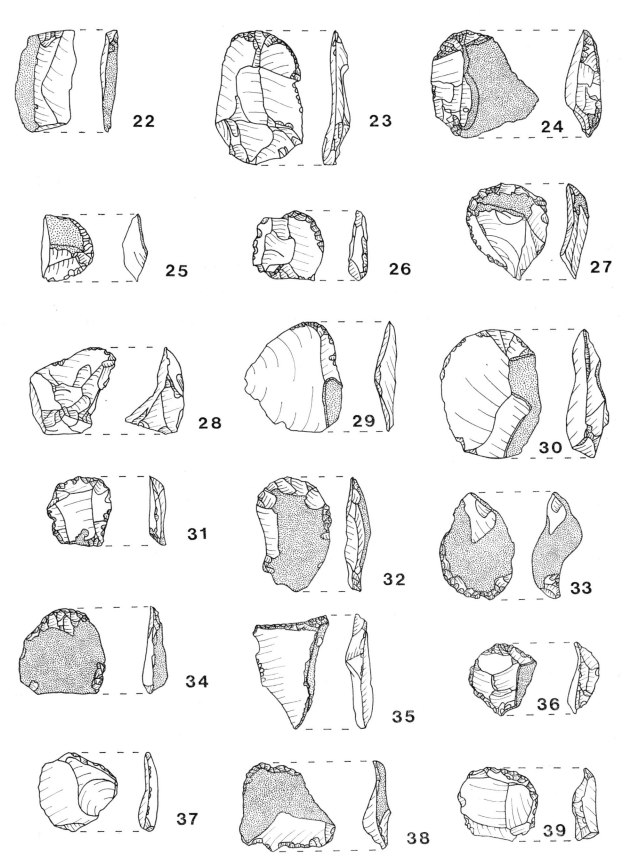

Fig. 8. *Neolithic flint implements* (½), *Baston Manor, Hayes (Site 1).*

No. 24.   End scraper half cortexed on dorsal face, with fairly steep retouching at one end (from A3-4).

No. 25.   End scraper, broken, half cortexed on dorsal face, which has steep retouching most of the way round (from B2-4).

No. 26.   End scraper, no cortex, retouched at about 45° (from C4-4).

No. 27.   End scraper, some cortex on dorsal face, which is steeply retouched along the end curve below the cortex (from D5-3).

No. 28.   End scraper, very little cortex, but some patination. Rounded end retouched at about 45° (from C3-2).

No. 29.   End scraper with some cortex. 45° edging flake removed down part of longer side and 45° retouching on rounded point (from C3-3).

No. 30.   End scraper with cortex along steep edge with steep and shallow retouching along rounded end (from D5-5).

No. 31.   End scraper, irregular, with fairly rough and shallow retouching at end and down one side of dorsal face (from A3-3).

No. 32.   End scraper almost entirely cortexed on dorsal face, but coarsely retouched around half of circumference furtherest from bulb (from D4-5).

No. 33.   End scraper, with cortex, almost 90° retouching round the curved end (from F4-1).

No. 34.   End scraper, mostly cortexed on dorsal face, with 45° retouching on rounded end (from C3-4).

No. 35.   Side scraper, with cortex down one side and short side worked at about 45° for the whole of its length. Both faces singly struck with about 12 mm. of fine secondary flaking midway on longer uncortexed side, which includes a worked notch (from D3-3).

No. 36.   Side scraper with some cortex; edge irregularly broken except for small area of steep working on right of dorsal face (from B2-4).

No. 37.   Side scraper with one or two strikes on dorsal face. Extremely fine pressure flaking down one side and signs of use on the other (from E4-2).

No. 38.   Side scraper, partially cortexed, with shallow retouching and broken edge (from D5-5).

No. 39.   Side scraper, edged by flaking at differing angles with retouching round half the circumference (from D5-3).

No. 40.   Side scraper with a little cortex at end of dorsal face. Fairly shallow retouching along one side and signs of use on opposite sharp edge on flake face (from A3-4).

No. 41.   Side scraper, one spot of cortex on dorsal face. Almost 90° retouching along thicker part of straight side (from E4-3).

No. 42.   End and side scraper, probably broken, cortexed almost entirely on dorsal face which has some retouching or use abrasions round most of the edge (from B3-2).

No. 43.   End and side scraper heavily cortexed on most of dorsal face. Considerable retouching at 45° along thickened edge; steeper at rounded end (from C4-2).

No. 44.   End and side scraper, probably hafted, with fine 45° retouching round at least half of circumference (from C3-3).

No. 45.   End and side scraper, triangular, steeply retouched along two sides and round point (from C5-4).

No. 46.   End and side scraper, half cortexed on dorsal face, with fairly steep retouching on about three-quarters of the circumference (from E4-2).

No. 47.   End and side scraper mostly cortexed on dorsal face. Non-bulbar end retouched at about 45° and some coarser retouching on one side of other end (unstratified).

No. 48.   End and side scraper, some cortex on dorsal face, with fairly steep retouching on most of the edge (from E4-5).

No. 49.   White patinated polished axe, sharp, probably little used. This implement weighs 7½ oz. and its maximum measurements are approximately 120 mm. by 55 mm., tapering down to 30 mm. Its maximum thickness is 27 mm., which is reached about 55 mm. back from the cutting edge. It is not symmetrical in section. For 30 mm. or so from the edge it is perfectly smooth, but thereafter numerous shallow flakes have been removed.

It has a greyish-white patina all over and it is not possible to say what colour the internal flint is. The narrow end and about 35 mm. of one side are cortexed, which at the end shows signs of abrasive indentation. The flint is unlike any other found on the site and may well have been imported. The cutting edge is quite sharp with a slight 'S' curve (from C3-4).

No. 50.   Leaf-shaped arrowhead. This measures 54 mm. by 23 mm. maxima and has some cortex in the middle of the lower half on one side. The profile shows a slight obtuse angle between the two halves such that the arrow would have tended to swerve in flight. The convex side, which has the cortex, has secondary flaking on about two-thirds of its area, while on the concave side the working is more confined to the edges. The outline is not quite symmetrical (from south-east of main area).

No. 51.   Hard, smooth sandstone object, possibly a burnisher. A pair of similar objects, described as polished stone plaques, were found with a primary inhumation in a bowl barrow at Winterbourne Stoke, Wiltshire (Ref. 39). It may possibly be a whetstone and was found near the polished axe (from D4-3).

No. 52.   Polished knife, broken and cortexed along short edge. No retouching as such, but signs of use. The dorsal face has two long bands consistent with having been polished (from B5-2).

No. 53.   Typical keeled Neolithic flake, with serrated edge, no silica gloss. Serrations diminish progressively in size, but average about 1 mm. Cortex down opposite side (from B4-4).

No. 54.   Small core-rejuvenation flake or broken blade, 'S' curved, cortexed at sharp end with fine angled retouching along the straight edge. Could be a small sickle, though no gloss (from B4-4).

No. 55.   Small flake with retouched notch (from F4-2).

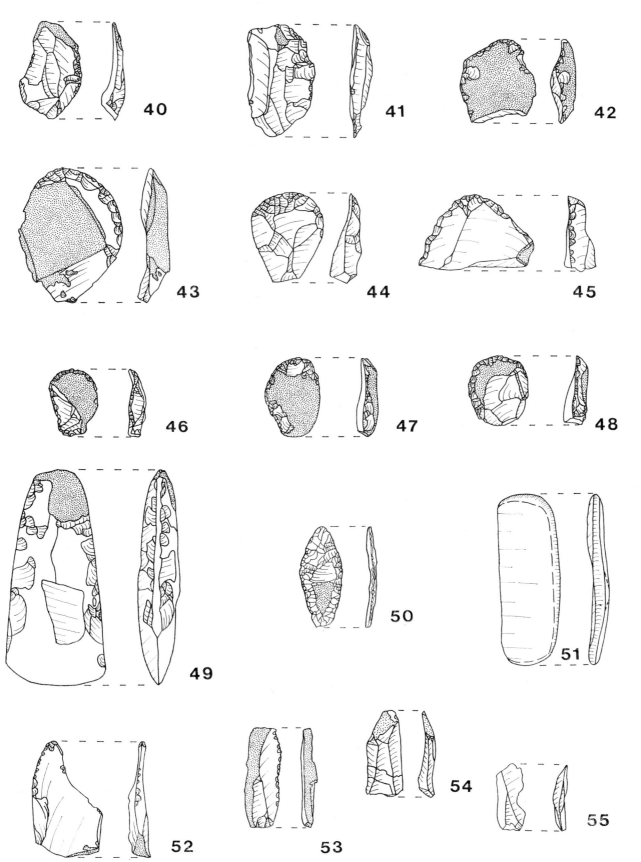

Fig. 9. *Neolithic flint implements and sandstone object* ($\frac{1}{2}$), *Baston Manor, Hayes (Site 1)*.

SITE 2. A Neolithic or Bronze Age Site near Fox Hill, West Wickham, Kent

This site (N.G.R. TQ. 3860.6410) lies on Wickham Court Farm, in the parish of West Wickham, Kent about a ⅓ of a mile south of the parish church. It occupies an open field (O.S. parcel 7714) on a gentle north-facing slope on the east side of Fox Hill and Birch Wood (Fig. 20). It is situated on brickearth and Upper Chalk and the elevation is about 300–350 ft.

The site was discovered in 1961 after Mr. K. Austen, of Upper Norwood, reported finding worked flint on the surface of the field. The Group undertook intensive surveys of the area in the winter of 1961–62.

The Group wishes to record its thanks to Mr. E. E. Pallant of Wickham Court Farm for his ready co-operation in allowing the work to be carried out. Of the various members who worked for extended periods special mention must be made of Mrs. M. Woolven; Miss Janet Weeks and Messrs. A. Appleby, B. Brandham, C. Hart, G. Richardson and C. Terry. The illustrated flints have been drawn by Miss R. Chatters and Mr. D. Broadfoot has kindly examined and reported on the flint material.

The survey revealed that the flint material covered an area of at least ten acres on the west side of the field. The area extended for about 900 ft. from the north margin of the field and about 650 ft. eastwards from the edge of the wood. The worked flint tended to be in local concentrations within this area and generally there was less at the northern and southern limits. By the end of the survey more than 12,000 items had been collected from the surface of the field. These were counted, examined and the majority discarded on site. There were more than 6,000 'pot-boilers' and more than 5,000 waste flakes and nodules, the latter both representing residual material from a flint industry. Only 1,650 pieces were retained for classification. The bulk of the material appears to represent an industry of Neolithic or Bronze Age date. Some of the tools are broadly similar to those from the Neolithic site at Baston Manor, Hayes (Site 1), though one core, at least, appears to be a Mesolithic type.

Limited trial-excavations in the field, including a 237 ft. mechanically excavated trench, running north-south, failed to locate any related features. At the south end of the area 5 ft. of brown loam, probably hillwash, capped the underlying chalk. Worked flint was found throughout this loam deposit and near its base were specks of carbon and burnt clay, the latter perhaps representing crushed potsherds.

It is clear from the overall evidence from this site that an important prehistoric site exists near Fox Hill, probably of Neolithic or Bronze Age date. The large quantity of material indicates a flint industry and it is even possible that evidence of flint mining may exist in the area. The specks of carbon and possible pottery at the base of the loam at the south end of the site may indicate a deeply buried occupation-site relating to the industry. What is clear is that only properly conducted, large-scale excavation is likely to substantially increase our knowledge of this site.

THE FINDS

1. THE FLINT MATERIAL (Fig. 10)

By D. N. Broadfoot

A total of 6,139 pieces of worked flint was recovered from this site which has probably been ploughed for several centuries. This action has damaged much of the material, some of which is crude, though there is a high degree of good, secondary retouching on many of the pieces.

It is possible to identify 345 implements and hammerstones in this collection which represents about 5½% of the total assemblage (excluding 'pot-boilers'). This closely compares with the totals of implements from Baston Manor, Hayes (Site 1) and Durrington Walls, Wilts. (Ref. 36b), both of which represented 4% of the total assemblages. At Hurst Fen, Suffolk (Ref. 36a) the implements seem to have represented about 10% of the total assemblage. It is not possible to comment on the density of the material from Fox Hill as it was recovered from the surface and not by excavation.

The flint may be classified as follows:

Tools	Knives and blades	65	
	Scrapers	146	
	Notched flakes	49	
	Borers	78	338
Hammerstones			7
Waste	Cores	121	
	Flakes	585	
	Misc. (retained)	599	
	„ (discarded)	4,489	5,794
			6,139

TABLE A

Classification of the flint material from the Neolithic/Bronze Age site at Fox Hill

The knives and blades (Nos. 56 and 57) have little cortex and many are keeled and of triangular section. Of the 146 scrapers (Nos. 58–65) 28 are end-scrapers, mostly monofacial, 13 having a convex working edge. Forty-three are side-scrapers nearly all of which are cortexed, 23 having straight and 16 convex worked-edges. All but one of the 29 discoid scrapers are cortexed, 22 of them being steep-angled.

The 12 concave scrapers are the best of the series. Six are steep angled and there is a classic 'spokeshave' (No. 66), 3·5 in. across with 'handles', one of which is also retouched.

The remaining 34 miscellaneous scrapers, except one, are cortexed and the majority steep-angled. There is an oval tortoise-core scraper about 2·2 in. by 1·5 in. and 0·75 in. thick with steep edges all round. About 16 downward flakes have been removed from this, though there is no fine retouching.

The 49 notched flakes (Nos. 67 and 68) are a group of large, flattish flakes of all shapes, but all with concave re-entries from 0·1 to 1·5 in. in width, most being finely retouched.

Of the 78 borers (No. 69) 16 are very crude lumps of flint from 2 in. to 5 in. long, mostly with cortex and thermal scars. All have blunt and retouched beaks. Another 19 smaller pieces, with little or no cortex, are quite fine with sharp, sometimes broken points. Eighteen others are finely retouched with fairly sharp points and all cortexed. Nineteen of the remaining 25 are mostly cortexed with fairly coarse retouching and reasonably sharp points, or beaks. Four of the remainder are both borers and scrapers.

Six of the seven hammerstones are roughly spherical, all with cortex and varying from 2 in. to 4 in. in diameter. Two of the smaller ones have been subjected to heat, while one large one has a blue-white patina. Another is flatter, resembling a core, with several flakes missing, probably removed by natural causes.

Cores (Nos. 71–74) amount to 121 and include 11 pyramidal with little cortex, about 1·5 in. across the base and with many flake beaks. Four of the 18 spherical cores have no cortex and had many square and discoid flakes removed. Their average diameter is 2 to 2·5 in. There are two good tortoise cores with flat bases, about 3 in. long, in grey-white flint. Most of the 90 miscellaneous cores are crude and include six blunt borers and four possible palaeoliths. Many are rough and angular and of all shapes. Two appear water-rolled and many have been used as pounders, judging by the abrasions.

There are 585 flakes (No. 75) which have been classified into four groups. A total of 103, with cortex and two strikes or less, are mostly flat and have bulbs. Though crude a few might be rough scrapers. Another 275, with more than two strikes, are only slightly less crude yet several have short lengths of fine retouching. Thirty-three of these could be scrapers, knives or borers though they are too rough for this to be certain. Another 53, without cortex and two strikes or less, are unremarkable. The uncortexed flakes with several strikes, totalling 154, are mainly rough and of these about 23 might be implements.

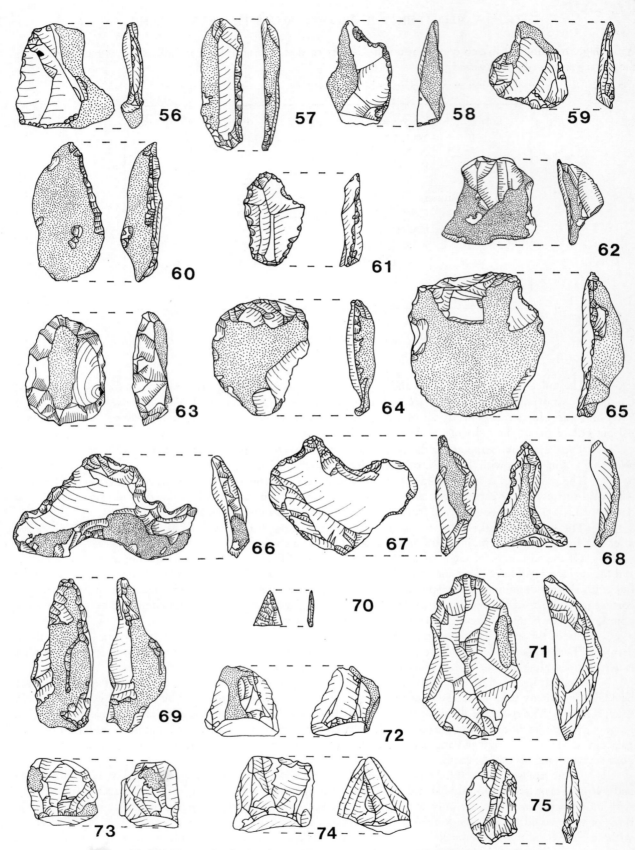

Fig. 10. *Neolithic–Bronze Age flint implements, cores and flakes* ($\frac{1}{2}$), *Fox Hill, West Wickham (Site 2).*

The 599 pieces of retained miscellaneous waste consist of broken nodules, half-pebbles and thermal fractures. Almost all are cortexed and many have cones of percussion.

Catalogue of Illustrated Flint from Fox Hill, West Wickham (Fig. 10)

No. 56. Flake with part-cortex. Possibly a knife (FH-15B).

No. 57. Probable core-rejuvenation flake, three facetted dorsal faces, one of which is cortexed. Rough retouching on non-cortexed edge, possible knife (FH-B12).

No. 58. Irregular flake, part cortexed, with slightly notched and roughly worked short edge (FH-E1).

No. 59. Flake, slightly cortexed, with four strikes on dorsal face (FH-F1).

No. 60. Plano-convex nodule with cortexed and possible rough, steep retouching down one side (FH-J4).

No. 61. Plano-convex flake, multi-struck dorsal face, a doubtful scraper (FH-I3).

No. 62. Plano-convex flake, part cortex, with small amount of steep retouching on one side and several flakes removed from cortexed dorsal face (FH-F2).

No. 63. Plano-convex scraper, steep-sided with some cortex down middle of back, fairly rough and steep retouching on three sides (FH-G3).

No. 64. Plano-convex scraper, cortexed and steep-angled, coarsely retouched (FH-R7).

No. 65. Plano-convex probable pot-lid, but with a small amount of retouching on the edge (FH-F1).

No. 66. Large flake, very irregular and partly cortexed, with steep retouched notch. A tapered spokeshave (FH-1).

No. 67. Irregular flake with some cortex and large roughly worked notch (FH-E1).

No. 68. Irregular flake, with cortex, a combined awl and rough scraper (FH-C1).

No. 69. Irregular core-like piece cortexed and beaked at one end, with several flakes removed. Probably an awl (FH-R5).

No. 70. Broken end of possible leaf-shaped arrowhead, finely worked (FH-A1).

No. 71. Tortoise core with white patination (FH-12A).

No. 72. Small core, rough with part-cortex (FH-B1).

No. 73. Small core, roughly spherical and slightly cortexed, with at least 12 irregular flakes removed (FH-16).

No. 74. Blade-core, of Mesolithic type, in grey flint with about 12 strikes (FH-B38).

No. 75. Small flake, plano-convex with no cortex, in light grey flint (FH-J4).

SITE 3. A Neolithic or Bronze Age Site at Mill Hill, Farnborough, Kent

This site (N.G.R. TQ.4394.6390) lies immediately to the east of Mill Hill, Farnborough about a ⅓ of a mile south-west of the parish church. It occupies the top north-west corner of an open field (O.S. parcel 139) on the upper, west slope of a wide, dry valley. It stands on Thanet Beds at an elevation of about 400 ft. O.D.

Flint implements were collected from the surface of this field in 1944–7 (Ref. 40) and then identified as mostly of Neolithic or Bronze Age date. Surveys by the Group in March, 1967 and again in January, 1970 eventually relocated the site and defined its approximate limits. Another 652 flints were recovered from the site and these have been studied by Mr. D. N. Broadfoot, whose report appears below. The Group gratefully acknowledges the help of the farmer Mr. A. J. Wilson of Mace Farm, Cudham and the work of Mrs. M. Luyke-Roskott and Miss Rowena Chatters in drawing the published finds.

The surveys revealed that although worked flint was found over much of the field the main concentration was in the north-east corner. This extended for about 200 ft. eastwards from the edge of the wood and about 220 ft. southwards from the north hedge (since removed).

It is difficult to offer definite dates for this fairly small collection of material. Much of it is rough and somewhat similar to the flint from Fox Hill, West Wickham (Site 2), which has been classified tentatively as Neolithic or Bronze Age. There are, however, some cores and a small tranchet axe of Mesolithic form. On balance it seems best to suggest that this material relates to a site of mainly Neolithic or Bronze Age date. A flint industry of uncertain size appears to be represented and an adjacent occupation-site may be indicated.

THE FINDS

(1) THE FLINT MATERIAL (Fig. 11)

By D. N. Broadfoot

A total of 652 pieces of flint was recovered from this site during the surveys and this can be classified as follows:

Tools	Scrapers	37	
	Blades	54	
	Notched tools	6	
	Borers	16	
	Fabricator	1	
	Tranchet axe	1	115
Hammerstones			10
Waste	Cores	48	
	Flakes	169	
	Misc.	310	527
			652

TABLE A

Classification of the flint material from the Neolithic/Bronze Age site at Mill Hill

Tools

These are a very mixed collection with few really good types. There are 13 side scrapers (Nos. 76 and 77). One is keeled and elongated with a single-strike flake face and cortex down one side with secondary working at the bulb. Another is on a rough cortexed flake, rather similar, with secondary working on the uncortexed concave side. A third is a rather better bluish discoid with a single-strike flake face and many flakes removed from the dorsal face; the worked side is angled at about 75°.

There are also eight end scrapers (No. 78). One is similar to the last mentioned side scraper, but smaller and cruder with an angle of only about 35° and some cortex on the upper surface. Another is similar, but larger and whiter, more discoid, no cortex and the secondary working at about 90°. A third is a large flattish flake, maximum 3 by 2 in., fan shaped with some fine retouching on the flake side beneath the bulb and a possible steep retouch on the otherwise cortexed edge. Two more elongated scrapers, possibly off cores, crude but the larger (2·7 in.) has had many flakes removed. Both perhaps were also used as knives.

There are also another 16 scrapers of various shapes. One is crude, but much flaked, triangular in section, 2·3 in. long with about 0·5 in. of retouch on the otherwise rough, shortest edge. Another is a shiny black, flattish flake face with several strikes. It is discoid with many flakes from the dorsal face, one end of which has a worked point. The opposite edge, 0·5 in. thick, is completely right-angled and worked all along the edge. A third is large, 3 by 2 in., cortexed on one side, one primary strike, and has an edge worked all the way round. Another is triangular, about 2·5 in. high, is in grey-brown translucent flint with a little cortex and about seven flake beds on the dorsal face. It is finely worked all the way round, with a blunt point and a notch. Finally, there is one about 2·5 in. square which has steep retouching all the way round.

Of the 54 knives and blades (No. 79), 16 are very assorted and mostly blue-grey. Of these four small blades have flakes running the whole length. The remainder are larger, averaging 2 in. in length, some nicely flaked and all with one flake removed down the whole of one side. Of these six are also pointed. The remaining six are quite distinct and possibly arise from core rejuvenation. All have the typical single strike arched flake side and several long flakes have been removed down the keeled back. Two are fine and very sharp.

There are six notched tools, all but one greyish-white, singly struck on the flake face with worked concavities. There are also 16 various borers (No. 80) all with one or more points suitable for grooving or boring. One good example appears to have broken off a larger implement. Another resembles a core rejuvenation flake with arched single strike flake surface, triangular in section, 2·3 in. long and tapering to quite a fine elongated point very suitable for grooving. One large example resembles a punch or chisel.

The other tools include a fabricator (No. 81) made from a fine rejuvenation flake and a small tranchet axe (No. 82) of Mesolithic form (see below).

Hammerstones

There are ten of these of which six are large and between 3 and 4 in. in length. One is very crude and two are cores with circular flakes removed. The other four are considerably smaller and are also cores. They must have been used for very fine work, especially the smallest which resembles an end scraper and is triangular in section, measuring 2 by 1 by 1 in. and has very fine abrasions at the steep end.

Waste material

This includes 48 cores (Nos. 83–86), all but ten with cortex. Of these ten are black and the remainder grey with occasional blue patination. Of the ten uncortexed most are grey and not more than 2 in. long with a minimum of six flakes removed, except for two which are cylindrical with flat ends and have had eight or more fine, long narrow flakes removed. One crude example is entirely white patinated and may be Palaeolithic whilst at least two are of Mesolithic type.

Of the 38 cortexed cores 22 are fairly crude, mostly roughly spherical with from five to eight flakes removed. Three, also small but crude, have areas of fine abrasions and may be small hammerstones. Another six have flat single-strike flake surfaces and hemispherical dorsal surfaces with at least five irregular flakes removed. They could be roughouts for large scrapers. The remainder are fine, somewhat pyramidal types, most with long flakes removed and of grey-blue flint.

There are also 169 flakes (No. 87). Of these ten have cortex and a single-strike scar. Two are white, five are blue-white and three grey. Most could have been used as knives or scrapers and one is possibly a broken awl.

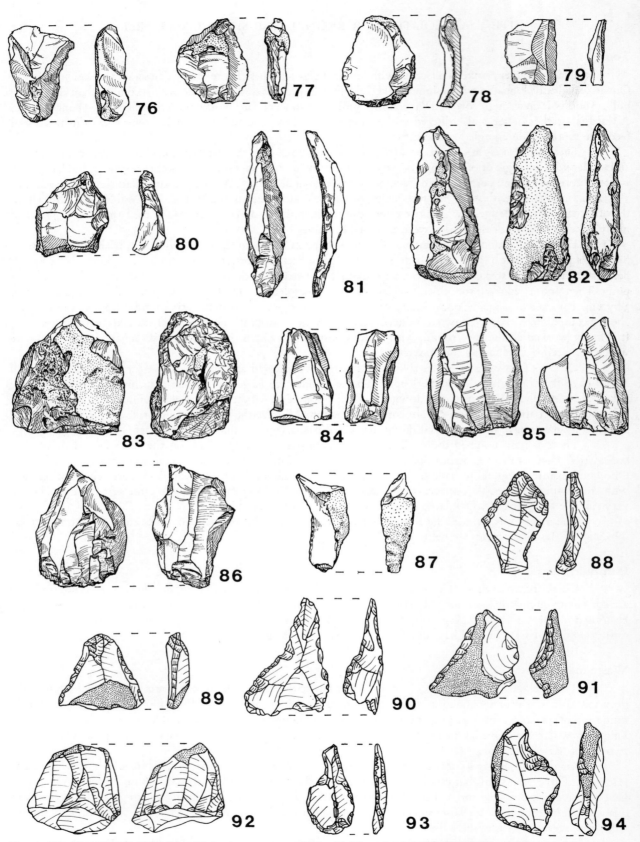

Fig. 11. *Mesolithic, Neolithic–Bronze Age flint implements, cores and flakes* (½) *(Nos. 76–87), Mill Hill, Farnborough (Site 3) and (Nos. 88–94), Homefield Farm, Sutton-at-Hone (Site 4).*

Another 64 have cortex and two or more strike scars. Of these six are white, ten blue and white mottled and the remainder are mostly grey or black. Three of these are more than 2·5 in. long, but most are about 1·2 in. They are fairly crude and not many would be usable. Another eleven have no cortex and a single strike-scar and are mostly under 1 in. Finally, there are 84 with no cortex and two or more strike-scars. Of these six are black, twelve are mottled blue, 15 are white and the remainder grey-white. They are mostly discoid and one or two could have been used as knives. Not many have more than three flakes removed or are particularly noteworthy.

Catalogue of the Illustrated Flint from Mill Hill, Farnborough (Fig. 11)

No. 76.   Side and end scraper combined, roughly made.

No. 77.   Possible side scraper, lightly retouched, in translucent grey flint with many flakes from dorsal face, which still has some cortex. The bulbar face also has several scars.

No. 78.   End scraper, steeply retouched, with a single-strike bulbar face.

No. 79.   Probably a broken knife with retouch blunting on the shorter edge and five flake-beds on the dorsal face.

No. 80.   Borer with many flakes from dorsal face. The bulb has broken away leaving a vertical retouched face opposite the point.

No. 81.   Fabricator made from a large core rejuvenation flake; double ended, with six flake removals.

No. 82.   Small Mesolithic-type tranchet axe, almost entirely cortexed on one side which has most of the fairly good retouching. The tranchet flake bed is an excellent example and runs the full length of the cutting edge.

No. 83.   Core, roughly pyramidal, subsequently used as a hammerstone.

No. 84.   Blade core, cylindrical Mesolithic type, in light blue-grey flint. At least eight blades have been removed.

No. 85.   Blade core, Mesolithic type, larger than above and in similar flint. Perhaps originally pyramidal, but most of one half has broken away. Seven flakes have been removed from the good side.

No. 86.   Blade core, similar to above.

No. 87.   Flake, cortexed and rough, with an awl at one end and retouching along one edge. The bulb has broken away.

SITE 4. A Neolithic or Bronze Age Site at Homefield Farm, Sutton-at-Hone, Kent

This site (N.G.R. TQ.5490.6870) lies just in the parish of Sutton-at-Hone, Kent on Homefield Farm, about 1 mile south-west of the parish church. It occupies part of three fields (O.S. parcel 0006) on gently sloping ground on the west side of the Darent valley. The bed-rock is Upper Chalk, here capped with one or two feet of brown clay and the elevation is between 175 and 225 ft. O.D.

The site was discovered on 11th November, 1969 during 'Operation Gaspipe East'. Very little appeared in the actual pipe-trench, which cut across the area roughly north-south, but about 180 struck flints were found in the topsoil which had been bulldozed into heaps. These came from a stretch of ground about 1,000 yards in length lying immediately east and south-east of the farmhouse (from TQ.5491.6823 to about 5485.6916).

The bulk of the flint is waste with each piece having one or more flake-beds. Only about 50 pieces are of special interest and these include scrapers, blades, notched tools and a borer (Nos. 88–94). The flint from this site has been studied by Mr. D. Broadfoot who has kindly supplied a short report (below). The illustrated flints have very kindly been drawn by Miss Rowena Chatters.

The material from this site was recovered in a limited time and it represents only that which had been exposed by rain in the bulldozed topsoil. Even so it is clear that the occurrence of flint implements and waste was very much greater here than anywhere else along the pipe-line. Had time been spent on turning over the spoil-heap it seems highly likely that several hundred other struck flints would have been recovered. Presumably the finds extend to both east and west of the pipe-line area. If so, then a large site covering several acres appears to be indicated. The flint recovered from the site lacks specific implements that are readily assignable to particular periods. In spite of a single Mesolithic piece there is a broad similarity to the flint from the site at Fox Hill, West Wickham (Site 2), and it is probable that this material also represents a Neolithic or Bronze Age site.

THE FINDS

(1) THE FLINT MATERIAL (Fig. 11)

By D. N. Broadfoot

A total of 179 pieces of worked flint was recovered from the site and this may be classified as follows:

Tools	Blades	4	
	Scrapers	28	
	Notched tools	11	
	Borer	1	44
Hammerstones			—
Waste	Cores	9	
	Flakes	88	
	Misc.	38	135
			179

TABLE A

Classification of the flint material from the Neolithic-Bronze Age site at Homefield Farm

28

The flint from this site is crudely worked and there is a general lack of well-known types. It is similar in some respects to the material from Fox Hill, West Wickham (Site 2) and indeed both sites have probably been ploughed for centuries, with the likelihood that some of the retouching and notching may be accidental. There are four end scrapers, two with steep retouching and two with very delicate work on thin perpendicular edges. Of 13 side scrapers four are triangular and double-sided. The other nine are assorted, some with fairly steep retouching and the rest with very fine work on thin edges. The notched flakes are also mainly crude, cortexed pieces, but six of them are notched and have scraper-type retouching as well. A single borer, on a multi-keeled flake, is broken. The group is far too small to allow a statistically significant comment.

Catalogue of the Illustrated Flint from Homefield Farm, Sutton-at-Hone (Fig. 11)

No. 88.   Scraper with blunt point, keeled dorsal face and retouching on three sides.

No. 89.   Scraper with cortex on dorsal face and rounded end, with retouching on two sides.

No. 90.   Scraper with retouching down both the longer sides, a notch in the middle of the longest side and a shaped point. The dorsal face is keeled.

No. 91.   Scraper, patinated and cortexed, with steep retouching on two sides.

No. 92.   Core of grey flint with some cortex and at least 14 flake beds all struck from the flat base, only five of which would have produced short blades. Not typically Mesolithic.

No. 93.   Possible microlith with worked notch on one side and working on other. The narrow 'handle' is worked across the top and compares broadly with a Mesolithic tool from Surrey (Ref. 41).

No. 94.   Scraper with cortex down left side of keeled dorsal face, the upper half of one side forming a blunt hook, concavely and convexly worked, the lower half fractured.

SITE 5. A Bronze Age Site (and other sites) on Hayes Common, Hayes, Kent

SUMMARY

The excavations established the existence of prehistoric settlement on Hayes Common. The evidence for this consisted of two ditches, 30 small pits, four flint-packed post-holes, worked flint, pottery, quernstones and loom-weights. The datable material, where assignable with any accuracy, appears to be Bronze Age and Neolithic.

Most of the flint appears to be Neolithic and its distribution, both in the main area and over part of the Common north of Croydon Road, suggests a widely spread site. Just possibly some of the pottery could also be Neolithic and its association with Bronze Age material would then suggest that it was redeposited following disturbance.

The identifiable Bronze Age material such as the cinerary urn, the distinctive loom-weights and also the majority of the quernstones, all came from the Occupation-Area and the ditches and pits. There can be very little reasonable doubt that these features and the dated finds in them relate directly to each other and together represent a hitherto unknown Bronze Age occupation-site.

It seems likely that the site was a farmstead which the two ditches, meeting at 65°, may have partially delimited. The lined pits may have been used to store water or grain and it is possible that some of the pottery was manufactured on the site. The presence of saddle-querns suggests that corn was grown and the loom-weights prove weaving and suggest that sheep were reared for their wool. The site appears to have covered at least ½ an acre and it is possible that the flint-packed post-holes represent a rectilinear structure, or hut. As regards dating the broadly comparable sites at Itford Hill, Sussex (Ref. 44) and Weston Wood, Surrey are regarded as either Middle or Late Bronze Age. From this it seems likely that the Bronze Age site on Hayes Common dates, on present knowledge, somewhere in the range 1400–500 B.C.

The excavations away from the main area, although producing only limited evidence, suggest that the Linear Earthwork is not earlier than the Iron Age; that the Defensive Earthwork may date from 1570–80; that the Circles, in at least one case cut by the Field System, may date between 1400–1797 and that the Field System itself may date from between 1580 and 1797.

It is clear that the Bronze Age site on Hayes Common is one of the most important in the area, being one of the very few of this period known in Kent. Only large-scale excavations are likely to advance substantially knowledge of this site and this would involve considerable clearance. The site is not at present threatened.

INTRODUCTION

This site (N.G.R. TQ.4047.6520) lies on Hayes Common, Kent about 1,200 yards south of the parish church of St. Mary the Virgin, Hayes. It lies within the area (O.S. parcel 753) bounded by Preston Road, West Common Road and Croydon Road, being about 500 ft. south of Hayes Court (Fig. 12). The site is on a gently sloping plateau of the Blackheath and Woolwich pebble-beds at an elevation of about 310 ft. O.D. It is now covered by ever increasing vegetation with a predominance of gorse and silver birch. There are patches of heather and a noticeable spread of oaks from the north.

The Bronze Age site was discovered by the Group in June, 1962 during trial-excavations on the Common. Work, largely of a training nature, had started in 1960 when several so-called 'hut-circles' were examined. In 1961 the Group examined two more circles and in 1962 cut sections across some banks of a nearby Field System. In 1963 the Group turned its attention to the Bronze Age site when it located and excavated two ditches (Ditches 1 and 2) and in 1964 a Linear Dyke, to the south and east, was examined at several points. In 1965 an area-excavation (Figs. 13 and 14) was carried out on part of the Bronze Age site, adjacent to the ditches, during which time three flint-packed post-holes and 30 small pits were found (Ref. 42). In 1966 a series of long trenches was dug all around the Bronze Age site in an attempt to determine its limits, but this failed to reveal any other pits or ditches. This Report

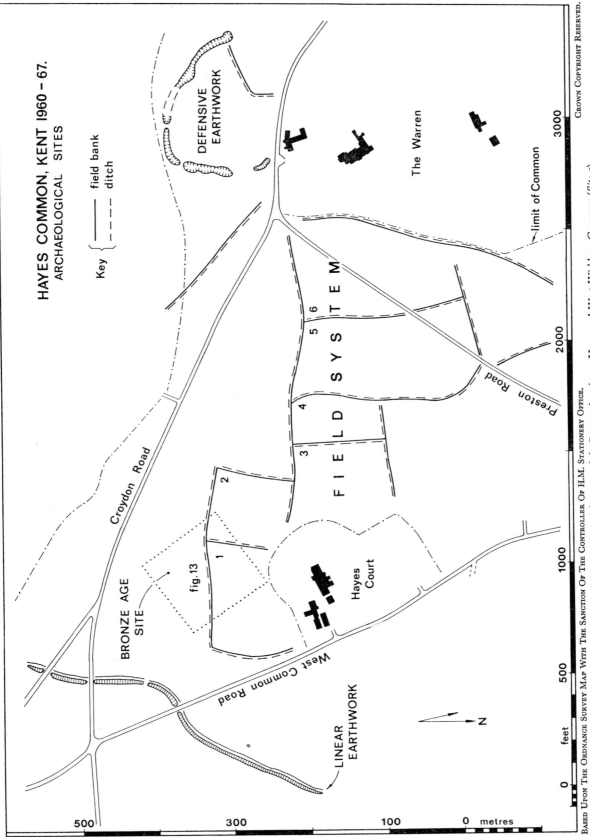

HAYES COMMON, KENT 1960 – 67.
ARCHAEOLOGICAL SITES

Key { field bank
      ditch

DEFENSIVE EARTHWORK

The Warren

limit of Common

3000

FIELD SYSTEM

4

3

2

5 6

Preston Road

2000

1

fig.13

BRONZE AGE SITE

Croydon Road

West Common Road

Hayes Court

1000

LINEAR EARTHWORK

N

500

feet

0

500

300

100

0 metres

BASED UPON THE ORDNANCE SURVEY MAP WITH THE SANCTION OF THE CONTROLLER OF H.M. STATIONERY OFFICE.

Fig. 12. *Plan showing archaeological features and the Bronze Age site on Hayes and West Wickham Commons (Site 5).*

deals mainly with the work on and the finds from the Bronze Age site, but brief notes on some of the other features examined have been included.

The excavations were severely hampered throughout by conditions imposed on the work by the public nature of the Common. All single trial-holes had to be completed, backfilled and restored before nightfall and in only four cases was it possible to erect fences so that more extensive excavation could be undertaken. No plant, tree or bush could be removed and all sites had to be restored to their natural state. The pebble-beds under these sites varied considerably from area to area. Sometimes compact, undisturbed pebble was encountered at 8–10 in., but disturbance by roots, animals, weather and even bombs had caused deep pockets of loose pebbles and soil, often resembling archaeological features. On one site it was necessary to excavate to a depth of nearly 6 ft. to ascertain that the loose pebble-beds were in fact a natural deposit and not a man-made feature. It is also possible that post-holes, pits, and stake-holes may have been disturbed beyond recognition. The acid nature of the soil appears to have removed all trace of bone and corrodes even recently deposited metal.

ACKNOWLEDGEMENTS

Thanks are due to the Commons Committee of the Bromley Council (Ref. 43) for permission to excavate on various parts of Hayes Common and in particular to Mr. C. R. Stock and Mr. J. F. Adsett for their help and interest. Mrs. E. Healey (née Warman) deserves a very special mention, not only for taking an active part in much of the excavation on the Common, but also for drafting the preliminary report on the work and for a detailed study of the finds. Mr. R. Robertson-Mackay has kindly contributed the report on the pottery and given valuable assistance throughout the classification of the other finds.

Mr. P. Bolton has kindly prepared most of the site-plans, assisted by Mr. F. Rebbeck and Mrs. M. Luyke-Roscott and Miss R. Chatters have drawn the majority of the published flints. Mr. R. Gierth and Mr. G. Clewley have drawn most of the other finds at the Bromley Archaeological Research Centre. To all concerned considerable thanks are due.

Of the many who helped on the excavation special mention must be made of those who worked for extended periods. These included Mrs. S. Brandham, Mrs. M. Broadfoot and Mrs. M. Woolven; Misses M. Last, E. Mynott (now Mrs. Philp), G. Price; Messrs. A. Appleby, D. Bartlett, B. Brandham, D. Broadfoot, G. Clewley, R. Ellis, N. Field, R. Gierth, C. Hart, J. Horne, H. Robinson and the late C. Jones.

THE EXCAVATIONS
(1) THE BRONZE AGE SITE (Fig. 13)

A series of scattered trial-holes, their positions largely determined by bushes, trees and paths, eventually located two joining ditches (Ditches 1 and 2), containing Bronze Age and perhaps Neolithic material. An area-excavation (Fig. 14) about 100 ft. to the north of these ditches located three flint-packed post-holes and 30 small pits, several of which produced Bronze Age material.

Ditch 1 (Plate IVa)

This was traced with difficulty in a straight line, running roughly north-east by south-west for a distance of 182 ft. It was approximately V-shaped in section, about 7 ft. wide at the top, about 5 ft. deep and had a narrow, flat base between 10–16 in. wide (Fig. 15). Its lower part had been cut through hard pebble-beds, but its upper part had been cut through a zone of mixed brown loam, sand and pebble, almost identical to the filling of the ditch. The primary layer (layer 6) consisted of compact pebbles capped by a layer (layer 5) of loam and pebble. This in turn was sealed by a black hard-pan layer (layer 4) almost certainly caused by leaching. It is possible that the ditch was deliberately filled, but the nature of the soil made this difficult to judge. In almost every case the trees and under-growth prevented the ditch being sectioned by a trench long enough to include the area where any bank may have been. Where this was possible no bank or other structure was found.

Nothing at all was found in the eastern two-thirds of the ditch, but the west end contained a large amount of archaeological material discarded as domestic rubbish. The primary layer was archaeologically sterile and all the

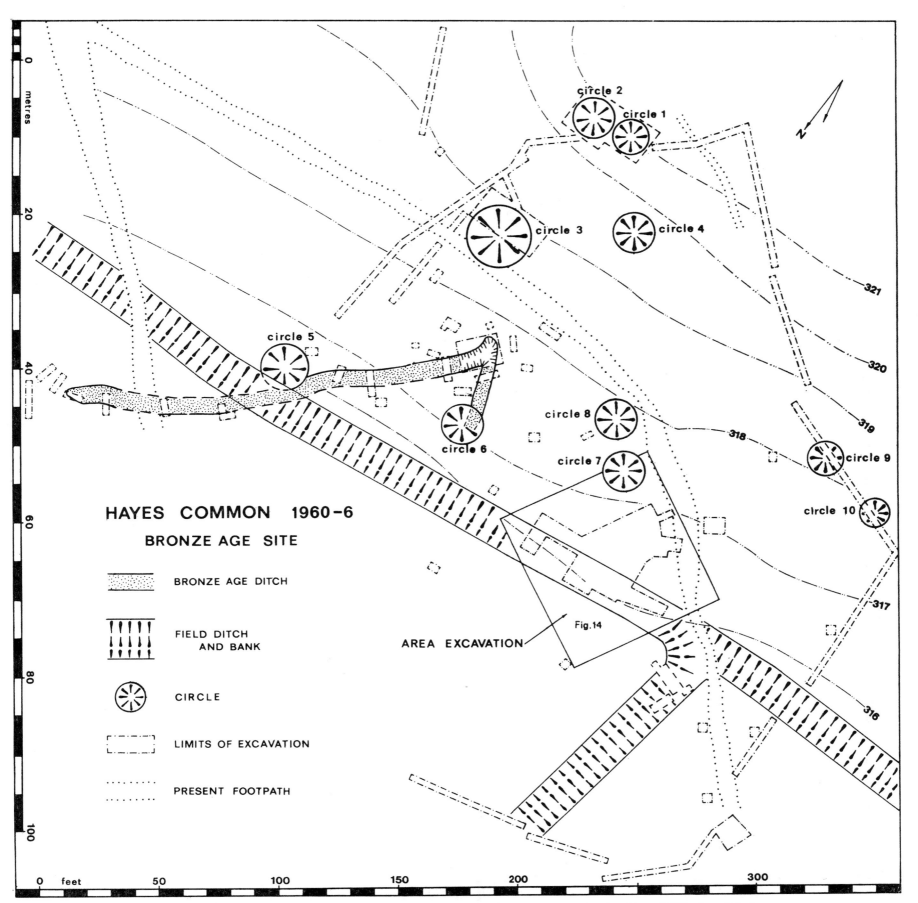

HAYES COMMON 1960–6

BRONZE AGE SITE

	BRONZE AGE DITCH
	FIELD DITCH AND BANK
	CIRCLE
	LIMITS OF EXCAVATION
	PRESENT FOOTPATH

circle 2
circle 1
circle 3
circle 4
circle 5
circle 6
circle 8
circle 7
circle 9
circle 10

321
320
319
318
317
316

Fig. 14
AREA EXCAVATION

Fig. 13. *Plan of the Bronze Age site on Hayes Common (Site 5), showing ditches, area-excavation (inset) and later Field Banks and Circles.*

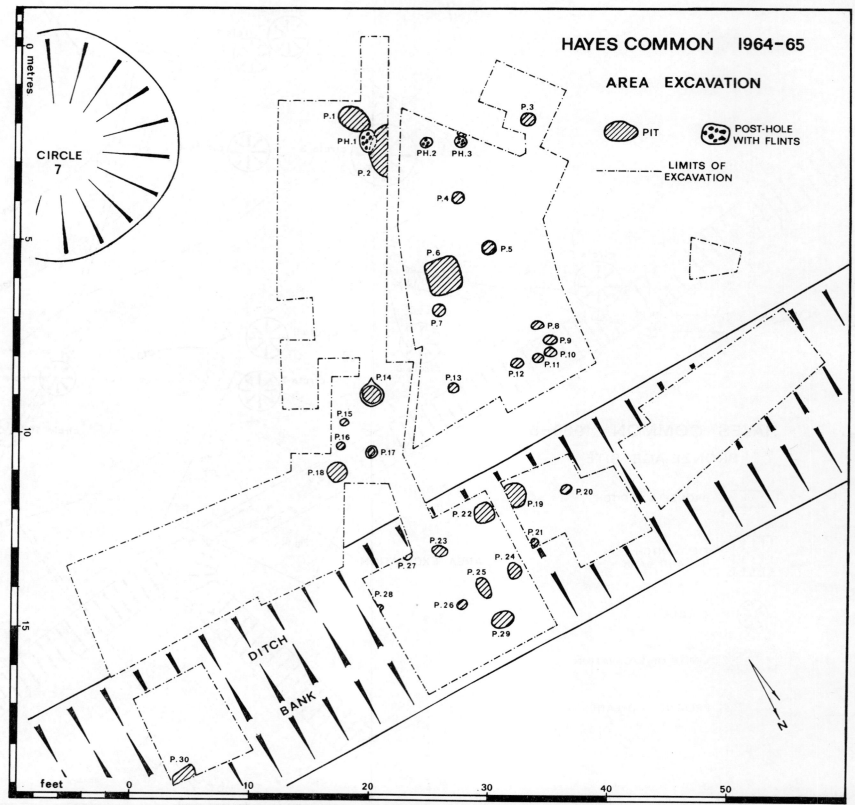

HAYES COMMON   1964-65

AREA EXCAVATION

PIT

POST-HOLE
WITH FLINTS

LIMITS OF
EXCAVATION

CIRCLE
7

P.1
PH.1
P.2
PH.2 PH.3
P.3
P.4
P.6
P.5
P.7
P.8
P.9
P.10
P.11
P.12
P.13
P.14
P.15
P.16
P.17
P.18
P.19
P.20
P.22
P.21
P.23
P.24
P.25
P.27
P.28
P.26
P.29
P.30

DITCH

BANK

N

0 metres

5

10

15

feet   0   10   20   30   40   50

Fig. 14. *Plan of the area-excavation of the Bronze Age site on Hayes Common (Site 5), showing pits and post-holes.*

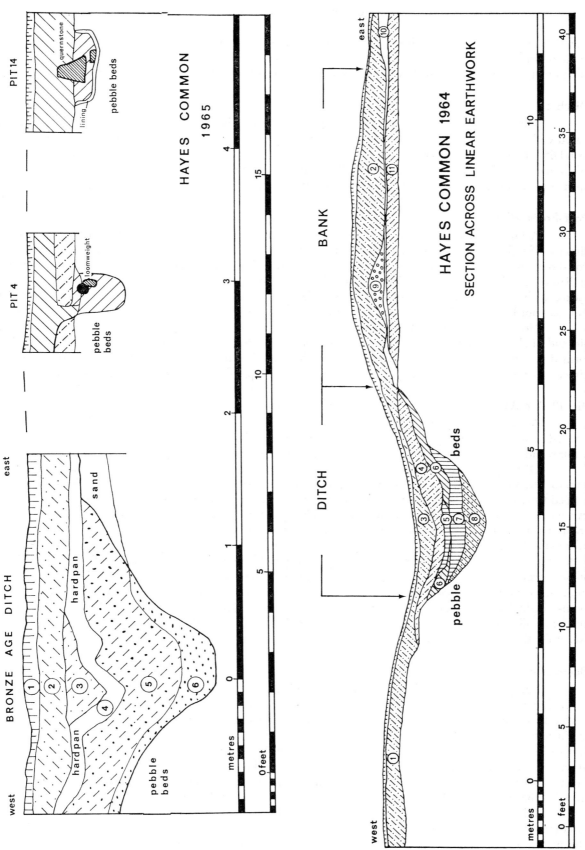

PIT 14

quernstone

lining

pebble beds

PIT 4

loomweight

pebble beds

HAYES COMMON

1965

west east

BRONZE AGE DITCH

① ② ③ ④ ⑤ ⑥

hardpan

hardpan

sand

pebble beds

metres 0 1 2 3 4

0 feet 5 10 15

east

⑩

BANK

② ⑪

⑨

DITCH

④ ⑥

beds

③ ⑤ ⑦ ⑧

⑥

pebble

①

west

HAYES COMMON 1964

SECTION ACROSS LINEAR EARTHWORK

metres 0 5 10

0 feet 5 10 15 20 25 30 35 40

Fig. 15. *Sections across the Bronze Age Ditch and Pits and across the Linear Earthwork on Hayes Common (Site 5).*

material came from the upper filling. This included three types of pottery (Nos. 139–142 and 142b–146), fragments of quernstone (Nos. 148 and 149), a hammerstone and worked flint (Nos. 103, 105, 109, 123 and 137). The majority of this material can be identified as Bronze Age, but some appears to be Neolithic.

Ditch 2

This appeared to join Ditch 1 at an angle of about 65°, but the junction was disturbed by roots. It was traced with difficulty for 42 ft. where it had been cut away by the construction of Circle 6. It was generally smaller than Ditch 1 and U-shaped in profile, being about 5 ft. wide and $3\frac{1}{2}$ to $4\frac{1}{2}$ ft. deep. It also contained a small quantity of domestic rubbish (Nos. 100 and 117), similar to that found in Ditch 1, which suggests that both ditches were open at about the same time. Again most of this material appears to be of Bronze Age date.

Post-holes (Plate Va)

A line of three flint-packed post-holes was found about 100 ft. north of Ditch 1. These cover a total distance of 8 ft., the space between Nos. 1 and 2 being $4\frac{1}{2}$ ft. and the space between Nos. 2 and 3 being $3\frac{1}{2}$ ft. Post-hole 1 was 2 ft. in diameter, 1 ft. 5 in. deep and was packed with six large flints. Post-hole 2 was only 10 in. in diameter, 10 in. deep and packed with eight flints. Post-hole 3 was about 11 in. in diameter, 1 ft. 3 in. deep and packed with five flints. A fourth post-hole (Post-hole 4) was found 140 ft. to the north-west in a random trial-hole and may not have related to the others. It was 1 ft. 1 in. in diameter, 8 in. deep and was packed with six flints.

No datable finds were found in direct association with these post-holes, but as these occurred close to the pits and ditches containing the Bronze Age material on an otherwise barren plateau, the probability is that they formed part of the Bronze Age site. Just possibly they could relate to the Neolithic material found in the area. Either way they probably represent a wooden structure, perhaps of rectilinear form, rather than free-standing posts.

Pits (Table A).

A total of 30 small pits, or hollows, was located in the area-excavation and all of these are shown on the detailed plan (Fig. 14). Only 19 of these pits contained material to suggest that they were certainly archaeological features and it seems likely that the rest were hollows formed by natural agencies.

Of the pits 16 are circular and between 6 in. and 23 in. in diameter. Eleven are oval ranging in size from 9 in. to 4 ft. 8 in. by 2 ft. and the other three are sub-rectangular (see Table A). The majority have steep sides and cupped bases and their depths vary from 4 in. to 3 ft. Seven have linings of yellow clay about an inch thick and two others contain slight traces of similar clay. It is likely that the lined pits were probably intended to hold either grain or water. Storage pits of broadly similar size, though unlined, were found in the Bronze Age settlement at Itford Hill, Sussex (Ref. 44). The pits at Hayes were filled with loam, pebbles, specks of carbon and a small amount of domestic rubbish including pottery (No. 142a), some possible potter's waste, fragments of quernstone, fragments of loom-weights, struck and worked flints and a number of burnt or fire-cracked flints ('pot-boilers'). Pit 14 (Plate IVb and Fig. 15) in particular contained large fragments of quernstone (Nos. 147 and 150) and Pit 4 half a cylindrical loom-weight (No. 152). All this material is similar to that recovered from the two adjacent ditches and it seems highly likely that all of it was discarded at about the same time. It seems from this that both ditches had gone out of use, except for the disposal of rubbish, at the time when at least some of the pits were open.

Occupation Area

The general area of the pits, ditches and adjacent circles produced an interesting assemblage of flint material. It includes struck flakes, implements (Nos. 95–8, 101, 106–7, 110–113, 115a, 116, 119–122, 124–127, 130–134 and 138) and numerous 'pot-boilers'. The retouched flint does not appear to belong to a homogeneous industry and includes a flake struck from a ground and polished axe (No. 131), scrapers and other tools which show general similarities to some Neolithic and Early Bronze Age types. It may be significant (see Table C) that only 196 rather large, crude flakes, five hammerstones and ten scrapers and knives were recovered from the pits and ditches in direct association with the later Bronze Age material. From this evidence it seems likely that a Neolithic site preceded the Bronze Age features coincidentally occupying part of the same area.

Trial-holes over many acres of the Common showed that it was generally fairly barren, except for an area of uncertain size flanking Croydon Road south of the Bronze Age site (hereafter referred to as 'Croydon Road'). This produced worked flint, including a leaf-shaped arrowhead (No. 129) and the usual mass of 'pot-boilers'. This may mark an extension of Neolithic activity on the Common. The same area is marked on the six-inch O.S. map *'flint implements found about here 1879-1908'* and this presumably refers to the work of George Clinch (Ref. 45).

Pit No.	Shape	Size (in.)	Depth (in.) below present ground level	Clay lining	Char-coal	Pottery	Loom-weight	Quern	Flint	Pot-boilers	Notes
1	O	32×24	32	—	—	—	x	—	1	—	Pit
2	O	56×24	36	—	—	—	—	—	—	—	Pit
3	C	16	25	—	x	—	—	—	—	—	Pit
4	C	12	28	—	x	—	x (No. 152)	—	1 (Hammer-stone)	—	Pit
5	O	16×14	21	—	x	—	—	x	—	18+	Pit
6	S.R.	34×34	24	—	—	—	—	—	—	—	Pit
7	C	13	16	—	—	—	—	—	—	—	—
8	O	8×12	17	—	—	—	—	—	—	—	—
9	O	8×12	16	—	—	—	—	—	—	—	—
10	O	13×9	19	—	—	—	—	—	—	—	—
11	C	11	24	—	—	—	—	—	—	—	—
12	C	11	24	—	—	—	—	—	—	—	Pit
13	C	10	13	x	x	—	—	—	—	—	Pit
14	C	23	6	x	x	Group 1b and potter's waste	Trace	x (Nos. 147, 150)	9 (1 knife, No. 118, 1 ham-merstone)	1	Pit
15	C	10	6	—	—	—	—	—	—	—	—
16	C	10	4	—	—	—	—	—	—	—	—
17	C	10	18	x	—	—	—	—	—	—	Pit
18	C	20	29	—	x	Group 1b (No. 142a) and potter's waste	x	x	1	2	Pit
19	C	22	20	x	x	—	x	—	1	3	Pit
20	O	10×12	26	—	x	—	x (above)	—	—	—	—
21	C	6	34	—	—	—	—	—	—	—	—
22	S.R.	22×18	31	—	—	—	—	—	2 (1 knife)	—	Pit
23	O	12×16	24	—	—	—	x	—	—	—	Pit
24	O	16×12	29	—	x	—	—	—	—	—	Pit
25	O	12×24	33	—	x	—	—	—	1	—	Pit
26	C	10	28	—	x	—	—	x	—	—	Pit
27	C	8	19	x(?)	—	—	—	—	—	—	Pit
28	C	7	25	x(?)	x	—	—	—	—	—	Pit
29	O	16×24	17	—	—	—	—	—	—	—	—
30	S.R.	24×24	21	—	—	—	—	—	—	1	—

O = Oval;   C = Circular;   S.R. = Sub-Rectangular

TABLE A

Pits found on the Bronze Age site on Hayes Common

(2) THE LINEAR EARTHWORK

A single bank-and-ditch earthwork can be traced for about 1,500 ft. across Hayes Common. This follows a somewhat irregular course on a north-east/south-west line with the ditch on the north-west side. It travels across gently sloping ground apparently without taking advantage of natural features. Its south-west end now finishes about 150 ft. short of the steep valley side and limited excavation suggested that it was not continued beyond this point. The apparent north-east end was not tested by excavation. A causeway across the ditch about half-way along its length, shown on a plan published in 1941 (Ref. 46), was found to be a deliberate fill consisting of flints, gravel and 18th century pottery.

Several sections cut along the bank and ditch showed that the bank is now between 1 and 2 ft. high and 10 to 15 ft. wide. The ditch was about 3 to 4 ft. deep and 10 to 15 ft. broad. The most extensive examination of the bank and ditch was made 55 ft. south of the centre of Croydon Road and 138 ft. north of the centre of Baston Manor Road (Fig. 15 and Plate Vb). Here the bank, constructed of material dumped from the ditch, was about 2 ft. high and 15 ft. wide. It sealed a hardpan layer, most probably the pre-bank land-surface. The ditch was a wide U-shape in section and had been cut through the hard pebble-beds. Originally it had been about 15 ft. wide and 4 ft. 6 in. deep. Over the primary filling of pebble (layer 8) was a deep deposit of mud-silt (layer 7), which in turn was sealed by pebbles and brown loam (layers 3–5). Allowing for considerable erosion of the bank it seems likely that the combined overall vertical height of the bank and ditch must have been between 7 and 10 ft.

None of the excavations along the bank and ditch produced any readily datable material. Only four struck flints and seven 'pot-boilers' were recovered from beneath the bank and 23 from the filling of the ditch (Nos. 102, 128 and 135). These probably represent a scatter of flakes relating to the Neolithic or Bronze Age sites in the area and they simply indicate the bank to be of a later date. Although there was no other evidence to date this earthwork, the fact that the bank is now largely flattened and the ditch largely silted would suggest that it may be at least several hundred years old. Its function seems to be that of a boundary rather than a defensive work, and it is broadly similar to another linear bank on Keston Common, about ¾ mile to the south (Ref. 47). It is anyway unlikely to be earlier than the late-Iron Age though it could equally well be of Saxon or early-medieval date. Just possibly it may be an outlying boundary of the large Iron Age hillfort in Holwood Park (Ref. 48).

(3) THE CIRCLES

The existence of more than 150 'Pit Dwellings' on Hayes Common was first published in 1880 (Ref. 49). At least six were excavated inconclusively by George Clinch between 1878–1886 (Ref. 45), who by 1906 had identified a Neolithic village (Ref. 50). Another circle was excavated in 1934 (Ref. 46) and two more in 1950 (Ref. 51), without conclusive results.

In reality the 'Pit Dwellings' are circular depressions, varying from 10 to 30 ft. in diameter; from 6 in. to 1 ft. 8 in. deep and normally they are enclosed by a small bank composed of material scooped out from the central area. Although widely scattered they form two groups and there is a hint that they may fall into various alignments.

The Group selected three (Nos. 1–3) for detailed examination in 1960 and tested another five on different parts of the Common. The results were largely inconclusive, the only finds being occasional flint implements (Nos. 99, 104 and 136), both in the depressions and under the banks. This material almost certainly relates to the Neolithic and Bronze Age settlements which cover limited areas and which was deposited before the circles were formed. The depressions had been scooped out of the root-disturbed pebble subsoil which had then been deposited around the edges, though in one case (Circle 3) there was some evidence that turf had been incorporated into the banks.

Two circles (Nos. 5 and 6) lie over the completely filled Bronze Age ditches and are clearly of much later date. One of these (No. 5) also appears to be cut by a ditch of the Field System, probably laid out between 1580 and 1797 (see below), which implies an earlier date. The fairly sharp profile of the depressions tends to favour a comparatively recent date though their function was clearly unknown to local inhabitants in 1890. On balance a date somewhere between about A.D. 1400 and 1797 seems most likely.

Their regular form would suggest that they were dug for some functional purpose rather than for the extraction of gravel. It has been suggested that some may have been hollows dug to provide shelter for animals grazing on the Common. Others may represent the position of large trees, which have been extracted, though there are few large trees on this part of the Common today. Some or all could even relate to a military encampment and represent hollows dug for bivouacking. Certainly in the Napoleonic period extensive temporary military camps were formed on Dartford Heath and on other open sites in Kent and Sussex (Ref. 52). More than this cannot be said at present.

(4) THE FIELD SYSTEM

An extensive series of small banks and ditches can be traced across much of Hayes and West Wickham Commons. These create a number of sub-rectangular units of varying size in the vicinity of Hayes Court and delimit a large area to the south. The block of rectangular enclosures thus formed (numbered 1 to 6 on Fig. 12) appear to be field units and cover an area of about 26 acres. The following Table gives their dimensions and acreages.

Field	Dimensions	Acreage
1	500 × 340 ft.	3·8 acres
2	330 × 350 ft.	2·6 ,,
3	500 × 400 ft.	4·6 ,,
4	100 × 400 ft.	0·9 ,,
5	770 × 400 ft.	7·0 ,,
6	770 × 400 ft.	7·0 ,,

TABLE B
The field units on Hayes Common

The other banks, generally not forming regular units, alongside the Warren and on the south side of Croydon Road probably enclose another 25 acres. The banks are now generally 2 ft. high and 6–10 ft. wide and the ditches about 1½ ft. deep and about 5 ft. wide.

A section cut in 1957 (Ref. 53) showed the bank to be constructed of turf and material probably taken from the corresponding ditch. Four cuts were made through the banks and ditches near Hayes Court in 1962, but the results were inconclusive. Fragments of Bronze Age loom-weights (No. 151), waste flakes, flint scrapers (Nos. 108, 114 and 115), and several small pits were found under the banks. One particular bank crossed over a completely silted Bronze Age ditch (Ditch 1) and was clearly constructed some considerable time after the ditch was dug. This eliminates the suggestion that the banks formed ranch boundaries of Bronze Age date.

Apart from being much later than the Bronze Age ditch the same bank also appears to trim part of one circle (Circle 5) suggesting that at least some circles were of earlier date. This is supported to some extent by the apparent total absence of circles within the Field System, for outside the fields they occur in large numbers and their absence within suggests that they may have been removed by agricultural activity. In addition, the longest bank on the west side appears to avoid deliberately the Defensive Earthwork on West Wickham Common, implying that the bank was laid out after the construction of the earthwork. Another small bank-and-ditch crosses the inside of the Defensive Earthwork and seems to take advantage of the ditches on the south and west sides to form yet another enclosure. Again this could only happen if the defensive ditches were already in existence. The earthwork itself has not been properly excavated nor is it easy to guess its function or date from its character or the various mounds within it. The shallow fill noted in its south ditch during a probe in about 1934 (Ref. 46) and its still sharp profile tend to suggest it is very much post-Roman in date. Camden, writing in about 1600 (Ref. 54), records:

> '*As for the other small intrenchment not farre of by W. Wickham, it was cast in fresh memorie when old Sir Christopher Heydon, a man of great command in these parts, trained the country people.*'

If this reference relates to this earthwork, as it probably does, then it is likely that it was constructed about 1570–80. Finally, the Field System itself appears to be cut partly away by the grounds of Hayes Court, built in 1776 (Ref. 55) and extended in 1797. This particular area was then known as 'THISTLY FIELD' and this implies the existence of at least one field in the late-18th century. Local maps provide no extra clues either to the naming or enclosing of this large area and Sister Mary Baptist, who has kindly researched this matter, could find no further information. Significantly, some of the ditches and banks on the south and west sides of the Commons are followed by the present parish boundary of Hayes. These sections are described (Ref. 56) in notes on boundary perambulations of about 1797 and 1825 as 'old ditches' and this, too, implies a date no later than the 18th century.

From the relative positions of the various features it seems that the Field System was laid out after the Bronze Age ditches had completely silted; after the excavation of at least some of the circles (perhaps 1400–1800); later than the Defensive Earthwork (perhaps 1570–80) yet before the construction of Hayes Court (1776 and 1797). On balance it seems probable, therefore, that the Field System was laid out between 1580 and 1797. This dating conveniently embraces the period of land enclosure prevalent through much of the 18th and early-19th centuries. Such 'reorganisation' of farming methods was in many cases long established before 1760 and to which formal parliamentary enclosure often provided a rational conclusion (Ref. 57). That the field units at Hayes eventually reverted to common use may reflect either very poor soil or unusual local conditions.

THE FINDS

By Mrs. Elizabeth Healey

This section of the report was substantially completed early in 1970 and no account has been taken of material published after that date.

(1) THE FLINT

The assemblages of struck flint from the sites on Hayes Common cannot be assumed to belong to one industry, although it is likely that most of the material from Ditch 1 and the pits forms a homogeneous group.

Most of the flint selected for use is of good quality and the local pebble has been used in only a few instances. Chalk with flints, occurs within ½ a mile to the south-west and would provide a readily available and practically inexhaustible supply. The flint deposited in Pits 14 and 18 may have been struck from a single nodule since it is possible to rejoin some of the flakes. This flint is dark in colour, unweathered and the cortex is unrolled.

The secondary retouch is usually minimal and is little more than is sufficient to make a serviceable tool. Scale-flaiking of the type associated with arrowheads is noticeably absent. Description and comment has been confined mainly to artefacts. All the groups are treated together for descriptive purposes since no difference in typology was apparent, but the composition of each group is shown in Table C. No metrical analysis of the material was undertaksen a the assemblage is too small in size and is unlikely to belong to a single datable industry.

Cores (Nos. 123 and 124)

Few of the cores have been used consistently, or in a regular manner, the two illustrated ones (Nos. 123 and 124) being unusual in this respect. No detailed classification of the cores has been made. They vary in weight between 15 oz. and as little as ¼ oz. Some large flakes (e.g. No. 121) and some of the scrapers indicate the size of the nodule that must have been available. Both pebble flint and imported flint was selected for use and they occur together in Ditch 1. Few of the cores (as No. 123) have been used to their full potential. It is hard to see what use the flakes struck from the keeled core (No. 124) could have been, as there are no flake artefacts of a comparable size and the core has not been utilised.

In addition to the more regularly struck cores there are almost 300 pieces of raw material or waste flint, which have been brought to the site, some of which have one or more random flake scars.

Flakes

The struck flakes vary considerably in size and shape. The larger, thicker ones seem to have been preferred for retouch as implements. Blade-like flakes are rare. There is no apparent difference in size between flakes with

	Ditch 1	Ditch 2	Pits and post-holes	Occu-pation-area	Linear earth-work	Circles	Field system	Croy-don Road	Total
Nodules	4	—	—	—	—	—	—	—	4
Cores	50	5	2	223	13	7	3	12	315
Other raw material	38	3	3	241	7	4	—	3	299
Flakes	146	31	19	687	65	83	13	97	1,141
Scrapers	7	1	—	30	3	7	4	1	53
Knives	1	1	2	9	1	—	—	—	14
Arrowheads	—	—	—	1	—	—	—	1	2
Axes	—	—	—	1	—	—	—	—	1
Perforators	—	—	—	22	1	5	4	1	33
Notched flakes	—	—	—	12	1	1	—	1	15
Other types	—	—	—	1	1	—	—	—	2
Unclassifiable retouch	—	1	2	—	—	—	—	—	3
Hammerstones	2	1	2	13	1	4	—	2	25
Totals	248	43	30	1,240	93	111	24	118	1,907

TABLE C

The composition of the flint assemblage from Hayes Common

cortex and those without or those selected for utilisation. The utilised flakes show both the regular squills and more random spalling as noted at Windmill Hill (Ref. 58, pp. 92–3).

Scrapers (Nos. 95–115a)

Primary flakes, or those among the first to be struck from a core, are preferred for retouch as scrapers (e.g. Nos. 95, 96 and 111). Thermally fractured flakes were also used (Nos. 109 and 115a). The smaller flakes (like Nos. 102 and 105) and the more blade-like flakes (No. 101) are not common. The majority of the scrapers are between 40 and 60 mm. long and fall into the breadth to length ratio of 3 : 5 or greater; half are more than 19 mm. thick. They have been classified according to the system adopted at Hurst Fen (Ref. 59, p. 217). There is a consider-able variety of form among the scrapers found at the various sites, but the main forms are the end scraper and the end-and-side scraper. For the purposes of this classification end scrapers are defined as having retouch only across the end of the flake opposite the striking platform (that is across the main axis of the flake) and no retouch on the sides of the flake. The distinction between these and end-and-side scrapers, where the retouch continues along the side of the flake, may be empirical (in examples Nos. 104 and 105). Scraping edges on the side of a flake (i.e. with the retouched parallel to the main axis of the flake) are found on broken flakes (Nos. 103 and 112), but are not strictly classifiable as side scrapers. Thumbnail scrapers (Nos. 115 and 115a) and disc-like scrapers (No. 114) are rare. The numbers are too few and the provenance too varied to make any metrical analysis; however, the end scrapers were separated into long and short forms. In the long form the length is more than 1½ times the breadth and the results confirm the impression that squatter flakes were preferred. In view of the small numbers present and the uncertain nature of the sites this cannot be used to suggest any chronological or cultural difference. Table D shows the distribution of the various types.

On visual inspection it appears that the profile or contour (Ref. 60, p. 10) of the retouched scraping edge varies from the classic rounded and symmetrical type (Nos. 96 and 110) to a flattened version (Nos. 100 and 102) and to a narrow almost pointed form (No. 109). A few scrapers have an irregular edge (as No. 98) and are possibly unfinished. In several instances (e.g. Nos. 95 and 105) only sufficient cortex has been removed to allow the edge to be dressed. Wear of the sort described by Semenov (Ref. 61, p. 85) was noted on five scrapers, but 14 have step-fracturing or undercutting on the scraping edge, perhaps occasioned in the reconstitution of the edge rather than in use (Ref. 60, p. 14). The retouch is normally steep (as Nos. 96 and 97), whilst the flatter retouch (as No. 112) is

	End		Side	End-and-side or Compound	Thumb-nail	Thermal	Total
	Long	Short					
Ditch 1	2	1	1	2	—	1	7
Ditch 2	1	—	—	—	—	—	1
Post-holes	—	—	—	—	—	—	—
Pits	—	—	—	—	—	—	—
Area	1	11	2	10	1	5	30
Linear Earthwork	—	1	—	2	—	—	3
Circles	1	1	—	3	—	2	7
Field system	1	—	—	2	1	—	4
Croydon Road	—	—	1	—	—	—	1
Totals	6	14	4	19	2	8	53

TABLE D

The occurrence of scrapers from various sites at Hayes Common

unusual. The retouch is mainly non-convergent (Ref. 60, p. 15). The long edges of some of the end scrapers have been retouched or utilised (as No. 100). The bulb of percussion and the striking platform have been deliberately removed in some (Nos. 95 and 111), perhaps to assist in hafting.

The scrapers are of a type found throughout the Neolithic period (Ref. 59, p. 217 and Fig. 11; Ref. 58, p. 93 and Fig. 40; Ref. 62, p. 291 and Fig. 9; Ref. 63, p. 118 and Pl. XXXIX) and into the Early Bronze Age (Ref. 64, p. 272 and Figs. 3–5).

Knives (Nos. 116–120)

Large flakes of 60 mm. long or more were preferred for retouching as knives; many of these are among the first flakes to have been struck from a core and only enough cortex to make an efficient working edge has been removed. Good quality flint, grey or dark brown in colour, was frequently selected for these implements. Three types occur which are described below.

(a) Four flakes have one edge steeply blunted and the other showing regular squilling. However they are not bifacially worked as the blunted-back form at Windmill Hill and Hurst Fen (Ref. 58, p. 99 and Fig. 43; Ref. 59, p. 224 and F51 and F54). One (No. 117) from Ditch 2 has less edge retouch than the others, but is of similar form. The leaf-shaped knife (No. 118) from Pit 14 has intermittent bifacial retouching on one edge. Another (No. 119) although squarer in profile also belongs to this series.

(b) A further four knives have only one regularly retouched edge (No. 120); they are made usually on primary flakes. In addition there are four cruder flakes, two of which were thermally fractured, with one regularly retouched edge, in one instance bifacially.

(c) Apart from these heavy flakes there are two smaller, narrower, parallel sided flakes (both broken) with one steeply blunted edge and the other with regular squilling.

Edge-dressed Flakes and Blades (Nos. 121 and 122)

Many flakes show signs of utilisation, but in addition to these there are some flakes with a more regular retouch. Few blades (as No. 122) are to be found in the assemblages. One (No. 121) is exceptionally large.

Arrowheads (Nos. 129 and 130)

A triangular or leaf-shaped flake with a rounded base (No. 129) has both sides retouched and multi-directional scarring on the back. This may be analogous to the Class B or edge retouched form of leaf-shaped arrowhead noted at Windmill Hill (Ref. 58, p. 100, Fig. 108–12).

	Type			Totals
	a	b	c	
Ditch 1	—	1	—	1
Ditch 2	1	—	—	1
Pits	1	1	—	2
Occupation Area	2	5	2	9
Linear Earthwork	—	1	—	1
Totals	4	8	2	14

TABLE E

Occurrence of flint knives from Hayes Common

No. 130 is a broken *Petit tranchet* derivative arrowhead, probably Class C (Ref. 65, p. 36 and Fig. 1). It was found under one of the field banks in the general Occupation Area. One side has been damaged, but the other has steep retouch on the truncated edge characteristic of PTDs. Another broken flake with retouch on the transverse edge may be a broken PTD, but it is too fragmentary to be certain.

Flake from a Polished Flint Axe (No. 131)

A flake struck from a polished flint axe was found in a field-bank in the main Occupation Area. It is of white flint and probably struck from near the side of the axe. Several of the original scars have not been fully ground out and patches of the ground areas have escaped polishing. The striation marks are at an angle of about 75° to the long axis of the implement. Two other flakes of similar flint, but unpolished, were found in the area.

Perforators (Nos. 132–135)

Tools of this category were seemingly used for perforating or reaming some organic material. Three grades of point may be distinguished:

(a) On a thin flake with a fine sharp point (pricker).
(b) On a thicker flake with a well retouched point (piercer).
(c) The true rotating awl, retouched from alternate faces.

The flakes are often squat and chunky. Table F gives their distribution.

	Type			Totals
	a	b	c	
Occupation Area	1	14	7	22
Linear Earthwork	—	—	1	1
Circles	1	4	—	5
Field System	—	2	2	4
Croydon Road	1	—	—	1
Totals	3	20	10	33

TABLE F

Occurrence of perforators from Hayes Common

(a) Prickers

These are on small, thin flakes with regular squilling on the points. The delicacy of the point suggests that they were used to pierce or prick something soft.

(b) Piercers

Thick flakes (like No. 132) and smaller flakes with projecting spurs or points were selected for retouch as piercers. The point is always well retouched but varies in length; in some instances there are signs of abrasion. The end opposite the point may have cortex left on it or it may be retouched (as No. 132). The heavier flakes with thicker points may have been used as a boring implement. Four of these have notches on the sides.

(c) Awls

The retouch is from alternate faces and the points are usually squat (as Nos. 134 and 135). There is only one example with a longer point (No. 133); it is triangular in section and retouched on all faces.

Notched Flakes (Nos. 125 and 126)

These form a miscellaneous group. The flakes selected are usually squarish and often small and rather poor. The notch may be deliberately cut into the side of a flake (as No. 126) or a concave edge may be chosen for retouch. Notches are also found on the sides of three flakes used as scrapers (No. 125) and four flakes used as piercers. The depth of the notch ranges between 2 mm. and 6 mm. with an average depth of just over 3 mm., the diameter varies from 5 mm. to 21 mm. the average being 11 mm. The notch is frequently undercut by step fracturing of the type noted on the scrapers. Apart from this no sign of wear was detected. The sides of the flake are not usually retouched, one (No. 125) is exceptional in this respect. This and the squat shape of the flakes with notches, makes it unlikely that they were intended as part of a process in the manufacture of microliths. Their survival throughout the Neolithic period and into the Early Bronze Age is documented at Arreton Down (Ref. 62, p. 294) and Plantation Farm (Ref. 64, p. 272, Fig. 4, No. 56). In addition to the deliberately retouched notches advantage may be taken of a hollow or concave edge for utilisation.

Spurred Implement (No. 127)

A primary flake with three retouched notches forming two points or spurs. One of these points has spalling on the bulbar surface possibly occasioned in use. It is very similar to artefacts found among the Late Neolithic types from the upper levels at Windmill Hill and West Kennet Avenue (Ref. 58, p. 105, F.153–4 and p. 239, F.215).

Other Types (No. 128)

An artefact made on a thermally fractured piece of flint has a bevelled end, which has been retouched from both faces. It has suffered heavy bruising in use. Neither the sides nor the other end have been retouched. It might have been an adze or an axe and is perhaps a cruder form of F.40 at Arreton Down (Ref. 62, p. 291 and Fig. 10).

Other Retouched Flakes

Several flakes have secondary retouch on them but are not shaped as artefacts. One flake has regular retouch along the base, but is broken and unclassifiable. The back of another flake struck from an edge trimmed core has multi-directional flake scars and retouch along the edge especially in the hollows.

Hammerstones and Pounders (Nos. 136, 137 and 138)

There are nine complete hammerstones with abraded areas varying in extent (as Nos. 136 and 137). Four of these have been extensively used and parts of the abraded surfaces are almost smooth. Their weight varies from 8 oz. to $21\frac{1}{2}$ oz., but one large fragment now weighing 14 oz. was probably three times this size originally. One (No. 138) is a flake struck from a hammerstone, suggesting that some were subsequently re-used as cores. Cores were also used as hammerstones, but the battering on the edges of some core-platforms is probably due to difficulty in detaching flakes rather than the use of the core for percussing. A further 14 fragments with abraded areas represent shattered hammerstones.

Comments

It is clear that diagnostic types are absent, but there is no reason to suppose that any of the flint is pre-Neolithic. The flake struck from a polished flint axe, the leaf shaped arrowhead and some at least of the scrapers and knives might indicate an industry associated with the Neolithic Bowl Cultures (Refs. 59, p. 214 and 58, p. 85). There are no artefacts which would not occur in such a context. Transverse arrowheads are known from such a context for example at Hurst Fen (Ref. 59, p. 225, Fig. 48) and Whitehawk (Ref. 72, p. 78). Some of the flint could, however, equally well be found in an industry with Late Neolithic pottery associations (Ref. 62, p. 284), or with Early Bronze Age Ceramic styles (Ref. 64, p. 270–277). The quantity of struck flint present however, militates against a date later in the Bronze Age, where flint tends to occur only sporadically (Ref. 66, p. 202 and Ref. 67, p. 323 and Fig. 23).

The relationship of the worked flint to the other material with which it was associated and which may be attributed to a particular cultural tradition (the pottery, loom-weights and the saddle querns—see below) is not clear. The flint was found over a much wider area than this material and it seems that the flint artefacts provided a major part of the equipment of the inhabitants at some stage. It has already been noted that flint does not usually occur in great quantity after the Early Bronze Age and it seems likely that most of the struck flint together with some of the pottery belongs to the Neolithic period and that this either survived when the material attributable to the Bronze Age was in use, or was disturbed during this later activity in the same area and became redistributed amongst the material.

(2) THE POTTERY

About 200 sherds of prehistoric pottery were recovered from the site. All of these came from either Ditch 1, or Pits 14 and 18. The preservation is very poor and the sherds small, very few show identifiable characteristics. For these reasons the pottery is described, but it has not been possible to date all of the sherds with any degree of certainty. I am very grateful to Mr. R. Robertson-Mackay who has kindly examined the material and offered the following comments:

The sherds have been described in the catalogue and it is clear from the illustrated material that there are three diagnostic vessels present only one of which is reconstructable. The following forms emerge:

(a) Group Ia

Large cordoned cinerary urn (No. 139). The cordon has been applied and is decorated with fingertip impressions made at irregular intervals; these are shallow and poorly executed. The rim is irregular in form, but it is mainly plain or slightly flattened. The coil left on the outside of the rim is unusual; this is found on the inside of a few rim sherds also. The ware is tempered with calcined flint grits up to 3 mm. in size and unevenly distributed. The paste is a red-brown colour and poorly fired. There are 17 sherds including 13 rim sherds of similar fabric and more than 50 other unidentifiable sherds. The rim forms of some of these differ from the illustrated sherd and probably belong to different vessels. (All from Ditch 1.)

(b) Group Ib

Cordoned vessel, perhaps similar to Group Ia (No. 142, 142a, 142b). The cordon is probably decorated with thumbnail impressions, but the condition of the pottery is too poor to be certain. The cordon is applied to the shoulder below a cavetto neck. The rim is everted, thin and pointed in form. The ware is corky and extremely friable; the inside is a dark chocolate colour and the outside brick red. The flat base (No. 142c) is of similar ware and may belong to this group. There are also more than 40 unclassifiable sherds which may belong to this group. The distribution of this group is wider than the others. Ten sherds came from Ditch 1 and seven and eleven from Pits 14 and 18, respectively.

(c) Group II

This group comprises vessels with everted flaring rims pointed in form (Nos. 143 and 143a). The profile of the pot is relatively straight. Decoration consists of four vertical lines arranged in overlapping arcs (Nos. 143b, c and d). This has been executed with a four-pronged comb-stamp. The ware is tempered with fine flint grits and fairly well fired. It is burnished externally and internally. The section of one (No. 143c) suggests that this pot was made by the coil technique. There are a further 21 sherds of this group. (From Ditch 1.)

(d) Group III

The vessels in this Group have T-shaped rims (Nos. 145, 145a and 146). There appear to be diagonal incisions on the outside of the rim, but the surface of the sherd is too badly eroded to be certain. The walls are about 13 mm. thick. There are 22 sherds and about 60 fragments which may be assigned to this group. (From Ditch 1.)

(e) Unassignable Sherds

Three sherds (Nos. 140, 141 and 144) are not readily attributable to any of the above groups. In addition a further seven sherds (not illustrated) were found scattered in the Occupation Area, but it is not possible to assign any of these to the above groups.

(f) Potter's Waste

Clay lumps, perhaps potter's waste, were found in Pits 14 and 18.

The precise relationship of the four pottery groups is not clear. The small quantity and extremely poor condition of the pottery does not permit detailed discussion of the material. The sherds are mainly too badly eroded to determine the finishing techniques. The cinerary urn belongs in a Bronze Age context. The finger-tip impressions on the cordon are shallow and poorly executed and the presence of unfinished coil construction implies poor potting. T-shaped rims (similar to No. 145) are known to occur among Neolithic Plain Wares (Ref. 58, p. 48 ff).

The material directly associated with the pottery, or from a similar horizon, is mainly the struck flint and includes a flint scraper (No. 109) and two knives (Nos. 117 and 120), the saddle-querns (Nos. 147–150) which were found in Ditch 1 and Pit 14 and scattered in the Occupation Area. Only one small fragment of loom-weight was found in Ditch 1. It is likely that the flint represents some pre-Bronze Age activity in the area (see above) and it is possible that some of the ceramic material, particularly the sherds with Neolithic traits may be associated with this. Other groups of the pottery may be contemporary with the saddle-querns and the loom-weights. It is suggested therefore that at least some of the material deposited in Ditch 1 may be derived.

(3) LOOM-WEIGHTS (Fig. 19)

Three almost complete cylindrical loom-weights and fragments of others were found in a very restricted area; two being found together under one of the field-banks and one in Pit 4. They are made of baked clay, tempered both with sand and some organic matter which has decayed. Their condition is very friable. The colour of the weathered surfaces is a dull red-brown, but when freshly broken is brick red.

The complete loom-weights vary in height from 70 mm. to 91 mm. and are cylindrical in form; one tapers towards the top (No. 151); another is approximately straight-sided and the third (No. 152) is squatter and has more rounded corners than the others. Each has a more or less central perforation which is only about 9 mm. in diameter in the two larger loom-weights; however, the perforation in one (No. 152) is wider (up to 27 mm.) and appears to have been made from both ends, perhaps with a finger.

In several instances fragments were found associated with pottery, fragments of quern-stones and struck flint (e.g. Pits 14, 18 and 19). Loom-weights of a similar type occur in Middle to Late Bronze Age contexts, for example at Itford Hill (Ref. 66, p. 200), Park Brow (Ref. 68, p. 4) and Shearplace Hill (Ref. 67, p. 231). They differ markedly from triangular forms found on Iron Age sites like Staple Howe (Ref. 69).

(4) THE QUERNSTONES (Fig. 19)

Some 100 fragments comprising at least two complete querns of dark red or purple ferruginous sandstone, or carstone, were found in the general area of the Bronze Age site. These specimens were kindly identified by Mr. R. W. Sanderson of the Petrographic Department of the Institute of Geological Sciences. Their distribution is shown in Table G.

Fragments of broken querns were found scattered over a considerable area. The majority of fragments are too small to reconstruct or attribute with any certainty and only 24 have any milling surface on them, but this is usually too small to identify. The upper and lower stones (Nos. 148 and 149) were found together in Ditch 1 and parts of two more (Nos. 147 and 150) were found in Pit 14. Both querns seem to be of similar size, the lower

	No. of fragments	Surface fragments		
		Upper stone	Lower stone	Unidenti-fiable
Occupation Area	51	2	3	7
Ditch 1	9 (3 large)	1 (No. 148)	2 (No. 149)	3
Ditch 2	1	—	—	—
Pits	38	1 (No. 150)	5 (No. 147)	—
Circles	1	—	—	—
Totals	100	4	10	10

TABLE G

Occurrence of quernstone fragments from Hayes Common

stones being about 15 in. long and 7 in. wide. There seems to be no deliberate shaping of the under surface of the lower stones, as was noted on the lower quernstone from Winnall, Hants. (Ref. 70). They are approximately oval in shape, although one (No. 147) is slightly more tapered at one end than the other. One of the upper stones (No. 148) is surprisingly thin, but it may have been split; it is not a rider of the typical bolster shape, but it overhangs the edge of the lower stone; whereas the upper stone from Winnall is narrower than the lower stone (Ref. 70). The milling or grinding surfaces of the querns from Hayes Common do not show much wear, except for a narrow band of polishing around the edge of the surface probably caused by the stones rubbing against each other in use. The milling surfaces are not markedly convex and it seems likely that these stones were abandoned because they had broken, as their scattered distribution suggests, rather than because they were worn or were part of a ritual deposit.

Saddle-querns are characteristic of the Middle to Late Bronze Age in England. Other sites, with saddle-querns and cylindrical loom-weights include Itford Hill (Ref. 66, p. 204); Green Lane, Farnham (Ref. 71, p. 187 and 192), where complete querns were found and Park Brow (Ref. 68).

(5) CALCINED FLINTS

Calcined or fire-cracked flints (often termed 'pot-boilers') were present in every area. A total of 1,195 was found and their distribution is given below.

Ditch 1	39
Ditch 2	8
Pits	25 (and 9 small pieces)
Occupation Area	921 (and 230 small pieces)
Linear Earthwork	53
Circles	57
Field System	2
Croydon Road	90
Total	1,195

TABLE H

Occurrence of calcined flints from Hayes Common

The pattern of distribution is similar to that of the struck flint (see Table C) with a relatively dense occurrence in the Occupation Area and the Croydon Road area. There are no local concentrations. Few burnt flints seem to have got into the ditches and pits despite other apparently domestic refuse there and only in Pit 5 are they present in quantity. It is suggested, in view of the small numbers present and the fact that some implements are burnt (No. 118), that these are flints and pebbles which were lying about, became accidentally heated in fires and then scattered.

(6) OTHER STONE ARTEFACTS

Flat Pebble with Abraded Ends (not illustrated)

Both ends of a flattish, water-rolled pebble, of a type which may be found in the local gravels, are abraded, probably by percussion. It is likely that the entire circumference was abraded, but the pebble has been split, perhaps in use as a pounder. There is no indication of any perforation.

Other similarly shaped flat pebbles have been found both in pits, the Occupation Area and in the bank of the Linear Earthwork, but there is no sign of abrasion on them. The sporadic occurrence of the pebbles amongst other archaeological material, however, suggests that they may have been deliberately collected.

Catalogue of the Illustrated Material from Hayes Common, Hayes
1. The Flint (Figs. 16–18)

No. 95.   End scraper, with regular non-convergent retouch. Slight wear on scraping edge. Grey flint with unrolled cortex over most of dorsal surface. Bulb of percussion and striking platform removed. From Occupation Area (HC-DB).

No. 96.   End scraper on a primary flake of dark grey flint; utilisation along one edge. The scraping edge is abraded and undercut with some signs of wear. The retouch is non-convergent. From Occupation Area (HC-AV).

No. 97.   End scraper; retouch non-convergent, steep and irregular, but with regular trimming on edge. Concave edge of flake utilised or possibly lightly retouched. Cortex (unrolled) along other edge. A patinated scar has been used as the striking platform, but the flint is dark grey in colour when freshly struck. From Occupation Area (HC-CE).

No. 98.   End scraper; large and irregularly retouched, possibly unfinished as only one short part of the edge is regular. Unrolled cortex on the dorsal surface. Dark grey flint. From Occupation Area (HC-BZ).

No. 99.   End scraper with minimal retouch, on a core rejuvenation flake, waisted in shape. Concave edges retouched. No cortex, but there is a small inclusion. Flint is poor quality, opaque grey. From Circle No. 1 (HC-60-2).

No. 100.   End scraper on the end of a broken core rejuvenation flake. Retouch regular and almost semi-convergent in parts. Some step fracturing and slight wear. Utilisation on concave edge. Grey flint, with small area of unrolled cortex. From Ditch 2 (HC-932).

No. 101.   End scraper on a blade with two parallel flake scars and dark cortex on one edge. Retouch regular and non-convergent; some spalling on the under surface. The non-corticated side has regular retouch. From Occupation Area (HC-AP).

No. 102.   End scraper. Scraping edge damaged, but contour is flattened. Retouch non-convergent. One side of the flake utilised, other retouched. Parallel-sided flake of honey-coloured flint, rolled cortex and some patinated flake scars. From Linear Earthwork (HC-A67).

No. 103.   Small scraper. Retouched edge is at an angle to the main axis of the flake. Contour flattened and retouch on side is semi-convergent although non-convergent at end. Utilisation on sides and concave edge. Bulb and striking platform deliberately removed. Small area of (?)unrolled cortex on top. Dark brown-grey flint. From Ditch 1 (HC-CR-11).

No. 104.   End scraper with part of one side retouched. Retouch is short, regular and non-convergent. Possible wear. Cortex (weathered) along one side and two of the flake scars on the back are patinated. Grey-white flint. From Circle (HC-233).

No. 105.   End scraper with one side partially retouched as No. 104 above. Other side utilised, inversely on the concave edge. The retouch is short and non-convergent, with much step-fracturing. Dark grey flint, with patinated striking platform. From Ditch 1 (HC-C5).

No. 106.   End-and-side scraper (end damaged). Slight wear on the scraping edge. Possible use on side, but too damaged to be certain. Small area of unrolled cortex on back. One old flake scar patinated. Bulb and striking platform faceted. Dark grey flint. From Occupation Area (HC-A5).

No. 107.   Scraper with retouch extending along one end and partially along the sides of a thermally fractured flake. Retouch regular and mainly non-convergent. Flint is light grey in colour; cortex and patinated scar on back, some abrasion, perhaps due to rolling in gravels. From Occupation Area (HC-682).

No. 108.   End-and-side scraper. Retouch forms an irregular edge. One side partially bifacially retouched with flat trimming on the bulbar surface. Patch of cortex at end interrupts scraping edge. Flint grey-white. From Field System (HC-613).

No. 109.   Scraper on a thermally fractured primary flake. Both ends and sides retouched. Edges are steeply and irregularly trimmed all round. Abrasion and undercutting at top. Contour rather angular for scraper. Dark grey flint, unrolled cortex. From Ditch 1 (HC-768).

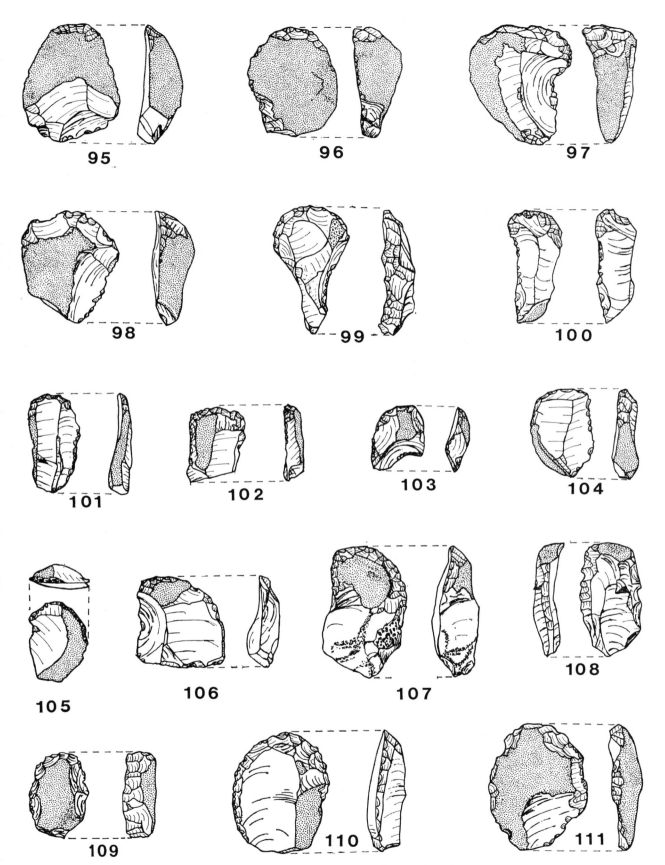

Fig. 16. *Flint implements* (½), *Hayes Common* (*Site 5*).

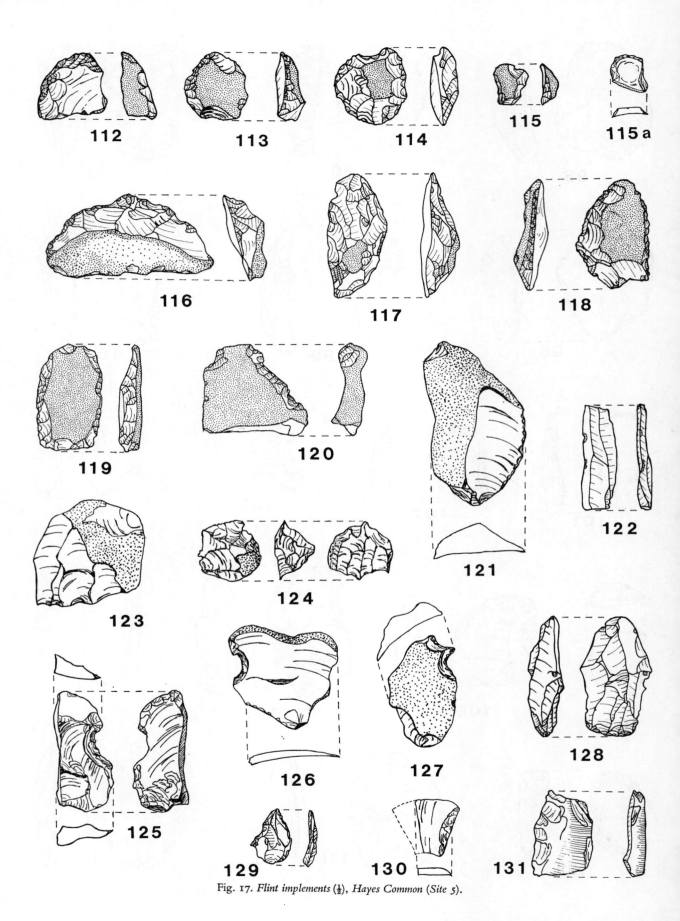

Fig. 17. *Flint implements* (½), *Hayes Common (Site 5).*

No. 110. Large end-and-side scraper. Scraping edge extends for three-quarters of circumference, and is slightly undercut. Retouch is semi-convergent in parts. The bulb of percussion has been removed and the striking platform retouched from the dorsal surface. Dark grey flint with a small area of unrolled cortex. From Occupation Area (HC-722).

No. 111. End-and-side scraper on a primary flake (unrolled cortex). One side damaged. Retouch is regular and non-convergent. End steeper than sides and undercut. Bulb and striking platform removed. Grey flint. From Occupation Area (HC-738).

No. 112. Scraper made on the side of broken flake. Retouch for a short length, regular and partially semi-convergent. Grey flint but with old flake scars patinated and cortex rolled. From Occupation Area (HC-88).

No. 113. Small end-and-side scraper. Retouch varies in steepness and may be unfinished; semi-convergent at bottom. Bulb of percussion and striking platform removed. Dark grey flint with fresh cortex all over back. From Occupation Area (HC-715).

No. 114. Compound scraper. Entire circumference of the flake is retouched, bifacially at the bulbar end (removing bulb of percussion and striking platform). Edge is irregular and slightly undercut in parts. The concave area is regularly and steeply retouched. Small patch of unrolled cortex on back; honey-coloured flint. From Field System (HC-606).

No. 115. Thumbnail scraper. Small irregularly shaped primary flake, retouched at side and partially at end. Bulb of percussion and striking platform removed. From Field System (HC-608).

No. 115a. Thumbnail scraper on a thermally fractured flake. Shallow retouch on three edges, cortex on fourth. One edge slightly concave. Probably pebble flint. From Occupation Area (HC-670).

No. 116. Knife with a steeply blunted back. Long flake with one edge steeply retouched, almost to centre of flake. The spur is carefully blunted. The other edge has minimal but regular retouch. Bulb of percussion and striking platform removed; primary flake, unrolled cortex, dark honey-coloured flint. From Occupation Area (HC-AV).

No. 117. Knife (?). Flake scars all over dorsal surface of flake, except for small area of cortex, meeting along a central ridge. Regular squill-like flakes removed along one edge; some step fracturing. Grey flint. From Ditch 2 (HC-N).

No. 118. Knife on a leaf-shaped flake. Both edges retouched, one steeply, producing an irregular outline; some abrasion on this edge. The other edge (the side of the striking platform) has flatter retouch. The butt end is damaged. Dark grey flint, unrolled cortex. Burnt. From Pit 14 (HC-AJ).

No. 119. Knife on the side of a broken primary flake. One edge steeply retouched, other flatter with regular squills removed along the edge and a small amount of bifacial trimming. The ends have not been retouched. Very dark grey flint, unrolled cortex. From Occupation Area (HC-AV).

No. 120. Knife (?). Retouch on one side and end of a large broken primary flake. Retouch on the end is short and steep. The side is truncated. The edge is fresh and may not have been used. Dark grey flint, unrolled cortex. From Occupation Area (HC-BA).

No. 121. Large edge-dressed flake. Regular squills removed along edge of main flake scar. Other scars at 90°, truncated by the flake. Dark grey flint, unrolled cortex. From Occupation Area (HC-BA).

No. 122. Blade with three parallel scars. End broken. Regular squill-like flakes removed along both edges and some gloss on top and edges. Light grey flint. From Occupation Area (HC-AX).

No. 123. Core, single platform. One old patinated flake scar suggesting the nodule had been previously used. Core platform is the scar of thermally fractured flake. Weight 9 oz. Light grey flint, unrolled cortex. From Ditch 1 (HC-864).

No. 124. Small core with keeled edge. Weight 1 oz. Multi-directional flake scars. Grey-brown flint with a small area of cortex. From Occupation Area (HC-748).

No. 125. Notched flake, with side and both ends of bulbar face retouched shallowly, as scraper (i.e. inversely to the notch). Some step fracturing inside notch. On core rejuvenation flake. Grey flint. From Occupation Area (HC-CX).

No. 126. Notched flake. Semi-circular notch steeply retouched from the dorsal surface; some undercutting. Edge of flake lightly and irregularly retouched. Unrolled cortex on end of flake, dorsal surface slightly patinated. Grey flint. From Occupation Area (HC-562).

No. 127. Spurred Implement. Primary flake with three notches at end forming two spurs, which are retouched; one point shows some spalling on bulbar surface. Dark grey-brown flint. From Occupation Area (HC-H).

No. 128. Chisel, chopper or axe (?). End of thermally fractured flake has been bifacially retouched. The edge is bevelled and abraded. Mottled grey flint with some old scars patinated. From Linear Earthwork (HC-119A).

No. 129. Small triangular flake, retouched to a point, one side more steeply than the other; multi-directional scarring on the back. Possibly an edge retouched leaf-shaped arrowhead (Windmill Hill Class B). The bulb and striking platform still remain. Light brown-grey coloured flint. From Croydon Road area (HC-302).

No. 130. *Petit-tranchet* derivative arrowhead (broken). One edge steeply retouched. Light brown-grey flint. From under field bank in Occupation Area (HC-CC).

No. 131. Flake (broken), from a ground and polished flint axe. Several of the flake scars are not completely ground out. Some striation marks. One edge utilised. Whitish grey flint. From Occupation Area (HC-CB).

No. 132. Piercer with wide point, steeply trimmed. Sides retouched as scraper; bulbar end damaged but also retouched. Old scars on the back patinated; dark grey flint. From Occupation Area (HC-AV).

No. 133. Awl with long point (broken); triangular in section, steeply retouched on three edges. Sides of flake retouched. Grey flint. From Occupation Area (HC-CM).

No. 134. Awl with short point retouched from alternate faces. Sides retouched; made on the bulbar end of a flake, cortex and some retouch on base. Dark grey flint. From Occupation area (HC-BC).

No. 135. Awl with very short point retouched from both faces. Concave edges of flake also retouched. Cortex left on base. Made on the side of a flake of dark grey flint. From Linear Earthwork (HC-A41).

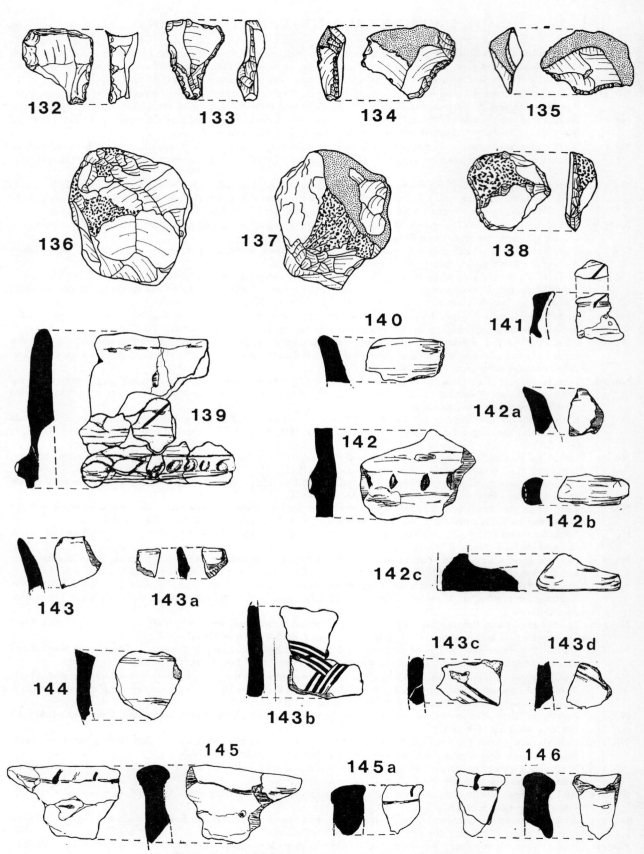

Fig. 18. *Flint implements and pottery* (½), *Hayes Common (Site 5).*

No. 136. Hammerstone of whitish-grey flint. Abraded on irregular points and in parts worn smooth. Weight 14 oz. From Circle No. 2 (HC-60-1).

No. 137. Hammerstone of whitish-grey flint. Corners and points abraded and worn smooth in parts. Some cortex remains. Weight 15·5 oz. From Ditch 1 (HC-872).

No. 138. Flake from a hammerstone of dark grey flint. Hammerstone subsequently used as core. Surface is very abraded. From Occupation Area (HC-M).

2. The Pottery (Fig. 18)

All the illustrated pottery is from Ditch 1, except No. 142a which is from Pit 18

No. 139. Rim sherd and cordon from a cinerary urn. The rim is irregular in form, with an external coil left in some parts. Possible diagonal incision on the neck above cordon. Applied cordon decorated with fingertip impressions at intervals varying between 3 mm. and 4·5 mm. Possibly vestigial lug on the cordon. Flint-gritted ware. (HC-CT).

No. 140. Sherd from a vessel with a very everted rim. Grit-tempered ware, similar to No. 139 (HC-CT).

No. 141. Rim sherd of uncertain type (damaged) but probably flattened. Decorated with diagonal incisions across the rim. Flint-gritted ware, similar to No. 139 and 140 (HC-CT).

No. 142. Wall sherd of a vessel, perhaps similar in form to No. 139. Cordon applied on the shoulder; cavetto neck above. The cordon is decorated with four probable thumbnail impressions. Condition very poor. Corky ware (HC-CT).

No. 142a. Rim sherd, pointed in form and everted. Corky ware similar to No. 140 (HC-CT).

No. 142b. Cordon with thumbnail impressions, probably similar to No. 142 (HC-CT).

No. 142c. Flat base from a vessel similar in ware to Nos. 142, 142a, 142b (HC-CT).

No. 143. Sherd from a vessel with an everted flaring rim, pointed in form, although the vessel profile is relatively straight. Slight vertical burnishing on the inside. Flint-gritted ware as Nos. 143a, b, c and d (HC-CT).

No. 143a. Rim sherd, pointed in form, like No. 143 but thinner and of a finer ware (HC-CT).

No. 143b. Wall sherd, broken just short of the rim (thickness of the wall decreases sharply) which was probably pointed in form like Nos. 143 and 143a. Decorated with a four-pronged comb in what seems to be a series of arcs. Flint-gritted ware similar to No. 143 (HC-CT).

No. 143c. Wall sherd with some markings, probably three parallel incised lines as Nos. 143b and 143d (HC-C5).

No. 143d. Wall sherd, probably from the same vessel as No. 143c. Some slight markings, probably three incised lines (HC-C5).

No. 144. Sherd broken just beneath the rim (profile flaring out). High finish, some burnishing. Flint-gritted ware, dark grey-black in colour. (Four other sherds of this type); (HC-C5).

No. 145. Rim sherd T-shaped form. Diagonal incisions on rim. Corky ware, black in colour. 145a and 146, probably from same or similar vessels (HC-C5).

No. 145a. Rim sherd T-shaped in form, with incision on rim. Similar to No. 145 (HC-C5).

No. 146. Rim sherd T-shaped in form, with incision on rim, similar to 145 and 145a (HC-C5).

3. The Querns and Loom-weights (Fig. 19)

No. 147. The lower half of a saddle-quern of purple limonited cemented sandstone, or carstone. Four fragments of a roughly oblong stone, about 1 ft. 4 in. long, 7·5 in. wide and 3·2 in. thick. The upper surface is only slightly concave and little worn; the slight trace of polishing around the edges suggests that the stone was little used. The fragments together weigh about 20 lb. and when complete the stone probably weighed about 30 lb. From Pit 14 (HC-AJ and HC-AE).

No. 148. A fragment of the upper stone of a saddle-quern of an identical stone to No. 147 and perhaps being the corresponding member. Slight convexity and slight traces of polished edges again suggest limited use. This was probably almost square when complete, about 7 by 7 in. and at least 1·5 in. thick. It weighs 4·15 lb. and when complete may have weighed about 7 lb. From Ditch 1 (layer 5) (HC-817).

No. 149. An almost complete lower stone of another saddle-quern of identical stone to Nos. 147 and 148. Two fragments of a roughly ovoid stone, about 15 in. long, 7·4 in. wide and 1·7 in. thick. Slightly concave with patches of polishing on edges and centre indicating wear. Together the fragments weigh about 8 lb. and when complete the stone must have weighed about 10 lb. From Ditch 1 (layer 5) (HC-809 and 818).

No. 150. A fragment of saddle-quern of identical stone to Nos. 147-9. Flat surface and only slight traces of wear. It is 3 in. thick and weighs 4·18 lb. When complete it may have weighed about 15-20 lb. From Pit 14 (HC-AJ).

No. 151. Several joining fragments of a cylindrical, orange-brown, baked-clay loom-weight. It is about 3·4 in. long, between 3·1 and 3·8 in. in diameter and has a central perforation about 0·5 in. for vertical suspension. The fragments weigh about 9 oz. and when complete the weight was probably about 25 oz. This weight is one of at least two found in many fragments under one of the field-banks immediately north-west of the Bronze Age site. These may have come from a small pit cut through by the ditch fronting the field-bank and re-deposited as the bank was made.

No. 152. A fragment of another orange-brown, baked-clay loom-weight, rather squat and roughly cylindrical. This is 2·9 in. long, about 2·8 in. in maximum diameter and has an uneven, central perforation about 0·7 in. wide. It weighs about 5 oz. and when complete may have weighed about 10 oz. From Pit 4 (HC-CD).

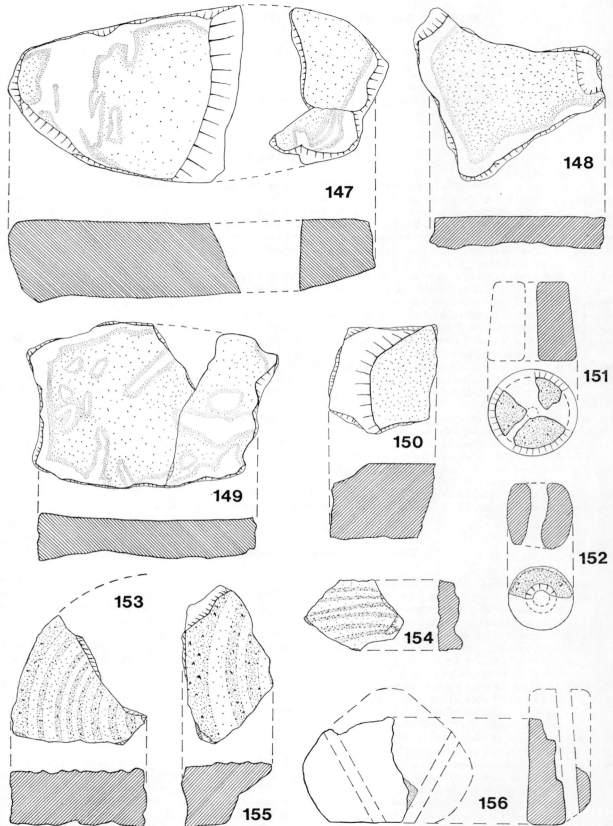

Fig. 19. *Bronze Age quernstones (Nos. 147–50) and loom-weights (Nos. 151–2), Hayes Common (Site 5); Roman quernstone (No. 153), Fox Hill, West Wickham (Site 8); Roman quernstone (No. 154), Elm Farm, West Wickham (Site 9); Roman quernstone (No. 155), Baston Manor, Hayes (Site 13); late-Iron Age loom-weight (No. 156), North Pole Lane, West Wickham (Site 10). (All at ¼.)*

SITE 6. A Probable Late-Iron Age Site at Pilgrim's Way, Westerham, Kent

This site (N.G.R. TQ.4560.5606) lies on the east side of the parish of Westerham, Kent, about 1¼ miles north-north-east of the parish church. It occupies part of two open fields (O.S. parcel 0005 and 4800), one each side of the Pilgrim's Way. The site is situated on hard Middle Chalk, beneath the scarp of the North Downs at an elevation of about 420 ft.

The site was discovered by the Group on 2nd September, 1966 during 'Operation Gaspipe West'. On the north side of the Pilgrim's Way the pipe-trench ran roughly north-south, but 70 ft. south of the road-centre it turned sharply to the east. Three features were recorded in the side of the pipe-trench and about 25 potsherds were recovered from the adjacent spoil-heaps.

Feature 1

Situated 93 ft. north of the centre of Pilgrim's Way and 83 ft. from the east hedge (O.S. parcel 0005). This was a large V-shaped ditch, cut obliquely by the pipe-trench, but running roughly north-east by south-west. It was about 15 ft. wide and at least 6 ft. deep. Its filling of brown loam and chalk wash contained specks of carbon, snail-shells, a single piece of burnt clay and an indeterminate potsherd.

An examination of the upcast soil representing the filling of this ditch produced 25 potsherds representing at least six different vessels, all too fragmentary for adequate illustration. One sherd was a coarse, black shell-loaded ware; two more were of Patch Grove type, one orange and the other brown, both with a mottled black-brown surface; another was of a fine, black burnished ware with at least two cordons and the fifth was a vessel of grey-brown ware with a hard, sandy light-brown surface. The sixth vessel was a soft dark-brown ware with curvilinear tooled decoration containing traces of white slip. This appears similar to several vessels from the Iron Age farmstead at Hawk's Hill, Surrey (Ref. 73) where it appears as one of the seven main classes of pottery. There it represents well-made jars with gentle outcurving rims tentatively assigned to the 3rd or 2nd centuries B.C. The majority of the other sherds appear to be late-Iron Age in character.

Feature 2

Situated 67 ft. south of the centre of Pilgrim's Way and about 60 ft. west of the east fence (field O.S. parcel 4800). This was a small bowl-shaped ditch, running approximately north-south and traced for at least 9 ft. It was about 7 ft. wide and 4 ft. deep. It was filled with chalk rubble and brown loam, but contained only one small piece of bone.

Feature 3

Situated 67 ft. south of the Pilgrim's Way and 3 ft. east of Feature 2. This was a small U-shaped gulley, or pit, 2 ft. 4 in. wide and about 2 ft. deep. Its filling of brown loam contained no finds.

It is difficult to say much about the nature and extent of this site. The various features and domestic pottery suggest an occupation-site and the large ditch may be defensive in character. The few potsherds mostly appear to be late-Iron Age in date and for this reason alone the site has been identified as Iron Age. The pottery was in fact from the upper filling of the large ditch which may have been dug centuries earlier, or indeed centuries later with the potsherds having been subsequently washed in with the silt. The exact relationship of the features to the Pilgrim's Way was not determined.

SITE 7. A Probable Iron Age Site at Goss Hill, Sutton-at-Hone, Kent

This site (N.G.R. TQ.5330.7080) lies in the north-west corner of the parish of Sutton-at-Hone, Kent, in a field (O.S. parcel 2800) about 1¼ miles west of the parish church. It is situated on the east side of the Goss Hill road on a south facing slope above Swanley Bottom. The subsoil of Upper Chalk is capped by about 8 in. of ploughsoil and the elevation is about 160–180 ft. O.D. It was discovered on 14th November, 1969 during 'Operation Gaspipe East'. The pipe-trench cut across the field south-east by north-west cutting through the southern hedge 188 ft. from the south-east corner. A group of four features was located on this site, but two other features more than 500 ft. further north may relate in some way.

Feature 1

85 ft. from the south hedge. A shallow U-shaped ditch, running north-east by south-west, about 5 ft. wide and 2 ft. deep. Its filling of brown loam contained animal bone, carbon, pot-boilers, and a single potsherd.

Feature 2

130 ft. from the south hedge. A small rectangular pit, 2 ft. wide and 2 ft. deep, with vertical sides and a flat base. Its filling of brown loam and chalk rubble contained a single potsherd.

Feature 3

163 ft. from the south hedge. A small U-shaped ditch running north-west by south east, 4 ft. wide and 2½ ft. deep. Its filling of black loam contained carbon specks, pot-boilers and three potsherds.

Feature 4

331 ft. from the south hedge. A small rectangular pit, 3 ft. wide and 3 ft. deep, with vertical sides and a flat bottom. Its filling of brown loam contained carbon and a single potsherd. Two pieces of burnt daub came from the corresponding spoil-heap.

Feature 5

869 ft. from the south hedge. The edge of a wide, bowl-shaped pit at least 7 ft. wide and 2 ft. deep. Its filling of brown loam contained no finds.

Feature 6

893 ft. from the south hedge. A small V-shaped ditch, running north-west by south-east, 3 ft. wide and 2 ft. deep with a flat bottom 1 ft. 2 in. wide. Its filling of brown loam and chalk rubble contained no finds.

Only six potsherds were found on the site and these came from Features 1, 2, 3 and 4 and all are too fragmentary for illustration. Five of these are from coarse, hand-made pots in a soft, black ware containing shell and with red-brown surfaces. The remaining sherd is from a much finer vessel with a slightly burnished surface. It seems likely that these sherds are of early-Iron Age date and that the first four features relate to an occupation-site, perhaps a farmstead. The shallow depth of soil overlying the very hard chalk should facilitate aerial surveys under ideal conditions when the extent and nature of this site might be revealed.

SITE 8. A Romano-British Site near Fox Hill, West Wickham, Kent

This site (N.G.R. TQ.3860.6410) lies within the limits of the Neolithic-Bronze Age (Site 2) on Wickham Court Farm, West Wickham, Kent. Its centre lies about 180 ft. from the edge of the wood on the west side of the field and about 300 ft. from the north hedge (Fig. 20). The subsoil is a soft brickearth and the elevation about 330 ft. O.D. The main London-Lewes Roman road passes only about 350 yds. east of the centre of the site.

It was discovered in January, 1962, during survey work on the Neolithic-Bronze Age site when about 20 Romano-British potsherds were found. During the severe winter of 1962–3 the Group excavated further to the east in an attempt to locate the course of the Roman road. A total of 466 ft. of trench was then dug and the line of the road, two quarries and one side-ditch eventually located. Very few finds were made during all this work and so in the winter of 1963–4 attention was returned to the Neolithic-Bronze Age area where the Romano-British potsherds had been found originally. During the course of this winter it was possible to excavate about 400 ft. of trench and about 25 small trial-holes before the field had to be restored in readiness for sowing. This work revealed six small ditches, seven irregular pits, a single post-hole and occupation-scatter over a limited area. The finds from all of these features were Romano-British and dated from about A.D. 80–140.

Thanks are again due to Mr. E. E. Pallant of Wickham Court Farm for his kind co-operation and for permission to excavate on his land. Of the diggers who worked for extended periods Mrs. M. Woolven, Messrs. A. Appleby, D. Bartlett, C. Hart and C. Jones deserve special mention. Thanks are also due to Mrs. M. Broadfoot, Misses G. Price and E. Warman (now Mrs. E. Healey), Messrs. D. Broadfoot, G. Cramp, N. Field, T. Greenwood, R. Gierth, J. Horne and H. Robinson for their hard work on various occasions.

As regards specialist help Mr. G. Clewley has described and drawn the pottery; Mrs. K. Hartley has kindly reported on the stamped mortarium and Mr. M. Henig on the finger-ring and intaglio. The site-plan is mostly the work of Mr. T. Woodman.

THE DITCHES

All six ditches had suffered to some extent from the effects of weathering and ploughing and in certain areas they were traced only with considerable difficulty. All had been V-shaped in section originally, but in each case the profile had weathered to a rounded U-shape. The depths varied from 12 to 34 in. even along the same length of ditch. It seems unlikely that any ditch was dug with such an intentional variation and the best explanation seems to be that the ground-level in Roman times was uneven and that the ditches were dug to a constant depth. Subsequent ploughing may have made the surface level and removed more of one part of a ditch than another. The filling in each ditch was an even light-brown loam similar to the disturbed soil beneath the ploughsoil and identical to that in all seven pits. It was impossible to differentiate between the fillings of the pits and ditches where these coincided. The depths given below are those taken from present ground-level.

Ditch 1

This followed a straight north-south course for a distance of at least 70 ft. Its south end touched Pit 1 and its north end must have stopped short at the end of Ditch 2. It was U-shaped in section, about 1 ft. 6 in. wide and 2 ft. 6 in. deep. Its filling of brown loam contained eight Romano-British potsherds.

Ditch 2

This followed an almost straight east-west line for a distance of at least 200 ft. Its east end was not found, but its west end terminated a few feet from the end of Ditch 1. It was U-shaped in profile and its width varied from 10 in. to 4 ft. 7 in. and its depth from 1 ft. 5 in. to 2 ft. 10 in. Its filling of light-brown loam contained only seven Romano-British potsherds, but the disturbed soil above contained numerous potsherds almost certainly ploughed from the filling.

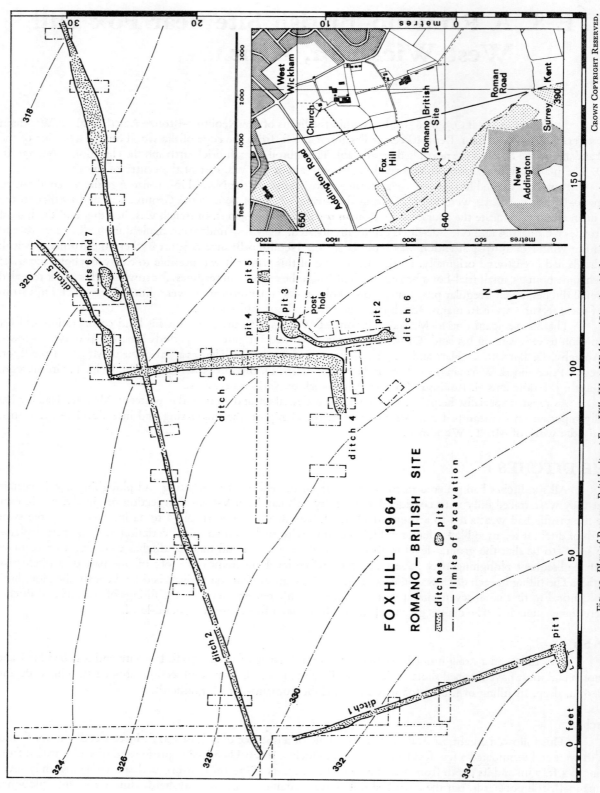

Fig. 20. *Plan of Romano-British site at Fox Hill, West Wickham (Site 8) with location map (inset).*

Ditch 3

This, too, ran in an almost straight line for a total length of only 60 ft. Its south end joined Ditch 4 and its north end joined Ditch 5. It was U-shaped in profile, between 2 ft. 2 in. and 3 ft. 5 in. wide and between 1 ft. 5 in. and 2 ft. 10 in. deep (Fig. 21). Its filling of brown loam contained 329 fragmentary Romano-British potsherds, including a little Patch Grove ware, the rims of several small sandy-ware jars, a chip of samian, a Roman tile and fragments of sandstone quern (No. 153).

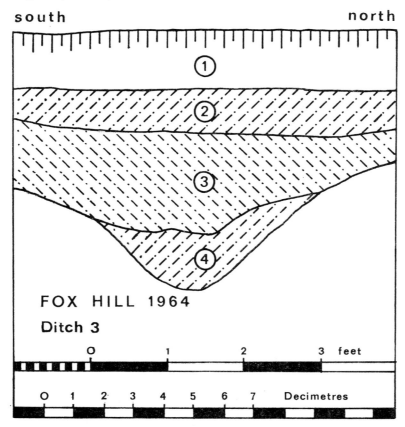

Fig. 21. *Section through Ditch 3, Romano-British site at Fox Hill, West Wickham (Site 8).*

Ditch 4

This was traced for only 15 ft., running in a straight line, roughly east-west. Its east end joined Ditch 3, but its west end was not located. It was U-shaped in section, about 2 ft. 8 in. wide and 2 ft. 6 in. deep. Its light brown loam filling contained 15 Romano-British potsherds.

Ditch 5

This joined the north end of Ditch 3 and from there ran in a slight curve eastwards for at least 42 ft. Its east end was not found. It was U-shaped in section, about 2 ft. 7 in. wide and 2 ft. deep. It was filled with brown loam containing seven potsherds, including a chip of samian ware and a fragment of an amphora.

Ditch 6

This lay south-east of Ditch 3 and it was traced for a distance of at least 35 ft. though neither end was found. The main part of it ran north-south, but the rest curved away to the north-east. On its line were Pits 2, 3 and 4. It was U-shaped in section, about 1 ft. 7 in. wide and between 1 ft. 7 in. and 2 ft. 6 in. deep. Its filling of light-brown loam contained 629 Romano-British potsherds (Nos. 157–168). These included Patch Grove ware, corky ware, numerous shouldered jars, reeded rim bowls, raised foot-ring bases, an amphora sherd, two chips of samian, fragments of sandstone quern and two pieces of slag.

THE PITS

The seven pits were all either sub-circular or irregular. None was well-cut and considering the soft nature of the natural brickearth it is possible that several were in fact large holes made by roots or burrowing animals. Only Pits 1 and 3 contained sufficient Roman material to suggest they had actually been open in Romano-British times. The filling of the pits was a light brown loam in each case, generally indistinguishable from the ditch-fillings and disturbed deposits elsewhere on the site. All had sloping sides and cupped or flat bases.

Pit 1

Irregular pit on line of Ditch 1, at least 6 ft. long, 3 ft. wide and 3 ft. 8 in. deep. Its filling of light brown loam contained pot-boilers, but no pottery.

Pit 2

Roughly circular pit on line of Ditch 6, 3 ft. 6 in. wide and about 2 ft. 6 in. deep. It was filled with brown loam and contained no pottery.

Pit 3

Oval pit on line of Ditch 6, about 4 ft. 6 in. by 3 ft. 4 in. and 2 ft. deep. Its filling of light-brown loam contained several flints, 303 sherds of Romano-British pottery (Nos. 169–182) and fragments of sandstone quern. The pottery includes Patch Grove ware, corky ware, sandy ware shouldered jars and at least one reeded-rim bowl.

Pit 4

An irregular pit east of Ditch 3 and probably on the continuation of Ditch 6. About 5 ft. wide and 1 ft. 10 in. deep. It contained 21 potsherds, mostly sandy wares.

Pit 5

A section of an irregular pit east of Ditch 6 about 2 ft. 4 in. wide and 2 ft. 8 in. deep. It was filled with brown loam and contained no finds.

Pit 6

Irregular pit between Ditches 2 and 5. About 4 ft. long, 3 ft. wide and 2 ft. deep. Its filling of light brown loam contained 35 potsherds, mostly Romanised sandy wares, including a stamped mortarium (Nos. 183–4).

Pit 7

An irregular pit immediately east of Pit 6. At least 4 ft. long, 3 ft. wide and 1 ft. 10 in. deep. It was filled with brown loam and contained no finds.

Post-hole

A roughly circular mass of flints and two Roman tiles, about 1 ft. by 1 ft. 6 in., was located by Pit 3. These filled a small vertical hole dug to a depth of 1 ft. 7 in. and had formed the packing around a wooden post 6 in. in diameter. No other post-holes were located and it is not known if this post formed part of a structure or building.

Unstratified Material

As could be expected from a shallow site ploughed for many years a large amount of the material recovered was unstratified. This included some 744 potsherds of a wide range of vessels (see Table A) and fragments of three quernstones. There were also several pieces of Roman tile and iron slag; part of a bronze brooch, an iron finger-ring (see specialist report) and a coin of Edward II (A.D. 1307–1327).

ROMAN ROAD

An east-west trench, 145 ft. in length, eventually cut the Roman road at a point about 350 yds. south of the track to the farm and about 300 yds. west of the track flanking the east side of the farm outbuildings. This revealed the line of the road, a quarry-ditch flanking each side and a single side-ditch, cut into solid chalk.

Progressing from east to west the first feature was the side-ditch, V-shaped in section, 3 ft. wide and 2 ft. deep. About 5 ft. west of this was a quarry-ditch 12 ft. 4 in. wide, 2 ft. deep, with steep sides and a broad, flat base. Its brown loam filling contained several hundred small round pebbles which covered its whole width. From the west lip of the quarry-ditch was a hard, flat platform of natural chalk just 17 ft. wide and covered by only 10 in. of ploughsoil containing more small pebbles.

From the west edge of this platform was a larger quarry-ditch 22 ft. wide, 2 ft. 9 in. deep with sloping sides and a flat base. This too contained brown loam which was capped by a mixed layer of loam and pebbles up to 8 in. thick. No trace of a west side-ditch was found.

There can be little reasonable doubt that the 17 ft.-wide platform of natural chalk represents the position of the Roman road, the metalling of which has been removed by ploughing. The wide quarries on the sides were probably dug for the extraction of the very hard chalk-rock in Roman times whilst the road was still in use. The large quantities of small pebbles in the upper filling of each quarry must have spilled off the road itself, either spread by traffic or by subsequent ploughing. The small east side-ditch was probably one of a pair with that on the west side having been eliminated by the larger quarry. The centre of the east ditch lay 27 ft. from the centre of the chalk platform and this suggests that if matching side-ditches did exist then they would have been about 54 ft. apart.

The small pebbles from the surface of the platform and in the quarry-ditches are typical of the metalling used for this road elsewhere. Similar pebble metalling has been observed by the Group at Sparrow's Den ($\frac{1}{2}$ mile to the north), King Henry's Drive (2 miles to the south) and at Titsey (Site 15—5 miles to the south). Extensive deposits of these natural pebbles occur nearby at West Wickham and Hayes.

DISCUSSION

The site chosen occupied good, light soil very close to the main arterial Roman road. It appears to have been occupied from about A.D. 80–140. This dating is based upon a study of the pottery where the predominance of sandy Romanised products is particularly significant (see below). On similar local sites the predominance of native wares normally dates a site to the second half of the 1st century A.D. From this it seems that the site was established towards the end of the 1st century and that it was probably occupied for no more than two generations, perhaps by a single family.

The total lack of building materials, other than a very few tiles, tends to prove that no masonry buildings existed here and suggests that any structures were of wood. The small amount of iron slag and the few possible wasters are the only hints of industrial activity and it seems likely that this was another farmstead. The pits and ditches are anyway typical of such farmstead sites and the finds generally reflect a modest establishment. The finger-ring may have been left by a passing traveller, the lavastone quern and the samian came from the Continent and the other querns and pottery from much nearer local markets. As with all the sites in this immediate area Fox Hill lay well within the orbit of Roman Londinium a mere 11 miles away. Why the site was abandoned is not known.

It seems clear that all stratified deposits, other than those in pits and ditches, have been totally destroyed by ploughing. The single post-hole may indicate that the outlines of structures yet survive, but this seems unlikely. The ditches are mostly rectilinear in form and either delimited fields, served as enclosures or for drainage. The bulk of the pottery was found in the vicinity of Ditches 3 and 6 adjacent to the post-hole and it may be that this represents the centre of the site and perhaps the position of a domestic hut. Ditches 1 and 2 appear to form two sides of a single rectangle and the fact that they do not quite join may indicate the position of an entrance. Ditch 3 appears to form the third side of the same rectangle giving a length of about 100 ft. If Ditch 4 formed part of the fourth side then the width of this area would have been about 45 ft. Ditches 5 and 6 are not regular and do not seem to form part of the basic rectilinear arrangement. It seems likely that more ditches and pits exist, or did exist, in the area and the whole complex must have covered at least an acre.

THE FINDS

(1) THE POTTERY

A total of 2,098 potsherds was recovered from the pits, ditches and unstratified deposits and these represent a minimum of 124 different vessels, of which 30 (Fig. 22) have been drawn. Although this pottery may not be a representative sample its classification provides some useful information. Four main groups emerge. The distribution of the pottery in these groups is given in Table A and the notes on each appear below.

Deposit	Samian ware	Patch Grove and related wares	Shell and corky wares	Romanised wares	Totals
Ditch 1	—	2	1	5	8
Ditch 2	—	—	—	7	7
Ditch 3	1	34	8	286	329
Ditch 4	—	1	3	11	15
Ditch 5	1	2	1	3	7
Ditch 6	2	31	73	523	629
Pit 3	—	8	6	289	303
Pit 4	—	1	—	20	21
Pit 6	—	3	—	32	35
Unstratified	8	116	37	583	744
Total sherds	12	198	129	1,759	2,098
Vessels represented (minimum)	4	12	10	98	124

TABLE A

Distribution and classification of pottery from the Fox Hill site

Group A. Samian Ware

Only 12 very worn sherds of samian ware were recovered and these represent a minimum of four vessels. These consist of the rim of a Form 29 and parts of two Form 27, all three probably of late-1st century date. The fourth vessel is the rim of a Form 35–36 and probably dates from the first half of the 2nd century. The four identifiable vessels all came from unstratified contexts, but indeterminate sherds were found in Ditches 3, 5 and 6.

Group B. Patch Grove and Related Wares

This group embraces here those vessels with a porridgy, blue-grey paste, often black speckled. The surfaces are orange, brown, grey or black. The ware feels soft and slightly soapy and most of the vessels are fairly thick and coarse. It also includes rather similar pottery, but with a poorer surface and orange-red specks in the paste. This type of pottery is well-known in West Kent and East Surrey though it has not yet been the subject of a detailed study, nor is it known where it was made. The term 'Patch Grove' was first applied in 1939 when pottery of this type from a site at Ightham was published together with similar pottery from other local sites (Ref. 74). The name is convenient to use though it must be remembered that it does not necessarily mean that this type of pottery was actually made at Patch Grove, Ightham. Three main types of vessel seem to be represented. Large storage-jars with simple outcurved rims and often one or two rows of stick-stabbing on the shoulder. Squat jars with simple outcurved rims and often burnished externally, sometimes with a simple lattice pattern. Thirdly, cooking-pots with bead-rims matching those in shell-loaded or sandy Romanised fabrics. All of these types were found at Eastwood, Fawkham (Ref. 75), Oldbury or Patch Grove, Ightham (Ref. 74), Baston Manor (Site 13) and Lullingstone, Eynsford (Ref. 76). It was suggested in 1944 (Ref. 77) that this pottery first appeared in the region just before the Conquest, in A.D. 43, though conclusive evidence is yet to come. It was certainly abundant throughout the second half of the 1st century A.D., where it is often the paramount native ware. Although it certainly survived into the 2nd century, as at Joyden's Wood (Ref. 78) and Baston Manor, it was rapidly superseded by Romanised products. It survived, however, until about the end of the 2nd century at least in the form of cinerary urns as found at Wickham Field, Otford (Ref. 79) and Warbank, Keston (Ref. 80).

A total of 198 sherds representing a minimum of 12 vessels was found at Fox Hill, all being too fragmentary for illustration. These consisted of fragments of seven storage jars and five bead rim cooking-pots. At least one storage jar was decorated with a single row of large stabs and another with a deeply incised chevron pattern along a raised band (similar to No. 287 from Eastwood). Sherds of Patch Grove pottery were recovered from all parts of the site.

Group C. Shell-loaded and Corky Wares

This group represents pottery containing varying amounts of crushed shell added to the clay, as a temper, before firing. It also includes similar pottery from which shell has dissolved out giving the surface a pocketed, or 'corky' appearance. The ware is normally fairly soft to the touch and in a wide range of colours from pink-orange to brown or black. The type occurs widely in West Kent appearing before the Conquest in exclusively late-Iron Age contexts as at Lower Warbank, Keston (now under excavation). It is common throughout the second half of the 1st century occurring almost invariably as cooking-pots with beaded rims. At Baston Manor (Site 13) and here at Fox Hill this shell-loaded pottery occurs in direct association with Romanised pottery of the early-2nd century. It seems probable that it did not extend beyond the middle of the 2nd century A.D.

Only 129 sherds of shell-loaded or corky pottery were found and these represent a minimum of 10 vessels (Nos. 157, 158, 160 and 187). Nine of these vessels are bead rim cooking-pots and the tenth a storage jar with a squared, thickened rim. These too were found on all parts of the site.

Group D. Coarse, Hard Sandy Romanised Wares

This group consists of a very wide range of vessels. They are generally hard and sandy to the touch and generally much better-fired than either the Patch Grove or shell-loaded wares. The paste and surface is mostly sandy and the colours, forms and functions vary. The term 'Romanised' is here used, following the description at Colchester (Ref. 81), as many of the types are copies of purely native vessels and others may be derived from Gallo-Belgic prototypes. Many represent the establishment of the ceramic tradition of Roman Britain. No distinction has been made here, as on some of the adjacent sites, between the finer sandy wares and those which are much coarser. This is because there are few finer wares represented, but also because of the pitted nature of the pottery.

In all 1,759 sherds were recovered and these represent a minimum of 98 different vessels, of which 26 have been drawn (Nos. 159, 161–186). The range of types is considerable though there is a preponderance of small shouldered jars with outcurved rims in grey ware with grey surfaces. About 40 different vessels of this type can be identified and it may be that the wall-sherds represent twice that number. At a glance they seem to be products of the same kiln and one (No. 159) is either a poor 'second' or even a waster. Sherds of at least five other vessels also show signs of distortion and the presence of a small kiln in the area must not be ruled out.

The other types represented include a mortarium; an amphora; a strainer; a carinated beaker; a storage jar; a jar with rusticated patterns; three raised footrings (probably from small jars); four flagons; at least five bead rim cooking-pots; at least six reeded rimmed jars and nearly 30 small jars with outcurved or faintly beaded rims. These came from every part of the site with large numbers coming from Ditch 3, Ditch 6 and Pit 3. The shouldered jars and reeded rims are typologically early-2nd century and are largely absent on sites in West Kent of the second half of the 1st century. The two flagons probably date to the end of the 1st century, or early-2nd, whilst the stamped mortarium has been dated A.D. 100–140. The Patch Grove and shell-loaded wares both occur in deposits of the second half of the 1st and the early-2nd centuries, whilst the small sherd of a carinated beaker probably dates earlier than A.D. 100.

The pottery from the various pits and ditches at Fox Hill is similar in type, range and character and can be treated as a single group. The pottery from no single deposit stands apart and all, it seems, can be encompassed within the dates A.D. 80–140 though the 2nd century types certainly predominate. This dating is also reflected in the proportion of Romanised products as compared with the distinctly native wares. The former certainly heavily outweigh the latter with the native Patch Grove and shell-loaded wares constituting only 18% of the total. This is in marked contrast to those sites of the second half of the 1st century, such as Eastwood (Ref. 82) where the Patch Grove and shell-loaded wares account for 58% of the total vessels recovered from the site.

(2) THE MORTARIUM STAMP

By Mrs. K. F. Hartley

This is an incomplete impression of a stamp (No. 184) which reads TMH and was used in conjunction with the usual counterstamp in the form of a leaf. The letters could be the initials of *tria nomina*, though not many mortarium potters were Roman citizens.

Other stamps of TMH have been noted from Colchester (2); London (2) and Verulamium (4). One of these was from a Trajanic-Hadrianic deposit at Verulamium and another, from Colchester, from a deposit containing Flavian and very early-2nd century material (Ref. 83). A date of *c.* A.D. 100–140 would accord well with the rim-forms used by this potter.

'TMH' is one of the small number of potters for whom there is evidence of migration, in this instance from the vicinity of Colchester to that of Verulamium. The fabrics produced in these two areas differ notably in texture and the apparent visual difference has been checked by spectrographic analysis (Ref. 84). The West Wickham mortarium, like the majority of his products, was made near Verulamium (from Pit 6).

(3) THE FINGER-RING WITH INTAGLIO

By Martin Henig

The ring found at Fox Hill, West Wickham was submitted to me for examination. The ring itself is made of iron and consists of a hoop rounded externally, but flat within (i.e. it has a D-shaped section), which expands very sharply at the bezel. The external diameter of the ring is 26 mm.; the width of the hoop about 4 mm. and the width of the bezel about 12 mm. It has now disintegrated into several fragments and the intaglio is very much crazed and seems to be held together largely by corrosion.

Similar rings may be noted from London (Ref. 85), Silchester (Duke of Wellington's collection in Reading Museum, 03022), Colchester (Ref. 86), Great Casterton (Ref. 87) as well as from Nymegen in the Netherlands (Ref. 88). All may be ascribed to the 1st century A.D.

The intaglio is of yellow glass, oval in shape with a flat face and the device being cast from a mould rather than engraved. Its length is 12 mm., its breadth 10 mm., and the thickness about 2 mm. It yields an impression of OMPHALE, Queen of Lydia, standing towards the right, draped in Hercules' lion-skin and holding his club over her left shoulder and his bow in her left hand. According to legend, Hercules was in love with Iole, the daughter of Eurytus, King of Oichalia. Eurytus refused to allow him to marry Iole and in a fit of madness Hercules murdered Iphitus, the king's son. In order to purify himself from the blood-guilt which he had incurred, Hercules consulted the oracle of Apollo at Delphi and although at first Apollo refused to help him, in the end he received the command to sell himself as a slave and give the purchase money to Eurytus. Hercules was bought by Omphale who made him do women's work as well as the usual deeds of prowess (Ref. 89).

The type appears on signets as early as the 4th century B.C. (Ref. 90), but only appears to have become popular in late Hellenistic times (Refs. 91–94). Pastes seems to be especially popular and apart from the three examples in the British Museum already cited (Nos. 3009, 3167 and 3168) and the one in West Berlin, there is a very large number now in the East Berlin collection (Ref. 95). Also note a paste in an iron ring from the Colonia Triana at Xanten (Ref. 96), probably 2nd century.

The significance of this intaglio at the Fox Hill site is problematic. Early Roman pastes with mythological subjects generally occur in Britain on military sites, although an amazonamachy is recorded on an intaglio from the possible official residence at Angmering and a representation of Hercules has been found at Verulamium where it *could* belong to the military phase (Ref. 97). An intaglio from Richborough, showing Hercules wrestling with Antaeus, is also moulded in yellow glass. It is virtually certain that the ring is an import from the Continent and likely that it was owned, at least originally, by a soldier. In view of its low intrinsic value its owner was an ordinary trooper, either legionary or auxiliary. To him it might have signified the fact that even the most glorious of heroes had to contend with a life of uncertainty, travail and degradation, even to the extent of being subjected to the power of a woman. As Hercules is said to have become much attracted to Omphale and even to have had a son by her, his fate may have seemed almost desirable to some men. As M. Masskant-Kleibrink has suggested with regard to a paste from Nymegen, showing a maenad, such intaglios could have served as 'pin-ups' (Ref. 98). Further speculations are that the ring reached Fox Hill by way of trade, through the visit of a passing soldier or that a veteran was settled there? (From ploughsoil—FH-1.)

(4) OTHER FINDS

Quernstones

Only 10 fragments of quernstone, representing at least four separate rotary querns, were recovered from Fox Hill in direct association with the pottery. Only one is illustrated the others generally being too fragmentary.

Quern A. Three pieces of friable lavastone imported from the Mayen district of Germany. Shape and diameter not determined, but at least 1·4 in. thick. From unstratified deposits (FH-18 and 51).

Quern B. A single piece of a flat stone of grey-white Millstone Grit. One surface visible and at least 1·6 in. thick. From unstratified deposit (FH-14).

Quern C. A fragment of a flat rotary quern (No. 153), probably an upper-stone, of grey-green calcareous sandstone from the Folkestone Beds, Lower Greensand. The top has been slightly tooled, the side has vertical tooled lines and the milling surface underneath has a series of concentric grooves. It weighs 3·12 lb. and the complete stone probably weighed about 25 lb. This piece is 2·6 in. thick and the original diameter was probably about 14 in. From Ditch 3 (FH-20B).

Quern D. A fragment of another stone, similar to Quern C. This is a tapered upper-stone with an uneven upper surface, but a lower surface much worn by use. At least 1·7 in. thick at the widest (outside) point and perhaps originally about 12–14 in. in diameter. From unstratified deposit (FH-15).

Four other fragments of sandstone, possibly parts of Quern C, were found in Ditch 3, Ditch 6, Pit 3 and unstratified respectively.

Roman Tile

Four fragments of flat Roman tile, or brick, were found at Fox Hill. They varied in thickness from 1 to 1·3 in. and probably represent at least two tiles. One was found in Ditch 3 (FH-15B) and the others were not stratified.

In addition 16 small pieces of iron slag were recovered. Of these 14 were unstratified and two came from Ditch 6 (FH-44). A large lump of baked clay, again not stratified (FH-11C), may represent a loom-weight of late-Iron Age type. A fragment of a bronze brooch and a silver penny of Edward II (A.D. 1307–1327) were also found in unstratified deposits.

Catalogue of the Illustrated Finds from Fox Hill, West Wickham (Figs. 19 and 22)

No. 153. A fragment of a grey-green rotary quern, probably an upper-stone of slightly calcareous sandstone from the Lower Greensand of the Folkestone Beds (see notes on quernstones). From Ditch 3 (FH-20B).

From Ditch 6

No. 157. Cooking-pot with bead rim of corky ware. Grey paste and buff-black surface (FH-52B).

No. 158. Cooking-pot with bead rim of corky ware. Grey-black paste and buff-black surface (FH-52A).

No. 159. Jar with outcurved rim of sandy ware. Grey paste and surface. Cordon and grooves on neck and faint burnished lines on shoulder. Warped rim suggests a waster or a 'second' (FH-52A).

No. 160. Cooking-pot bead rim of corky ware. Grey paste and buff-black surface (FH-52A).
Bead rim vessels of this type occur commonly on sites in West Kent and East Surrey dated to the second half of the 1st century A.D. (Ref. 99). The bead-rim, although popular with the Belgae (Ref. 100), does not seem to have reached West Kent much before the end of the Belgic period (Ref. 101). It remained popular after the Conquest even appearing in the harder Romanised wares. It appears to be largely absent in deposits dated to the second half of the 2nd century A.D., but at Joyden's Wood (Ref. 102), bead rims were found in the filling of a ditch with a small amount of 2nd century pottery. At Fox Hill these bead rim vessels were found in direct association with early-2nd century Romanised pottery. Nos. 157-8 and 160 are of corky ware and No. 170 (below) in the harder, sandy Romanised ware.

No. 161. Complete jar with upright, 'collar' rim and small, beaded lip, of sandy ware. Grey paste and surface and slight footring around raised base (FH-52A). An unusual form.

No. 162. Jar with outcurved, slightly thickened rim of sandy ware. Grey paste and surface. Cordon and grooves on neck and angled shoulder. Broadly similar to No. 159 (FH-52A).

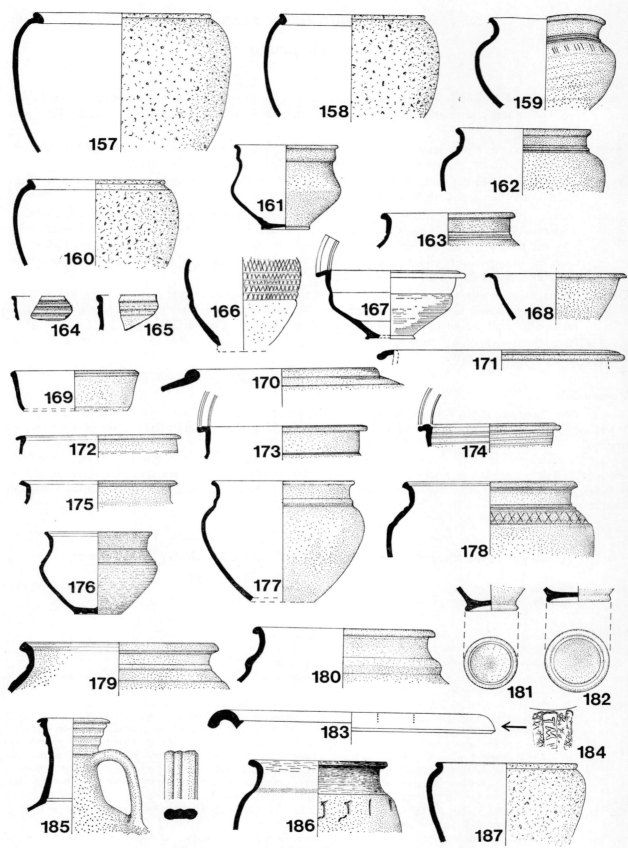

Fig. 22. Roman pottery ($\frac{1}{4}$), Fox Hill, West Wickham (Site 8).

No. 163. Vessel similar to No. 162, but with outcurved, angled rim (FH-52A).

        These shouldered jars (Nos. 159, 162, 163 and also 178 and 179) are largely absent on exclusively 1st century A.D. sites in West Kent and it appears that they were not introduced in the area before about A.D. 100. Pots with very similar profiles were being produced in a kiln at Highgate Wood, Highgate (Ref. 103) where they are regarded as typologically early-2nd century in date. Somewhat similar pottery, but generally without the distinctive cordons, occurs at Colchester in a deposit dated about A.D. 100 (Ref. 104).

No. 164. Jar or bowl with upright rim of sandy ware. Grey paste and buff surface. Slight trace of red-brown slip and three cordons below rim (FH-52A).

No. 165. Similar to No. 164, but with only two cordons and no trace of slip (FH-52A).

        These two vessels are probably wide bowls, perhaps in imitation of samian Forms 30 or 37, with upright rims. Again a likely parallel occurs at Colchester dated to about A.D. 100 (Ref. 105).

No. 166. Girth or butt beaker, with rim missing, of sandy ware. Grey paste and surface. Zone of oblique cross-hatching and a series of cordons on upper part (FH-44). The profile of this vessel is similar to the butt-beakers being imported into Britain (Colchester Form 112) before and after the Conquest. This example, in hard sandy Romanised ware, probably represents a native copy made some decades later.

No. 167. Carinated bowl with flanged, reeded rim of sandy ware. Buff paste, black surface and slight footring around raised base (FH-44). (For discussion see above.)

No. 168. Small bowl, or cup, with plain, outcurved rim of sandy ware. Grey paste and surface (FH-52A).

From Pit 3

No. 169. Dish with slightly thickened rim and chamfered base of sandy ware. Grey-black paste and black surface (FH-40). A similar vessel found at Brixworth has been dated about A.D. 100–140 (Ref. 106).

No. 170. Storage jar with bead rim of sandy ware. Grey paste and dark grey surface and incised line on shoulder (FH-40). This type is common on sites of the second half of the 1st century A.D., but does also occur slightly later (see above).

No. 171. Small bowl with flanged, reeded rim of sandy ware. Grey paste and black surface. Broadly similar to No. 167 (FH-40).

No. 172. Bowl with slightly down-turned rim of sandy ware. Buff paste and surface (FH-40).

No. 173. Bowl similar to No. 167 (FH-40).

No. 174. Bowl with flanged, reeded rim of sandy ware. Grey paste with grey surface and burnished lines inside and out (FH-40).

        These vessels with reeded rims are a type well known over much of Roman Britain. In West Kent they appear to be totally absent on 1st century rural sites though at Canterbury they are common from the late-1st to mid-2nd centuries (Ref. 107). In Northern Britain the range appears to be A.D. 80–125 (Ref. 108), at Leicester they occur in a deposit dated A.D. 125–130 (Ref. 109) and they were being made in a kiln at Highgate Wood, Highgate, where they are regarded as typologically early-2nd century (Ref. 110).

No. 175. Jar with out-turned rim of sandy ware. Grey paste and surface (FH-40).

No. 176. Jar with out-curved recessed rim of smooth ware. Grey paste, buff surface, coloured black, marked footring (FH-40). The profile is similar to vessels from Colchester (Form 225) which are about mid-1st century in date (Ref. 111). This Fox Hill example is a hard, sandy Romanised ware and thus likely to be of later date.

No. 177. Jar, or cooking pot, with outcurved slightly thickened rim of sandy ware. Grey paste and buff surface, coloured black. Cordon and grooves on shoulder (FH-40).

No. 178. Jar with outcurved, recessed, angular rim of sandy ware. Grey paste and surface, with cordon and grooves below neck and narrow band of hatched decoration above angled shoulder (FH-40).

No. 179. Wide jar, with recessed, angular rim of sandy ware. Grey paste and surface with cordon and grooves below neck (FH-40).

No. 180. Large jar with thickened, angular rim of sandy ware. Grey paste and surface with bold corrugation below neck (FH-40). Probably a copy of an earlier native vessel. It occurs at Canterbury in deposits dated late-1st to early-2nd century (Ref. 112).

No. 181. Jar with footring and raised base of sandy ware. Grey paste and surface (FH-40).

No. 182. Jar with footring and raised base of sandy ware. Buff paste and black surface (FH-40).

From Pit 6

Nos. 183–4. Flanged mortarium (and stamp) of coarse, sandy ware. Buff paste and surface. Rim stamped TMH (FH-30A). See specialist report above, A.D. 100–104.

Unstratified

No. 185. Flagon with ring-neck and three-ribbed handle of sandy ware. Cream paste and surface (FH-51A). Flagons of similar form, variously described, are common on sites of the late-1st and early-2nd centuries. Examples occur at Richborough dated A.D. 80–95 (Ref. 113); Colchester dated A.D. 70–130 (Ref. 114); Leicester late-1st to early-2nd centuries (Ref. 115); and Brixworth dated A.D. 80–120 (Ref. 116).

No. 186. Jar with outcurved, slightly thickened rim of sandy ware. Grey-black paste with buff-black surface and burnishing inside rim and on neck. Distinctive applied rusticated 'J' pattern on shoulder (FH-12). A broadly similar example from Brixworth is dated A.D. 80–120 (Ref. 116, No. 105).

No. 187. Small cooking-pot with slightly angular rim of shell-loaded ware. Mottled grey paste and orange-black surface (FH-1). See No. 160 above for comments.

SITE 9. A Romano-British Site at Elm Farm, West Wickham, Kent

This site (N.G.R. TQ.4014.6408) lies on Elm Farm, in the parish of West Wickham, Kent nearly a mile south-east of the parish church. It occupies almost level ground on the west side of a wide north-south valley on Woolwich and Blackheath Beds at about 330 ft. O.D. The centre of the site as located is in the south-west corner of an open field (O.S. parcel 2114, shown as 'Hazel Wood'), 25 ft. from the south-west hedge and about 40 ft. from the north-west hedge. The site very probably extends into the adjacent fields on both the south and west sides. The Roman arterial road, from London to Lewes, Sussex, lies nearly a mile west of the site.

The site was discovered on 28th October, 1962 during a survey by the Group, carried out with the ready agreement of Mr. W. Duff of Elm Farm. Two minute potsherds were then picked up on the surface of the field at the point plotted as the centre of the site. Trial-excavations were carried out during four days in February, 1963 during the 'Great Freeze' when the site was covered by more than a foot of snow. Two 30 ft. trenches were then dug at right-angles to each other in the form of a cross at the point where the pottery had been found. Several smaller trenches were dug nearby in March, 1963 before the farmer sowed the field. This work revealed three features, a small quantity of Romano-British pottery and other material of 1st century A.D. date.

Feature 1

This was a small V-shaped ditch, with a flat bottom, about 4 ft. wide and 3 ft. 6 in. deep from the present ground-level. This was traced for at least 25 ft. running roughly east-west and it appeared to curve to the south. Its west end continued under the hedge and its east end appeared to enter a pit (see below). Only the lower 1 ft. 8 in. of the filling could be regarded as stratified, the upper part having been thoroughly disturbed by roots. The filling, of light-brown loam, contained 43 potsherds (No. 188) and a fragment of greensand quernstone (No. 154).

Feature 2

A ditch of very similar size and form joined the first at right-angles near its east end and headed roughly north-west. This was traced with considerable difficulty for 17 ft. Its filling of light-brown loam contained another fragment of greensand, but no pottery.

Feature 3

The edge of a wide, perhaps circular, pit was found at the apparent east end of the first ditch, but was not fully examined. This had steep sides, was wider than 5 ft. and deeper than 5 ft. 3 in. Its filling of brown loam contained a single piece of burnt daub.

DATING AND DISCUSSION

In addition to the 43 potsherds from Feature 1 another five were recovered from disturbed deposits. Altogether at least five pots can be identified, but only one can usefully be illustrated (No. 188). The majority of the sherds, all from the bottom of the first ditch, are of black ware with a smooth burnished grey-brown surface. These appear to be from a well-made cooking-pot, probably of mid-1st century A.D. date. The bead rim cooking-pot (No. 188) from the upper fill of Feature 1, is of Patch Grove ware and very probably dates to the second half of the 1st, or early 2nd, century. The other sherds represent a corky ware vessel and another containing fine grit. Greensand quernstones occur commonly on early Romano-British sites in West Kent. The topsoil in this field contained a number of pot-boilers, flint flakes and a few implements. These may indicate the presence of another Neolithic or Bronze Age site in the vicinity.

Although the evidence from this site is slight the pattern of ditches and pit, associated with greensand quernstones, Patch Grove and 'corky' pottery, is a familiar one. At a number of other places in West Kent these all occur on Romano-British sites, mostly of the second half of the 1st century, where they suggest the presence of early farmsteads. The ditches may have formed parts of enclosures and the quernstone and pottery in them represent domestic rubbish. Just possibly this site may relate to that at North Pole Lane (Site 10), about 400 yards to the south, also occupied during the 1st century A.D.

Catalogue of Illustrated Finds from Elm Farm, West Wickham (Figs. 19 and 24)

No. 154.   A small piece of a flat, yellow-grey rotary quernstone, probably a thin upper-stone, broadly similar to No. 153 and probably a sandstone from the Folkestone Beds. Its milling surface carries roughly concentric grooves whilst its back is uneven. It weighs about 6 oz. and the complete stone probably weighed about 10 lb. and had a diameter of between 12–18 in. From the small ditch (Feature 1) in association with pottery of the second half of the 1st century A.D. (WW-34E).

No. 188.   Cooking-pot with bead rim of Patch Grove ware. Mottled grey-brown paste and buff surface. From the small ditch (Feature 1) (WW-34F). Vessels of this form and ware occur frequently in West Kent on sites dating to the second half of the 1st century A.D. For notes on Patch Grove ware see Fox Hill (Site 8).

SITE 10. A Romano-British Site at North Pole Lane, West Wickham, Kent

This site (N.G.R. TQ.4015.6408) lies on Nash Farm in the parish of West Wickham, Kent about 1 mile south-east of the parish church. It occupies parts of two fields (O.S. parcels 0063 and 0980), one on each side of North Pole Lane, just to the east of a small outbuilding which is itself situated about 250 yards east of Layhams Road. The site forms part of the crest of the west side of a wide north-south valley, on Clay-with-flints at an elevation of about 400 ft. O.D.

The site was discovered on 9th July, 1965 during Operation Gaspipe. The pipe-trench cut north-south across the road at a point about 30 ft. south-east of the corner of the outbuilding. Four features were noted, three deep pits and a small ditch. A quantity of late-Iron Age and Romano-British pottery was recovered from both the spoil-heaps and from the pits (see below). The field flanking the south side of North Pole Lane and containing Pits 2 and 3 and the Ditch, is shown on early maps as South Field. In 1889 an excavation (Ref. 117) was made at the highest point in the field when an area 8 ft. in diameter was found to contain many fragments of Romano-British pottery. It was then suggested that this represented a ploughed-out burial-mound which had contained a cremation. The site of this discovery must have been almost exactly that of Pit 2 and it is possible that the outline seen was this pit, or another nearby, containing domestic rubbish. Roman pottery and tile was said to have been found on this site some years before 1889.

Pit 1

This was 19 ft. north of the centre of North Pole Lane and 38 ft. north-east of the outbuilding. Only part of this feature was exposed by the pipe-trench, but it appeared to be a U-shaped pit about 9 ft. wide at the top and about 7 ft. 3 in. deep. Its filling largely consisted of almost horizontal layers of black and brown loam which seemed to represent silting over a long period rather than deliberate filling at one attempt. A thick band of orange-yellow clay near the base could represent a collapsed lining. The lower half of the filling contained only twelve potsherds which represented four vessels. All are native wares and date to the middle decades of the 1st century A.D. The upper filling contained 32 sherds from at least another ten vessels (No. 189), which included native and Romanised wares. It is clear from this that the pit was open and used for dumping domestic rubbish in the second half of the 1st century A.D. and it seems likely that it was dug at about the time of the Conquest in A.D. 43.

Pit 2 (Fig. 23, layers 3–10)

This was 26 ft. south of the centre of North Pole Lane and about 45 ft. from Pit 1. It had been sliced across the centre by the pipe-trench, but it is probable that it had been about 11 ft. in diameter and deeper than 6 ft. It had cut through Pit 3, only the bottom of which survived. In Pit 2 a small primary deposit (layer 10) contained carbon, animal-bone and a large loom-weight (No. 156). This was sealed by a thick deposit (layer 9) of grey-brown loam, perhaps representing silt forming over a lengthy period. This was in turn sealed by successive deposits (layers 5–8) of black-brown loam containing chalk rubble, bone, pottery and carbon deposited as domestic rubbish. This lower filling produced another 83 potsherds representing at least twelve vessels (Nos. 191–5). All the pottery is of native origin and it includes jars, beakers and a cup with burnished surfaces or cordons which are distinctly Belgic in character. The whole group appears to date from A.D. 30–50 and it also seals the loom-weight, a distinctive late-Iron Age type.

The upper two deposits (layers 3 and 4) of the filling of the pit contained five pieces of Roman tile, a chip of blue-green Roman glass and 74 potsherds representing at least twelve vessels. Two of these are samian vessels (Forms 27 and 35) of late-1st or early-2nd century date. The others include seven 'Romanised' ware cooking pots and jars and some native wares. It seems clear from this that Pit 2 was finally filled at about A.D. 80–120 and like Pit 1 it seems probable that it was dug several decades earlier, perhaps even just before the Conquest.

Pit 3 (Fig. 23, layers 11–14)

This had been partially destroyed by Pit 2 which may well have been a deliberate re-cutting following silting. From what survived it appeared to have steep sides, a flat base and may have been about 5 ft. wide and about 8 ft. deep. It had traces of a clay lining (layer 13) on one side, but contained only animal bone. Judging by the dating evidence for Pit 2 it seems likely that this pit was dug in pre-Conquest times, perhaps between A.D. 10–40.

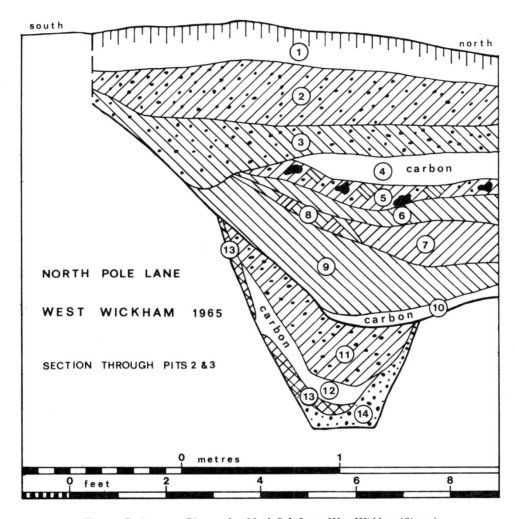

Fig. 23. *Section across Pits 2 and 3, North Pole Lane, West Wickham (Site 10).*

Ditch

This was 133 ft. south of the road-centre. It appeared in both sides of the trench as a U-shaped ditch about 3 ft. wide and 3 ft. deep. It was filled with light-brown sandy loam and produced no finds.

In addition to the limited work allowed on the pits some considerable effort was made to excavate the huge mound of soil thrown up by the contractors. Their giant rotary excavator had sliced right through the centre of Pit 2 leaving only narrow sections on each side. This work was rewarded by the recovery of another 356 potsherds (Nos. 190, 196–222), many of special interest, which gave a much fuller picture of the overall site. Nine more pieces of Roman tile (including four tegulae), a piece of daub and a pair of corroded bronze tweezers were also found. No fragment of a quernstone was found on this site.

DATING AND DISCUSSION

The evidence from this site is confined to three deep pits, a small ditch, some 557 potsherds, a few other finds and vague 19th century references.

The bulk of the pottery is largely typical of native and Romanised wares found on Romano-British farmsteads in West Kent of the second half of the 1st century A.D. (Ref. 118). Some, however, date from the early-2nd century and thus this site, in common with Fox Hill (Site 8), Baston Manor (Site 13) and Leafy Grove (Site 14), may have continued in use during the second or third decades of the 2nd century. In contrast to other local sites its origins are clearly pre-Roman and for the first time there is evidence of a local farmstead having been established prior to the Conquest. The imported platters and beakers, the distinctive burnished and cordoned vessels of Belgic character and even the triangular loom-weight suggest occupation on the site starting no later than about A.D. 10–40.

From this evidence it seems that, although the site is here listed as Romano-British, it was established immediately preceding the Conquest and survived for either three or four generations. The pits were probably dug for storage of water or grain early in the history of the site and subsequently used for dumping domestic rubbish. The small ditch may have delimited the main occupation-area on the south side and the absence of Roman building materials, other than a few tiles, implies wooden structures with daub walls. The pattern, in terms of finds and features, is largely typical of Romano-British farmsteads in West Kent. A study of the animal bones from the site proves the existence of cattle, sheep, pigs and at least one horse.

Exactly what relationship this site had in pre-Conquest times to the nearby major settlement at Lower Warbank, Keston and by what routes the imported pottery was reaching the site are problems yet to be answered. Certainly after the Conquest the site lay only ¾ of a mile east of the arterial Roman road from London to Lewes and was well within the orbit of Roman Londinium, about 11 miles to the north. It is possible that the site may have been connected in some way with the Romano-British site found on Elm Farm (Site 9), about 400 yards to the north.

THE FINDS

(1) THE POTTERY

A total of 557 potsherds was recovered from the site and these represent a minimum of 56 vessels, of which 34 have been drawn (Fig. 24). The most interesting and complete profiles came from the large group of unstratified pottery recovered from the contractor's spoil-heap close to Pit 2. Although the sample may not be representative of the site in general it does form an important group. The six main groups are shown in Table A and discussed below (for discussion of terms see Fox Hill—Site 8).

Group A. Samian Ware

Only seven sherds of samian, representing three vessels, were recovered from the site. Of these a Form 27 and a Form 35, both of late-1st or early-2nd century date, came from the upper filling of Pit 2. The rim of another Form 27, of 1st century date, was found in the contractor's spoil.

Group B. Imported (pre-Conquest) Wares

Eleven sherds, representing nine different vessels, of fine imported pottery of pre-Conquest date were recovered from the site. Three tiny sherds of coloured flagons were found in the pits and other fragments of flagons, butt-beakers and two Gallo-Belgic platters came from unstratified contexts. The latter includes a Terra Nigra rim (No. 215) and a highly polished black base with a token footring. These Gallo-Belgic vessels were imported into Britain a full generation before the Conquest and in Claudian times, but they are rare in post-Claudian deposits.

Group C. Patch Grove and Related Wares

Of the 174 potsherds from all deposits on the site, a minimum of eleven different vessels can be identified (Nos. 189, 199, 201–3, 206, 207, 209 and 210). The range includes the usual bead rim cooking-pots and the squat

Deposit	Samian ware	Imported (pre-Conquest) wares	Patch Grove and related wares	Shell and corky wares	Native (local) burnished wares	Sandy 'Romanised' wares	Total sherds	Total vessels
Pit 1								
Lower filling	—	—	2	8	2	—	12	4
Upper filling	—	2	14	6	1	9	32	10
Pit 2								
Lower filling	—	—	24	38	21	—	83	12
Upper filling	4	1	16	11	5	37	74	12
Unstratified	3	8	118	99	34	94	356	18
Total sherds	7	11	174	162	63	140	557	—
Total vessels	3	9	11	10	7	16	—	56

TABLE A

Distribution and classification of pottery from the North Pole Lane site

jars with outcurved rims. One unusual vessel (No. 189), of Patch Grove type, is a native imitation of samian Form 29 and dates from the second half of the 1st century.

Group D. Shell-loaded and Corky Wares

Just 162 sherds representing a minimum of ten vessels (No. 191, 192, 196–8, 200 and 205) were recovered from all deposits. The usual type is again the bead rim cooking-pot, but three vessels are of special interest. Two (Nos. 196 and 197) are almost rimless and slightly burnished and the third (No. 205) is part of a large vessel with a blunt, squared rim. All three are of very simple character unusual in this area and probably reflecting a non-Belgic ceramic tradition. Another much finer vessel (No. 192) has a bold cordon and a burnished surface and is clearly Belgic in character. All four are likely to be of pre-Conquest date. Most of the remaining shell-loaded vessels probably date to the second half of the 1st, or early-2nd, century.

Group E. Native (local) Burnished Wares (other than Patch Grove)

This group falls outside the scope of the pottery study of most local sites, being seldom represented. Some 63 sherds were recovered from the pits and unstratified deposits and these represent a minimum of seven vessels (Nos. 193–5, 204, 208, 213, 214 and 222). These may be described as having Belgic characteristics and most appear to be of pre-Conquest date. They cover a wide range of forms from small beakers, jars, bowls and perhaps even a pedestalled urn. All are native products, but probably from a variety of sources.

Group F. Sandy 'Romanised' Wares

As usual this group covers a very wide range of types and forms all generally sandy, well-fired, mass-produced pottery in the process of becoming the standard wares of Roman Britain. Just 140 sherds came from the upper fillings of both pits and from the spoil and these represent a minimum of 16 vessels (Nos. 190, 211, 212, 216–21). These include several bead-rim cooking-pots, jars with thickened or outcurved rims, two mortaria, an amphora, a butt-beaker and two sherds of a vessel with an applied rusticated pattern similar to the 'J' design on another vessel from Fox Hill (No. 186).

The pottery from North Pole Lane is an interesting and varied group though not a statistically critical collection. The whole can be embraced by the dates A.D. 10–120, rather longer that is than the majority of farmstead sites. The earliest pottery is the burnished ware in Belgic style and perhaps some of the very simple shell-loaded wares. All of these appear to be pre-Conquest in date and within the limits A.D. 10–40. This dating is to some extent supported by the Gallo-Belgic imports though some of these could be Claudian. Together the native burnished and the imported wares represent about 28% of the vessels from the site.

The rest of the pottery is typical of what is found in the area on simple Romano-British farmstead sites of the second half of the 1st century A.D. The usual Patch Grove and related wares and the shell-loaded wares account for another 38% of the vessels and the samian and sandy Romanised wares another 34%. Several vessels probably date from the late-1st, or early-2nd, century.

(2) THE MAMMALIAN BONES
By Mary Harman

All of the bones from this site were examined. Most were identifiable and in a good state of preservation. Only stratified bones have been considered and since the number of bones is extremely small the number of animals present is not always estimated. Those figures which are given are derived from the most frequently occurring bone of each species, considering also differences in age. The age of the animals at death is based on the evidence of the dentition, using figures given by Silver (Ref. 119). Goats may be represented among the sheep, but it has not been possible to distinguish them.

Three pits were found on this site. The material from these pits thus forms three groups each of which is considered separately. Only the Group from Pit 2 is large enough to be worthy of tabulation.

Pit 1 (A.D. 40–100)
      Cattle: Left mandible, M2, 3 worn
                Scapula fragment
      Pig: Right humerus

Pit 3 (A.D. 10–40)
      Cattle: Right frontal fragment, horned.
                Right scapula.
                Right tibia.
      Sheep: Left scapula.

Pit 2 (A.D. 40–120)
Table C shows the number of different bones of each animal present and the minimum number of animals. Table B shows the age of the animals at death. Both sheep frontals were horned. The sample is an isolated one, probably representing the domestic animals kept in the area, but is too small for further useful comment.

	Tooth eruption sequence and wear	Modern figures	Old figures	Number of examples
Cattle	(Pm2, 3, 4, erupting or erupted) M1, 2, (3 unerupted)	2–2½ yrs.	c. 2½ yrs.	8
	M1, 2, 3 worn	Over 2½ yrs.	Over 5 yrs.	2
Sheep	Dm1, 2, 3, M1	c. 3 m.	c. 6 m.	1
	(Pm3, 4 erupting) M1, 2, broken	c. 2 yrs.	c. 2½ yrs.	1
Pig	Pm3, 4 M1, 2, (3 erupting)	c. 1½ yrs.	c. 3 yrs.	1
	M2, 3 worn	Over 2 yrs.	Over 3 yrs.	1

TABLE B
Age of animals at death, Pit 2, North Pole Lane

Plate II. *The training-excavation at Lower Warbank, Keston*

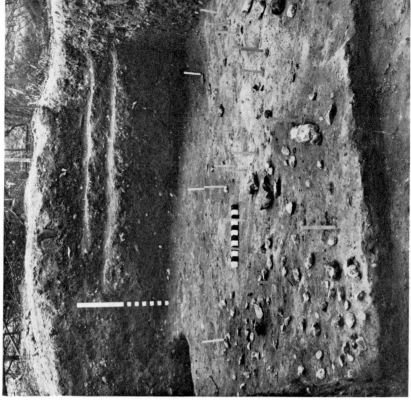

Plate IIIB. *Scatter of Neolithic flints and pottery (indicated by wooden markers) on the west side of the site. Baston Manor, Hayes (Site 1)*

Plate IIIA. *Rescue-work at North Pole Lane, West Wickham, during 'Operation Gaspipe' in 1965*

Plate IVA. *Ditch 1. Bronze Age site, Hayes Common (Site 5)*

Plate IVB. *Pit 14. Bronze Age site, Hayes Common (Site 5)*

Plate VB. *Section across Linear Earthwork south of Croydon Road, Hayes Common (Site 5)*

Plate VA. *Flint-packed post-holes. Bronze Age site, Hayes Common (Site 5)*

	Cattle		Sheep		Pig	
	L	R	L	R	L	R
Skull			2		1	
Maxilla	1	2				1
Mandible	1	2		2		1
Scapula					1	
Humerus	1		1			1
Radius	1		1			
Metacarpal	22					
Pelvis	1	1				
Femur		2	1			
Tibia	4	1		1		
Metatarsal	1		1			
Phalanx I		1				
Totals	21		9		5	
Minimum number of animals	4		3		2	
+ Horse: one splint bone						

TABLE C

Frequency of bones from each species and minimum number of animals present, Pit 2, North Pole Lane

Catalogue of Illustrated Finds from North Pole Lane, West Wickham (Figs. 19 and 24)

No. 156.   Almost half of a baked-clay loom-weight of broadly triangular form. The surface is grey-brown and smooth, whilst the under-fired paste is orange-red and contains at least three small pebbles. The left corner is rounded, the base flat and there were two diagonal perforations, about 0·5 in. in diameter, running from the base to the sides for suspension. This piece weighs about 1½ lb. and the complete weight must have weighed about 3 lb. From the lower filling of Pit 2 (layer 10) (GP-6-10). Fragments of similar loom-weights occur in association with mid-1st century pottery on local sites at Lower Warbank, Keston (Ref. 120), Layhams Road (Site 11) and Higham's Hill (Site 12). They are common on late-Iron Age sites in the South-East and at Verulamium they occur in Belgic deposits dated A.D. 5–35 (Ref. 121), but were entirely absent from sites in the Roman city.

No. 189.   Beaker with vertical wall and cordons below slightly beaded rim. Mottled grey paste as Patch Grove ware and buff surface containing slight flecks of red. From upper filling of Pit 1 (GP-6-22). This is a native copy of samian Form 29, perhaps modelled on a Gallo-Belgic imitation rather than the samian prototype as the devolved form suggests. This occurs at Colchester as Form 68 (Ref. 122) where it is predominantly A.D. 43–61, though it lasts later. Another vessel of this type, though not of the same ware, was found at Eastwood, Fawkham in 1957 (Ref. 123) in direct association with pottery dated to the second half of the 1st century A.D.

No. 190.   Cooking-pot with slightly thickened rim of sandy ware. Grey paste and black-brown surface. Unstratified (GP-6-1). A thoroughly Romanised vessel, perhaps part of a wide-shouldered jar or cooking-pot. Probably late-1st, or early-2nd, century.

No. 191.   Cooking-pot with bead rim of shell-loaded ware. Black paste and grey-black surface. From lower filling of Pit 2 (GP-6-7). Common throughout the second half of the 1st century and lasting into the early-2nd century (see notes on Fox Hill pottery—Site 8).

No. 192.   Squat jar with simple outcurved rim of shell-loaded ware. Black paste and grey-brown surface. Bold cordon on neck and traces of external burnishing. From lower filling of Pit 2 (GP-6-11). This native vessel is distinctly Belgic in character and whilst difficult to parallel precisely it reflects vessels at Verulamium (Ref. 124) in deposits dated A.D. 5–35 and others of probably much the same date at Colchester (Ref. 125) and Swarling, Kent (Ref. 126).

No. 193.   Cup with upright rim of burnished ware. Grey paste and grey-brown surface with exterior totally burnished and decorated with two faint horizontal grooves. From lower filling of Pit 2 (GP-6-5). This cup matches another recently found by

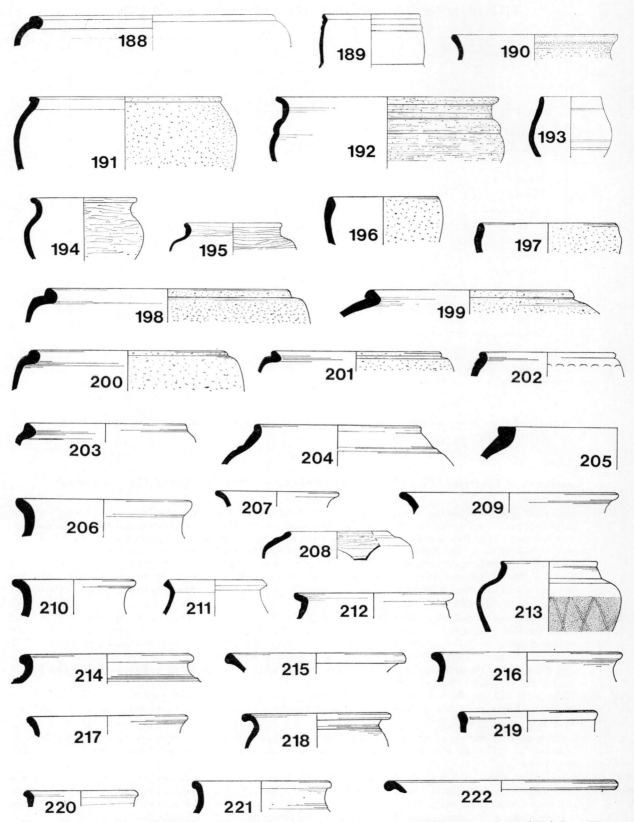

Fig. 24. *Roman pot (No. 188), Elm Farm, West Wickham (Site 9) and Roman pottery (¼) (Nos. 189–222), North Pole Lane, West Wickham (Site 10).*

the Group near Farnborough, Kent (publication pending) found in association with mid-1st century pottery. It seems to be derived from the Belgic beakers as at Verulamium (Ref. 127).

No. 194. Squat jar with tapered, outcurved rim of soft burnished ware containing slight traces of shell-filling. Grey paste with brown surface and burnished exterior. From lower filling of Pit 2 (GP-6-7). The paste and colouring of this vessel are similar to No. 192 above and it may be that they are the products of the same kiln. The simple S-profile recalls the foot-ring bowls at Oldbury and indeed a small footring of an almost identical vessel was found in the spoil alongside the pipe-trench. Its possible analogy with pottery of Oldbury type and its close similarity to No. 192 suggests that it dates from the first half of the 1st century A.D.

No. 195. Small jar with slightly thickened outcurved rim of burnished ware. Grey paste and black surface. From lower filling of Pit 2 (GP-6-4).

No. 196. Hand-made bowl with slightly thickened incurved rim of shell-loaded ware. Black paste and surface. Unstratified (GP-6-1). This is a crude, almost characterless, vessel reminiscent of some of the pottery of the early Pre-Roman Iron Age.

No. 197. Hand-made bowl with slightly thickened, incurved rim of corky ware. Black paste and surface. Unstratified (GP-6-1). Another crude vessel similar to No. 196.

No. 198. Cooking-pot with bead rim of corky ware. Grey-buff paste and buff-black surface and angled shoulder. Unstratified (GP-6-1). Second half of 1st, or early-2nd, century.

No. 199. Cooking-pot with bead rim of ware almost identical to Patch Grove. Light grey paste and speckled orange-buff surface, similar to No. 189. Unstratified (GP-6-1). Second half of 1st century, or early-2nd, century.

No. 200. Cooking-pot with bead rim of corky ware. Grey paste and buff-black surface. Unstratified (GP-6-1). Second half of 1st, or early-2nd, century.

No. 201. Cooking-pot with tapered bead rim of Patch Grove ware. Black paste and buff-brown surface. Unstratified (GP-6-1). Probably second half of 1st century A.D.

No. 202. Cooking-pot with small bead rim of hard Patch Grove ware. Grey paste and orange-brown surface and incised decoration on shoulder. Unstratified (GP-6-1). The type is common in the South-East. Again likely to be second half of 1st century and frequent at Colchester (Ref. 128).

No. 203. Cooking-pot with slightly beaded rim of Patch Grove ware. Mottled blue-grey paste and orange surface. Unstratified (GP-6-1). Similar to No. 202.

No. 204. Large jar with faintly beaded rim of burnished ware. Brown paste and brown surface with burnished exterior and also inside rim. A narrow-necked vessel with bulbous profile and cordons on shoulder, perhaps even with a pedestalled base. Unstratified (GP-6-1). This vessel appears to be directly linked with the Belgic urns found in pre-Conquest deposits such as at Verulamium (Ref. 129) and Canterbury (Ref. 130). A date either side of the Conquest is possible at North Pole Lane.

No. 205. Cooking-pot with broad, flattened rim of shell-loaded ware. Brown-black paste and brown surface. Unstratified (GP-6-1). This unusual vessel is presumably related to the more normal bead rim series, but its great squared rim is more reminiscent of the pre-Belgic Iron Age as seen at Hawk's Hill, Surrey (Ref. 131) than on any local West Kent site.

No. 206. Large jar with outcurved, thickened rim of Patch Grove ware. Mottled blue-grey paste and brown surface. Unstratified (GP-6-1). One of the basic Patch Grove types current throughout the second half of the 1st century A.D.

No. 207. Jar or small cooking pot with outcurved rim of overfired Patch Grove ware. Orange-grey paste and orange surface. Unstratified (GP-6-1). A smaller version of No. 206.

No. 208. Carinated jar with plain rim of hard burnished ware. Grey paste and black surface burnished externally. Unstratified Pit 2 (GP-6-32). This is an unusual shape and only vaguely paralleled at Colchester (Ref. 132) in pre-Conquest deposits.

No. 209. Jar or cooking-pot with outcurved rim of burnished Patch Grove ware. Grey paste and black surface burnished both sides. Unstratified (GP-6-1). The same as Nos. 206 and 207.

No. 210. A rather larger version of No. 206. Unstratified (GP-6-1).

No. 211. Butt beaker of fine sandy ware. Cream paste and cream-buff surface. Unstratified Pit 2 (GP-6-30). Probably a good native copy of a Gallo-Belgic vessel. This appears to be a variant of the well-known Colchester Form 113 (Ref. 133) dating from about A.D. 30–60.

No. 212. Butt beaker of sandy ware. Grey paste and grey-brown surface. Unstratified (GP-6-1). A Romanised version of the imported Gallo-Belgic prototype and probably dating from about A.D. 50–70.

No. 213. Small jar with upright, thickened rim of burnished ware. Grey paste and black surface. Rim and shoulder burnished and simple burnished lattice pattern on body. Unstratified (GP-6-1). This vessel appears to be a close relation of Colchester Form 221 (Ref. 134) with the cordons almost totally suppressed. Known in both pre-Conquest and post-Conquest contexts.

No. 214. Cooking-pot with rounded rim of hard, burnished ware. Grey-brown paste and surface with lightly burnished exterior and faint cordon on neck, Unstratified (GP-6-1). A common form in late-Belgic deposits at Verulamium (Form 61) (Ref. 135) and Canterbury (Ref. 136).

No. 215. Terra Nigra platter of Gallo-Belgic ware. Pale grey paste and surface, highly burnished all over. Unstratified (GP-6-1). A.D. 10–65.

No. 216. Cooking-pot with outcurved, thickened rim of sandy ware. Grey-brown paste and surface. Unstratified (GP-6-3). Another Romanised product, perhaps part of a shouldered vessel. Probably late-1st, or early-2nd, century.

No. 217. Cooking-pot with outcurved rim of sandy ware. Grey-buff paste and surface. Unstratified (GP-6-1). Probably the same date as No. 216.

No. 218. Jar with cavetto-type rim of sandy ware. Grey-buff paste and buff surface. Slight cordon on neck. Unstratified (GP-6-1). This vessel appears to be related to the shouldered jars found at the Fox Hill site (Site 8) and there dated late-1st, or early-2nd, century, though a slightly later date may also apply.

No. 219. Jar or bowl with thickened rim of sandy ware. Grey paste and surface. Unstratified (GP-6-1). A thoroughly Romanised product.

No. 220. Jar or bowl with thickened out-turned rim of sandy ware. Grey-brown paste and black surface. Unstratified (GP-6-1).

No. 221. Jar with outcurved, rounded rim of sandy ware. Orange-brown paste and grey-black surface. Unstratified (GP-6-1). Very similar to the shouldered jars being produced at Highgate Hill, Highgate, London (Ref. 137), and typologically late-1st, or early-2nd, century.

No. 222. Cooking-pot with rounded rim of burnished ware. Black-brown paste and surface burnished all over. Unstratified (GP-6-1). A native vessel with a well-developed rim, probably second half of 1st century A.D.

SITE 11. A Romano-British Site near Layhams Road, West Wickham, Kent

This site (N.G.R. TQ.3982.6146) lies in the parish of West Wickham, Kent, close to the County boundary and about 2 miles due west of Downe parish church. It occupies parts of two fields (O.S. parcels 8261 and 7427), on a high plateau flanked by north-south valleys. The site is on Clay-with-flints at an elevation of about 540 ft. O.D. The centre of the site lies about 1,200 ft. north-east of King Henry's Drive cross-roads and about 480 ft. east of Layhams Road.

The site was discovered on 7th August, 1965, during Operation Gaspipe. The pipe-trench cut through the fields roughly north-east to south-west and revealed nine small pits or ditches. Several potsherds, flint flakes and part of a loom-weight were recovered from these features. The pottery appears to be Romano-British and of 1st century A.D. date, whilst the loom-weight is a late-Iron Age type. The following table describes the features with measurements taken from the hedge dividing the two fields.

Feature	Profile	Width	Depth	From hedge	Notes
1	U-shaped	2½ ft.	2 ft.	393 ft. North	Ditch, E-W
2	V-shaped	2½ ft.	3 ft.	337 ft. ,,	Pit, W side. Pot and loom-weight
3	,,	3 ft.	3 ft.	308 ft. ,,	Ditch, NW-SE
4	,,	2 ft.	2 ft.	289 ft. ,,	Pit E side. Potsherd
5	U-shaped	2 ft.	3 ft.	267 ft. ,,	Gulley, NW-SE
6	V-shaped	1½ ft.	2 ft.	258 ft. ,,	Pit, W side
7	,,	4½ ft.	4 ft.	238 ft. ,,	Ditch, NW-SE
8	U-shaped	3 ft.	2½ ft.	174 ft. ,,	Ditch, E-W
9	,,	4½ ft.	3 ft.	91 ft. South	Ditch, SW-NE

TABLE A

Features sectioned near Layhams Road

The fillings of these features ranged through grey-brown loam, clay, pebble and carbon. Flint flakes were recovered from most though not in any quantity. Ten potsherds were recovered, seven from Feature 2, one from Feature 4 and two from the topsoil. Fragments of a large loom-weight were also found in Feature 2. The ten potsherds represent at least three vessels and all are too fragmentary for illustration. One jar rim in black ware is wheel-turned and similar to pottery from deposits on other local sites dating to the second half of the 1st century A.D. The other vessels appear to be native cooking-pots with a corky texture and these also occur in similarly dated contexts. The loom-weight is a late-Iron Age type and it appears similar to one (No. 156) found at North Pole Lane (Site 10) about 1½ miles to the north.

The arterial Roman road, from London to Lewes (Ref. 138), lies only 400 yards to the west of the site. The pipe-trench eventually cut this road on its known alignment about 400 ft. south-west of the adjacent cross-roads. It showed as a 5 in. pebble-band resting on a 10 in. bed of flint and pebble, with an overall width of at least 14 ft. 9 in. and capped by 1 ft. 5 in. of sandy loam and ploughsoil. Two possible side-ditches, cut into the thick underlying clay, were faintly discernible. One was 38 ft. west of the road edge and the other about 37 ft. east of the road edge. The overall distance between the ditches (centre to centre) was thus about 87 ft. which accords fairly well with 84 ft., known to be a standard spacing (Ref. 139). Neither ditch was well-defined, but the west one appeared to be about 3 ft. wide and 4 ft. deep.

It is difficult to say much of the extent and nature of this site owing to the limited nature of the evidence. The ditches and pits suggest an occupation-site covering a length of nearly 500 ft. The small amount of pottery appears to be Romano-British of the second half of the 1st century A.D. and the loom-weight, although a late-Iron Age type, could be the same date. The close proximity of the Roman road may be significant and the absence of building materials tends to suggest only wooden structures. This site may relate to the probable farmstead site 400 yards to the south at Higham's Hill (Site 12).

SITE 12. A Romano-British Site near Higham's Hill, Downe, Kent

This site (N.G.R. TQ.3978.6111) lies in the parish of Downe, Kent about 1½ miles south-west of Keston parish church and only about 400 yards south of the Romano-British site near Layhams Road (Site 11). It occupies the same high plateau, but looks across to a north-south valley and Higham's Hill to the east. The site is on Clay-with-flints at an elevation of about 540 ft. O.D. The centre of the site as found lies close to a narrow strip of woodland (since partially removed) between two open fields (O.S. parcels 7427 and 9214) into both of which the site extends.

The site was discovered on 20th November, 1964 during a three-month watch on a trench dug for a 33,000-volt electric-cable between Addington and Biggin Hill. The trench, about 2 ft. wide and 4 ft. deep, ran roughly east-west about 12 ft. from, yet parallel to, the north edge of Sheepbarn Lane. It cut three features and revealed a thin occupation-scatter which together yielded pottery, tile and quernstone of late-Iron Age and Romano-British date.

Feature 1

At 367 ft. east of the cross-roads and 23 ft. from the west edge of the wood. A shallow, V-shaped ditch, or pit, running north-south and about 2½ ft. wide and 3½ ft. deep from the present ground-level. Its filling of black loam contained a fragment of Roman tile and 14 potsherds. The pottery represents at least three vessels, a poppy-head beaker, a bowl (No. 223) and the other a Patch Grove ware bead rim cooking-pot (No. 224), all probably of late-1st century date.

A thin band of black loam, at a depth of about 1 ft. 9 in., was traced for several feet on each side of the ditch and was found to contain six more potsherds. At least one of these represented a vessel of Patch Grove type and another was in a hard, Romanised fabric. The adjacent spoil-heap contained another 65 sherds including a chip of samian (form not determined), fragments of a beaker, a flagon, at least three more sandy Romanised cooking-pots and more Patch Grove ware, mostly too fragmentary for illustration (Nos. 227–230).

Feature 2

At 621 ft. east of the cross-roads and on the east side of the strip of woodland. A roughly V-shaped pit, or ditch, about 2 ft. wide and 2 ft. deep. Its filling of light-brown loam contained specks of carbon, but no finds.

Feature 3

At 650 ft. east of the cross-roads and also east of the woodland. A circular pit with steep sides and a flat bottom. Its diameter was about 3 ft. 3 in. and its depth 2 ft. 3 in. from the present ground-level. Its filling consisted of two layers, a 2 in. primary deposit of light-brown loam sealed by a 6 in. band of black loam and carbon. These layers produced another 50 fragments of pottery, twelve pieces of greensand quernstone and three small pieces of loom-weight. At least four large vessels are represented the most interesting one being the upper part of a large jar (No. 225) of Patch Grove type with a simple burnished pattern. The other vessels are probably cooking pots, one being a Patch Grove vessel, another a sandy ware (No. 226) and the third a gritty black ware. All are hard to date with precision, but the absence of later Romanised wares suggests a date no later than about A.D. 60 and the two illustrated vessels may be pre-Conquest. The loom-weight fragments are probably from a weight of triangular shape and closely resemble those from nearby sites at Layhams Road (Site 11) and North Pole Lane (Site 10).

The site lies about 400 yards east of the arterial Roman road from London to Lewes, Sussex. The agger of the road is plainly visible on the north side of King Henry's Drive where it still forms the boundary between Kent and Surrey. The cable-trench cut the line of the Roman road at this point and a thin band of pebble confirmed its existence. Side ditches were not seen, but the irregular sides of the trench may have masked any variation in the sticky clay subsoil.

DATING AND DISCUSSION

It is only possible to comment briefly on the nature and extent of this site owing to the limited evidence. The pits or ditches and domestic rubbish all imply an occupation-site extending over a length of at least 280 ft.

The pottery in the east pit (Feature 3) seems to be the earliest on the site and this could reflect a small settlement established just before the Conquest. It may, however, represent an immediate post-Conquest site and certainly all the other finds date from the second half of the 1st century, or early-2nd, century.

The fragments of greensand quernstone are similar to those from distinctly Romano-British contexts at Fox Hill (Site 8), Baston Manor (Site 13) and Eastwood, Fawkham (Ref. 140). The loom-weight, normally regarded as a late-Iron Age artefact, was in fact found in the east pit with the earlier pottery.

The evidence from Higham's Hill thus shows it to be in some respects typical of many others located in West Kent in recent years, most of which appear to be simple Romano-British farmsteads (Ref. 141). The absence of building materials, other than roof tile, suggests as elsewhere, any structures were of wood with walls of wattle and daub. The ditches and pits are constant features too, the former often delimiting the farmstead enclosure. The pottery is again mostly native and from local sources, but as usual there is a small admix of distinctly Romanised products, including a little samian. Unlike the majority of these early farmstead sites, which normally occur on good well-drained soil, this site is on dense clay. A heavy plough would certainly be needed here and there would have been problems with drainage. Perhaps the close proximity of the Roman arterial road made this otherwise difficult site rather more attractive?

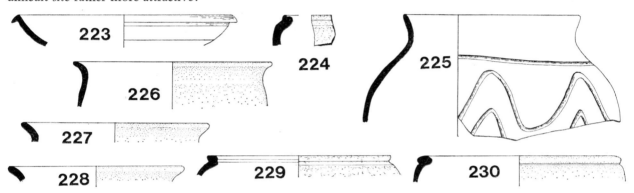

Fig. 25. *Roman pottery* ($\frac{1}{4}$), *Higham's Hill, Downe (Site 12).*

Catalogue of the Illustrated Pottery from Higham's Hill, Downe (Fig. 25)

No. 223. Bowl with angular out-turned rim of smooth ware. Grey paste and grey-black surface. From Feature 1 (HH-2). This appears to be a good native copy of a Gallo-Belgic bowl of the type recorded at Eastwood, Fawkham (Ref. 142) and Richborough, Kent (Ref. 143) where they date to the second half of the 1st century A.D.

No. 224. Cooking-pot with recessed, beaded rim of Patch Grove ware. Mottled grey-black paste and dark grey surface. From Feature 1 (HH-2). The Patch Grove bead rims are common throughout the second half of the 1st century and perhaps into the early-second century A.D. (see notes on Fox Hill—Site 8).

No. 225. Large jar with outcurved rim of Patch Grove or allied ware. Mottled grey-brown paste and surface with curvilinear pattern formed by two broad parallel burnished grooves. From Feature 3 (HH-4). This very interesting vessel is difficult to parallel on any local site. It is clearly a native product in the Iron Age tradition. It is so far absent at the nearby Lower Warbank, Keston site where there is both pre-Conquest and post-Conquest pottery. The associated pottery is all native and the total lack of distinctly post-Conquest types tends to favour a date in the first half of the 1st century A.D. The bold curvilinear pattern is known in Wessex in the pre-Roman Iron Age and it occurs in particular at Maiden Castle, Dorset (Ref. 144), in deposits dated securely to the last quarter of the 1st century B.C.

No. 226. Cooking-pot with wide outcurved rim of coarse, slightly sandy ware. Dark grey paste and buff surface. From Feature 3 (HH-4). This simple vessel is a native form resembling the combed vessels of Belgic type as found at Verulamium (Ref. 145) in deposits dated A.D. 5–35.

No. 227. Jar with everted rim of fine sandy ware. Light grey paste with buff surface coated black. Unstratified from Feature 1 area (HH-1). A thoroughly Romanised vessel, perhaps from a shouldered jar, dating from the late-1st, or early-2nd, century.

No. 228. Jar with everted rim of fine sandy ware. Light grey paste and surface. Unstratified from Feature 1 area (HH-1). Another Romanised product probably of the same date as No. 227.

No. 229. Cooking pot with slightly squared rim of Patch Grove ware. Mottled grey-black paste and brown surface. Unstratified from Feature 1 area (HH-1). See notes on No. 224 above.

No. 230. Cooking-pot with bead rim of coarse sandy ware. Light grey paste and black surface with groove below rim. Unstratified from Feature 1 area (HH-1). This is the Romanised version of the native bead rim cooking-pot common through the latter part of the 1st century and during the early part of the 2nd century (see notes on Fox Hill pottery—Site 8).

SITE 13. A Roman Bath-Building near Baston Manor, Hayes, Kent

This site (N.G.R. TQ.4090.6460) lies very close to the Neolithic site (Site 1), near Baston Manor, Hayes, Kent, about 1 mile south of the parish church. It occupies the south-eastern corner of an open field (O.S. parcel 8865), originally forming part of Nash Farm, about halfway up the fairly steep east side of a wide valley. The centre of the bath-building (Fig. 4) lies about 40 ft. north-west of the fence bordering Keston Court Riding School and about 150 ft. from the fence on the south-west side. The site is on Woolwich and Blackheath pebble-beds at an elevation of about 305 ft. O.D. The site lies nearly $1\frac{1}{2}$ miles east of the arterial London-Lewes Roman road and about 1 mile north-west of the major villa-complex at Warbank, Keston.

The site was rediscovered (Ref. 146) by the Group on 25th October, 1964, after a search which had lasted for several years. The existence of a Roman building in the general vicinity was reported by Mr. G. R. Corner in 1854 (Ref. 147) who recorded:

'I must not omit to mention, that in a
field at a short distance from Keston Court
Farm, near Baston Court, . . . there exist,
about four feet below the surface, the
foundations of a (Roman) building which we found
by probing the ground, having had the spot pointed
out to us by an old inhabitant of the place; but
we were obliged to defer further research until some
future period.'

It seems that the energetic Mr. Corner never returned to pursue his researches and that the site remained lost and undisturbed for another 110 years.

The lack of precise data regarding the exact position of the alleged Roman building proved somewhat inconvenient. Surveys by the writer were started independently in 1957 and these were continued by the Group in 1960. In a period of about seven years all fields in the Baston Manor area were searched and a number tested by excavation. One trial-hole, excavated in 1963, was actually within 40 ft. of the Roman building, but no trace of Roman material was then found. In 1964 another series of trial-holes was dug in the area which resulted in the discovery of the Neolithic site (Site 1). Eventually, trial-hole No. 7, excavated and refilled three times as a precaution against involuntary quadrupedal intrusions, located Roman tiles, mortar and shaped chalk blocks at a depth of 4 ft. 2 in. This represented rubble from the demolition of the bath-building which was itself soon located. Work continued steadily throughout the winter months, except for a brief pause for the excavation of Faversham Abbey in January and February, 1965. Work resumed on the site in September and was concluded in February, 1966. In July of that year the original work was supplemented by a series of mechanically excavated trial-holes over a wide area. The only other Roman features to be uncovered during all this work were four small ditches all of which produced material of late-1st, or early-2nd, century date. No trace of any other Roman structures, timber or masonry, was located. All trenches were back-filled on completion of the work.

ACKNOWLEDGEMENTS

Thanks are due first and foremost to Mr. P. H. Legge, owner of the site for kindly allowing the un-restricted use of his land. Secondly, to Mr. P. Hewings, the farm manager, for his considerable interest and help. Of the many members who worked at Baston for extended periods special mention must be made of Mrs. M. Broadfoot, Misses J. Buckle, M. Last, E. Mynott (now Mrs. Philp) and E. Warman (now Mrs. Healey), and Messrs. A. Appleby, D. Bartlett, D. Broadfoot, G. Clewley, N. Field, C. Hart, J. Horne and C. Jones.

Mr. G. Clewley and Mr. P. Bolton have kindly drawn the pottery from the site, which Mr. Clewley has also described. Most of the small finds have been drawn by Mr. W. Jeffries, the bath-building plan by Mrs. C. Batchelor, the overall site-plan by Miss M. Funnell and Mr. T. Woodman, and the two sections by Mr. K. Elton and Mr. J. Tedbury. Mrs. K. Hartley has kindly reported on the two stamped mortaria fragments from the site, and Mr. G. Clewley on the wall-plaster.

THE EXCAVATION
(1) THE BATH-BUILDING (FIG. 26)

No attempt was made to excavate the entire structure just sufficient work being done to reveal the broad outlines of the plan. The building comprised at least six rooms and had a stoke-hole on the south-east side. The overall length was about 40 ft. and the width was between 16–30 ft. From the plan it is clear that the building was a small Romano-British bath-building of common type. It contained most of the main structural characteristics and in addition spring-water flowed into the cold-plunge bath during the excavation.

The building was well-constructed with walls of flint, brick and chalk blocks held in a hard white mortar containing fine pea-gravel. The walls were normally about 2 ft. thick and although heavily robbed survived to a maximum height of 4 ft. 1 in. in Room 3 and about 2 ft. 8 in. in Room 5. The internal walls of Rooms 5 and 6, where seen, were built entirely of bricks and roof tiles, probably to withstand the considerable heat coming from the adjacent furnace. Elsewhere tile was sporadically used. Small, roughly squared chalk blocks, many about 6 in. by 5 in. by 2½ in., were freely used in most of the walls and in particular formed part of the external, north-east wall of Room 6. This external face showed little sign of weathering, but it could be that it was covered though there was no sign of any external rendering. Chalk blocks taken from the rubble inside the building during the excavation split open when left exposed to frost. Chalk could be obtained within 200 ft. of the building and it is just possible that the deep shaft to the south-west (see Site 1), certainly cut through hard chalk, was the source of supply. Flint could be obtained in large quantities in the nearby valley bottom and pea-gravel, used in the mortar, could be obtained from within 500 yards of the site on what is now Hayes Common.

There was no evidence of the type of roof this building had, but it could have been vaulted or flat. It is, however, clear that some of the rooms had been rendered internally with a variety of treatments and this could reflect work at different times. The rendering had been mostly coated with thin white plaster which in turn had been coloured either plain red or plain white. In only three cases did fragments of plaster show evidence of repainting and these showed that red had replaced red and white had replaced white. The only plaster found *in situ* was in Room 3 where it took the form of an *opus signinum* rendering painted red.

In the three heated rooms (Rooms 4, 5 and 6), only three pilae bricks were found *in situ* to represent the hypocaust. Fragments of several oblong box-flue tiles, originally each about 14 in. by 6 in. and 3½ in. deep (No. 252) and iron clamp-nails about 3 in. long (No. 251) were found in Rooms 4 and 6 and must also have related to the hypocaust.

Room 1 (Dressing Room?)

Only part of the north-east wall of this room survived, but the robber-trenches of the other three indicated an internal measurement of about 8 by 7 ft. A thin line of white wall-plaster marked the east wall and a robbed drain crossed through its centre, but no trace of floor or hypocaust was found. It is difficult to identify this room with any certainty, but from its position and the lack of heating its seems likely that this was a small dressing-room. The rubble and loam deposits in this room contained tile and pottery (Nos. 232, 233 and 236–8).

Room 2 (Cold Room)

Parts of the south-east, south-west and north-west walls of this room were found surviving to a maximum height of 2 ft. 1 in. The robber-trench of the north-east wall was found and also the robbed drain passing downhill to Room 1. The internal measurements were about 12 by 8 ft. and the north-west wall showed signs of having at least a partial *opus signinum* internal rendering painted red. The floor had been totally removed and as undisturbed natural was found at a depth of only 4 ft. 5 in. it seems clear that this room had not contained a hypocaust. The absence of underfloor heating and the position of this room adjacent to both the cold-plunge bath (Room 3) and a hypocausted room (Room 4) suggests this was the cold room of the bath-building.

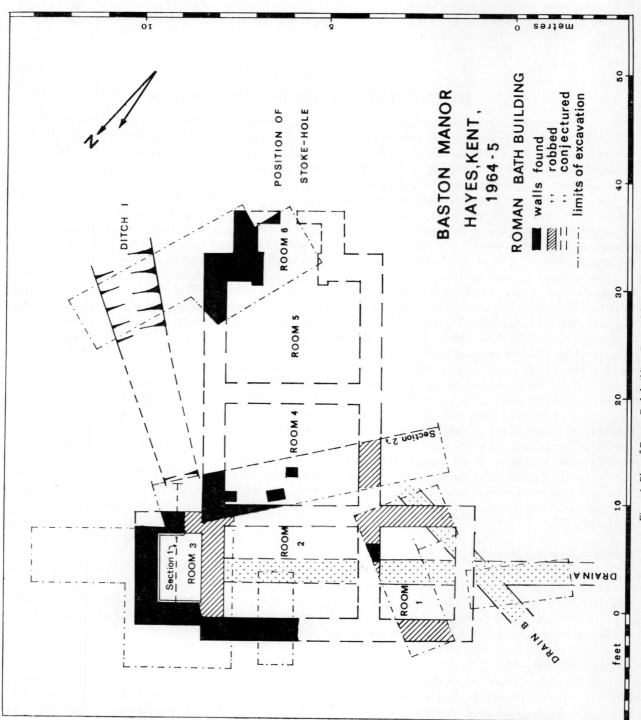

Fig. 26. *Plan of Roman Bath-building, Baston Manor, Hayes (Site 13).*

Room 3 (Cold-plunge Bath) (Fig. 27, Section 1)

This was the most complete room in the bath-building and it measured exactly 6 ft. by 4 ft. internally (Plate VIA). The north-west, north-east and south-east walls all survived, the latter to a maximum height of 4 ft. 1 in. The internal faces had all been rendered with a 1 in. layer of *opus signinum*, painted red. The floor had also been lined with *opus signinum* and the joint between wall and floor sealed with a thin triangle of orange mortar. The floor was located at a depth of 6 ft. 10 in. (O.D. 302.27) from the present ground-level and it is clear that originally it formed a deep bath lower than any other floor in the building. Clear spring-water flowed into this bath during the excavation and it is possible that it was deliberately sited over or very close to a spring. The absence of the south-west wall allowed a close examination of the method of construction. The walls had been constructed of tiles, chalk blocks and flints set in hard, pebbly white mortar. A bed of irregular chalk blocks had been laid in a grey-green sand layer (layer 11). The walls had then been coated with a coarse *opus signinum* rendering. A single layer of typical Roman bridging-tiles, about 22 in. square and at least 2 in. thick, was then laid and this covered by a 5 in. layer of pebble (layer 10). A 1 in. layer of tile-chippings was then spread over this solid base and the floor of *opus signinum* 1 in. thick was then laid. There was evidence to suggest that the walls were rendered again with *opus signinum* at the same time as the floor was laid. The final stage was the application of red paint to all the surfaces. Patches of a thin skin of white mortar, or plaster, may indicate an additional surfacing of the walls at a subsequent date.

The total absence of any means of heating this bath, or tank, suggests that the water in it was normally cold. In addition, the position of the room relative to the heated rooms and the distant furnace makes it clear that this was the cold-plunge bath. The entrance to the bath and the outlet for the water both must have been in the missing south-west wall, the latter probably consisting of a lead-pipe. A drain (Drain A) was in fact found running from the robber-trench of this wall downhill beneath Rooms 1 and 2. The drain had also been robbed, but it had been built in a U-shaped gulley about 2 ft. 6 in. wide, about 1 ft. 6 in. deep and with a clay-lining. A similar drainage gulley (Drain B) was found running roughly east-west beneath Room 1, but its exact function and relationship with the drain from the cold-plunge bath were not determined. Both drains were filled with a mixture of brown loam and rubble.

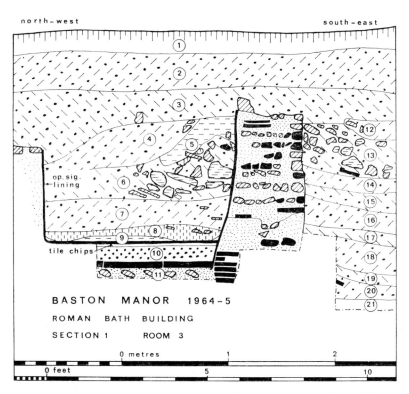

Fig. 27. *Section through Room 3, Roman Bath-building, Baston Manor, Hayes (Site 13).*

The floor of the cold-plunge bath was covered with carbon, mortar and fragments of plaster (layers 8 and 9), probably deliberately thrown in as rubble. This was sealed by a 13 in. layer (layer 7) of black loam, pebble, quernstone, tile and pottery (No. 241), certainly representing a domestic rubbish dump. This was covered by a 2 ft. layer (layer 6) of large rubble, including chalk blocks, mortar, plaster and flints probably representing the main demolition of the building. Covering this were deep layers of pebble and loam washed down from the slope above (layers 2–5). A fine bronze nail-cleaner was recovered from close to the bottom of the bath (layer 8).

Room 4 (Tepid Room) (Fig. 28, Section 2 and Plate VIB)

Only the north corner of this room was found intact, the south-west wall having been robbed and the south-east wall as shown on the plan being conjectural. The internal size, as drawn, is about 12 by 9 ft. and the clay-bonded walls only survived to a height of 11 in. above the floor. The room had contained a hypocaust, subsequently largely robbed, which explains the absence of *in situ* wall-plaster and of any trace of a floor. The hypocaust had been built on a compact bed of flints located at a depth of about 6 ft. 6 in. from the present ground-level and therefore about 2 ft. deeper than the floors of Rooms 1 and 2. The tile pilae had been constructed on this flint base, but of these only three had partially survived (Plate VIIA). Of these two measured about 11 in. square and the third about 1 ft. 4 in. by 11 in. The base was found covered by a thin layer of carbon (layer 9), no doubt deposited whilst the hypocaust was still in service. This was capped by a 2½ ft. layer of rubble (layers 6 and 8) containing chalk blocks, tile, red and white wall-plaster, smashed box-flue tiles, iron clamp-nails and some pottery (Nos. 239 and 240). This layer appears to represent the demolition of the building in two phases, the first including the removal of the north-east wall of this room and the second including the removal of the south-east wall. The rubble was covered by a layer of mud-silt (layer 4) about 1½ ft. thick and hillwash (layers 2 and 3) about 2 ft. thick. It is clear that this room was excavated into the natural hill-side and also partially through the filling of Ditch 1 (see below).

This room, whatever its exact length, clearly formed part of the main heated section of the bath-building. Its distance from the furnace and its position close to the unheated rooms makes it likely that this was the tepid room.

Room 5 (Hot Room)

Only the eastern corner of this room (Plate VIIB), constructed of brick and chalk blocks, survived to a maximum height of 2 ft. 8 in. The north-west and south-west walls are again conjectured. The internal measurements probably matched those of the adjacent tepid room being about 12 by 9 ft. As in Room 4 a flint base was found at a depth of about 7 ft. and this too must certainly have supported the pilae of a hypocaust. No trace of pilae was found here, but a thin layer of soot and carbon drawn in from the stoke-hole again covered most of the flint base. Similarly, the interior contained a mass of demolition rubble including wall-plaster painted red and white and more fragments of box-flue tiles. It seems highly probable that this part of the heated section of the building, being much nearer to the furnace, was the hot-room.

Room 6 (Hot Bath)

This room was really an extension of Room 5. They shared a common flint base and clearly the original hypocaust must have extended into Room 6. No trace of the pilae remained, but the north-east and south-east walls were intact, built entirely of large bricks and tiles internally and chalk blocks externally. Slight traces of the robbed south-west and north-west walls were observed and from these it seems that the room measured internally about 6 by 3 ft. On the south-east side the wall was broken by a partially robbed furnace-arch, 1 ft. 10 in. wide, which must have led into the furnace and stoke-hole. A layer of pebble and loam outside Room 6 and sealed by the demolition rubble contained pottery (Nos. 231, 234 and 235) and a quernstone (No. 155).

Ditch 1

A small U-shaped ditch (Fig. 28) about 3 ft. wide and about 2 ft. deep was found just outside the north-east wall of Room 4. A similar, but wider ditch was also located north-east of Room 5 and it seems highly likely that they relate and form a single ditch at least 24 ft. in length. It contained a filling (layer 18) of brown loam and pebble in which were two small sherds of corky ware cooking-pot and two sherds of samian. The latter included a Form 18 and a fragment of a platter both dated to the second half of the 1st century A.D. The ditch had been cut partly away when the bath-building was constructed and then sealed by a dump of clay (layers 12 and 13) about

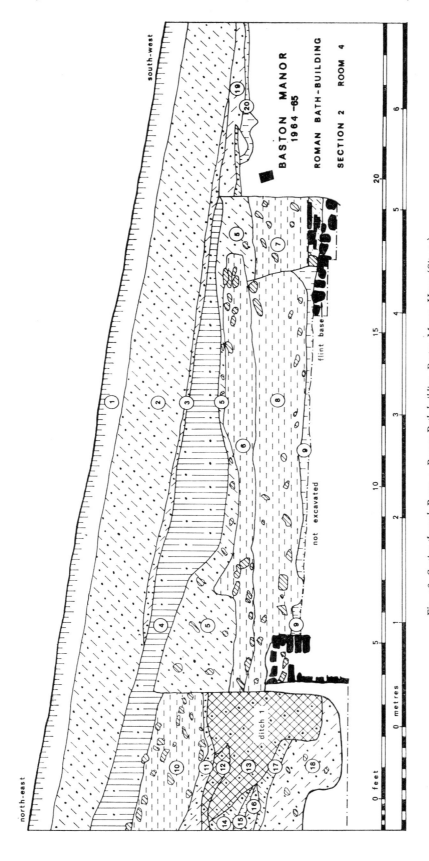

Fig. 28. *Section through Room 4, Roman Bath-building, Baston Manor, Hayes (Site 13).*

3½ ft. thick. The dump was covered by a thin layer of hillwash (layer 11) and also rubble resulting from the demolition (layer 10).

Ditch 2

Another small ditch V-shaped in section, at least 5 ft. 6 in. wide and originally 2 ft. 6 in. deep was found in a random test-hole about 100 ft. west of the bath-building. It ran uphill on a roughly north-south axis and its filling of loam and carbon contained several small Roman potsherds and fragments of tile. One vessel (No. 250) appears to be a finely finished native pot probably dating from the late-1st century.

Ditch 3

Another Romano-British ditch was found in Square A3 on the edge of the Neolithic area and about 150 ft. south-west of the bath-building. This was a broad, shallow ditch, about 9-10 ft. wide, with steep sides and originally not more than 3 ft. deep. It ran roughly north-west by south-east and was entirely filled with a grey-black mud-silt. The ditch was covered by a 1 ft. layer of brown loam and pebble hillwash which in turn was covered by about 6 in. of black loam topsoil. The mud-silt contained more than 130 potsherds, fragments of Roman tile and brick and part of a glass bottle. The pottery included samian Forms 18, 33 and 35 of the late-1st and early-2nd centuries, a mortarium stamped by SEXTUS (No. 243) and a strainer (No. 246).

Ditch 4

A fourth ditch was located in one of the random trial-holes about 180 ft. north-west of the bath-house. Only one side of it was seen and the bottom appeared to be at least 3 ft. 3 in. deep from present ground-level. The filling of grey-black loam contained single fragments of tile, bone and quernstone and small potsherds of late-1st, or early-2nd, century date.

Other Material from the Site

The four trial-holes dug on the uphill north-east side of the bath-building produced only a single Roman potsherd between them. Two more dug in the Riding School, one about 85 ft. to the south-east and the other about 150 ft. to the south-west likewise produced nothing of Roman date. The 17 trial-holes, the deep shaft (see Site 1) and the Neolithic area on the downhill, west side of the bath-building, however, all produced some material of Roman date. The hillwash cleared from over the Neolithic site contained more than 100 worn potsherds including cooking-pots (No. 247), bowls (No. 248) and a storage jar (No. 249). It also produced a worn coin of Vespasian (A.D. 70-3), four of the identifiable quernstones and pieces of vessel and window glass. All the pottery can be dated between A.D. 70-140.

The open field north of the bath-building was covered by a pattern of 21 trial-holes in the hope of finding related Roman structures. None was found and the total absence of rubble and mortar in this and other areas seems to suggest that no second Roman masonry building existed at Baston. Although the majority of these trial-holes produced no Roman material, six contained one or more small Romano-British potsherds and tile even as far as 250 ft. north-west of the bath-building and from this it seems likely that Romano-British debris is scattered over an area of two or more acres.

DATING AND DISCUSSION

The site chosen was a well-drained west-facing slope astride clear spring-water and close to good soil and flint and chalk for building. It appears to have been occupied from about A.D. 70 to about A.D. 140. This dating is based upon a study of the pottery where the total lack of Iron Age types and of Romano-British pottery of the second half of the 2nd century, or later, is particularly significant. From this evidence it seems that the site was probably established within about two decades of the Conquest of A.D. 43 and occupied for two or three generations, perhaps by a single family. The total lack of any industrial activity implies that this site was a farmstead, though the presence of a fine bath-building suggests a degree of prosperity not shared by many of the other farms in the area.

The finds also provide some evidence of the farm's links with local markets. The native pottery, the greensand querns and the Thames Estuary oysters all suggest good connections with local traders or markets. The imported samian, glass and lavastone querns tend to reflect bigger markets and highly organised trade. For both the presence of the nearby Roman arterial road gave ample facility for the transport of crops and cattle and the exchange of goods. The site also lay well within the orbit of Londinium.

The evidence from the site suggests that at least two periods are indicated. The first is represented by a shallow ditch (Ditch 1) and the second by the substantial masonry bath-building which was built partially over the ditch. The finds in all four ditches date from the end of the 1st and the beginning of the 2nd centuries and it seems likely that all formed part of a complex more extensive than revealed by the limited excavation. At other early Romano-British sites in the area similar ditches formed either farmstead enclosures or field boundaries.

Whatever the exact function of the ditch-system it is clear that the Roman bath-building superseded at least Ditch 1, already partially silted. Only four potsherds were found in this ditch and all date from the second half of the 1st century. They suggest that the bath-building was not constructed before about A.D. 100. The rubbish and rubble in the ruins of the bath-building clearly indicative of its disuse and partial destruction, dates no later than about A.D. 140. The building, as the site, thus appears to have been short-lived and this is reflected by the general lack of rebuilding or redecorating on any scale.

The available evidence suggests that no other Roman masonry building existed at Baston and this tends to eliminate the possibility of a nearby villa of the normal type. Isolated bath-buildings, however, do occur frequently elsewhere in Roman Britain and in Kent alone examples occur at Boughton Monchelsea (Ref. 148), North Cray (Ref. 149), Plaxtol (Ref. 150) and Little Chart (Ref. 151). A study (Ref. 152) of the development of early Romano-British rural sites in West Kent suggests that most began as humble farmsteads of no great size and that only some developed into villas with a rectilinear plan and at least mortared foundations. It is quite possible that these detached bath-houses relate to developing farmsteads not yet evolved into the full villa-class. Perhaps in these cases the bath-house was the first major refinement, which of necessity had to be built of stone and mortar owing to the presence of a furnace. If so the owners were still content to live a while longer in their simple un-mortared wooden buildings of which hardly any trace survives. Certainly the ditches, domestic rubbish, querns and tile attest an occupation-site in the close proximity of the bath-building and on the present evidence it seems likely that a pre-villa type farmhouse existed here too. Had the occupation at Baston continued into the later-2nd century then perhaps a substantial villa would have been constructed.

What is clear, however, is that the bath-building appears to have followed a familiar pattern consisting of a furnace, hot-bath, hot-room, tepid room, cold plunge, cold room, dressing-room and drains in the normal way. The principles used in the construction, the clever use of local materials and the internal *opus signinum* and plaster renderings all point to craftsmanship normally beyond the average country farmer. There is also slight evidence of replastering of some of the internal surfaces and from this it seems that the building must have been used for at least several years. Just how and why the building fell into disuse, how it became used for tipping rubbish and when it was so thoroughly demolished are problems which may never be solved.

THE FINDS

(1) THE POTTERY

A total of 1,097 potsherds was recovered from the site excluding the 225 pieces of prehistoric pottery (Site 1). These sherds represent a minimum of 83 vessels of which 20 have been illustrated (Fig. 29). Although this pottery may not be a representative sample from the site some useful conclusions can be drawn from its classification. Five main groups emerge. The distribution of the pottery in these groups is given in Table A and the descriptive notes appear below (for discussion of terms see Fox Hill—Site 8).

Group A. Samian Ware

Only 26 pieces of imported samian ware were found on the site and although mostly fragmentary at least nine vessels appear to be represented. Of these a Form 18 and a Form 33, both probably of late-1st century

Deposit	Samian ware	Patch Grove and related wares	Shell and corky wares	Roman coarse wares	Roman fine wares	Total
Ditch 1	2	—	2	—	—	4
Ditch 3	10	38	36	36	15	135
Hillwash over Neolithic	4	37	33	43	3	120
Bath-building	2	103	42	185	24	356
Test-holes and Ditches 2 and 4	—	5	12	18	5	40
Unstratified	8	120	75	216	23	442
Total sherds	26	303	200	498	70	1,097
Vessels represented (minimum)	9	15	15	35	9	83

TABLE A

Distribution and classification of pottery from the Romano-British site near Baston Manor

date, together with a Form 35 of the first half of the 2nd century, came from Ditch 3 (BM-A3 and A4). A fine Form Curle 11 (No. 238), of late-1st or early-2nd century date, came from the rubble in the bath-building (BM-Z11-3). A Form 18 (BM-Z2-7) and a fragment of a platter (BM-Z4-23), both of the second half of the 1st century A.D., were found in the filling of Ditch 1. Finally, a Form 18 (BM-B8-1), a burned Form 27 (BM-Z10-3), and a burned Form 29 (BM-Z13-4), all of the second half of the 1st century A.D., were found in unstratified contexts.

Group B. Patch Grove and Related Wares (see Fox Hill, Site 8, for discussion)

A total of 303 sherds was recovered representing a minimum of 15 different vessels of which five have been drawn (Nos. 234, 235, 239, 241 and 249).

Of the identifiable vessels four are large storage jars, with the usual stick-stabbing on the shoulder, of which one has a bead rim and the others have rims which are outcurved. Seven more are cooking-pots with bead rims and the remaining four are squat jars with outcurved rims. The Patch Grove pottery was found in the bath-building, in Ditch 3 and almost everywhere else on the site.

Group C. Shell-loaded and Corky Wares

This ware is normally fairly soft to the touch and in a wide range of colours from pink-orange to brown and black. The paste contains varying proportions of crushed shell or small irregular holes (where the shell has dissolved out) giving a corky appearance. Just 200 sherds were recovered, representing 15 vessels of which four have been drawn (Nos. 232, 237, 247 and 248). Almost all of the vessels are cooking-pots with bead rims though at least one is a bowl with a flanged rim. These too were found in the bath-building, in Ditch 1 and from most parts of the site.

Group D. Coarse, Hard Sandy Romanised Wares

This group consists of a wide range of vessels. They are generally much harder and better-fired than either the Patch Grove or shell-loaded wares and their pastes and surfaces are mostly sandy to the touch. The colours, forms and functions vary considerably. A total of 498 sherds represents a minimum of 35 vessels of which 8 have been drawn.

The vessels represented include two globular amphorae, four mortaria (Nos. 243 and 244), two flagons, a small pie-dish, 13 jars (Nos. 233 and 242), including at least three with developed shoulders, ten cooking-pots

Plate VIB. *The north corner of Room 4 and the adjacent wall of Room 3 at a higher level. Roman bath-building, Baston Manor, Hayes (Site 13)*

Plate VIA. *Room 3 (flooded by spring-water). Roman bath-building, Baston Manor, Hayes (Site 13)*

Plate VIIB. *The east corner of Room 5. Roman bath-building, Baston Manor, Hayes*
(Site 13)

Plate VIIA. *Traces of the hypocaust in Room 4. Roman bath-building, Baston Manor, Hayes*
(Site 13)

Plate VIIIB. *The site after excavation showing the full extent of the Roman aisled building, Darenth Roman Villa, Darenth (Site 21)*

Plate VIIIA. *The site before excavation showing the wall of the Roman aisled building uncovered by the contractor's bulldozer. Darenth Roman Villa, Darenth (Site 21)*

Plate IXA. *View across Room 1 to Room 3. Roman bath-building, Darenth Roman Villa, Darenth (Site 21)*

Plate IXB. *The Period IV aisled building from the south-west showing the main hall (marked by horizontal rods) and adjacent rooms. Darenth Roman Villa, Darenth (Site 21)*

(No. 231), two squat jars (Nos. 236 and 250) and a strainer (No. 246). Again these were found on most parts of the site.

Group E. Fine Roman Wares

This group consists of the much finer pottery (excluding samian) which is generally well-fired and finely finished. Much of it may be imported and again the colours, forms and functions vary. A total of 70 sherds representing a minimum of nine vessels, of which two have been drawn (Nos. 240 and 245), was found on the site. The group includes a ringed-neck flagon, several beakers (some with studs and poppy-head type rims) and other fine flagons. These too came from most parts of the site.

The pottery from Baston Manor consists, with few exceptions, of types familiar on Romano-British sites in West Kent, of the 1st and early-2nd centuries. The native types and their dating have been discussed under the description of the Fox Hill pottery and the Romanised products, where illustrated, are individually dated where this has been possible. All the pottery from this site can be placed within the date-limits A.D. 70–140. This dating is confirmed by the general absence of pottery types which were being imported into Britain in great quantities (such as beakers, flagons and platters) at about the time of the Conquest in A.D. 43. So too is there a general absence of samian and coarse pottery types assignable to the second half of the 2nd century, or later.

The purely native wares, such as Patch Grove and shell-loaded pottery, account for 36% of the total from the site. The finer Roman wares, including samian, account for another 22%. The coarse, sandy Romanised wares, probably all made in Britain, account for the remaining 42%. On sites in West Kent of the 1st century (such as Eastwood), native wares predominate and at Baston the higher proportion of Romanised products probably reflects the continuation of the site well into the 2nd century. The possibility that the native wares were exclusively 1st century and the Romanised products largely 2nd century is not supported by the stratigraphy at Baston. Both types were often found in close association and clearly the native wares did survive into the 2nd century.

(2) THE MORTARIUM STAMPS

By Mrs. K. Hartley

(a) A mortarium (No. 243) in sandy, greyish cream fabric with traces of pale buff slip surviving and small-sized, grey, red-brown and black trituration grit, worn away by use in the lower half. The piece has suffered some burning after fracture. This fabric is typical of the potteries at Verulamium, Radlett and Brockley Hill.

The broken stamp reads SEX, retrograde; when complete it would read SEX·VA·IVS ('s' reversed), for Sex(tus) Va(lerius) Ju(stus?). Ju(stus?) is one of a group of at least five potters, all Roman citizens and sharing identical *praenomen* and *nomen*, who had a workshop at Colchester in the period, *c.* A.D. 60–105.

In fact, although a Colchester fabric is their primary one, at least two of them also used the different fabric described above (Ref. 153). The rim-forms used by Sex(tus) Va(lerius) Ju(stus?) suggest that he was the latest of the group and also indicate that his work in the Verulamium area was later than his work at Colchester. Two of the fourteen mortaria now known for him are in the fabric of the Verulamium potteries. I would expect this example to date to A.D. 70–100.

Roman citizens are in a minority among mortarium potters though they are perhaps to be expected in a *colonia*. The Sexti Valerii, sharing *praenomen* as well as *nomen*, are perhaps likely to be the freedmen of one *patronus*, although a father and son relationship could also be involved. From the mud-silt of Ditch 3 (BM-A3-4).

(b) Another mortarium (No. 244) in sandy, greyish cream fabric with buff slip; grey and red-brown trituration grit. The diagonally impressed stamp is from one of the several dies of Albinus. Albinus was the most important single mortarium-maker working in the potteries near Watling Street and south of Verulamium (including Brockley Hill and Radlett). A number of his stamps are recorded from closely-dated Flavian contexts at Inchtuthil, Verulamium, Baginton and Wroxeter. A date of A.D. 65–95 is indicated (Ref. 154). From the deep shaft north-west of the Neolithic area (BM-B8-1).

(3) OTHER FINDS

Quernstones

A total of 15 fragments of quernstone, representing at least seven separate rotary querns, was recovered from the site. Although mostly too fragmentary for adequate illustration these form an interesting group for study and comparison can usefully be made with those found at Eastwood, Fawkham in 1957 (Ref. 155). Although several of the fragments were found in the hillwash overlying the Neolithic site there can be little doubt that all relate to the Romano-British site situated slightly higher up the slope. The hillwash also contained a large amount of Roman pottery and tile derived from the same source.

Quern 1.   Three small pieces of friable lavastone imported from the Mayen district of Germany. Thickness and size not determinable. From hillwash over Neolithic (BM-C5-3 and B4-2).

Quern 2.   A fragment of a flat stone of grey-white Millstone Grit. About 2·5 in. thick and originally about 12–15 in. in diameter. From hillwash over Neolithic (BM-E4-5).

Quern 3.   A fragment of a flat lower-stone of grey-green calcareous sandstone from the Folkestone Beds, Lower Greensand. Traces of tooling on all surfaces and parts of three deep concentric grooves appear on the milling-surface. About 2 in. thick and originally about 16–18 in. in diameter. From hillwash over Neolithic (BM-A3-1).

Quern 4.   Very similar to 3, but at least 3 in. thick. Just possibly the upper-stone of Quern 3. (See No. 155.)

Quern 5.   A fragment of a tapered upper-stone of iron-stained calcareous sandstone from the Folkestone Beds, Lower Greensand. The side is sloping, the stone tapers towards the centre and the lower surface is slightly concave due to wear. The sloping top constitutes a shallow hopper for the grain. Between 1·3 and 2·5 in. thick and originally about 15–18 in. in diameter. From hillwash over the Neolithic (BM-D5-2).

Quern 6.   A fragment of a flat upper-stone of iron-stained sandstone. The top appears to be untreated, the side has vertical tooled lines and the lower surface is worn and scored. About 2·8 in. thick and originally about 16–18 in. in diameter. From Room 3 of the Roman bath-building (BM-Z4-16).

Quern 7.   A fragment of a large upper-stone of iron-stained sandstone, similar to 6. Again the top appears to be untreated, the side has near-vertical tooling and the unworn lower surface has one clear concentric groove. About 3·2 in. thick and originally 16–20 in. in diameter. From the Roman bath-building (BM-Z10-12).

Glass

Only 9 small fragments of glass were found on the site of which four came from vessels and five from windows. At least three different vessels are represented; the rectangular base of a pale-green bottle from Ditch 3 (BM-A3-3); a pale green vessel from the bath-building (BM-Z10-3) and a small rim (?) of a fine white vessel from the hillwash over the Neolithic area (BM-E4-5). Of the window-glass, all pale-green in colour, two pieces have bevelled edges to fit a wooden frame. One piece has both surfaces matt and the others are matt one side and smooth on the other. Three pieces came from the bath-building (BM-Z10-3, Z10-2 and Z4-4) and the other two came from the hillwash over the Neolithic (BM-D5-2).

Coin

A worn, bronze sestertius of Vespasian was the only coin found on the site. It depicts ROMA standing left and it has been examined and dated by Mr. E. W. Tilley to A.D. 70-3. From the hillwash over the Neolithic area (BM-D5-2).

Bones and Oyster Shells

Only 40 fragments of bone were recovered during the excavation and these are of little value for statistical study. Part of the lower-jaw of a young dog was found in the bath-building as was the tooth of a mature sheep or goat.

Eight oyster shells were also found. Six came from the bath-building and two from the hillwash over the Neolithic area.

Bronze and Iron Objects

A flat, bronze nail-cleaner 2·1 in. long and about 0·2 in. wide was found in the bottom of the cold-plunge bath (Fig. 27, Layer 8). It has a circular hole at one end for suspension on a ring, two small zones of horizontal lines and the normal forked-end (BM-Z4-16). This object was published in 1973 (Ref. 156).

Ten iron nails and six iron clamp-nails were found in the rubble of the bath-building. The nails are square in section and either between 2·5 in. and 3·0 in. or about 5·4 in. in length. The heads are mostly circular or ovoid. The clamp-nails are T-shaped (No. 251), square in section and about 3·3 in. in minimum length. The horizontal cross-bar is about 3·6 in. long. Their purpose was to clamp the vertical box-flue tiles (No. 252) to the walls and iron-staining from these nails was found on some of the flue-tiles in the rubble.

(4) THE WALL-PLASTER

By Gerald Clewley

A total of 175 fragments of painted wall-plaster was recovered from the rubble inside the bath-building. Apart from the intact areas of red-painted *opus signinum* lining the cold-plunge none was found *in situ*. The fragments can be divided into ten types, each type receiving a different treatment. This suggests that either different treatments were required for the various rooms or that the work was not carried out as a single operation. Repainting was certainly undertaken in some cases with evidence of red replacing red and also white replacing white. Of the fragments found 78 were painted plain red, 84 were painted plain white and only four pieces which showed red and white adjacent, could possibly suggest a pattern.

It seems that most of the walls which were to be treated were first coated with a layer of rendering 0·1 to 0·5 in. thick, to which a very thin skin of plaster was later applied. The paint was probably applied whilst the plaster was still wet.

It is not possible to say with any certainty which fragments of plaster came from which particular room owing to the very extensive nature of the robbing and subsequent disturbance. The various types are listed below.

Type 1.   White plaster on coarse red *opus signinum* on white pebbled mortar.

Type 2.   White plaster on fine pink *opus signinum* on white mortar.

Type 3.   White plaster on grey mortar.

Type 4.   White plaster on grey-pink *opus signinum* over white plaster on pink *opus signinum*.

Type 5.   White plaster on red *opus signinum* on pink *opus signinum*.

Type 6.   White plaster on grey mortar on grey-pink mortar.

Type 7.   Pink *opus signinum* on red *opus signinum*.

Type 8.   Pink *opus signinum* on white mortar *opus signinum* over pink on cream mortar.

Type 9.   White plaster on cream mortar.

Type 10.   White mortar *opus signinum* on pink *opus signinum*.

Catalogue of the Illustrated Finds from Baston Manor, Hayes (Figs. 19 and 29)

No. 155.   A fragment of a grey-green rotary quernstone, probably an upper-stone, of calcareous sandstone from the Lower Green-sand. Its working surface carries roughly concentric grooves and its back is damaged. It weighs 2 lb. and the complete quernstone may have weighed as much as 30 lb. with a diameter of about 18–20 in. From loam layer sealed by demolition rubble outside Room 6 (BM-Z2-4). Similar to Nos. 153–4 from Fox Hill (Site 8) and Elm Farm (Site 9), respectively.

No. 231.   Cooking-pot with everted rim of coarse grey ware. Light grey paste and surface with groove on shoulder. From loam outside Room 6 (BM-Z2-4). A distinctive type occurring elsewhere in early-2nd century deposits as from a 2nd century kiln at Stoneyfield, Farnham, Surrey (Ref. 157) and see No. 272.

No. 232.   Cooking-pot with slightly beaded rim of shell-loaded ware. Dark grey paste and surface. From Room 1 (BM-Z11-8). A native product, but much sandier than the normal shell-loaded pottery. Probably early-2nd century.

No. 233.   Jar with small, upright rim of fine sandy ware. Buff paste and black surface with broad groove at girth. From Room 1 (BM-Z11-9). An unusual form.

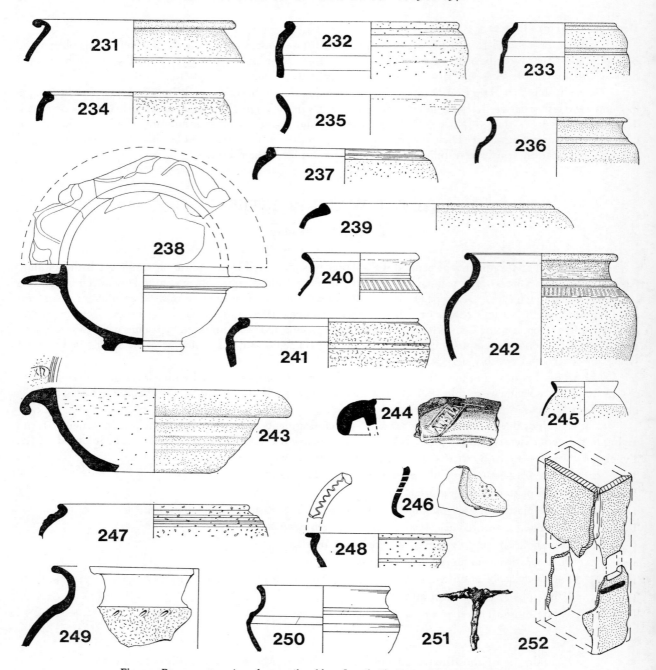

Fig. 29. *Roman pottery, iron clamp-nail and box-flue tile* ($\frac{1}{4}$), *Baston Manor, Hayes (Site 13).*

No. 234.   Jar with slightly recessed, bead rim of Patch Grove ware. Mottled grey-black paste and buff-black surface. From loam outside Room 6 (BM-Z2-4). A native product common in the second half of the 1st and early-2nd centuries, but found here with early-2nd century pottery (No. 231).

No. 235.   Cooking-pot with outcurved, thickened rim of Patch Grove ware. Mottled grey-black paste and buff-brown surface. From loam outside Room 6 (BM-Z2-4).

No. 236.   Small cooking-pot with outcurved, angular rim of fine sandy ware. Light grey paste, black surface, faint cordon and wide hollow on shoulder. From Room 1 (BM-Z11-10). This vessel appears to be related to the squat jars found at Eastwood, Fawkham, Kent (Ref. 158) in association with other pottery dated exclusively to the second half of the 1st century. This example has a much less pronounced cordon and rim and is perhaps slightly later in date.

No. 237.   As No. 232, same deposit.

No. 238.   Samian ware bowl (Form Curle 11) with broad flange decorated with *en barbotine* ivy-leaf pattern. From Room 1 and Room 2 (BM-Z11-3 and BM-Z14-5). Late-1st, or early-2nd, century A.D. (Ref. 159).

No. 239.   Cooking-pot with bead rim of Patch Grove ware containing slight traces of grit. Mottled grey-black paste and buff surface. From Room 4 (BM-Z4-10). See notes on Fox Hill pottery (Site 8).

No. 240.   Jar with outcurved rim of smooth ware. Dark grey paste and surface with white slip on rim and shoulder. Zone of diagonal burnished lines on shoulder. From Room 4 (BM-Z4-10). Very similar vessels were being produced in a kiln at Highgate, London (Ref. 160) during the early-2nd century. Compare with vessels from Fox Hill and with a vessel from Greenhithe (Ref. 161) found in a 2nd century context.

No. 241.   Jar with recessed rim of Patch Grove ware. Mottled grey-black paste and buff-black surface with faint groove below shoulder. From Room 3 (BM-Z4-16). A variant of No. 234. Its presence in the rubbish in the cold-plunge bath suggests very strongly that this too dates from the early-2nd century.

No. 242.   Cooking-pot with outcurved, thickened rim of coarse sandy ware. Light grey paste and dark grey surface. Cordon and grooves above zone of vertical burnished lines. Unstratified (BM-1). Again very similar to vessels of the early-2nd century made in the Highgate kiln (Ref. 160) and also to shouldered pots from Brixworth (Ref. 162) dated A.D. 70–120.

No. 243.   Mortarium with down-turned, rolled flange of fine sandy ware. Retrograde stamp of SEX(TUS). See specialist report. From Ditch 3 (BM-A3-4). A.D. 70–100.

No. 244.   Mortarium with down-turned, rolled flange of fine sandy ware. Stamped ALBINVS. See specialist report. From shaft by Neolithic area (BM-B8-1). A.D. 65–95.

No. 245.   Beaker with everted rim of smooth ware. Light grey paste and surface with dark grey slip on neck and shoulder. Poppy-head type, but no trace of applied studs. Unstratified (BM-1). This type probably appeared in the late-1st century and is common on very many sites throughout the 2nd century.

No. 246.   Wall sherd of wide, spouted bowl of fine sandy ware. Light grey paste and buff surface. A series of neat circular perforations facilitated straining through a spout (now missing). From Ditch 3 (BM-A3-3). Known on a number of Roman sites in Britain, as at Colchester in a deposit dated c. A.D. 100 (Ref. 163).

No. 247.   Cooking-pot with bead rim of corky ware. Grey paste and buff-black surface. Cordon and grooves on shoulder. From hillwash over Neolithic (BM-C6-2). The marked cordon and grooves and perhaps also the lack of a recess on the rim suggest that this vessel dates from the late-1st century.

No. 248.   Bowl with flanged rim of corky ware. Light grey paste and buff surface. Incised wavy line on top of rim and groove below shoulder. From hillwash over Neolithic (BM-C7-3). An unusual type for a native corky ware, perhaps in imitation of the Romanised reeded-rim of the early-2nd century.

No. 249.   Storage jar with outcurved rim of Patch Grove ware. Mottled grey-black paste and buff-orange surface with stick-stabbing on shoulder. From hillwash over Neolithic (BM-E5-2). Second half of 1st century or 2nd century.

No. 250.   Jar with outcurved rim of fine sandy ware. Light grey paste and buff surface, coated dark brown. From Ditch 2 (BM-Z7-5). This vessel is of the same type as No. 236 and appears to be a finely finished native product. Probably late-1st century.

No. 251.   Iron clamp-nail, rectangular in section. Used to secure box-flue tiles to the wall of the bath-house. From Room 4 (BM-Z4-4).

No. 252.   Plain box-flue tile of fine sandy texture. Length about 14 in., width about 5·5 in. and depth about 3·5 in. Sub-rectangular hole in centre of long side about 2 by 1·5 in. Iron staining from clamp-nail on side. From Rooms 4 and 6 (BM-Z2-5 and Z4-6).

SITE 14. A Romano-British Site at Leafy Grove, Keston, Kent

This site (N.G.R. TQ.4136.6388) lies in the parish of Keston, Kent about 1,000 yards north-north-west of the parish church and forms part of Foxhill Farm (Fig. 30). It lies within Leafy Grove, a woodland (O.S. parcel 3800), on the crest and shoulder of a low north-west spur projecting from the east side of a wide valley. The site is on Thanet Beds at an elevation of between about 350 and 400 ft. The centre of the site lies about 210 ft. due east (uphill) of the bungalow on the south side of the buildings now forming Foxhill Farm.

The site was discovered on 16th March, 1969 by Stephen and Richard Groves, the young sons of the farm manager, whilst digging casually in the wood by their home. Four sherds of pottery found by the boys were shown to the Group, then undertaking field surveys about ½ a mile to the west. As a result of the discovery a trial-excavation, in heavy rain, was undertaken on 30th March and further limited excavation on 6th and 7th April. This work produced Roman pottery and tiles, pieces of quernstone and five cremation-burials. The bulk of the material from the site appears to date from about A.D. 50 to 120.

The Group gratefully acknowledges the help and interest of Miss I. Groom of Foxhill Farm. Thanks are also due to Mr. A. Appleby for reporting the initial find, to Mr. R. Cockett for drawing some of the pottery, to Mr. R. Gierth for examining the cremated bones and to Mr. T. Woodman for the plan.

THE EXCAVATION

About 200 ft. east of the bungalow the steep slope tends to level off as it reaches the crest of the spur, which is itself overlooked by a steeper east slope leading up to Keston Common. Trial excavation here revealed a concentration of more than 230 pieces of Roman pottery and tile in an area of only 120 sq. ft. (just 210 ft. east of the bungalow) on a heavy clay subsoil. Slight traces of a very shallow east-west gulley were detected, but this was badly disturbed by roots. A series of five trial-holes in an arc around this point, at distances of from 42 to 99 ft., together produced only another 18 pieces of pottery and tile. From this it seems likely that the first concentration of occupation debris probably represents the approximate centre of the site. The steep slope beneath this apparent centre was found to be strewn with a light scatter of potsherds and tile, probably washed down from above. More than 260 items were collected here from an excavated area of about 600 sq. ft.

At a point 80 ft. down the slope from the centre of the site and 130 ft. east of the bungalow, was a small Romano-British cremation cemetery (Fig. 30). Five burial-groups were found in the small area cleared of bushes and trees and it is possible that others exist nearby. All were found at a shallow depth and had suffered severely from the effects of weathering, root-action and perhaps even ploughing.

Burial 1

This consisted of a single, badly crushed Patch Grove pot (No. 253), containing cremated bone, placed in a small hollow only 12 in. in diameter and covered by only 7 in. of soil.

Burial 2

This comprised two fragmentary vessels, crushed together, lying sideways and covered by only 6 in. of soil. One was the lower part of a Roman flagon, or beaker (No. 254) and the other consisted of about 33 sherds of a Patch Grove vessel without either base or rim. No bones were found in association with these vessels.

Burial 3

This consisted of two damaged pots and an adjacent compact mass of cremated bone, perhaps placed within a container since perished. All were within an area no more than 11 in. in diameter and again only covered

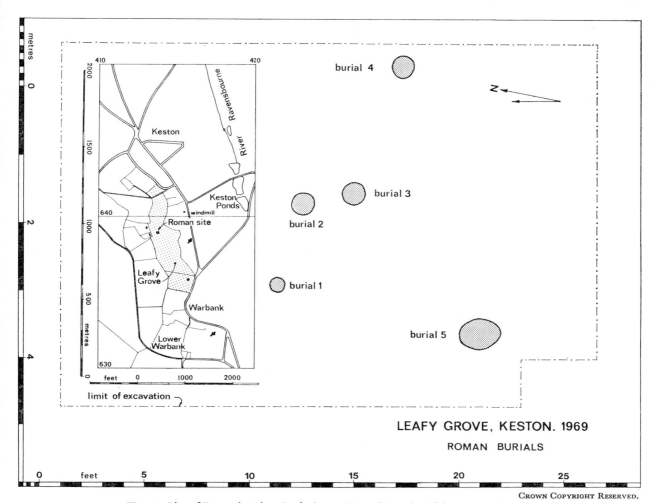

Fig. 30. *Plan of Roman burials at Leafy Grove, Keston (Site 14) with location map (inset).*

by a few inches of soil. One vessel, a fine carinated beaker (No. 256), lay on its side and the other, a small cup (No. 255) was in an upright position.

Burial 4

This comprised a single vessel, crushed into 56 pieces and with the upper part completely missing. The fragments lay in a faint hollow, 1 ft. 6 in. by 10 in. and were in direct contact with a small quantity of cremated bone. Again they were only covered by a few inches of soil. The vessel is a well-fired, grey-brown cooking-pot with a grey-black surface, no trace of decoration and a base about 3½ in. in diameter. Four additional fragments of another vessel, of blue-grey ware with an orange-brown surface, were found with the cooking-pot and could represent a second vessel in the group.

Burial 5

This consisted of five vessels, all touching, placed in an irregular pit 1 ft. 11 in. by 1 ft. 2 in. and about 1 ft. 6 in. deep and representing the most important burial-group on the site. The largest vessel was a fine Patch Grove cinerary urn (No. 258) which contained cremated bone and was placed at the centre of the group. On the west side of the urn there was a samian platter (Form 18) with its makers-stamp obliterated by the acid soil. On the north side was a small, poppy-head beaker (No. 259) crushed into 70 pieces. Inverted on top of this beaker was a small samian cup (Form 46 or variant) with a section of its rim missing and no maker's-stamp (No. 257). On the east side there was a shattered flagon of sandy ware (No. 260) with a buff surface and narrow neck.

DATING AND DISCUSSION

A study of the pottery from the cemetery suggests that all five burials were deposited between about A.D. 50–120. The earliest appears to be Burial 3 which consists of a fine native copy of a carinated beaker (about A.D. 40–70) and a cup probably copied from an early samian vessel (A.D. 30–60, or a little later). Both vessels have distinctive Belgic characteristics, but the slightly evolved profile of the beaker, at least, favours a slightly post-Conquest date.

The flagon, or beaker, in Burial 2 and the cooking-pot in Burial 4 are both distinctively Roman in character and are thus perhaps several decades later (A.D. 70–120). The Patch Grove vessels in Burials 1, 2 and 5, probably all cinerary urns, are of a type being produced from about the time of the Conquest to about the end of the 2nd century (see notes on Fox Hill pottery—Site 8). The later vessels in the series were sometimes rather taller and flatter in profile than the earlier ones and this suggests that the Leafy Grove urns date from the second half of the 1st century. This dating is anyway supported by the other vessels in Burial 5. The samian platter (Form 18) shows signs of evolving into Form 18/31 and must surely date to the last quarter of the 1st century. The samian cup (Form 46 or variant), an uncommon form, normally occurs, however, in contexts dated A.D. 50–80. The flagon and beaker are again Roman in character and likely to date to the last quarter of the 1st century. From this it seems probable that Burial 5 was deposited about A.D. 70–100.

The unstratified material recovered from the slope, from the central concentration and from the adjacent area may be studied as a whole. It includes 97 fragments of Roman tile, of which nine are certainly tegulae and 422 potsherds representing at least 24 vessels. Of these ten are of Patch Grove type, four are bead rim cooking-pots and six probably storage jars, all datable to the second half of the 1st, or early-2nd, century. The finer wares include two very worn samian bases, a cup and a bowl; a mortarium, a flagon, a dish, two beakers, two flanged bowls and at least five cooking-pots in hard, sandy-textured Romanised wares (Nos. 261–267). The great majority of these are datable to the late-1st, or early-2nd, century. The flanged bowls, however, are more common to the late-3rd and 4th centuries and seem out of place at Leafy Grove, but their damaged condition makes exact identification difficult.

In addition to the tile and pottery a single piece of slag and nine small fragments of quernstone were recovered from unstratified contexts. Three types of rotary-quern can be identified; greensand from the edge of the Weald, lavastone from the Mayen district of West Germany and a silicified flint-conglomerate probably from a local source.

The available evidence suggests that the site at Leafy Grove was typical of the many Romano-British sites in West Kent occupied during the second half of the 1st century A.D. The majority of these appear to have been farmsteads (Ref. 164) established shortly after the Conquest in A.D. 43. The number of finds, the burials and even the small gulley all point to it being an occupation-site and the absence of substantial building materials, other than roof-tile, suggests that any structures must have been timber-framed with walls of wattle and daub. Any buildings probably occupied the crest of the spur close to where the highest concentration of material was found and overlooked the wide valley. The related cremation cemetery was only 80 ft. down the slope below the crest and from this it seems that the site was fairly compact. The farmstead pattern of wooden structures, related ditches, a small attached cemetery, quantities of native coarse and fine pottery, small amounts of samian and a few quernstones is thus well-evidenced at Leafy Grove.

As regards the actual siting it may be significant that a small stream now flows along the north-east side of the spur about 200 ft. from the supposed centre of the site. The existence of a constant source of spring water probably dictated the position of the site which is otherwise on thick clay, when much lighter and better-drained soils could be found in the nearby valley. The main arterial Roman road lay about 1½ miles to the west and the later, major villa-complex of the area, at Warbank, Keston about 800 yards to the south.

The finds suggest that the site was probably established shortly following the Conquest and that it expired about A.D. 120, in common with the majority of farmsteads in the area. This allows for two, or just possibly three, generations of a single family, the earlier reflected by Burials 3 and 5 and the later by Burials 2 and 4. Here, as elsewhere, the family unit appears to have been small and the inevitable abandonment due to either economic, financial or social reasons. The small amount of pottery of possible late-3rd or 4th century date may indicate a much later re-occupation of at least part of the site.

This interesting site might repay further attention at some future date and it should certainly be investigated if ever threatened with development. It is clear that the area has been adversely affected by erosion on the steep slope and elsewhere by numerous tree-roots. What is equally clear is that only extensive and large-scale, properly conducted excavation is likely to increase substantially knowledge of the site.

Catalogue of the Illustrated Pottery from Leafy Grove, Keston (Fig. 31)

No. 253. Cinerary urn of Patch Grove ware. Mottled grey-black paste and buff-brown surface. Burnished zone beneath simple burnished lattice decoration. Burial 1 (LG-B1). This vessel is similar to another cinerary urn found at Eastwood, Fawkham (Site 17) some 11 miles to the east. That from Eastwood (No. 283) was found in direct association with a Roman flagon and is thus likely to be of post-Conquest date.

No. 254. Flagon, or beaker, of sandy ware. Buff paste and surface with girth grooves and footring. Burial 2 (LG-B2).

No. 255. Carinated cup with upright, slightly beaded rim of fine sandy ware. Grey-brown paste and grey-black surface. Broad convexity above carination, raised base and pronounced footring. Burial 3 (LG-B3). This is a very interesting vessel, probably a native copy of an early samian cup (Ritterling, Form 5) which generally failed to survive the Claudian period. The Leafy Grove version is somewhat more developed above the carination and may in fact be based on a Gallo-Belgic copy of the samian original. Either way it is likely to have been made about A.D. 30–60, though the possibility that it was copied later cannot be ruled out.

No. 256. Carinated beaker with outcurved rim of fine sandy ware. Grey-brown paste and grey-black surface. Broad convexity above carination and slight footring. Burial 3 (LG-B3). This form is more familiar than No. 255. Its basic profile, in the form of wider Belgic bowls, is known at Verulamium (Ref. 165) in a deposit dated A.D. 5–35. It occurs, again in a rather wider version, at Colchester (Ref. 166) in deposits dated A.D. 10–61. Although it may be regarded as a mainly pre-Conquest type the narrow mouth and more upright profile reflect the finer Romanised post-Conquest vessels. On balance it is perhaps best to regard this vessel as dating from about A.D. 40–70. The similarity of Nos. 255 and 256 may indicate that they are the products of the same kiln and were perhaps purchased together specifically for burial purposes.

No. 257. Small cup with upturned rim of samian ware (Form 46 or variant), worn, but unstamped. Probably made at La Graufesenque in the second half of the 1st century A.D. Burial 5 (LG-B5-P4).

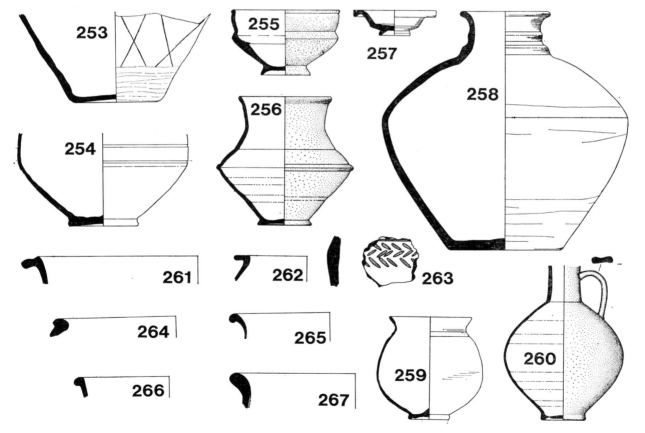

Fig. 31. *Roman pottery* (¼), *Leafy Grove, Keston (Site 14).*

No. 258. Cinerary urn with outcurved rim of Patch Grove ware. Mottled grey-black paste and grey-brown surface. Globular shape, two cordons on neck and traces of burnishing. Burial 5 (LG-B5-P1). A broadly similar vessel was found in the Belgic cemetery at Swarling (Ref. 167) where it probably dates to within a decade or two of the Conquest. Another similar vessel was found in a well at Colchester (Ref. 168) where it appears to have been deposited between about A.D. 43–70. The type is clearly in the pre-Roman native tradition, but considering its association here with post-Conquest pottery it either dates between about A.D. 50–100, or is an earlier survival.

No. 259. Poppy-head beaker with outcurved rim of smooth ware. Grey-brown paste and black surface. Faint trace of studs on surface and cordon on shoulder. Burial 5 (LG-B5-P5). These beakers are common through much of the 2nd century (Ref. 169), but they are known in contexts of the later 1st century as at Eastwood, Fawkham (Ref. 170). Judging by the associated vessels this example must be of late-1st century date.

No. 260. Single-handled flagon with straight, cylindrical neck of sandy ware. Buff paste and buff surface. Broad two-ribbed handle and slightly raised base. Burial 5 (LG-B5-P3). The vertical neck appears to be an early Roman form and occurs in mid-1st century deposits at Colchester (Ref. 171), but it probably continued for most of the second half of the 1st century A.D.

No. 261. Dish with flanged rim of sandy ware. Grey paste and grey surface. Unstratified from cemetery area (LG-2-1). Almost invariably a 3rd and 4th century form as at Jewry Wall (Ref. 172) and Reculver (Ref. 173) and seemingly out of place at Leafy Grove.

No. 262. Cooking-pot with flanged rim of sandy ware. Grey paste and grey surface. Unstratified in gully in occupation-area (LG-8-4). At a glance this vessel resembles a medieval pot, but its shape and texture do not match the local Limpsfield products. The same basic profile does, however, appear at Farnham (Ref. 174) where kilns producing this pottery seem to have been in production during the first half of the 2nd century.

No. 263. Wall sherd of large storage jar of soft-soapy texture, probably a Patch Grove or allied ware. Buff core and orange-brown surface. Incised chevron pattern on shoulder. Unstratified from cemetery area (LG-2-2). A form common in West Kent on sites of the second half of the 1st and first half of the 2nd centuries.

No. 264. Cooking-pot with bead rim of sandy ware. Grey-brown paste and black surface. Unstratified from cemetery area. This is the Romanised version of the native bead rim cooking-pot and it seems to have appeared in the late-1st century and continued into the first half of the 2nd century. For discussion see Fox Hill (Site 8).

No. 265. Jar with outcurved, thickened rim of sandy ware. Grey paste and grey-brown surface. Unstratified from occupation-area (LG-8-2).

No. 266. Dish with bead rim of sandy ware. Grey-brown paste and brown surface coated black. Unstratified from occupation area (LG-8-2). A common form in the late-2nd and early-3rd centuries as at Reculver (Ref. 175) and Faversham (Ref. 176).

No. 267. Cooking-pot with thickened outcurved rim of Patch Grove ware. Mottled grey-black paste and grey-brown surface. Unstratified from cemetery area (LG-2-2). Second half of the 1st, or first half of 2nd, century.

SITE 15. Romano-British Burials at Tatsfield Road, Titsey, Surrey

This site (N.G.R. TQ.4080.5608) lies in the parish of Titsey, Surrey about ½ a mile west of Tatsfield parish church. It occupies part of an open field on the north side of Clarks Lane and east of Tatsfield Road. It is situated on the crest of the North Downs scarp overlooking the Greensand ridge to the south. The site is on Clay-with-flints at an elevation about 825 ft. O.D. The Roman arterial road from London to Lewes passes only 500 ft. to the east and the North Downs Ridgeway must have passed very close to the site.

The site was discovered by the Group on 13th August, 1966 during 'Operation Gaspipe West'. The pipe-trench had been cut roughly east-west along the crest of the Downs about 710 ft. north of Clarks Lane and roughly parallel to it. An examination of the trench revealed that it had sliced in half a Roman flagon placed upright in a small hollow. This had formed part of a cremation burial and further work revealed two more burials just beyond the south lip of the trench. The Roman road and six other pits, or ditches, were also revealed by the pipe-trench in the same general area and these were duly recorded.

Burial 1

At 147 ft. 6 in. east of the centre of Tatsfield Road. This originally had consisted of a Roman flagon and a large cinerary urn. Half of the smashed flagon was found in the north side of the pipe-trench and most of the rest, together with dozens of pieces of the cinerary urn in direct association, were recovered from the adjacent spoilheap. Significantly, small pieces of cremated bone were found adhering to the inside of the urn. The base of the flagon was located at a depth of about 1 ft. 8 in. from the present ground-level and it had been set into the upper filling of a shallow gully (Feature 5).

Both vessels are too fragmentary for illustration. The flagon, of uncertain profile, has a pink-brown surface, a small handle and was originally about 8 in. high. The cinerary urn, with a grey-black paste and a soft grey-brown surface, is of Patch Grove type. On examination the mass of soil and bone found with the urn was found to contain three iron nails with broad, flat heads, of square section and 0·8 (broken?), 1·6 and 2·2 in. in length, respectively. These appear to have been burnt and it seems likely that they were collected with the bones from the funeral-pyre after cremation (Ref. 177). It may be that they represent part of a couch or frame upon which the body had finally rested. The remaining cremated bones weighed about 500 grams.

Burial 2

At 150 ft. east of the centre of Tatsfield Road. This was found on the south side of the pipe-trench just 4 ft. away from the first burial. It consisted of a single, crushed cinerary urn, standing upright and filled with cremated bones. Its base is 4½ in. in diameter, its maximum girth is about 10 in. and it was probably about 9 in. high. It is decorated with at least two faint horizontal, burnished lines with perhaps a stabbed decoration on the shoulder. The core of this vessel is the same as the Patch Grove urn in Burial 1, though the surface is rather more brown. The pot had been placed in a shallow, irregular hole, cut into the underlying clay, of just sufficient size. Its base lay at a depth of about 1 ft. 8 in. from the present ground level. The contents of this vessel have been left as a compact mass for exhibition purposes and it is not known, therefore, if it contained anything other than cremated bones.

Burial 3

At 153 ft. east of Tatsfield Road. This burial consisted of a cinerary urn filled with cremated bones and a small Roman flagon (No. 268), both badly crushed. The urn is again of the Patch Grove type, with a base about 4¼ in. in diameter, a maximum girth of about 10 in. and a probable height of about 9 in. It appears to have had a narrow neck about 2½ in. in diameter and a bulbous profile.

The vessels were touching, with the flagon laying on the south-east side of the urn. They were packed around with flints and the base of the urn was found at a depth of about 2 ft. from the present ground level. The contents of this vessel have been left as a compact mass for exhibition purposes.

Feature 1

At 572 ft. west of Tatsfield Road. A wide U-shaped ditch, about 7 ft. wide and about 5 ft. 6 in. deep, running roughly north-south. Its filling of clay and loam contained nine small potsherds of a vessel of black ware of indeterminate date.

Feature 2

At 375 ft. west of Tatsfield Road. A U-shaped pit on the south side of the pipe-trench, 11 ft. wide and 4 ft. 6 in. deep. Its filling of brown loam contained chalk specks, but no finds.

Feature 3

At 121 ft. 6 in. east of Tatsfield Road. A U-shaped pit, on the north side of the trench, about 2 ft. wide and about 3 ft. deep. Its filling of brown loam contained a single indeterminate potsherd.

Feature 4

At 141 ft. 6 in. east of Tatsfield Road. A V-shaped pit on the south side of the trench, about 3 ft. wide and 2 ft. deep. Its filling of clay, loam and carbon contained pieces of local ironstone and two indeterminate potsherds.

Feature 5

At 147 ft. 6 in. east of Tatsfield Road. A V-shaped gulley both sides of the pipe-trench, 3 ft. wide and 2 ft. deep and running roughly north-south. Its brown loam filling contained no finds, but was cut by Burial 1.

Feature 6

About 640 ft. east of Tatsfield Road. A band of small pebbles, 25 ft. wide and up to 5 in. thick, was revealed under the east hedge of the field and this must certainly represent the known London-Lewes Roman road. This is anyway its suggested line (Ref. 178) and indeed the agger can be seen along the hedge further north. No trace of side ditches was found.

Feature 7

About 640 ft. east of Tatsfield Road. A U-shaped ditch, both sides of the trench, running roughly north-south, about 4 ft. wide, 3½ ft. deep and sealed by the Roman road. Its filling of orange clay and brown loam contained several sherds of a large vessel with a thin, squared rim of late-Iron Age type, too fragmentary for illustration.

DATING AND DISCUSSION

Although the evidence from this location is limited, an unusual site seems to be indicated. At least two periods of occupation appear to be represented, one possibly Iron Age and the other certainly Romano-British. One small ditch (Feature 7) seems to be of late-Iron Age date and if all the other undated pits and ditches are too, then an extensive site, covering a length of at least 1,200 ft., may be indicated. In two cases earlier features (Features 5 and 7) are sealed by Roman deposits, one by Burial 1 and the other by road metalling.

The simple, squared Iron Age rim is of a type found at Lower Warbank, Keston (excavation still in progress) in contexts dated to the first half of the 1st century A.D. The two fragmentary Roman flagons are unlikely to be earlier than about A.D. 50 or later than about A.D. 100. The three cinerary-urns are all of Patch Grove ware and should, therefore, date between about A.D. 40–200 (see notes on Fox Hill—Site 8). The profiles are bulbous and these tend to be early in the Patch Grove series. The nearest parallel to these urns is from Leafy Grove, Keston (4 miles to the north) in a burial group dated to about A.D. 70–100 (Site 14). On balance it seems likely that the burial-groups from Titsey represent a small cemetery dating from about A.D. 60–100.

The very high altitude of this site and the heavy soil are not features typical of either Iron Age or Romano-British sites in the area. Perhaps the close proximity of the prehistoric Ridgeway (Ref. 179) was a significant factor in Iron Age times, whilst the Roman cemetery probably relates to a small settlement situated close to the intersection of the trackway and the Roman arterial road. The comparatively early date of the Romano-British material tends to imply an equally early date for the construction of the road and this is supported by evidence from other local sites.

Catalogue of the Illustrated Pottery from Tatsfield Road, Titsey (Fig. 32)

No. 268. Single-handled flagon of sandy ware. Buff paste and surface. Burial 3 (GPW-4-5). Though clearly a Roman flagon this vessel is difficult to date exactly on its own merits. Its profile resembles that of a very similar vessel from Burial 5 at Leafy Grove, Keston (Site 14) which was found in direct association with two samian vessels, a Patch Grove cinerary urn and a poppy-head beaker and there dated to about A.D. 70–100.

SITE 16. A Romano-British Site near Oakley House, Bromley Common, Kent

This site (N.G.R. TQ.4188.6635) lies about 800 ft. south-south-east of Oakley House in the parish of Bromley, Kent about ¾ of a mile east of Hayes parish church and west of the main A21 road. It occupies part of two fields (O.S. parcel 0038) on a gentle south facing slope close to the River Ravensbourne. It stands on thick orange-grey clay forming part of the Woolwich and Blackheath pebble beds and the elevation is about 230 ft. O.D.

The site was discovered on 20th June, 1965 during 'Operation Gaspipe'. The pipe-trench, cutting north-east to south-west, passed through the wire fence on the west side of the field at a point about 121 ft. from the south-west corner. A small ditch was observed and examined and Romano-British pottery recovered from it, from the spoil-heaps and from the adjacent area.

The Ditch

This was found 14 ft. north-east of the fence. It was U-shaped in section, about 4 ft. wide and 3 ft. deep and it appeared to run on a north-south axis. Its filling of brown loam, carbon and grey clay contained 219 Romano-British potsherds with fragments of almost identical vessels in both the upper and lower fillings. From this it seems likely that the ditch was filled over a short period of time. Of the various vessels represented, both native and imported, several appear to date from the middle of the 1st century A.D. and others to the first half of the 2nd century (Nos. 269–272, 274, 276–8 and 281). If the ditch was filled over a short period then this could not have been done earlier than about A.D. 120–150. This suggests that either 1st century types were still in circulation much later or that rubbish survivals had found their way into the ditch. The ditch also contained two fragments of Roman tile and small pieces of a Mayen lava quernstone.

The contractor's spoilheap adjacent to the ditch also produced a quantity of archaeological material. Several more potsherds were also recovered from the area 100 ft. to the west, both from the spoil-heap and from a layer of brown loam sealing the undisturbed natural clay. All the material from these sources is regarded here as unstratified and studied as a second group (see Table A). It consists of another 420 Romano-British potsherds, five fragments of flat Roman tile, a broken imbrex and a fragment of the same quernstone. The pottery is almost identical to that recovered from the ditch and again it ranges in date from about A.D. 50–150 (Nos. 273, 275, 279–280 and 282).

DATING AND DISCUSSION

The evidence from this site is confined to a small ditch, some 639 potsherds (representing at least 39 vessels) and fragments of tile and quernstone. The site was not ideal being situated on heavy clay, but it lay close to the Ravensbourne stream and only about 2 miles east of the main Roman London-Lewes road.

It was clearly a Romano-British site and although some of the pottery seems to be of mid-1st century A.D. date, none need be pre-Conquest. A large amount of the pottery dates from the first half of the 2nd century, some even as late as about A.D. 150. The range is thus about A.D. 50–150. Of this pottery 38% is of native origin and the remaining 62% of imported or Romanised wares.

Although the sample is small it does seem that two main groups of pottery can be identified, one mid-1st century and the other 2nd century. In addition the absence of native shell-loaded wares and also of shouldered jars and reeded-rim vessels on a site of this date range may be significant. One possible explanation is that the site was not continuously used, but was abandoned and subsequently reoccupied. It is anyway difficult to explain the pottery of differing dates in the same context and it is probable that the circumstances are exceptional and may not be representative of the site as a whole.

The ditch probably formed part of an enclosure, or field system, as on other rural sites in West Kent of similar date. The absence of industrial activity must again imply a farmstead site and the finds are entirely consistent with this suggestion. The absence of building materials, other than a few roof tiles, again suggests timber-framed buildings. The Mayen quernstone proves, as at Eastwood, that German exports were reaching rural markets in Kent during the 1st and perhaps early-2nd centuries.

It seems that the site was established within a decade or two of the Conquest and the occupation, if continuous, lasted for three or even four generations. If so, a small cremation cemetery must await discovery nearby.

THE FINDS

(1) THE POTTERY

A total of 639 sherds was recovered from the site and these represent a minimum of 39 vessels of which 14 have been illustrated (Nos. 269–282). They came either from the small ditch or from unstratified contexts. The pottery has been classified into the four main groups shown in Table A and discussed briefly below (for discussion of terms see Fox Hill—Site 8).

	Samian ware	Patch Grove and allied wares	Shell-loaded and corky wares	Romanised wares	Total sherds
From the ditch	1	65	—	153	219
Unstratified	5	218	2	195	420
Total sherds	6	283	2	348	639
Minimum vessels	3	14	1	21	39

TABLE A
Distribution and classification of pottery found near Oakley House

Group A. Samian Ware

Only six sherds, representing three vessels, were recovered from the site. Two of these, a Form 27 and a small sherd of a Form 37, came from unstratified contexts and a Form 18/31 was found in the ditch. All probably date from the end of the 1st, or first half of the 2nd, century.

Group B. Patch Grove and Allied Wares (see notes on Fox Hill pottery)

Some 283 sherds of a minimum of 14 vessels (Nos. 275, 276, 280–2) were recovered from the site. These consisted of five squat jars with outcurved rims, fragments of five large storage jars, the base of a pedestal urn, a bead rim cooking-pot, a squat carinated bowl and a cooking-pot with a squared rim. Three of the storage jars are represented by body sherds with broad chevron patterns incised on the upper shoulder. The pattern on the largest of these runs along an applied band 1·2 in. wide, similar to the one from Eastwood (No. 287). Two more of the Patch Grove vessel sherds retain marked pre-Roman characteristics and must date to within two or three decades of the Conquest. The others are typical of vessels dating to the second half of the 1st century and into the 2nd century.

Group C. Shell-loaded and Corky Wares

It seems highly significant that only two sherds of shell-loaded pottery from a single vessel were recovered from the site. It may be that this reflects freak circumstances of some sort, though elsewhere in the area this ware is prolific on sites of this period. It is possible that the predominance of Romanised and 2nd century products may indicate that the native shell-loaded wares were rapidly being superseded by about the end of the 1st century.

Group D. Romanised Wares

Both the fine and coarse wares, either local or imported, have been included under this heading. Much is fragmentary and all badly marked by the acid nature of the soil. Some 348 sherds, representing a minimum of 21 vessels (Nos. 269–274, 277–279) were recovered. These include three mortaria, an amphora, a fine beaker with an outcurved rim, a fine flagon, a poppy-head beaker, three cooking-pots with outcurved rims and five small bead rim dishes. Of these the beaker and flagon may be mid-1st century imports, whilst the poppy-head beaker, cooking-pots, mortaria and dishes are mostly of the first half of the 2nd century.

The pottery from Oakley House spans a period of at least a century, ranging from about A.D. 50 to at least A.D. 150. Two groups seem to emerge, one dating from the middle years of the 1st century and the other to the first half of the 2nd century, though the distinction may not be representative of the site as a whole. The earlier group includes fine beakers, imported or copied from imported vessels, a pedestal-urn and the two pots (Nos. 269 and 280) with Belgic characteristics. The later group includes mortaria and small dishes some of which may even date to the decade or so after A.D. 150.

It may be significant that shouldered jars and reeded rim vessels are seemingly absent, particularly as these are abundant at Fox Hill, West Wickham, only three miles to the west (occupied from about A.D. 80–140). In addition the absence of native shell-loaded wares is noteworthy.

Catalogue of the Illustrated Pottery from Oakley House, Bromley (Fig. 32)

No. 269.   Beaker with angled rim of fine, hard ware. Dark grey paste and orange surface with traces of buff coating. From the ditch (GP-2-5). This appears to be a wide-mouthed version of a flask noted at Colchester (Ref. 180, Form 234) in mid-1st century contexts, either an import or a good quality native product.

No. 270.   Dish with angular rim of sandy ware. Grey-black paste and black surface. Curved wall, slightly chamfered base and zone of nearly vertical burnished lines. From the ditch (GP-2-8). See No. 273 for comments.

No. 271.   Dish with bead rim of sandy ware. Grey-black paste and surface, probably originally burnished. From the ditch (GP-2-5). See No. 273 for comments.

No. 272.   Jar with out-turned, thickened rim of sandy ware. Grey paste and black surface with band of burnishing on shoulder. From the ditch (GP-2-7). Noted in early-2nd century context at Baston Manor (Site 13, No. 231) and common at Leicester (Ref. 181) during the 2nd century.

No. 273.   Dish with bead rim of sandy ware. Grey-black paste and black surface originally burnished. Unstratified (GP-2-4). The dishes Nos. 270, 271 and 273 belong to the range of low-walled vessels, normally with rims of triangular or rounded form, having lattice or burnished exteriors. They normally date to the first half of the 2nd century, as at Leicester (Ref. 182), being notably absent from sites of the second half of the 1st century in West Kent. They are common within the Classis Britannica fort at Dover, but rare in the early-3rd century fort at Reculver (Ref. 183) and at Faversham (Ref. 184) where a more developed form is common.

No. 274.   Mortarium with broad, down-turned flange and small rim of sandy ware. Grey paste and orange surface with few traces of grit. From the ditch (GP-2-1). Dated to A.D. 100–140 in Northern Britain (Ref. 185, Gillam Type 243).

No. 275.   Cooking-pot with slightly recessed, undercut bead rim of Patch Grove ware. Mottled grey-black paste and buff surface. Unstratified (GP-2-1). This is one of the more distinctive variants of native bead rim vessels common in the second half of the 1st and early-2nd centuries. It occurs at Eastwood (Ref. 186) and perhaps at Charlton (Ref. 187) in late-1st century deposits.

No. 276.   Jar or small cooking-pot with squared rim of Patch Grove ware. Mottled grey-black paste and buff surface. From the ditch (GP-2-1). This is an unusual squared version of the native bead rim and it looks back to pottery of the pre-Roman Iron Age (Ref. 188). Probably second half of 1st century A.D.

No. 277.   Mortarium with down-turned flange and small, splayed rim of sandy ware. Pink paste and cream surface containing multi-coloured grits. From the ditch (GP-2-1). Similar to vessels in Northern Britain dated A.D. 80–110 (Ref. 185, Gillam Type 277).

No. 278.   Bowl with thickened, slightly down-turned rim of sandy ware. Grey paste and surface with traces of external white slip. From the ditch (GP-2-1). Similar to types dated to the end of the 1st and early part of the 2nd centuries (Ref. 189).

No. 279.   Mortarium with broad, thickened flange and upright rim of smooth ware. Grey paste and orange surface with multi-coloured grits. Unstratified (GP-2-3). Broadly similar to vessels found in Northern Britain dated A.D. 140–180 (Ref. 185, Gillam Type 245).

No. 280.   Squat carinated jar or bowl with angled recessed rim of Patch Grove ware. Mottled grey-black paste and buff-orange surface. Unstratified (GP-2-2). This is a distinctly native form reminiscent of pre-Roman vessels found in Dorset (Ref. 190) and of mid-1st century vessels at Colchester (Ref. 180, Form 250). Probably second half of 1st century.

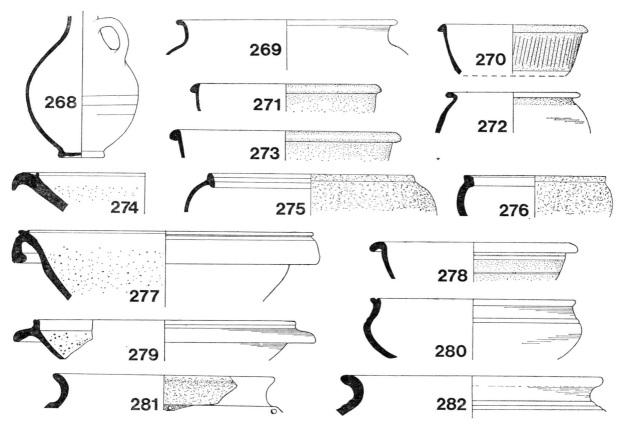

Fig. 32. *Roman flagon (No. 268), Tatsfield Road, Titsey, Surrey (Site 15) and Roman pottery (Nos. 269–282) (¼), Oakley House, Bromley (Site 16).*

No. 281. Storage jar with outcurved rim of Patch Grove ware. Mottled grey-black paste and orange surface. Series of small indented marks decorating edge of shoulder. From the ditch (GP-2-1). A typical product of the second half of the 1st and first half of the 2nd centuries.

No. 282 Storage jar with thick outcurved rim of Patch Grove ware. Mottled grey-black paste and orange-brown surface. Unstratified (GP-2-2). Pair of heavy cordons on shoulder. This vessel recalls the late-Belgic jars from Canterbury (Ref. 191) and Wheathampstead (Ref. 192). In view of the lack of pre-Conquest material on this site and the more developed rim a date of about A.D. 50–80 seems likely for this vessel.

SITE 17. A Romano-British Site at Eastwood, Fawkham, Kent

This site (N.G.R. TQ.5886.6466) lies in the parish of Fawkham, Kent on farmland about 2 miles south of the parish church and just under a mile west of the church at Ash. It occupies parts of a field, farmyard and garden of Eastwood Farm owned by Mr. George Self (O.S. parcel 43). It lies about half way up the steep west side of a narrow north-south downland valley in what appears to be an isolated position. The site is mostly on Upper Chalk, containing numerous pockets of clay and the O.D. is about 380–400 ft.

The site was discovered by chance on 25th October, 1957 by Mr. Self and excavations which started then, by Mr. M. Kellaway and the writer, were concluded in 1961. These revealed part of the outline of a ditched enclosure and recovered nearly 3,000 potsherds, brooches, quernstones and animal bones. The evidence, which was published in 1963 (Ref. 193), indicated a Romano-British farmstead dating to about A.D. 45–100.

One puzzling feature not fully explored at the time was a wide, circular shaft situated within the area enclosed by the farmstead ditches. This was selected as a special project by some members of the West Kent Group and excavated by them during the winter of 1962–3. The original work had also suggested that a small family cemetery relating to the farmstead might exist nearby and in October, 1963 this was found during the construction of a bungalow on the farm (Fig. 33). The immediate area was later excavated with the aid of members of the Fawkham Historical Society when evidence of two cremation burials was found. This report deals with the excavation of the shaft (probably a chalk quarry) and the burials, which constitute a small cemetery.

Thanks are due first and foremost to Mr. Self for again allowing unrestricted access to his land and to Mrs. Self for her many kindnesses. Of the sixteen members of the West Kent Group who helped excavate the shaft under arctic conditions, particular thanks must be given to Miss G. Price; Messrs. A. Appleby, D. Bartlett, A. Casement, R. Casement, G. Cramp, R. Ellis, C. Hart and C. Roadnight for their sustained efforts. Of the fourteen members of the Fawkham Historical Society who helped with the excavation of the burials Mrs. S. Keen and Mrs. J. Wiseman; Misses M. Chuter, J. Keen and S. Payne; Messrs. J. Barrow, J. Keen, L. Keen, R. Walsh, R. Wattenbach and F. Wiseman deserve a special word of thanks.

The late Rev. H. E. J. Biggs kindly reported on the mollusca from the shaft whilst the various drawings have been prepared by members of the Group at the Bromley centre.

THE EXCAVATIONS

(1) THE CHALK QUARRY (Fig. 33)

The total excavation of the circular shaft entailed the removal, by hand, of about 80 tons of soil. Work began on 3rd November, 1962 as a normal part of a winter programme without the knowledge of the severe arctic conditions to follow. By Christmas about one half of the filling had been removed and a vertical section left across the centre. Snow began to fall in quantity before the close of work on Boxing Day to mark the beginning of the 'Great Freeze', which was to last about nine weeks and said to be the worst for 200 years. The obligation to the farmer to complete the excavation and backfill by early Spring, however, remained and work continued. All minor roads to the site, situated high in the North Downs, were blocked by snow-drifts 6–10 ft. deep and access was often almost impossible. Three feet of snow drifted over the canopies covering the shaft and nearly as much had to be removed from the bottom. The filling and sides of the shaft froze solid to the full depth (13 ft.) and the vertical section was coated with a 1 in. layer of clear ice through which the layers were recorded. Throughout most of this period the temperature remained at or below freezing-point and on ten actual working days it failed to get above 32 °F even at midday. The lowest daytime temperature recorded in the shaft was 10 °F below freezing.

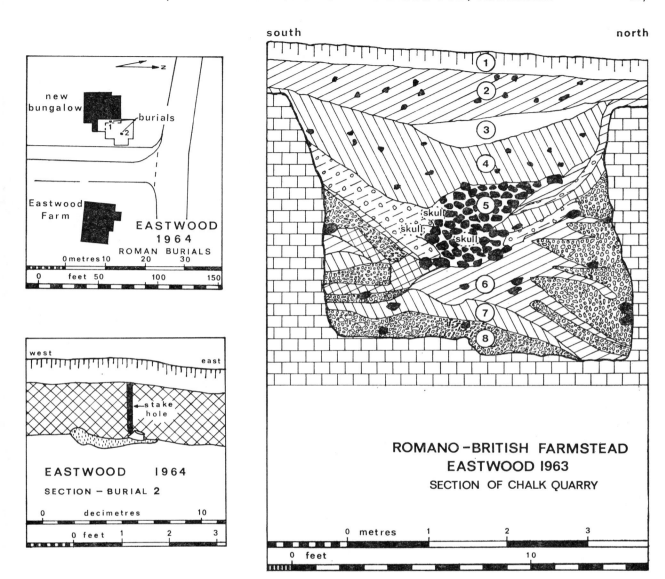

Fig. 33. *Plan showing burials, section through Burial 2 and a section through the Chalk Quarry, Romano-British site, Eastwood, Fawkham (Site 17).*

The thaw started in March and by the 15th the excavation was completed. By 19th April the shaft had been back-filled and the site restored.

The original excavation had suggested that the shaft was about 13 ft. wide and deeper than 9 ft. The total excavation showed that it had originally been 12 ft. wide and 13 ft. deep. It was circular and had been dug through a thin band of orange-brown clay into solid chalk below. Flints still protruded from the original sides and a ragged step had been left across the centre. It was clear that the shaft had been dug by men using metal picks, the impressions of the points of which were clearly visible. These showed that the pick-points had been rectangular in section, about ½ in. square and that the points had been rounded through prolonged use.

The filling of the shaft suggests that it was not deposited at one attempt, but had accumulated over a period of time. Only about 10% was chalk and most of this had probably fallen in from the sides and clearly the large amount of chalk extracted had never been returned. The lower filling (layers 6–8), of brown loam and chalk rubble, may represent alternate collapses and silt accumulations, perhaps forming annually. This was covered by a deep deposit (layer 5) of large flints deliberately thrown in and containing the crushed skulls of five oxen, several potsherds and various mollusca. The flints were in turn sealed by a thick layer (layer 4) of brown loam, which, in the absence of tip-lines, probably formed by natural silting. A layer of black loam (layer 3), containing carbon and more potsherds, was then thrown into the hollow marking the position of the partly filled shaft. Finally, another layer of brown loam (layer 2) formed across the area so that the shaft was invisible on the surface. The date and function of the shaft are discussed below.

(2) THE CEMETERY (Fig. 33)

This was located in October, 1963 just to the west of the original farmhouse at Eastwood. A mechanical excavator had dug out the foundation-trenches for a new bungalow and left the soil in heaps from which Mr. John Lynn recovered fragments of Roman pottery and pieces of cremated bone. It was clear that these had formed part of a cremation burial and as others might exist nearby the area was excavated in the summer of 1964. Members of the Fawkham Historical Society helped clear an area of 1,400 sq. ft. during which one more cremation burial and further pieces of pottery from the original burial were found.

Burial 1 (removed by machine)

Only the approximate position of this burial could be determined and it appears that it had contained two vessels, a cinerary urn and a flagon (Nos. 283–284). Although removed by the machine the cinerary urn still had traces of calcined bone stuck to its inner side. Its form shows it to be a native product of a type common in West Kent in the second half of the 1st century A.D. The flagon is a distinctly Roman type, either imported or a good native copy. Although fragmentary it too can be dated to the second half of the 1st century and it seems that this burial-group was deposited sometime between about A.D. 50–100.

Burial 2

This burial, partly disturbed, contained parts of a beaker and a cooking-pot (Nos. 285–286). The cremated bones had been placed in the beaker originally standing in an upright position. Only fragments of the other vessel survived. Both vessels had been placed in a sub-rectangular pit about 1 ft. 8 in. square and now only 1 ft. 10 in. deep. The bottom of the pit was found to be covered with a 2-in. layer of carbon, perhaps collected from a nearby funeral pyre. The sides of the pit could not be detected owing to either root or animal disturbance, but the impression of an upright stake, 1 in. in diameter and with a tapered point, was observed. It seems likely that this was a marker projecting above ground-level and it is probable that most burials would be marked in some way.

The carinated beaker occurs frequently in cremation-groups of the later 1st century A.D. as at Leafy Grove, Keston (Site 14). The form occurs at Camulodunum (Form 120) where it is dated A.D. 43–65 and one other was found at Eastwood in 1967. The cooking-pot is also a very common type in West Kent and indeed at least 56 of the vessels from the original Eastwood excavation had bead rims. Again this vessel can be dated to the second half of the 1st century and it seems that this burial-group must have been deposited at about the same time as Group 1.

DATING AND DISCUSSION

The dating of the shaft rests on a total of about 30 potsherds recovered from the filling at two main levels (layers 3 and 5) and probably representing domestic rubbish. All the sherds are of similar type and fabric to the pottery recovered from the nearby enclosure ditches and dated to the second half of the 1st century A.D. There can be little doubt that this shaft was dug and filled during this time. The ox skulls probably represent the discarded heads of farm animals slaughtered for meat.

Many hundreds of deep shafts dug through chalk are known in Kent the great majority of which can be identified as either deneholes or chalk-wells of medieval or later date (Ref. 194). Besides the Eastwood shaft, discovered in 1961, two others in West Kent can claim to be of Roman date. One was discovered at Keston in 1962 (Ref 195) when it was found to be 16 ft. deep and 11 ft. in diameter. It contained several potsherds of Roman date and the cremated bones of two small dogs. The excavator suggested that it might have had a ritual function.

Another shaft, found accidentally near Lullingstone in 1964 (Ref. 196), appeared to be circular with a diameter of about 18 ft. and of uncertain depth. Its function was not ascertained, but 1st century Roman pottery was found in the upper part of the filling.

The function of the shaft at Eastwood now needs to be considered. Clearly it was not dug for flint as no attempt had been made to extract those projecting from the sides or to collect those lying in the loose rubble at the bottom. Neither was there the slightest evidence to suggest that the shaft had been inhabited or had a burial or ritual function. Certainly much smaller pits in chalk were used for storage in Iron Age times, but the Roman equivalent was an underground cellar such as occur in Kent at Burham (Ref. 197), Chalk (Ref. 198), Faversham (Ref. 199), Lullingstone (Ref. 200) and Whitstable (Ref. 201). The absence of a ready means of access and no trace of any feature or find relating to storage in the shaft at Eastwood makes this solution unlikely. The probable answer is that the shaft was simply a quarry dug for the extraction of chalk. At least 60 tons of chalk must have been extracted and used. The roughly hewn sides and the ragged step across the bottom are more reminiscent of quarrying than of a finely-finished functional pit. Quarried chalk blocks were used for construction purposes in Roman Britain. In West Kent alone chalk blocks were incorporated into Roman buildings at Hayes (Site 13), Lullingstone (Ref. 202) and Springhead (Ref. 203) and at the latter site numerous Roman floors and rafts of rammed chalk have been found in recent years. At Dover excavations, in 1970, revealed very extensive Roman military buildings built almost exclusively of chalk blocks (Ref. 204). Certainly the chalk in the lower part of the shaft at Eastwood was very hard and it broke away in irregular blocks from which more regular shapes could have been made.

There is also some documentary evidence that chalk was quarried in Britain during the 1st century A.D. for the purpose of 'marling'. Pliny, writing in about A.D. 70, remarks that the Belgae dug deep shafts for chalk to spread on their land (Ref. 205). Certainly at Eastwood the close proximity of heavy clay soil might have made this a necessity. On balance it seems probable that the shaft at Eastwood was a quarry capable of producing both chalk blocks for any of the buildings on the site and chalk rubble for spreading on the land.

The two burial-groups constitute a small cemetery and it seems clear that they were both deposited between A.D. 50–100. They lay 250 ft. north of the known enclosure and it is possible that other burials remain to be found at Eastwood. Similar cremation cemeteries occur at other 1st century sites in West Kent, but none contains more than a dozen burials (Ref. 206).

The apparently isolated position of the site at Eastwood had always puzzled the excavators. Survey work in 1958 in the wood immediately north of the road outside Eastwood farm did, however, reveal a pronounced east-west bank. This is remarkably similar to the agger of a Roman road and this could be evidence of a branch road to which the Eastwood site might relate. In 1970 the possible westward continuation of this road was recorded by Mr. R. Hetherington (Ref. 207) and further work is now being undertaken.

Finally, the few finds from the shaft and the small cemetery in no way contradict the earlier conclusions that this was the site of a small Romano-British farmstead dating from about A.D. 45–100.

THE FINDS

(1) THE NON-MARINE MOLLUSCA FROM EASTWOOD

By the late H. E. J. Biggs

During the excavation of the Romano-British site at Eastwood, Fawkham in 1963 a number of non-marine mollusca were found in the flint filling of a chalk shaft at a depth of between 6 and 10 ft. (layer 5). This has been dated to the second half of the 1st century A.D. The following list of species found in the shaft is arranged in taxonomic order.

1. *Pomatias elegans* (Müller). 50 examples. A thermophilic species preferring dry, open situations; a calcophile.
2. *Cecilioides acicula* (Müller). 2 examples only and these are juveniles. This is a blind burrowing snail, quite small and often found by archaeologists on account of its habits.
3. *Discuc rotundatus* (Müller). 3 examples and a juvenile. A widely distributed species found in many varied habitats; said to be an anthropophile (i.e. a species usually found near human habitations).

4. *Helicella itala* (Linné). 1 fragment. A calcicole and xerophile species.

5. *Hygromia hispida* (Linné). 1 example. A hygrophile.

6. *Arianta arbustorum* (Linné). 1 example. The species is indifferent to habitat. Stratton (Ref. 208) has shown that, contrary to some suggestions, this species is at home in damp or dry conditions and that in Britain today its habitat is largely determined by its intolerance of cultivation. This fact is not sufficient to be a reliable guide to the type of habitat it occupied in Roman times.

7. *Cepaea hortensis* (Müller). 3 examples. No special habitat preference.

8. *Cepaea nemoralis* (Linné). 6 examples. Boycott (Ref. 209) says that it prefers lime. There were also 11 juvenile examples of this genus *Cepaea*, but it is impossible to refer them with any certainty to either of these species, but most likely they are *nemoralis*.

9. *Retinella nitidula* (Draparnaud). 5 examples of various ages. The species is indifferent to lime, but can live with it.

10. *Retinella pura* (Alder). 1 example. Prefers a calcareous habitat.

11. *Oxychilus cellarius* (Müller). 36 examples of various ages. A thermophile which prefers dryish places.

The two most numerous species (Nos. 1 and 11) in this collection suggest a general facies of a fauna living in a warm and dry habitat. Most of the others are species with such a wide tolerance of various habitats that they would not demand any modification of this suggestion. *Pomatias elegans* is definitely a calcophile and *Helicella itala* the same, but as the latter species is only represented by one example it may have been a chance introduction. My thanks are due to Dr. M. P. Kerney for help and advice with the determinations.

Catalogue of the Illustrated Pottery from Eastwood, Fawkham (Fig. 34)

No. 283. Cinerary-urn with outcurved rim of Patch Grove ware. Grey-black paste and black-brown surface. Burnished zones on exterior and simple burnished lattice pattern and horizontal bands on lower half. Slightly raised base and cordons on neck. Burial 1 (EW-B1). The squat form, cordons and the bulbous profile all suggest that this vessel is early in the Patch Grove series and on its own merits should date to the second half of the 1st century A.D. A very similar native cinerary-urn was found at Leafy Grove, Keston (No. 253). Its association at Eastwood with the flagon makes a post-Conquest date almost certain.

No. 284. Flagon of sandy ware with white paste and surface and small footring. Burial 1 (EW-B1). In the absence of the mouth and neck precise dating is difficult. The vessel is coarse and rather thick and is a British product rather than an import. Although flagons, based on imported types, were being produced at Camulodunum (Ref. 210) prior to the Conquest it is more likely that this vessel is one of the versions mass-produced during and after the Claudian period.

No. 285. Carinated beaker with outcurved rim of smooth ware. Black paste and grey-brown surface. Faint trace of rouletted decoration and small footring. Burial 2 (EW-B2). Probably a very good native copy of an imported vessel. As Form 120 at Camulodunum where it is dated A.D. 43–65 and here likely to be before A.D. 100.

No. 286. Small cooking-pot with bead rim of shell-loaded ware. Black paste and orange-black surface. Burial 2 (EW-B2). The squat form suggests a date early in the bead rim range, almost certainly in the second half of the 1st century.

No. 287. Wall sherd of very large storage jar of Patch Grove ware. Mottled grey-black paste and orange-brown surface. Girth diameter about 2 ft. Broad chevron decoration applied to raised band on girth or shoulder. From Ditch I of the 1957–61 excavations, but not previously illustrated (EW-A). From the associated finds (samian, brooches and coarse pottery) there can be little doubt that this vessel dates from the second half of the 1st century A.D. Similarly decorated sherds have come from Charlton (Ref. 211) there described as Bronze Age; Baston Manor, Neolithic (Site 1, No. 21), Fox Hill (Site 8, not illustrated), Bromley Common (three specimens, not illustrated) and Leafy Grove (Site 14, No. 263). All of these sites are within a radius of 14 miles of Eastwood and it is likely that this was a local specialisation with a limited distribution.

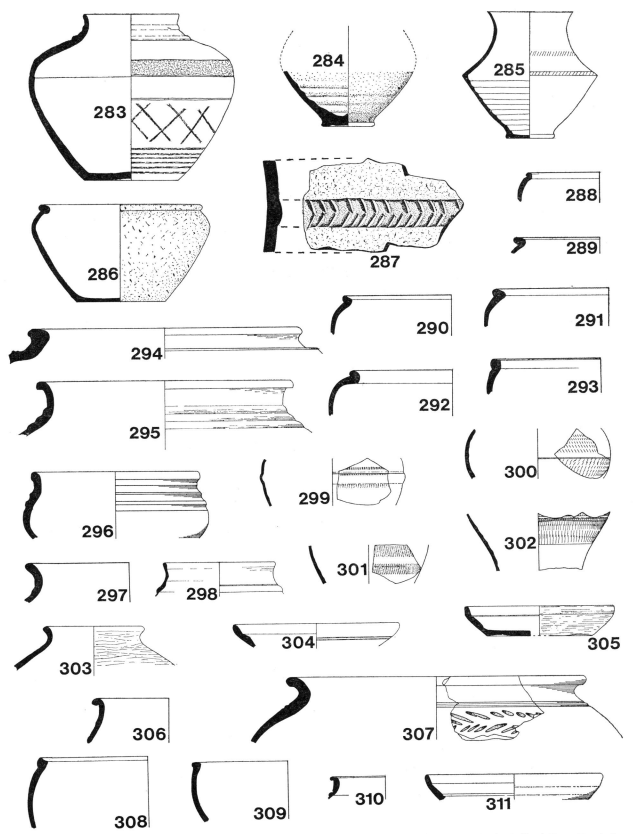

Fig. 34. *Roman pottery (Nos. 283–7), Eastwood, Fawkham (Site 17) and Roman pottery (Nos. 288–311) (¼), Calfstock Lane, Farningham (Site 19).*

SITE 18. A Romano-British Site near Eglantine Lane, Farningham, Kent

This site (N.G.R. TQ.5615.6682) lies in the parish of Farningham, Kent on farmland about one mile east of the parish church. It lies across two fields (O.S. parcel 0083) on the actual crest of the east side of the Darent valley and about half a mile north-west of Site 21. The site is on very hard Upper Chalk and the O.D. is about 310 ft. The centre of the site lies at the wire fence between the two fields about 230 ft. from the north hedge.

The site was discovered on 4th November, 1969 during 'Operation Gaspipe East'. The pipe-trench, running south-east to north-west, cut through three features.

Feature 1

At 39 ft. east of the fence. A small pit or ditch, 5 ft. wide at the top, 2 ft. 6 in. deep with steep sides and a flat base 3 ft. wide. It was filled with brown loam, flint, chalk rubble and a fragment of Roman tile was found in the corresponding spoil heap.

Feature 2

At 105–129 ft. west of the fence. A large pit, probably rectangular, with vertical sides and a level flat base 2–3 ft. deep. It was cut obliquely by the trench so that 9 ft. showed in the south face and 24 ft. in the north face. Its filling of brown loam, chalk rubble and flints produced eight pieces of Roman roof-tile, four potsherds and several small, animal bones, the latter including those of a sheep. Of the sherds three were of Patch Grove type and the fourth a rim of a 2nd century vessel.

Feature 3

At 141 ft. west of the fence. A small pit in the south face of the trench, 4 ft. wide and 2 ft. deep, with steep sides and a flat base 2 ft. wide. The filling of brown loam and light chalk rubble contained a small chip of Roman samian ware of 1st century A.D. date.

It is difficult to say much about the extent and nature of this site. The presence of Roman tile and pottery precludes a pre-Roman date, but it need not preclude a post-Roman date. On this admittedly slender evidence, however, it seems likely that the site may have been that of a Romano-British hilltop farmstead of 1st or 2nd century date. Air surveys by the writer have failed to reveal any further clues to this site, though under ideal conditions there is a good chance that much more would be revealed. Certainly the potential of this site must not be ignored when the proposed M20 Motorway is eventually constructed a few hundred feet to the south.

SITE 19. A Romano-British Site near Calfstock Lane, Farningham, Kent

This site (N.G.R. TQ.5504.6775) lies in the parish of Farningham, Kent on the west side of Dartford Road, just to the south of Calfstock Lane and about ½ a mile north-east of the parish church. It lies in the north-west corner of an open field (O.S. parcel 0665) about halfway up the west slope of the Darent valley. The site is on hard Upper Chalk and the O.D. is about 200–220 ft. The centre of the site is about 113 ft. from the west hedge and just 46 ft. from the north hedge at a point where the bottom end of a private garden projects into the field.

The site was discovered on 6th November, 1969 during 'Operation Gaspipe East'. The pipe-trench, running south-east to north-west, cut through four features. Pottery, of Romano-British date, was recovered from only two of these and from their corresponding spoil-heaps.

Substantial Roman buildings exist in the immediate vicinity. About 500 yards to the east is the villa at Franks (Ref. 212); 1,200 yards to the south is the villa at Oliver Crescent (Ref. 213) and only 200 yards to the west is the reputed site of another villa in Farningham Wood (Ref. 214).

Feature 1

At 69 ft. from the centre of the west hedge. An irregular pit about 4 ft. wide and 5 ft. deep. It contained a very loose filling of brown loam and chalk rubble, but no finds.

Feature 2

At 108 ft. from the centre of the west hedge and aligned roughly north-east by south-west (Fig. 35). A U-shaped ditch, about 7 ft. wide and 3 ft. deep, with steep sides and a flat bottom about 2½ ft. wide. The primary filling of chalk rubble (layer 6) contained sherds of three vessels, two burnished pots and the base of a large shell-loaded cooking-pot, all of mid-1st century date. This was sealed by sterile layers of light brown loam with chalk specks (layer 5) and grey loam (layer 4). These layers reduced the ditch to a shallow hollow into which had been tipped a layer of fine black loam (layer 3) containing quantities of domestic rubbish. This included oyster shells, small pieces of daub, a bronze brooch (No. 449), an iron brooch (No. 450) and nearly 300 potsherds of native and imported ware (Nos. 288–306). The pottery dates from about A.D. 50–100, the bronze brooch to the end of the 1st century and the iron brooch to either side of the Conquest (see below).

Feature 3

At 125 ft. from the west hedge. Another small ditch or pit, 4 ft. 6 in. wide at the top and 2 ft. deep. It had steep sides, a flat base 3 ft. wide and was filled with brown loam and chalk rubble. This too contained more than 200 pieces of pottery, most of the same type as that from Feature 2 (Nos. 307–311).

Feature 4

At 156 ft. from the west hedge. The north edge of a pit at least 8 ft. wide and deeper than 1 ft. 6 in. Its filling of chalk rubble and brown loam produced no finds.

DATING AND DISCUSSION

The evidence from this site is confined to a pit, two ditches, some 535 potsherds (representing at least 43 vessels), two brooches, oyster shells and daub. A study of the finds suggests that all date from about A.D. 50–100 and are thus of the Romano-British period. Although some of the pottery has Belgic characteristics none is certainly

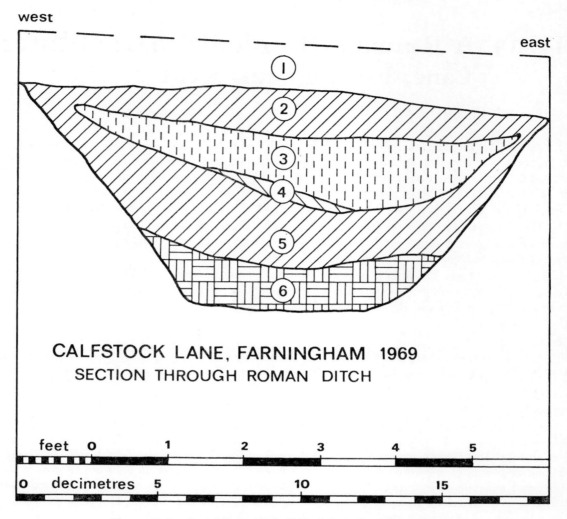

Fig. 35. *Section through Roman ditch, Calfstock Lane, Farningham (Site 19).*

of the pre-Roman Iron Age and none appears to be 2nd century. Most of the pottery is either native ware or represents good quality native copies of Roman products. If the sample of material is representative of the site as a whole it does seem that the site could have been abandoned before the full development of the truly Romano-British pottery industry, typified by the hard, sandy wares largely absent at Calfstock Lane. The contrast between the pottery on this site with that from Fox Hill, West Wickham (Site 8) is most marked with the latter, dating to about A.D. 70–140, strongly reflecting the rapid development of the Romano-British pottery industry.

In the absence of evidence to the contrary it seems likely that this site was that of yet another farmstead on the Eastwood (Site 17) scale. The ditches probably formed part of an enclosure which defined the living area and the total absence of building materials (even tile) suggests timber-framed structures. The site was largely typical in its setting being on well-drained soil, on a south-east facing slope though still some 400 yards from the river. The similarity of much of the pottery and the bronze brooch with those from Eastwood (three miles to the south-east) is most marked and it seems clear that each was served by the same market. As at Eastwood oyster shells show that the oyster industry was already operating in the 1st century A.D.

From the available evidence it seems likely that this site was occupied for about two generations. Again a small family cremation cemetery may await discovery nearby and it is likely that quernstones, samian ware and groups of animal bones survive. As elsewhere this site must be fully explored if ever threatened with development, but only properly organised work under skilled direction will substantially increase our knowledge.

THE FINDS

(1) THE POTTERY (Fig. 34)

The pottery from Features 2 and 3 and from the unstratified deposits is essentially of the same character and is here studied as a single group. A total of 535 sherds represents a minimum of 43 vessels of which 24 have been drawn (Nos. 288–311). This pottery has been classified into the four main groups listed in Table A and discussed below (for discussion of terms see Fox Hill—Site 8).

	Patch Grove and allied wares	Shell-loaded and corky wares	Native (local) burnished wares	Romanised wares	Totals
Feature 2 (lower)	—	2	2	—	4
Feature 2 (upper)	106	90	1	101	298
Feature 3	52	78	—	85	215
Unstratified	11	4	—	3	18
Total sherds	169	174	3	189	535
Minimum vessels	12	10	3	18	43

TABLE A
Distribution and classification of pottery from the Calfstock Lane site

Group A. Patch Grove and Allied Wares

A total of 169 potsherds, representing a minimum of 12 vessels (Nos. 294–297, 307 and 311) was recovered from the site. There are at least five squat jars, three of which have distinct cordons of Belgic form and are thus early in the Patch Grove series. The jars with the outcurved rim are typical of those from Eastwood (Ref. 193, Nos. 1 and 4), where they were found in direct association with material dated A.D. 50–100. There are at least six large jars of which five have outcurved rims and one has a thickened, beaded rim. Of the five, one (No. 295) is a harder, more evolved version of a jar common in late-Belgic deposits and similar to one from Bromley Common (No. 282). Another, a large storage jar (No. 294) has an angular rim of unusual type whilst another storage jar (No. 307) has the typical incised chevron pattern on the shoulder. Finally, there is a platter (No. 311) in imitation of the Gallo-Belgic original (Camulodunum Forms 12–14).

Group B. Shell-loaded and Corky Wares

A total of 174 sherds represents a minimum of ten vessels (Nos. 288–293, 308–309). Eight of these are small cooking-pots with beaded or thickened rims of wide range. All are typical products of the second half of the 1st century A.D. and it seems probable that the flatter, roughly squared rims are earlier than the more developed rounded rims. In addition there is a base of what appears to be a pedestal-urn made with a single hole in its base, perhaps to serve as a strainer. Finally, there is the base of a large, coarse storage vessel from the lower filling of Feature 2.

Group C. Native (local) Burnished Wares

Only three sherds of three different burnished vessels were found on the site and these seem to stand apart from the Patch Grove, shell-loaded and Romanised products. It is likely that they represent the better finished native pottery to which the burnished Patch Grove vessels seem to relate. One particular vessel (No. 306) is a wide-mouthed jar with burnishing on the exterior and inside the rim.

Group D. Romanised Wares (mostly fine)

This group embraces all the pottery that is not local, but which may usefully be regarded as reflecting Roman markets in Britain or Gaul. Some 189 sherds represent a minimum of 18 vessels (No. 298–305 and 310). Of these there are fragments of four flagons, not sufficient for illustration. One is a white sandy-ware flagon, two are of soft orange ware of different sizes with traces of white slip and the fourth is a fine red-brown ware with a thick cream-coloured external slip.

There are eight girth or butt beakers in grey, orange, brown or buff ware. Six of these are fine vessels, either Gallo-Belgic imports or good native copies and four have external rouletted decoration. Another is a large, coarse native copy of a butt beaker and one other has a red-brown surface reminiscent of Terra Rubra.

Five more vessels are more distinctly Romanised and have a sandy texture. These are an amphora, two native platters copied from Gallo-Belgic imports, a narrow-mouthed flask and a squat jar.

Although the sample of material from this site is not large several interesting points emerge. Most significant is the general lack of Romanised sandy wares common on many local sites of the late-1st and early-2nd centuries. Some 58% of the pottery recovered is distinctly local native ware and the bulk of the remaining 42% is either imported or good native copies. Not more than six vessels (14%) can be described as sandy wares and these seem to represent the very beginning of the Romano-British pottery industry.

The bulk of the pottery appears to date from the three decades following the Conquest, but the presence of a few later types and the bronze brooch infer occupation until the Flavian period. The absence of samian, never abundant on early rural sites, may not be significant, but the total absence as at Eastwood (Site 17) of mortaria and 2nd century pottery is particularly noteworthy.

(2) THE BROOCHES (Fig. 46)

By M. R. Hull

(a) A large iron brooch (No. 450), being the iron version of the bronze 'Nauheim derivative', such as found at Camulodunum (Ref. 215) and as such may occur with a flat or round bow. Since the original Nauheim brooch did not appear until about 50 B.C. all the derivatives may be fairly late in La Tene III. In Britain they occur chiefly on sites which can be safely regarded as occupied before the Conquest and they were probably still current at the time of the Conquest. In the South-West most of the brooches of this class, in both bronze and iron, are hinged. The above remarks apply to these and several are dated to pre-Roman levels at, for example, Maiden Castle (Ref. 216). Indeed, I call the hinged series the 'Maiden Castle' type. Until recently it had been thought that iron brooches scarcely survived the Conquest, but two large batches of brooches recently found in Lincolnshire in which iron brooches figure strongly, suggest a more definite survival, though not for long. From Feature 2, layer 3.

(b) A complete bronze brooch (No. 449) of the Colchester BB type. It is one of two developments which arose out of making the Colchester brooch in two pieces, i.e. with separate spring and pin. The first one, Colchester B was common at Camulodunum (Ref. 217), but the second form, Colchester BB was not, although it is a very common form. It must, therefore, begin later than A.D. 65, possibly even not before A.D. 70. It would be a reasonable approximation to describe it as a Flavian introduction. Similar brooches to this occur at Richborough, Kent (Ref. 218), where one was in a deposit dated A.D. 80–100 and three more were found at Eastwood, Fawkham, Kent (Ref. 219) associated with pottery of the late-1st century. From Feature 2, Layer 3.

Catalogue of the Illustrated Finds from Calfstock Lane, Farningham (Figs. 34 and 46)

From the Upper Filling of Feature 2 (all GPE-3-B1)

No. 288. Small cooking-pot with bead rim of shell-loaded ware. Grey paste, black external surface and brown internal surface. Probably second half of 1st century A.D.

No. 289. Small cooking-pot with flanged, recessed rim of shell-loaded ware. Black paste and black surface. Probably the same date as No. 288.

No. 290. Small cooking-pot with angular, slightly recessed rim of shell-loaded ware. Grey paste and grey-black surface. Second half of 1st century A.D.

No. 291.   Small cooking-pot with flattened, bead rim of shell-loaded ware. Brown paste and black-brown surface.

No. 292.   Cooking-pot with bead rim of shell-loaded ware. Black paste and black-brown surface with groove on shoulder. This appears to be a developed type of rim probably arising from the more angular, flattened rims of the late-Iron Age which Nos. 288–290 reflect. A larger, but otherwise very similar vessel was found at Eastwood, Fawkham in direct association with brooches and samian of Flavian date (Ref. 219, No. 9).

No. 293.   Small cooking-pot with squared, recessed rim of shell-loaded ware. Black paste and grey-black surface with faint cordon below rim. Probably mid-1st century.

No. 294.   Storage jar with angular rim of Patch Grove ware. Mottled black-brown paste and buff surface. A common native type in Kent, in both pre- and post-Conquest deposits, though the rim here is rather more angular. More rounded rims occur on Belgic vessels at Canterbury (Ref. 220) and Faversham (Ref. 221), but at Leicester (Ref. 222) similar storage jars occur in deposits assigned to the Claudian-Neronian period. These vessels are large and strongly made and it is likely that they remained in use for many years. If this vessel is a pre-Conquest product it is likely that it was not discarded as rubbish until two or three decades later.

No. 295.   Storage jar with out-turned rim of Patch Grove ware. Mottled grey-black paste and orange buff surface. Three cordons on neck. The profile is similar to Belgic vessels from Canterbury (Refs. 220, Nos. 10 and 12), but here has a sharper, more everted rim and harder fabric. Probably mid-1st century A.D.

No. 296.   Squat jar with thickened, upright rim of Patch Grove ware. Mottled grey-black paste and buff-black surface with external burnishing. Two bold cordons on shoulder. This vessel is also a distinctly Belgic type comparing with vessels from Canterbury (Ref. 220, No. 17) and Faversham (Ref. 221, No. 204) in pre-Conquest deposits. If found out of context it might normally be dated to the first half of 1st century, but its association here with post-Conquest pottery suggests that it dates from no earlier than the mid-1st century A.D. The identification of 'Belgic' sites on the evidence of a few similar sherds has been a common failing of archaeology in West Kent in post-war years.

No. 297.   Jar with slightly thickened, out-turned rim of Patch Grove ware. Mottled grey-black paste and surface. Two cordons on neck and burnishing on inside rim and exterior. This appears to be the slightly evolved form of No. 296. It corresponds with a vessel found at Fawkham (Ref. 219, No. 4) in direct association with brooches and samian of Flavian date.

No. 298.   Beaker with upright rim of smooth ware. Black paste and buff-brown surface. Bold cordon on shoulder. This seems to be a good native copy of a Gallo-Belgic girth-beaker. Mid-1st century A.D.

No. 299.   Butt-beaker of smooth ware. Grey paste and grey surface. Bold cordon at girth and bands of vertical rouletting. Probably a native copy of a Gallo-Belgic import. Perhaps A.D. 50–70.

No. 300.   Globular beaker of smooth ware. Grey paste and surface. Faint groove at girth and zones of diagonal rouletting. Similar to vessels found at Colchester (Ref. 180, Forms 108–109). Common throughout the second half of the 1st century A.D.

No. 301.   Butt-beaker of smooth ware. Grey paste and surface. Oblique zones of rouletting. Very similar to No. 300 and possibly even from the same kiln.

No. 302.   Butt-beaker of smooth ware. Orange-grey paste and orange surface. Zones of vertical rouletting and narrow horizontal groove A. good native version as at Colchester (Ref. 180, Forms 112–115). A.D. 40–70.

No. 303.   Jar with narrow neck and out-curved rim of slightly sandy ware. Grey-black paste and grey-brown surface lightly burnished. A more finely finished version of the Belgic jars often provided with pedestal bases.

No. 304.   Platter with almost upright rim of sandy ware. Grey-black paste and surface. Broad internal quarter-round moulding and burnished all over. Native copy of Gallo-Belgic platter as at Colchester (Ref. 180, Forms 24–26a) mostly found in post-Conquest deposits.

No. 305.   Platter with upright rim of sandy ware. Grey paste and black surface. Broad internal quarter-round moulding and burnished all over. No trace of footring. Similar to No. 304; as at Fawkham (Ref. 219, No. 5) found in association with Flavian samian and brooches.

No. 306.   Beaker with out-turned, angular rim of burnished ware. Orange-brown paste and buff-brown surface. Burnished exterior and inside rim and faint cordons on neck and shoulder.

No. 449.   Bronze brooch, complete with coiled spring and pierced catch-plate. From Feature 2, layer 3 (GPE-3-B1). See specialist report. About A.D. 70–100 (Colchester type BB).

No. 450.   Iron brooch with coiled spring, solid catch-plate and pin missing. From Feature 2, layer 3 (GPE-3-B1). See specialist report. Normally 50 B.C. to A.D. 50.

From Feature 3 (all GPE-3-C)

No. 307.   Storage jar with thickened, outcurved rim of Patch Grove ware. Mottled grey-black paste and buff surface. Irregular stabbed chevron pattern on shoulder. This is a common form in West Kent and East Surrey and it seems likely that the out-curved rim is a development from the Belgic thickened rim as No. 294. Dated at Ightham (Ref. 223) to the 1st century A.D. and at Leicester (Ref. 222, Fig. 37, No. 3) to the earliest Roman levels of the mid-1st century.

No. 308.   Small cooking-pot with angular, recessed rim of shell-loaded ware. Grey paste and orange-brown surface. Similar to 293.

No. 309.   Small cooking-pot with flattened rim of shell-loaded ware. Black paste and buff-brown surface.

No. 310.   Small jar with recessed, out-turned rim of sandy ware. Grey paste and grey-black surface. Bold cordon and incised groove on shoulder. Almost identical with the squat jars from Fawkham (Ref. 219, Nos. 13 and 14) found in association with Flavian samian and brooches.

No. 311.   Platter with upright rim of Patch Grove ware. Grey-brown paste and surface. A native copy of a Gallo-Belgic platter. similar to Nos. 304 and 305.

SITE 20. A Romano-British Site at Ship Lane, Sutton-at-Hone, Kent

This site (N.G.R. TQ.5445.6960) lies in the parish of Sutton-at-Hone, Kent on farmland about 1 mile south-west of the parish church and about ½ mile north-west of Site 4. It occupies part of an open field (O.S. parcel 0081) on the north side of Ship Lane on slightly sloping ground on the west side of the Darent valley. The site is on Woolwich Beds and the O.D. is about 160 ft. The pipe-trench cut across the field on a south-east and north-west axis cutting the centre of Ship Lane immediately adjacent to the south-east corner of the field. The west limit of the site was 545 ft. along the pipeline from the centre of Ship Lane at a point 192 ft. north of the centre junction of a farm-track which joined Ship Lane on its south side. This junction is 520 ft. west of the point where the pipeline crosses the centre of Ship Lane.

The site was discovered on 11th November, 1969 during 'Operation Gaspipe East'. The pipe-trench cut three features, each with a filling of light brown loam and pebble.

Feature 1

At 433 ft. from where the trench cut the road-centre. This was probably a pit, 5 ft. wide and 4 ft. deep, with vertical sides and a flat bottom. The adjacent spoil-heap produced only pot-boilers and a flint flake.

Feature 2

At 481 ft. from the road. This was a pit with steep sides, about 4 ft. wide and deeper than 3 ft. It was probably similar to Feature 1. Three worn potsherds of late-Iron Age or early-Roman date were found in the corresponding spoil and a badly corroded Potin coin (Ref. 224) was found 3 ft. down in the filling of the pit. The pottery and coin probably date from the 1st century A.D.

Feature 3

At 545 ft. from the road. A large ditch about 20 ft. wide, with steep sides and deeper than 6 ft. The adjacent spoil-heap produced a worn sherd of a Roman samian platter, a sherd of Patch Grove ware of 1st or early-2nd century A.D. date and several struck flint flakes and pot-boilers.

It is difficult to say much about the nature and extent of this site. The few datable finds all suggest a 1st or 2nd century A.D. date and in the absence of other evidence the site may tentatively be regarded as Romano-British. It is possible that aerial surveys carried out under ideal conditions could reveal more of the extent and nature of this promising site.

SITE 21. The Roman Villa at Darenth, Kent

SUMMARY

The excavations established that the Darenth Roman villa-complex extends for another 400 ft. to the south-west and includes at least two more masonry buildings. The complex can now be seen to spread over an area of about 800 ft. by 400 ft. and to cover about seven acres.

The extensive buildings discovered in 1894–5 appear to represent the principal elements of the villa-estate, forming in effect the country-house of the owner and his family. The baths, guest-house, swimming-pool, tessellated floors, ornamental pools and walled gardens all reflect a considerable degree of wealth and social standing. The lesser known buildings found south of these may represent farm out-buildings placed at a suitable distance from the main range.

The newly-discovered buildings include a detached bath-building and a very large structure, probably a house for the bailiff and farm-workers, to which the bath-house may have related. The bailiff's house began life, perhaps in the middle of the 2nd century, as a simple rectangular block at least 94 ft. by 20 ft. (Period I). Its south end was subsequently altered on two occasions. The last, involving the construction of a pair of matching rooms at the south end forming small external projections, was probably carried out in the second half of the 2nd century (Period II).

The structure was totally rebuilt, probably in the first two decades of the 3rd century, when a wide main block and east corridor were constructed (Period III). This increased the building to at least 110 ft. by 44 ft. which more than doubled the area of the Period I building. Sometime about the middle of the 3rd century, the structure was again almost totally rebuilt this time in the form of a vast aisled building at least 160 ft. by 58 ft. (Period IV) and more than four times the size of the Period I house. The central feature was a wide hall, 76 ft. by 26 ft. internally, with seven bays on each side, the central one being wider than the others and forming an entrance. Wide, 12 ft. aisles flanked the hall which had large rooms at its two ends. The east aisle contained two small rooms, flanking the entrance, whilst two large corn-drying ovens were built in the southern end of the main block. A drain was built outside the east wall of the building and a large functional pit made inside the hall in the centre of the west side. The exact function of this pit is uncertain, but it later contained a small drain which presumably flowed into the nearby river.

The final phase (Period V) probably dates from the second quarter of the 4th century and represents a major reduction in the plan of the building. The northern half of the aisled building was abandoned and a new north-end wall added to include just three bays. The aisles were partly blocked to create small rooms and a new drain built through the demolished walls at the north end. Several other minor structural alterations were detected and the latest evidence from the building appears to date to about the end of the 4th century.

A narrow metalled track and a single burial, both of Roman date, were found east of the bailiff's house. The absence of 1st century pottery is noteworthy as is the presence of a small group of 13th or 14th century pottery from just north of the Roman grave.

INTRODUCTION

This famous site (N.G.R. TQ.5635.7065) lies within the parish of Darenth, Kent, about 800 yards south-south-east of the parish church (O.S. parcel 3368). It occupies a gentle slope on the east bank of the River Darent about 2 miles south of the arterial Roman road, later known as Watling Street. The elevation is about 60 to 80 ft. O.D. and the subsoil is gravel, brickearth and chalk. The site was discovered on open farmland towards the end of the 19th century and largely excavated under the direction of George Payne in 1894–5 (Ref. 225). His work revealed (Fig. 36) an extensive series of buildings and gardens covering 414 ft. by 370 ft. (about 3½ acres), which at the time was claimed to be the largest known villa-complex in Britain. The site was subsequently left open for visitors, but eventually it was partially reburied and became a mass of weeds and bushes. The site was later scheduled as an Ancient Monument and by 1969 the vegetation had expanded into a dense wood with trees standing to a height of more than 50 ft. The consequent root-damage and perennial illicit digging by pseudo-archaeological groups rate as one

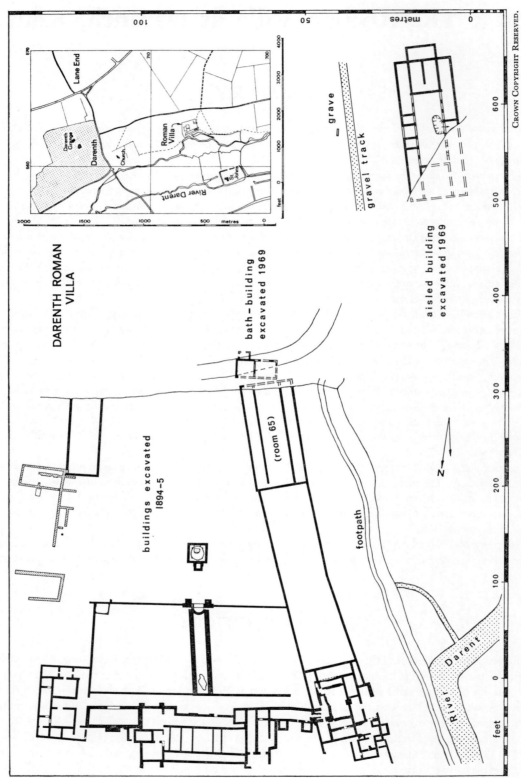

Fig. 36. Overall plan of the Roman Villa complex at Darenth (Site 21), with location map (inset).

of the scandals of Kentish archaeology. The wood was felled in January, 1972 and between March and June of that year more than 2,000 tons of soil were pushed over the more exposed walls by the C.I.B. Archaeological Rescue Corps during the 'Darent Valley Rescue Operation'.

A Government Report published in February, 1969 (Ref. 226), stressed the need for regular inspection of scheduled sites. As a direct result of this the writer began to visit a number of scheduled monuments in Kent and in March, 1969, inspected the villa-site at Darenth. On arrival it was found that a bulldozer had just cut an east-west track from Roman Villa Road, downhill past the south edge of the villa-complex, to a gravel-pit just being opened about 300 ft. to the south-west. The topsoil had been removed and the subsoil was left exposed. As the 1895 plan showed possible walls crossing the line of this track the area was closely examined. A wall of Roman date was then found running roughly north-south in line with 'Room 65' of the original plan. Immediate rescue-work by the Group on 4th, 5th, 12th and 13th of April, 1969, to fit in with the contractor's access, revealed the outline of a small detached bath-building and also located the south end of 'Room 65'. An area of black loam and Roman and medieval pottery was also revealed at the edge of the gravel-pit to the south-west. All of this was duly recorded and the archaeological sites back-filled.

A site-meeting took place in late-April, with an Inspector of the Ministry of Public Building and Works, when the possibilities of further discoveries in the gravel-pit were discussed. Watch was kept on the contractor's operations throughout May and June. On 17th June, the bulldozer clearing more topsoil in the new gravel-pit area, about 500 ft. south-west of the centre of the villa-complex, hit a masonry wall (Plate VIIIA). This was detected the same evening by the writer and permission from the owner to excavate and financial backing from the Ministry, obtained, next day. Emergency excavations began on 20th June and continued non-stop for 46 days (Plate VIIIB). These revealed a substantial Roman building more than 160 ft. in length and 58 ft. in width, a single grave and a metalled track (see below). The site was then backfilled by mechanical means and the local Council invited to consider the purchase of this corner of the gravel-pit and thus save the building from total destruction (Ref. 227).

ACKNOWLEDGEMENTS

Thanks are due first and foremost to the Dartford and Horton Ballast Co. Ltd. for permission to carry out the excavation and in particular to Mr. H. A. Ludlow for his sympathetic understanding of what was a difficult excavation under trying conditions. Particular thanks are also due to Mr. F. Wiseman, of Sutton-at-Hone, who helped the work in a variety of different ways.

The hard-core of the team came from the West Kent Border Archaeological Group. These were supported by a strong contingent from Queen Elizabeth's School at Faversham, continuing the tradition started in 1965 when a Roman villa was found under similar conditions in the school playing-field (Ref. 228). In addition, support was forthcoming under the Council for Kentish Archaeology emergency-scheme and members of the Faversham, Fawkham, Gravesend, Lower Medway, Otford, Reculver, Ruxley, Sittingbourne and Upchurch groups assisted at various times.

Of the total of 105 volunteers special thanks must be made to those who worked for extended periods. Notably to Mr. Richard Garnett and Mr. Derek Garrod who acted as assistant-supervisors for some of the time and to Mrs. Jennie Lock, Misses Pam George and Edna Mynott (now Mrs. Philp); to Messrs. Tony Ijzendoorn, Peter Knivett and Simon May. Of the school-party Misses Pat Fettes, Shirley Jenner, Melody Montgomerie, Joy Nuttall, Ann Sim, Paula Smith, Jacquie Wildash and Messrs. Mike Hale, Roger Mainwood, Martin Montagne and Mark Thompson deserve a special mention.

Sincere thanks are also offered to the team responsible for the work on this section of the Report. In particular all the plans are the work of Mrs. J. Lock and the sections are the work of Mr. R. Tedbury. Mr. G. Clewley has described some of the pottery from the site, most of which was drawn by Mr. J. Thorn of the Ancient Monuments drawing-office. Mr. W. Jeffries has drawn some of the small finds. Mr. E. Tilley assisted by cleaning and identifying the coins which were then confirmed by Mr. R. Merrifield. Miss M. Harman has written a short report on the animal bones and Mrs. C. Keepax has reported on the human skeleton.

The total cost of the excavation was about £800. The Ministry of Public Building and Works, through Miss S. Butcher, kindly provided £600 before expiring in the economic squeeze! Immediate appeals brought in another £153, including a most generous contribution from Mrs. Martin of the Martin Welding and Cutting Co. Ltd. of Dartford and eventually the balance was kindly provided by the Dartford Rural District Council.

9

THE EXCAVATIONS

(A) THE BATH-BUILDING (Fig. 37 and Plate IXA)

The April, 1969 excavation revealed the outline of a small detached bath-building with an overall length of 46 ft. 6 in. and a width of about 20 ft. A projection on the south side, an integral part of the original structure, probably increased the width to about 30 ft. The walls varied in thickness from 2 to 2½ ft. and were built of coursed flint set in a white mortar. Only three rooms were detected, but had the excavation been more extensive it is likely that other internal divisions would have been found. The arrangement is likely to have followed the normal pattern such as that used in other local bath-buildings as at Baston Manor, Hayes (Site 13) and Beden's Field, North Cray (Ref. 229). It seems probable that Room 1 served as a cold-room. Room 2 was almost certainly the cold bath and Room 3 was probably a combined hot and tepid room, perhaps sub-divided.

Room 1 (Cold Room and Dressing Room?)

This room measured 17 ft. 7 in. by 16 ft. internally and its walls still survived to a height of about 1 ft. 6 in. It was filled with chalk blocks, flint and broken tile. No trace of any floor remained, but slight traces of *opus signinum* plaster were found inside the south wall and suggest the level of the floor. Near the south-west corner was a 4 in., U-shaped slot in the wall which originally may have contained a drain-pipe. Any water collecting in this room could have passed through such a pipe into the external drain beyond.

Room 2 (Cold Bath)

This room projected on the south side of the bath-building, partly beyond the limits of the excavation. It measured internally 8 ft. 7 in. in length and had a width greater than 4 ft. 7 in. This room was in a remarkably good state of preservation with one wall still standing to a height of 3 ft. 6 in. above the floor. The entire bottom and sides of the bath were lined with a 2-in. layer of *opus signinum* painted red, thus matching closely the cold bath at Baston (site 13). On the north side were three steps, each about 6 in. wide, which allowed bathers to descend into the bath. The bottom of the bath was probably at least 2 ft. lower than the floor of Room 1 (missing) and access from one to the other must have been through a wide opening in the wall common to both. The loam and rubble filling this bath contained large pieces of plaster painted white.

Room 3 (Tepid and Hot Rooms)

This large room measured about 22 ft. by 15 ft. 6 in. internally and contained traces of a hypocaust buried by layers of rubble. It seems likely that this room had originally formed two separate compartments, each about 15 ft. by 10 ft., though this was not proved by excavation. Parts of large masonry piers survived, separated by narrow channels and these must have formed part of a channelled hypocaust. The channels varied in width from 7 in. to 1 ft. 6 in., some being parallel-sided and others tapering towards the south. The piers varied in form and size, but owing to the limited nature of the excavation it was not possible to determine the exact arrangement. The stoke-hole for this hypocaust was not found and it seems probable that it was somewhere on the north or west side. If this room did contain both the tepid and hot rooms then a small hot plunge-bath may have existed close by. This should have been close to the furnace-arch and may have formed another projection on the north or west side. A ragged gap in the south-west corner of the room must almost certainly have contained a lead-pipe serving to remove surface water to the external drain to the south.

Other Features

A small rectangular gulley, 1 ft. 3 in. wide and about 1 ft. 6 in. deep, was found flanking the south side of the bath-building. This appears to have served as a drain for Rooms 1 and 3 and perhaps also for Room 2 though no trace of a drain-hole was found in the latter. No evidence was found to suggest that the drain was either lined or capped.

A small U-shaped ditch, about 4 ft. wide and 3½ ft. deep, with a flat bottom 1 ft. wide was found beneath the east wall of the bath-building. Its filling of brown loam contained several struck flints and a damaged Roman

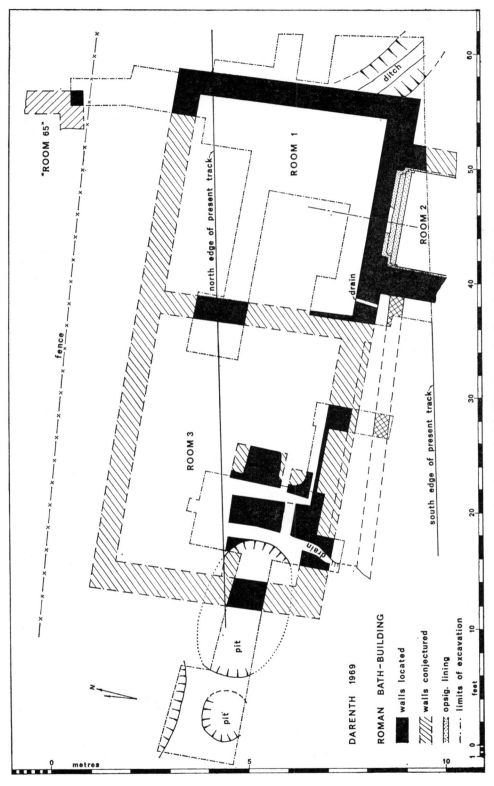

Fig. 37. Plan of Roman Bath-building discovered at Darenth, 1969 (Site 21).

bronze spoon in an upright position. The ditch clearly pre-dates the building and may have been an enclosure or field-ditch associated with an early phase of the Roman occupation on the site. Judging by its position the spoon was probably an intrusion. The ditch was also sealed by a rough metalled surface flanking the east side of the bath-building. From this came several potsherds of 2nd century date.

Beneath the west wall of the building was a large oval pit, about 12 ft. in length and about 4 ft. deep. It was filled with brown loam containing a few flints and fragments of tile. It, too, pre-dates the building, but it was not possible to determine its function in the limited time available.

'Room 65'

The 1894-5 excavations revealed a substantial building in the south-west corner of the complex (Room 65). The April, 1969 excavation located the external south-east corner of this building about 8 ft. from the bath-building. This wall was built of flints set in yellow mortar. A small trial-excavation also located the north-east corner of the building and it is now clear that the overall length of the building was about 108 ft. George Payne reported that the internal measurements had been greater than 101 ft. 10 in., which allowing for end walls each 2 ft. thick, was only 2 ft. 2 in. less than the actual measurement.

No dating evidence was found inside the bath-building and only a few largely indeterminate 2nd century potsherds came from the metalled area on the east side. These could imply that the bath-building was in use during the 2nd century. The similar bath-building at Baston Manor (Site 13) was probably constructed and abandoned during the first half of the 2nd century and another at North Cray may have been built at about A.D. 100. That at Darenth appears to have the same axis as the main range and contrasts with that of 'Room 65'. Judging by its position it seems likely that it pre-dated 'Room 65' for had the latter already been in existence, it seems probable that the bath-building would have been either attached to it, aligned on it or placed several feet further to the south. Perhaps this detached bath-building was superseded by the massive bath-complex at the north-west corner of the main range or it may have related to one of the buildings under the 3rd century aisled house. Either way it was eventually demolished. This operation removed all of the floors, most of the superstructure and the lead-pipes and left behind a thick layer of rubble.

(B) THE AISLED BUILDING (Figs. 38 and 39)

The wall hit by the bulldozer in the new gravel-pit area was the east wall of a very substantial Roman building of aisled form, running roughly north-south. The area of the Roman building had been buried initially by large heaps of topsoil moved from other parts of the site. It was whilst this was being loaded into lorries that the bulldozer struck the wall. The developing situation called for emergency action and the rest of the topsoil was stripped mechanically with the minimum of delay. This work revealed the tops of several walls and at once a rapid archaeological excavation, by both mechanical and manual means, was pursued as appropriate.

By the end of the excavation it was clear that five major periods of construction had taken place (Fig. 40). What had started out as a simple block had gradually evolved into a great aisled building larger than the nearby villa at Lullingstone.

PERIOD I (Fig. 40, Plan I)

The first building on this site was a simple rectangular structure, of which only the east and west side walls were found. These revealed an oblong structure 23 ft. in overall width with mortared flint walls about 1 ft. 6 in. wide and an internal width of about 20 ft. The minimum length was 73 ft., but flints at the south end of Room 1 probably mark the south limit and increase the minimum length to about 94 ft. This would give an overall minimum area of about 2,160 sq. ft. The north end lay beyond the limits of the excavation.

The unmortared flint foundations, mostly only two courses high (about 8 in.), were set in an orange-coloured mortar and were quite smooth on top (sections 1-4). They had the appearance of sleeper-walls upon which had rested a timber frame. From this it appears likely that the whole superstructure was timber-framed, probably with a long ridged roof. There was no trace of any tile associated with the building and it may not have had a roof of tiles. The internal floor area was covered with compact layers of rammed chalk and loam varying from 6 in. to 1 ft. 4 in. thick to offset the slope of the ground (section 2, layer 19; section 3, layers 22–25 and section 4, layer 29). Another primary dump of chalk on the east side of the east wall appears to have been a rammed surface outside the building. It is, however, just possible that this represented another internal floor relating to a third wall of which no trace was found. Such a wall could have been totally replaced by the construction of the Period III east wall or it may have been entirely timber-framed. The total absence of finds either under or on the floor makes dating difficult, but Period I probably dates from the middle of the 2nd century A.D. (see Discussion).

PERIOD IA

The first structural change was a minor one and apparently confined to the south end of the Period I building. New sleeper-walls were added inside the existing ones, perhaps because of instability in the original structure. The new walls were similar in construction to Period I, but 1 ft. 11 in. in width. They were built of flints set in a yellow-white mortar containing small pebbles and their effect was to decrease the internal width of the block to about 18 ft. (section 4). One wall was inserted immediately inside the west wall and this was traced for a distance of at least 24 ft. The other was a transverse wall which must have created a room at the south end about 20 ft. in internal length. A new chalk floor appears to have been laid (section 4, layer 26).

PERIOD II (Fig. 40, Plan II)

The next structural change resulted in the demolition of about 26 ft. of the south end of the Period I building, including most of the Period IA alterations. This time a pair of square rooms was added to the shortened end of the block, each being 11 ft. square internally. The walls were 2 ft. thick, of flint set in a yellow-white mortar and again appeared to have supported a timber-framed superstructure. The new walls cut through the pre-existing masonry and created small wing-like projections on each side of the main block. It seems probable that the original south end of the Period I building was now abandoned and this reduced the overall area to a minimum of about 1,920 sq. ft. There was no dating evidence to suggest when this alteration took place, but it probably dates to the second half of the 2nd century (see Discussion).

PERIOD III (Fig. 40, Plan III)

The next structural change was a totally new masonry building comprising a large central range with an eastern corridor. The old wooden building must have been totally demolished and new walls, of flint set in orange mortar, 1 ft. 9 in. thick, were built well beyond the original structure on the south, east and west sides. This increased the length of the building to a minimum of 110 ft. and expanded the width to 44 ft. (sections 1–4). The new house thus covered an overall area of at least 4,840 sq. ft. which was more than twice the area of the Period I building. The new external walls still survived in places to a maximum height of 3 ft. 6 in. and the south-east corner was found to have been quoined externally with tiles. Of the new internal walls very much less survived due largely to the superimposition of the massive sleeper-walls of Period IV. The original east wall of the Period I plan was replaced by a new wall 4 ft. further west and the original west wall seems to have been abandoned. It seems clear that the pair of square rooms at the south end (Period II) must have been demolished at this time. These changes gave the main range an internal width of 27 ft. and the east corridor an internal width of about 11 ft. 9 in. No internal divisions were detected.

The floor level was again raised with dumped material, including orange clay and chalk (section 2, layers 16 and 17), chalk and mortar (section 3, layers 12–18) and orange clay and *opus signinum* (section 4, layers 22 and 23). A thin skin of *opus signinum* was then applied as a floor surface over most, if not all, of the interior of the building. A thin band of brown loam (section 3, layer 16) may indicate either an earlier floor in the corridor or simply an interval in the make-up of the floor. The dumped material and the *opus signinum* floor generally sealed the walls and foundations of Periods I, IA and II, thus proving beyond all reasonable doubt that Period III had entirely superseded all previous structures.

Against the external face of the east wall was a low ramp of rammed chalk (section 3, layer 8 and section 4, layer 10). This it seems was intended to keep surface water away from the foot of the wall. A thick deposit of black loam and carbon subsequently collected over the chalk ramp (see below).

The South Ditch

About 15 ft. to the south of the Period III south wall, but not quite parallel to it, was a V-shaped ditch (Section 5). This was 6 to 7 ft. wide, about 3½ ft. deep and it had a flat, squared bottom about 1½ ft. wide. Its lower

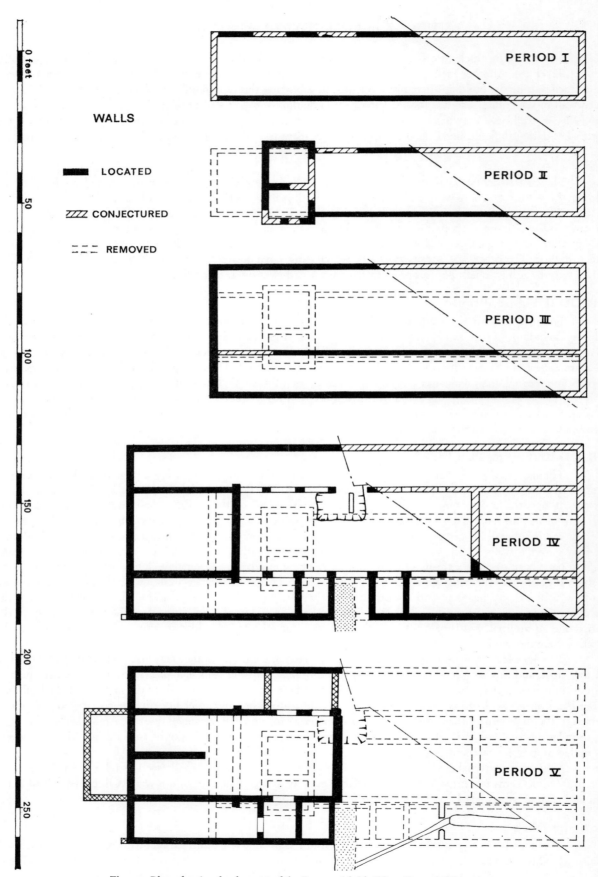

WALLS

LOCATED

CONJECTURED

REMOVED

PERIOD I

PERIOD II

PERIOD III

PERIOD IV

PERIOD V

0 feet

50

100

150

200

250

Fig. 40. *Plans showing development of the Roman aisled building, Darenth (Site 21).*

part was filled with a thick mud-silt (layer 6) which was capped by dumped clay, flint, carbon and gravel (layers 2–5). It seems likely that this ditch was open during the earlier period of occupation and that it was filled in at the beginning or during the Period III occupation. The filling included pottery (Nos. 314–322), a fragment of a bone pin and part of a rectangular glass bottle.

There was at least some dating evidence for the Period III building. Fragments of a small cup (No. 323), dating from about A.D. 200, were found sealed by the main floor and this suggests that the Period III floors, at least, were laid sometime after this date. Two vessels (Nos. 312–13), dating to about A.D. 190–240 were found sealed by the chalk ramp against the east wall and prove that the ramp was constructed sometime after that date. Nine more vessels (Nos. 314–22), were recovered from the mud-silt of the South Ditch and most of these were probably discarded at about A.D. 200–240. On this slight evidence it seems clear that the Period III building was not constructed earlier than about A.D. 200 and probably in the first two decades of the 3rd century.

PERIOD IV (Fig. 40, Plan IV)

The next structural change involved another major rebuilding of almost the entire structure, but this time incorporating some of the earlier walls. This work converted the Period III corridor house into an aisled building of great size (Plate IXB). A new matching corridor (or aisle), nearly 12 ft. wide, was added to the west side. In addition the external south wall was demolished and the whole building extended southwards by another 26 ft. The central range was converted into an aisled hall of seven bays with the piers resting on broad sleeper-foundations directly over the Period III walls. The new walls, mostly built of coursed flint and yellow-brown mortar were about 2 ft. thick and the piers of brick and pink mortar. New tiled floors were laid in the flanking corridors and a very solid rammed chalk floor laid in the main hall. The effect of these sweeping changes was to increase the width of the building to 58 ft. and the overall (minimum) length to 160 ft. The overall area was now increased to at least 9,280 sq. ft., nearly twice the area of the Period III building and at least four times the area of the Period I building. The various rooms are described in detail below.

As regards dating the construction of Period IV there is again not very much evidence. The new south extension totally sealed the filled-in South Ditch and must, therefore, have been constructed sometime after A.D. 200–240 (see above). Two more vessels (Nos. 324 and 325) were sealed beneath the new floor of the west aisle and these too probably date from about A.D. 200–240. A group of coins (Nos. 1–11) was found scattered about the floor of Room 8 and had been sealed by the demolition rubble of this section of the building. It seems likely that these were deposited at about A.D. 270–300. From this evidence it seems likely that the Period IV structure must have been constructed about the middle of the 3rd century and was superseded by the Period V work sometime after A.D. 270–300.

Room 1 (The Central Hall)

This room was the major element of the new house and it took the form of a large aisled hall 76 ft. by 26 ft., internally. It occupied the exact width of the central range of the Period III house and both ends were formed by new walls across the width. Each side incorporated a row of six detached rectangular brick piers resting on a heavy sleeper-wall about 3 ft. wide and 1½ ft. deep which in turn sat directly over the remains of the Period III walls. The piers were 2 ft. 8 in. square and built of bricks set in pink mortar. Those at the north end had been largely destroyed, but Piers 4E, 5E and 6E survived to a height of 1 ft., 1 ft. 2 in. and 1 ft. 8 in. respectively (Plate XA). Six of the seven east bays formed by the piers were of the same width, about 8 ft. 6 in., but the central bay had been increased to 10 ft. 6 in. to form an entrance. It seems likely that a similar arrangement had also existed on the west side. The corners of the hall were formed by additional corner piers supported by substantial buttresses. The end walls were 2 ft. 4 in. to 2 ft. 6 in. wide and it seems likely that they were partitions dividing the hall from the north and south ends. The south cross-wall was found to butt against the base of the two southern corner buttresses.

The floor of the hall was made of two layers both of which had survived remarkably intact (Plate XB). The lower, up to 6 in. thick, was made of chalk rubble rammed down and the upper, also up to 6 in. thick, comprised a compact mixture of chalk and yellow loam. Of the superstructure there was little evidence. It seems likely that the piers rose to a height of somewhere between 10 and 20 ft. and that the bays were spanned by heavy wooden lintels. The hall itself must have been roofed as certainly there was no trace of weathering of the floor and indeed an area of smashed roof-tiles lay over a wide zone at the north end. In all probability the central hall rose rather higher than the flanking aisles and light came in through high-level windows. This imaginative reconstruction constitutes a basilica of familiar type which gave rise to the original term 'basilican villa' (now termed aisled villa).

Room 2 (The West Aisle)

This room formed the western aisle of the new building. Its walls were 2 ft. thick, its internal width 11 ft. 9 in. and its minimum internal length was 67 ft. There can be little doubt that it extended along the entire length of this side, thus originally being at least 135 ft. in length. Two walls across its width appear to be later additions (see below). Its floor, like the main hall, was made of layers of chalk and chalk-loam totalling 5 in. in thickness. A thin bed of orange-red *opus signinum* had been laid over this base and on this had been set a tiled floor. Only slight traces of the bedding and floor survived, but several of the complete tiles were 11 in. square. On the outer, west side of the aisle was a group of largely complete tegulae tiles measuring 1 ft. 6 in. by 1 ft. These lay flat and had the appearance of having slipped off the roof of the aisle. The external south-west corner of the aisle was partly quoined with large fragments of millstone.

Under the floor was a thin layer of black loam (section 4, layer 31) which contained several potsherds dating from about A.D. 200–240 (Nos. 324 and 325). At the south end the floor dipped into the subsided filling of the underlying ditch. The floor was covered by a thin band of loam containing domestic rubbish (see Period V).

Rooms 3 and 4 (South End)

These two rooms were contained within the southward extension of the main hall, but divided from it by a substantial cross-wall. This extension measured internally 31 ft. in length and 27 ft. in width. It was divided into two equal parts (Rooms 3 and 4), separated from each other by a wall which ended in a badly damaged brick pier some 7 ft. short of the cross-wall. The south, east and west walls of Rooms 3 and 4 were all 2 ft. thick and built of coursed flint set in a yellow-white mortar. The dividing wall between the two rooms butted to the end south wall and was clearly added to it, but even so it may have formed part of the original scheme. It also cut across the line of two demolished earlier walls, one the original south end of the Period III building and one of uncertain function (see below).

Both rooms contained a large corn-drying oven of almost identical construction (Plate XIB), but of which only the bases survived (Fig. 41). It seems clear that each oven consisted of two long flues, one on each side of a narrow, central spine wall. In both cases one flue was narrow and the other broad, being about 1 ft. 9 in. and 2 ft. 7 in. in width, respectively. All four flues seem to have been at least 10 ft. in length and the broader ones opened out into rectangular chambers about 7 ft. by 4 ft. at the south ends. Here possible gaps in the superstructure may indicate the positions of vertical flues and it is possible that each pair of horizontal flues joined. At the other end of the long flues were rectangular areas of tiles, about 4 ft. by 4 ft. which were damaged by intense heat. It seems clear that these mark the points where small fires were regularly made from which warm air was drawn along the flues to the chambers and possible vertical flues at the south end. Although more elaborate than the normal T-shaped corn-drying ovens the principle of drying was probably much the same. Elsewhere, as at Hambledon, Buckinghamshire (Ref. 230), Atworth, Wiltshire (Ref. 231) and Great Casterton, Rutland (Ref. 232) it seems likely that the corn was spread out on one or two floors constructed over the flues to facilitate drying.

In detail the beds of the flues, chambers and hearths were made of a mixture of bricks, roofing tiles and bridging-tiles laid flat. The spine walls were mostly built of chalk blocks, but they only survived where there was settlement into the underlying ditch. There, two courses of chalk blocks, each about 3 in. high, were capped with a single course of brick. The sides of both ovens were packed with flint, chalk and loam.

Room 5 (South End of East Aisle)

This part of the building formed the aisle on the east side of the south end of the hall and Room 4. It was similar to the west aisle in that its internal width was 11 ft. 4 in. and all its walls were 2 ft. thick. Its internal length was originally 52 ft. It differed from the west aisle in that it made use of part of the pre-existing Period III corridor and the junction between the two was clear (Plate XIA). Its floor was made up of a base of chalk and loam 3 in. thick, upon which was laid a bed of orange-red *opus signinum* up to 2 in. thick. Set on this was a floor, largely complete, of bricks mostly 8 in. square, but including several larger ones up to 15 in. square (Plate XIIA). The floor had settled into the underlying ditch and also into the slots caused by rotted timbers relating to the Period III

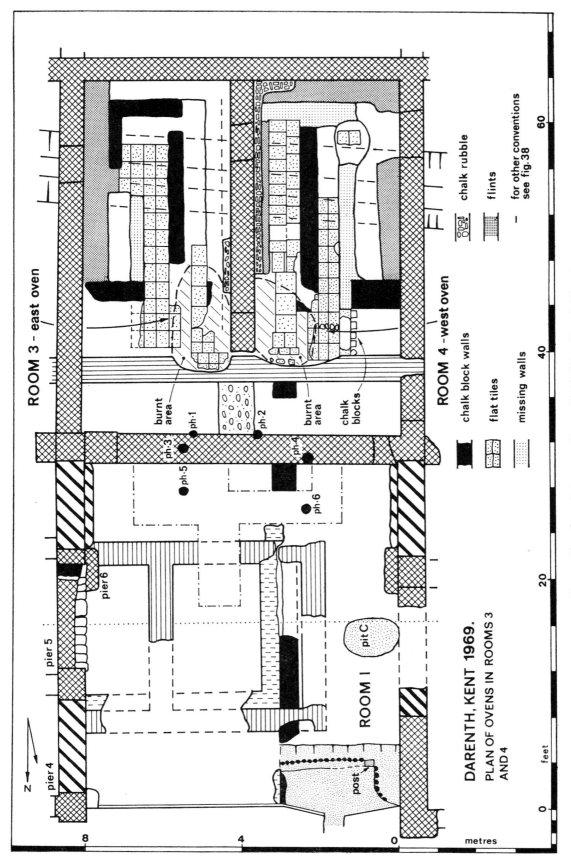

ROOM 3 - east oven

ROOM 4 - west oven

burnt area

ph-1

ph-3

ph-5

ph-2

ph-4

ph-6

N

pier 4

pier 5

pier 6

ROOM I

pit C

post

burnt area

chalk blocks

DARENTH, KENT 1969.

PLAN OF OVENS IN ROOMS 3 AND 4

chalk block walls

flat tiles

missing walls

chalk rubble

flints

for other conventions see fig.38

metres

feet

Fig. 41. *Plan of corn-drying ovens, Roman aisled building, Darenth (Site 21).*

floor. A thick layer of black loam over much of the floor contained domestic rubbish (see Period V). The internal face of the east wall had a thin lining of *opus signinum* only small traces of which survived. The external south-east corner was also partly quoined with fragments of large millstones.

Room 6

This room was framed between the east aisle and the main entrance and measured 11 ft. 9 in. by 8 ft. 9 in. internally. Each side wall was 1 ft. 9 in. thick and both walls butted against the pre-existing Period III east wall and against the two corresponding brick piers. It seems clear that these walls formed part of the Period IV scheme. It is noteworthy that the tile floor in Room 5 ends against the south wall of Room 6 indicating that it had already been built when the floors were laid. The floor of Room 6 consisted of yellow mortar up to 2 in. in thickness. This covered both the Period I and Period II foundations, but it had partially collapsed into one of the cavities left by a rotted timber of Period III.

Room 7 (The Entrance)

This division corresponds with the wide bay at the centre of the hall and appears to have formed the main entrance into the building during Period IV. It measured 11 ft. 6 in. by 11 ft. 9 in. internally. The sleeper-wall on this side of the hall was not taken to its full height and the pre-existing outer Period III wall was partly demolished to allow access. The level was made up with dumped soil and this was then capped by a thin layer of gravel metalling (section 3, layer 4) laid across it to a point at least 5 ft. beyond the outer wall and also covering the East Drain. A line of large flints set in the metalling on the outer line of the external wall probably formed a sill against which large, internal wooden doors may have closed. In addition two 9–10 in. diameter holes, 4–5 in. deep were found in the metalling and these may indicate wooden posts dividing the entrance. Three coins (Nos. 12–14), two of Constantius II (A.D. 337–354) and one of Helena (A.D. 324–330) were found on the metalling and were probably dropped in the entrance.

Excavation through the metalling and underlying layers revealed the Period I wall (1 ft. 6 in wide) separated from the Period III wall (1 ft. 9 in. wide), by a gap of 1 ft. 2 in. The reduced Period IV foundation sat across the remains of the Period III wall (Section 4).

Room 8

This room corresponds with Room 6 in that it flanks the main entrance, but this time on the north side. It measures 11 ft. 9 in. by 9 ft. 6 in. internally and its side walls had been about 1 ft. 9 in. thick. It too had a yellow mortar floor, 3 in. thick, which was cut through by two pits. An irregular one (Pit A) at the south-east corner was probably of post-Roman date and an oblong pit (Pit B) contained a complete, handled pot (No. 448) of late-17th or early-18th century date. In the north-west corner was a circular tile base, 3 ft. 9 in. in diameter, built of Roman bricks and tufa blocks set in clay. It rose at least 1 ft. 4 in. above the floor and appeared to have been a base, or podium, of an uncertain feature. The poor bonding, rough construction and its isolated position all tend to suggest a simple structure perhaps for domestic use. Just possibly this may have supported a small altar or votive object. Eleven coins (Nos. 1–11) were in fact found over the adjacent floor and it is possible that these were scattered offerings. The coins were probably deposited at about A.D. 270–300. Pottery found in Room 8 (Nos. 326–334) probably represents domestic rubbish discarded about the middle of the 3rd century.

Room 9 (North End of East Aisle)

This division had a width of about 11 ft., a minimum internal length of 44 ft. and it occupied much of the Period III corridor. Almost certainly it extended another 10 ft. or more further on beyond the limit of excavation. A rectangular block of masonry, about 2 ft. 9 in. by 2 ft. 1 in. against the inside face of the outer wall may have formed part of the original scheme.

The floor at the south end of this room had been surfaced with large rectangular tiles, each about 1 ft. 4 in. by 1 ft., subsequently partly destroyed by the west drain. The north end of this room had a patchy floor of yellow mortar into which had been cut a small hearth about 3 ft. long, 1 ft. wide and about 10 in. deep. It had been lined with fragments of tile, heavily scorched by intense heat and was generally sealed by a deposit of carbon.

Two broken imbrices placed at an angle in the east wall appear to have served as a water-gulley, perhaps even after this section of the building was destroyed. Room 9 contained quantities of domestic rubbish including bone, antler (No. 453), fragments of quernstone, pottery (Nos. 335–350) and four coins (Nos. 15–18). The coins are of Gallienus (A.D. 260–268), Carausius (A.D. 287–293), Constantius II (A.D. 337–341) and one is illegible. This material, of 3rd and early-4th century date, probably represents rubbish dumped both before and after the demolition of the north end of the Period IV building being partly sealed by demolition rubble. At some earlier date, the wall dividing Rooms 8 and 9 had been demolished and a new wall, 1 ft. 10 in. wide, inserted one bay further north. This increased the length of Room 8 to about 20 ft. 6 in. and shortened the north end of the east aisle by about 11 ft. 4 in.

Room 10

Only the extreme south-east corner of this room was located and of its size and function nothing can be said.

East Drain

This drain flanked the east side of the building running about 4 ft. from and parallel to the external face of the east wall (sections 1–4). Its width varied from 2 ft. to 2 ft. 3 in. and its depth from 1 ft. to 2 ft. 8 in. as it progressed northwards in the direction of its outlet. It was rectangular in section and had contained a wood-lining of which only a single timber of trough-shaped section, remained *in situ*. This was about 5½ ft. long, 1 ft. 6 in. wide and 2 in. thick. Its bed was only 1 ft. 2 in. wide and the two upright sides were each 2 in. thick and survived to a height of only 3 in. (Plate XIIB). Any other lengths of timber lining must have been removed when the drain was abandoned.

It is clear that the line of this drain respects the entire east wall of the building and this suggests that it relates to either Period III or Period IV. It was clearly superseded by the West Drain (see below) and filled with smashed tiles probably when the north end of Period IV was demolished during the Period V programme of work.

The drain was cut through a thick layer of carbon (section 1, layer 14; section 2, layer 4; section 3, layer 7; section 4, layer 9) containing pottery of about A.D. 150–250 (Nos. 351–366). It was sealed in part by a layer of black loam and carbon (section 4, layer 3) containing pottery (Nos. 367–9) of 3rd century date and the probability is that it relates to Period IV.

The Deep Pit (Plate XIIIA)

Sometime after the construction of the Period IV building a large, deep pit was dug adjacent to the widest west bay between what would have been the central pair of piers, opposite the main entrance (section 3). This was about 10 ft. wide, 4 ft. deep and at least 13 ft. in length. It extended from the main hall through the bay into the west aisle and perhaps even beyond the building to the nearby river. Its north and east sides had been vertical and were held by wooden stakes driven into the underlying gravel. Two of these were detected, one (Stake 1) being about 4 in. square and the other (Stake 2) pointed and about 1½ in. in diameter. On the west side was the faint impression of a third stake (Stake 3) about 9 in. in diameter. It seems likely that these stakes may have supported horizontal wooden planks around the sides.

On the south side of this deep pit was a smaller extension about 7 ft. long, 5 ft. wide and only 2 ft. deep. It too had been cut through the floor of Room 1 and its south and west sides appeared to have been revetted with flints, perhaps placed behind upright planks. A rectangular post, 10 by 8 in. at the south-west corner may have formed part of this arrangement. In effect this extension provided an intermediate stage, or platform, between the main hall and deep pit. They were linked by a sloping (or weathered) ramp.

Down the centre of the pit was a wood-lined drain 1 ft. 4 in. wide and at least 8 ft. 6 in. in length. It was made of wooden planks laid flat to form a base and others laid on edge to form vertical sides, up to 1 ft. 2 in. high. The drain rested on gravel which was presumably the original base, but as this was several inches below present water-level it was impossible to be certain.

The sides of the drain had been packed with flint, rubble, tile and soil which contained a coin (No. 19) of Licinius I (A.D. 320–321) and pottery (Nos. 370–377) of late-3rd to mid-4th century date. The drain itself and the lower 3 ft. of the pit were filled with fine black loam and carbon (section 3, layer 2). Worn Roman pot-sherds and tile chips were found on the bottom of the drain. In the rubble layer on the north side of the drain were two massive, rectangular wooden beams. The larger was a squared timber 5 ft. 7 in. by 1 ft. 1 in. by 6 in. with a rectangular socket, 4 by 3½ in., 4 in. from one end and a mortice 6 by 4 in. at the other end. The smaller beam, 2 ft. 8 in. by 1 ft. 1 in. by 7 in. contained a central hole 2½ in. square and 2 in. deep.

The exact function of this great pit is not clear. It occupies a central position on the west side of the main hall and surely must have had some specific purpose. A cess-pit might reasonably be more discreetly placed, perhaps at an extremity of the building, or even outside. It seems unlikely that this large pit was dug just for a small drain and anyway why put the drain 4½ ft. below floor-level? Clearly the drain must have had an outlet at a corresponding depth and it may be that this equated with river-level in Roman times. If so, it is also possible that the river flowed back at certain times, into the pit itself. It has been suggested that if the river did flow in then a narrow flat-bottomed vessel could have been floated out. If so the step and ramp could readily be explained as providing access and it might suggest a more likely solution as to the function of this unusual pit and better explain its central position in the great hall. In the absence of additional evidence it is impossible to be sure. The drain does seem to be a secondary feature as the wooden stakes holding the sides of the pit and its considerable width imply a different use. The large beams seem to have been thrown in with the rubble to form packing against the sides of the drain and may not be connected in any other way.

PERIOD V

The fifth and final major phase of construction resulted in a drastic reduction of the building. That part of the structure north of the central entrance appears to have been abandoned and a new cross-wall built to form a new north end. Other new flint walls blocked some of the south bays or helped create smaller rooms. The mortar in each wall was a light yellow and contained chalk specks.

In detail the new north wall, built of flint and containing fragments of *opus signinum*, was 2 ft. 4 in. thick. It rested on broader foundations, having two offsets 4 and 6 in. wide respectively. The new wall cut through the floors of Period IV and its east end partially clasped Pier 4E. Its west end over-ran the deep pit, then completely filled with fine black loam and carbon, the presence of which was presumably unknown to the builders. On excavation the west end of this wall was found to have collapsed into the pit and it had to be removed for safety. It is clear that the south cross-wall of the Period IV hall had also been removed at sometime and it seems probable that this was done during the Period V work. The overall effect of this would have been to create a new central hall, or room, about 64 ft. 6 in. in length internally and containing the drying ovens in its southern half.

The blocking of at least two bays on each side totally separated the aisles from the original hall and the building was no longer of the 'aisled' type. The blocks were uniformly 2 ft. 4 in. wide and survived in places to a maximum height of 1 ft. 8 in. The block between Pier 6E and the corner-pier rested on new, deeper foundations which also cut through the Period IV floors.

Room 11 (Plate XIIIB)

A new 2 ft. cross-wall of similar yellow mortar was inserted across the eastern aisle in line with Pier 6E. This created a new room (Room 11) exactly 10 ft. wide and it reduced the south end of the east aisle (Room 5) by a corresponding amount. The new wall rested on the tiles of the Period IV floor and the outline of a doorway, probably with a pair of wooden treaders, 5 ft. wide was found at 1 ft. 2 in. above floor-level. The floor of the new room was then filled with mortar, flints and broken tiles (section 4, layers 13–15) up to the level of the sill. A similar cross-wall may have been built in a corresponding position across the west aisle (see below).

Inside the remodelled building a 10 in. layer of black loam and carbon formed over the northern half of the new hall and in Room 11 from where it spread through the open doorway for several feet to the south. This layer was generally absent from the rest of the Period V building, but similar deposits were spread over a wide area east of the building. It seems likely that this was the residue from the two large drying-ovens. The black deposit in the new main hall (Room 1) and in Room 11 lay directly over the undamaged floor and sealed on it pottery (Nos. 378–391) of 4th century date.

The side rooms, now largely walled off from the main hall, may have been used for storage or even for accommodation. The floors of each were covered with a layer of black loam containing domestic rubbish never removed from the building. From this, in what had been the west aisle (Room 2), came three coins (Nos. 20–22), one of Constantius II (A.D. 337–341), one of Valerian (A.D. 253–260) and one illegible (*c.* A.D. 350) and pottery (Nos. 392–401 and 444) of late-3rd and 4th century date. What had been the east aisle (Room 5) also produced a coin (No. 23) of Constantius II (A.D. 341–346), pottery (Nos. 402–411) and an antler tool (No. 455) and Room 6 produced another group of pottery (Nos. 412–416). The coins and pottery all date from the late-3rd century to second half of the 4th century and represent the latest dating evidence from the building. It seems this represents domestic rubbish left behind just before the building was abandoned. The main hall and most of the rooms were sealed by a thick layer of flints representing the destruction of the building over an indeterminate period.

Beyond the Period V north-wall fallen roof-tiles lay over the floor of the north end of what had been Period IV floor and sealed a light scatter of rubbish, including pottery (Nos. 417–19) and a coin (No. 24) of Constantine I (A.D. 323–324). The Period IV drain (East Drain) was deliberately filled in with large roof-tiles, probably those from the abandoned north end of the building.

West Drain

A new rectangular drain was made to replace the East Drain and this cut through two walls and ran through Rooms 8 and 9. Clearly these walls had been largely demolished before the drain was built, very probably to supply materials for the Period V scheme. The drain flowed north and varied in width from 1 ft. 2 in. to 3 ft. and in depth from about 9 in. to 2 ft. 7 in. (sections 1, 2 and 3). Its depth and width suddenly increased at the south end of Room 9 where two small upright stakes may have retained a vertical cross-board. There was no trace of a wooden lining. The drain was filled with gravel, loam, chalk and rubble and contained pottery (Nos. 420–43 and 459) of late-2nd, 3rd or 4th century date.

The date of the Period V scheme clearly falls after the completion of the grand aisled building which was probably built sometime about the middle of the 3rd century (see page 127). Time had to elapse for the construction of the Deep Pit, for its re-use as a drain, for its abandonment and filling before the Period V wall could be built across it. The solitary coin of Licinius I in the filling of the pit beneath the wall suggests that Period V cannot date from earlier than A.D. 320. In addition the domestic rubbish and coins left lying about the building suggest abandonment during the second half of the 4th century. From this it seems likely that the Period V scheme probably dates from the second quarter of the 4th century A.D.

UNDATED FEATURES AND WALLS

Two walls were at sometime added across the west aisle. The north one, just 1 ft. 7 in. wide, butted against Pier W4 and also against the outer wall. It may have formed part of the Period IV plan to correspond with the wall dividing Rooms 6 and 7, but it had subsided partly sideways into the adjacent Deep Pit and its exact relationship was difficult to determine. The added south wall butted against the outer wall and also against Pier W6. Its foundation trench, 2 ft. 2 in. wide, cut through the Period IV floor and only a small section of this wall survived on the west side. From this evidence it seems likely that this wall formed part of the Period V plan.

Slight trace of another short east-west wall was found in Rooms 3 and 4, about 15 ft. from the south wall. It was 2 ft. 6 in. wide and barely 2 in. high. Not enough survived to suggest what structure this related to and it could be that it was not a continuous wall, but short lengths on each side to retain the ovens.

Room 12

At the extreme south end of the building was another large room which had been added to the Period IV south wall. It measured 27 ft. by 12 ft. 4 in. internally and its walls were 1 ft. 9 in. thick. There was no trace of a floor or of any doorway, though a small gap in the west wall may indicate the latter. The outer south-west corner was quoined with three large fragments of millstone, of pink sandstone and also of grey Millstone Grit. The outer face of the west wall and the adjacent outer face of Room 2 had been plastered. A 2-in. layer of soil was found between the wall and the plaster, which comprised an ½ in. layer of yellow mortar covered by an ½ in. layer of opus signinum, painted red. Exactly why the only painted plaster should be external is difficult to say, but similar external plaster is known on at least one other Romano-British site (Ref. 233).

A narrow U-shaped gulley, about 2 ft. wide and 9 in. deep and on an east-west alignment, was found running beneath Room 12. This contained a fragment of samian ware (Form 31) of mid-2nd century date.

A small pit (Pit C) 4 ft. 7 in. in length and about 1 ft. deep, found on the west side of the hall (Room 1), was not examined in detail. It contained chalk, mortar and loam (section 4, layers 19 and 20), but no finds.

A pair of circular, tapered post-holes (PH-1 and 2) about 5 ft. apart, were found about 9 ft. south of the twin rooms of Period II. They were 6 in. in diameter and at least 1 ft. 10 in. deep and 8 in. in diameter and at least 2 ft. 2 in. deep, respectively. Both were partially sealed beneath the new south wall of the Period IV building and must relate to an earlier structure. It may be that they related to the Period II building, perhaps forming part of a verandah or an extension on the south side.

Two more pairs of circular post-holes were found at the south end of Room 1. One pair (PH-3 and 4) which cut through the demolished Period IV south wall, were 10 in. diameter, 1 ft. 1 in. and 1 ft. 4 in. deep, with steep sides and flat or cupped bases. The other pair (PH-5 and 6), which cut through the Period IV floor of Room 1, were 9 in. in diameter, 6 in. and 8 in. deep with steep sides and flat bases.

The Metalled Road

The bulldozer also revealed a narrow band of flint and gravel metalling on each side of a deep cut made on the extreme east side of the proposed gravel-pit. This appears to represent a minor metalled road, or track, about 8 ft. wide and running roughly parallel to and about 45 ft. from the aisled building. It was 9 in. thick and the surface was located at a depth of about 2 ft. 9 in. below the present ground-level. It was sealed by the layer of black loam, containing late-Roman pottery and tile, which was found over a wide area on the east side of the Roman building.

The Burial (Plate XIVA)

At the extreme edge of the gravel-pit and at about 65 ft. east of the aisled building, just beyond the edge of the metalled road, the bulldozer revealed a rectangular cut in the subsoil. On examination this proved to be a grave, 8 ft. long and probably 3 ft. wide, containing the skeleton of an adult female aged about 20–30 years and about 5 ft. 5 in. in height. The body had been placed on its front with its arms and legs quite straight and the head towards the north. It had been buried in a wooden coffin, of which only the iron nails survived. These indicated that the coffin had been about 5 ft. 8 in. by 1 ft. 8 in. and at least 8 in. high. The nails had broad, flat heads and were about 2 or 3 in. long. There were no associated grave-goods. The base of the grave rested on chalk and gravel at a depth of about 2½ ft. below the approximate Roman ground-level and about 5 ft. from present ground-level. The grave was covered by the thick deposit of black loam, containing late-Roman material, which covered most of this area. It seems clear that the burial must date from Roman times, perhaps from the 3rd or 4th centuries, when unaccompanied inhumation-burials were more common. A careful search of the adjacent area failed to locate other graves, but it is possible that more await discovery nearby.

DISCUSSION

It seems clear that the various Roman buildings discovered at Darenth between 1894 and 1969 form a single, extensive complex which can be identified as the centre of a major villa-estate (Ref. 234). Groups of such buildings on varying scales, but seldom as large as at Darenth, were frequent in the Romano-British countryside and reflect the mainly agricultural function of the province (Ref. 235).

As regards dating it is difficult to provide exact dates for all the various structures on the site of the aisled building. As there were no finds from the Period I, IA or II structures it is easier to consider the Periods in reverse order. Period V cannot be earlier than the coin of Licinius I (A.D. 320–321) and was probably constructed in the second quarter of the 4th century and abandoned during the second half of that century. Period IV appears to have been constructed in the middle of the 3rd century and partially demolished later than A.D. 270–300. Period III cannot be earlier than about A.D. 200 and was probably built in the first two decades of the 3rd century. This leaves Periods I, IA and II which, considering the total lack of 1st century material on the site, probably date to the 2nd century. In the absence of other evidence Period I is here regarded as dating from the middle of the 2nd century and Period II from the second half of the 2nd century. This would allow each to be in use for a reasonable time and also allow for the Period IA work. It is possible, though rather less likely, that all this early work was carried out in the second half of the 2nd century. The finds from all deposits on the site do, however, include material dating from about the middle of the 2nd century A.D.

The large Roman building discovered at Darenth in 1969 may, if considered on the merits of its Period IV plan (Fig. 40), be identified readily as an 'aisled villa' of common form (Ref. 236). In size (at least 160 by 58 ft.) it tends to be larger than most and compares with broadly similar aisled structures at Norton Disney, Lincolnshire, about 120 by 50 ft. (Ref. 237) and Mansfield Woodhouse, Nottingham, about 140 by 45 ft. (Ref. 238). In terms of its central aisled section (about 76 by 26 ft.) no exact parallel comes to mind though the same basic arrangements are reflected at Clanville, Hampshire (Ref. 239) and Brading, Isle of Wight (Ref. 240). In detail the central entrance is a feature often noted (Ref. 241), but the two small rooms which flank the entrance are unusual. The spacious south end, with its two large corn-drying ovens, reflects simple work-rooms as on other sites. Of the destroyed north end we know little, but comparable plans suggest that a small suite of rooms may have existed to serve as modest accommodation as at Stroud, Hampshire (Ref. 242) and North Wanborough, Hampshire (Ref. 243).

Detailed studies of these aisled structures (Ref. 236) confirm that they incorporated some living-accommodation with large working areas, principally that of the nave which was certainly roofed. Here and in flanking aisles and rooms were covered areas for working, storage and perhaps farm vehicles. At Darenth the solid floor of the nave may well have been used for threshing corn which was subsequently dried in the large ovens in the adjacent rooms and perhaps stored in the projecting room at the south end. The wide, central entrance was probably a wagon-entrance and indeed it is otherwise difficult to explain the metalling. Hence it is easy to imagine wagons loaded with corn and straw trundling through the entrance into the spacious nave to be off-loaded under cover so that the threshing, drying and storing processes could begin.

The provision of mortared floors in the pair of rooms flanking the entrance is not surprising as these probably served a special function. What is surprising is that the side aisles were paved with tiles throughout their lengths and that the south end of the east aisle had at sometime been decorated with an internal rendering. These modest refinements tend to suggest that at least parts of the aisles were intended as living-accommodation. Certainly the Period V alterations sub-divided the aisles into smaller units and the domestic rubbish found on the floors tends to confirm that some of these new rooms were occupied for at least part of the 4th century.

Taken in isolation, then, the aisled building appears to be just another unpretentious Romano-British villa, lacking major refinements and reflecting a truly working farmhouse. Considered with the other buildings it takes on a new role. Happily, elsewhere in Britain similar aisled buildings also formed part of large villa complexes often being overshadowed by pretentious houses containing refinements lacking in the former. Almost invariably the aisled structures can be seen to be of secondary importance and often they are part of one side of a courtyard complex as at Llantwit Major, Glamorganshire (Ref. 244) and perhaps Great Casterton, Rutland (Ref. 245). Only occasionally, as at Ickleton, Cambridgeshire (Ref. 246), was it apparently a totally detached structure and this is very clearly the case at Darenth. Indeed at Darenth the main occupation-range with its swimming pool, tessellated floors, bath-wing, ornamental fish-pool, walled gardens and monumental entrance can be seen to be in splendid isolation at the north end of the site. Lesser buildings, perhaps stables and workshops, seem to flank an outer court whilst the aisled building and small bath-building are even further south (Fig. 36).

Studies of such arrangements on other large villa estates suggest that the pretentious houses were occupied by the wealthy villa-owner and that the adjacent aisled buildings were occupied by a bailiff and the farm-workers. This scheme would certainly explain the juxta-position of the buildings at Darenth. Again it is not difficult to imagine the land-owner living in gracious comfort and entertaining his family and friends at a suitable distance from the noise and smells of the working farm. The real nerve-centre was the aisled building 'a more primitive type of establishment which belonged to a lower grade of society' (Ref. 247) who lived and worked close to the land of what must have been a great estate. So too may the small detached bath-building have related to this lesser house rather than to the main house which anyway had its own arrangements.

The majority of recorded masonry aisled villas appear to have been constructed in the 3rd century and indeed that at Darenth was probably built in the middle of the 3rd century. Exactly what function the earlier, smaller structures beneath the aisled building served is difficult to gauge. Perhaps they too served to house an earlier bailiff and the farm-workers of the estate. More than this cannot be said, but clearly the drastic Period V reduction tends to imply a diminishing, or at least changing, system. Just how the evolution of the building from the 2nd to 4th centuries reflects the pattern of the main villa and estate in general only more work may tell.

Finally, of the many Roman villas along the Darent Valley the complex at Darenth is by far the largest known and it is likely that it represents a farming estate of several thousand acres. Today the immediate area is mostly arable and it is possible that in Roman times large quantities of corn were grown here too. This to be transported by the river to the nearby Watling Street or to the Thames and on the tide to London.

THE FINDS

(1) THE COINS FROM THE ROMAN AISLED BUILDING, DARENTH, 1969

A total of 30 coins was recovered during the 1969 excavation and these were submitted for cleaning and identification to Mr. E. W. Tilley and Mr. R. Merrifield, Guildhall Museum. Table A is based upon their notes.

No.	Obverse	Date A.D.	Notes	Deposit	Code
1	Marcus Aurelius	172	Sestertius (R.I.C. 1058–1062)	Floor, Room 8	SDV-KF7
2	Septimius Severus	194	Sestertius (R.I.C. 667 or 672)	,,	SDV-KF8
3	Severus Alexander	229	As (R.I.C. 494)	,,	SDV-KF6
4	Salonina	257–258	Antoninianus (R.I.C. 7). Mint of Lugdunum	,,	SDV-KF5
5	Valerian	254–260	Antoninianus (R.I.C. 106). Mint of Rome	,,	SDV-KF2
6	Victorinus	265–270	Antoninianus (R.I.C. 61). Southern mint	,,	SDV-KF12
7	Tetricus I	268–273	Antoninianus (R.I.C. 136)	,,	SDV-KF10
8	Tetricus I	270–273	Antoninianus (R.I.C. 90)	,,	SDV-KF3
9	—	Late-3rd century	Barbarous radiate. 16 mm.	,,	SDV-KF22
10	—	—	Illegible—Antoninianus. R Victory walking	,,	SDV-KF4
11	Sabina	c. 130	Sestertius (R.I.C. *Hadrian* 1026). Mint of Rome. Date uncertain—after early A.D. 128 and possibly posthumous under Antoninus Pius (see R.I.C. II, p. 318)	,,	SDV-KF13
12	Helena	324–330	Follis (L.R.B.C.I.35). Mint of Treveri	Metalling, Room 7	SDV-KF20
13	Constantius II	337–341	VICTORIAE DD AVGG QNN. Two victories type of A.D. 337–341. ? mint	,,	SDV-KF9
14	Constantius II	346–354	Barbarous copy. 12 mm. FEL TEMP REPARATIO. Fallen horseman type of A.D. 346–354	Metalling, Room 7	SDV-KF27
15	Gallienus	260–268	Antoninianus (R.I.C. 308). Mint of Rome	Rubble, Room 9	SDV-KF18
16	Carausius	287–293	Antoninianus. Pax type with transverse sceptre	,,	SDV-KF15
17	Constantius II	337–341	GLORIA EXERCITVS type with one standard. ? mint	,,	SDV-KF16
18	—	—	Illegible. Fragments only.	,,	SDV-KF17
19	Licinius I	320–321	Follis (R.I.C. *Siscia* 160). Mint of Siscia, mint mark A	Fill, Deep Pit	SDV-KF24
20	Constantius II	337–341	As L.R.B.C. I 130, but mint mark off plan	Floor, Room 2	SDV-KF28
21	Valerian	253–260	Antoninianus (R.I.C. ?86). (Broken)	,,	SDV-KF31
22	—	4th century	Illegible minim, 8 mm.	,,	SDV-KF26
23	Constantius II or Constans	341–346	Two Victories. ? mint	Floor, Room 5	SDV-KF29
24	Constantine I	323–324	Follis (R.I.C. *Trier* 429). Mint of Treveri	Under tiles, Room 1	SDV-KF23
25	—	4th century	Illegible	Unstratified	SDV-KF30
26	Constantine I	308–310	Follis (R.I.C. *Londinium* 103)	,,	SDV-KF11
27	Constantine I	330–335	Follis. (As L.R.B.C. I. 60. But mint mark off plan)	,,	SDV-KF25
28	Constans	346–350	Centenionalis (L.R.B.C. II.46). Mint of Trier	,,	SDV-KF32
29	George II	1752	Halfpenny	,,	SDV-KF19
30	Edward VII	1902	Halfpenny	,,	SDV-KF21

TABLE A
Coins found during the 1969 excavation at Darenth.

A list of only 53 Roman coins, recovered during the 1894–5 excavations at Darenth, was published by George Payne. In view of the extensive nature of the excavation it is highly likely that many others were in fact found. To these can now be added the 28 found in 1969, as shown in Table B.

Emperor	Date	1894–5 excavation	1969 excavation	Totals
Domitian	81–96	2		2
Trajan	97–117	1		1
Hadrian	117–138	1		1
Sabina	c. 130		1	1
Antoninus Pius	138–161	4		4
Marcus Aurelius	161–180		1	1
Septimius Severus	193–211		1	1
Severus Alexander	222–235		1	1
Philippus	244–249	2		2
Trebonianus	251–254	1		1
Valerian	253–260		2	2
Gallienus	253–268	1	1	2
Salonina	257–258	1	1	2
Postumus	260–269	1		1
Victorinus	265–271		1	1
Claudius II	268–269	2		2
Tetricus	268–273	19	2	21
Carausius	287–293		1	1
Constantius I	293–306	1		1
Allectus	293–296	1		1
Constantine I	306–337	2	3	5
Licnius I	308–324		1	1
Crispus	317–326	1		1
Helena	324–330	1	1	2
Constans	337–350		1	1
Constantius II	337–361	1	5	6
Decentius	351–353	1		1
Valentinianus	364–375	2		2
Valens	364–378	2		2
Gratian	367–383	2		2
Unidentified		4	5	9
Totals		53	28	81

TABLE B
Roman coins found during the excavations in 1894–5 and 1969 at Darenth

(2) THE ROMAN POTTERY FROM THE AISLED BUILDING, DARENTH, 1969

A total of 3,355 sherds was recovered from the site of the aisled building at Darenth and these represent a minimum of 262 vessels, of which 133 have been illustrated (Figs. 42–45). The pottery has been classified by members of the Group as shown in Table C and is discussed briefly below (for discussion of terms see Fox Hill—Site 8).

	Samian ware	Patch Grove ware	Shell-Calcite wares	Rhenish ware	Colour-coated wares	Roman coarse wares	Romano-Saxon ware	Totals
Pots	12	11	3	4	47	184	1	262
Percentages	5	4	1	1	18	71	—	100

TABLE C

Classification of Roman pottery from Darenth

Group A. Samian Ware

At least twelve vessels are represented and all are clearly of 2nd century date, mostly of the second half of that century. The total absence of standard 1st century forms is particularly significant. All the sherds are worn and several pieces burnt. The identifiable forms include two of Form 18/31; two of Form 31, of which one is dull orange; a small chip of a possible Form 32; two of Form 33 (including a base (No. 346) stamped]ANI·OF); the rim of a Form 36; four sherds of Form 37 and part of the flange of a Form 38. The majority of these are likely to be the products of the kilns of Central and Eastern Gaul.

Group B. Patch Grove and Related Wares

A minimum of eleven vessels is represented by a small number of sherds and it is clear that this ware was far from common on this site during the period represented by the pottery. All of the vessels have the normal mottled, blue-grey paste, ten have the typical orange-brown surface and one has a grey-brown surface. The latter, one of the standard Patch Grove forms, is a jar with an outcurved rim. There are three more jars (No. 359) and seven large storage jars at least three (No. 322) of which are decorated with a stabbed pattern on the upper shoulder. One vessel has an interesting graffito (VIII) on the shoulder.

Group C. Shell-loaded and Calcite-gritted Wares

Only three separate vessels (Nos. 374, 397 and 418) are represented and one contains shell filling and two contain particles of grit. None is similar to the shell-loaded and corky wares of the 1st and early-2nd centuries, so common on West Kent sites and it is highly probable that they are semi-local products of the 3rd and 4th centuries A.D. Statistically they are not significant on this site.

Group D. Rhenish Ware

Only four vessels of Rhenish ware were found on the site, none being large enough for adequate illustration. All are decorated either with white slip or fine bands of rouletting and date from the late-2nd or early-3rd centuries A.D.

Group E. Colour-coated Wares

A total of 47 vessels with a coloured slip, other than samian ware, is included in this group. Of these five have a white paste, either a dark brown or grey-black slip and are traditionally classed as 'Castor Ware'. All are small beakers or cups and decorated (Nos. 318 and 323) with applied patterns including hunting scenes. The bulk of the remainder had red, grey or black paste. Several have brown, grey-black or blue-green slips, but the majority has orange or orange-red slips. It is likely that most of these are the products of the New Forest, Nene Valley or

Oxfordshire industries. Apart from two flagons the great majority are bowls (Nos. 337, 378, 379, 389, 390, 393, 401, 405, 406, 409 and 444), either with bead-rims in imitation of samian Form 31; or with broad flanges in imitation of samian Form 38, or with wide down-turned rims in imitation of samian Form 36. Several, with coarse internal grits, are mortaria and others have occasional bands of rouletting. One of the most distinctive vessels (No. 396) is of Argonne Ware and is decorated with a geometric pattern.

Some of these colour-coated vessels may date from the end of the 2nd century, but the great majority probably date from the middle of the 3rd to the middle of the 4th centuries.

Group F. Romano-British Coarse Wares

A minimum of 184 vessels are here classified as Romano-British in contrast to the groups already described. The great majority has a sandy grey paste and surface, though a few are black or light-brown. About half of these are burnished. The total includes seven mortaria (Nos. 345, 353 and 398), five amphorae (too fragmentary for illustration) and an interesting face-urn (No. 420), four jars with recessed rims (Nos. 342, 362 and 433), a sherd of a poppy-head beaker and three simple hand-made pots (Nos. 388 and 391).

There are at least 71 dishes and at least 92 cooking pots. Of the dishes 18 have bead rims (Nos. 313, 315, 317, 333, 335, 336, 338, 339, 369, 371 and 435), 31 have flanged rims (Nos. 329, 368, 372, 373, 377, 383, 387, 392, 400, 403, 412, 414, 417, 432, 437, 440, 442 and 443) and 22 are straight-sided without bead or flange (Nos. 320, 321, 328, 350, 367, 381, 404, 425, 428, 429 and 439).

Of the cooking pots 22 have cavetto rims (Nos. 314, 332, 348, 349, 351, 375, 385, 413 and 423), 20 have everted rims (Nos. 316, 319, 324, 327, 334, 343, 344, 354, 356, 363, 366, 380 and 395), 9 have bead rims (Nos. 312, 331, 347, 360, and 361), 8 have squared rims (Nos. 340, 382, 408, 422 and 441) and 33 others have either out-curved, thickened or rolled rims.

As regards dating 1st century types are totally absent. There are a few vessels attributable to the 2nd century, but the majority again belongs to the 3rd and 4th centuries.

Group G. Romano-Saxon Ware

There is one squat bowl (No. 419) which has a grey paste, grey surface and black burnished exterior which is of a type sometimes classed 'Romano-Saxon' (Ref. 268). It appears to have had a series of indentations and vertical grooves around its girth and is decorated with stamped circles.

Medieval Pottery

A slight scatter of medieval pottery and tile was found near to the Roman grave and for about 60 ft. to the north, generally at a depth of about 2 ft. The twelve pieces of pottery include small sherds of cooking-pots and green-glazed jugs, probably of 13th or 14th century date (Nos. 446–7). Nearby were the remains of three damaged, circular hearth-bases, made of Roman tile fragments, but these could have been of either late-Roman or medieval date. One was about 5 ft. 9 in. in diameter, another had been largely destroyed by the bulldozer and the third was only exposed in section. All three overlay the thick black loam layer in this area and the third also overlay the Roman grave.

POTTERY DISCUSSION

It is at once clear that 1st century pottery is virtually absent on this site and this view is largely endorsed by the coins. Gallo-Belgic imports, 1st century samian and native wares are significantly absent and the contrast between this pottery and that found on early Romano-British sites in West Kent is most marked. Shell-loaded pottery, so prolific on 1st century sites, is largely absent and even Patch Grove ware, which persists until the end of the 2nd century, is represented by only eleven vessels.

Nor are common 2nd century types of pottery in abundance. There are a few reeded rims, several bead rim cooking-pots (all sandy wares), a poppy-head beaker and several Rhenish and Castor vessels which date to the end of the 2nd century.

In contrast, however, the 3rd and 4th centuries are well represented. There is a large number of cooking-pots and dishes which date from the first quarter of the 3rd century and these generally lack the lattice and burnished patterns common to their 2nd century counterparts. The 3rd century is also represented by the colour-coated wares, probably of the New Forest, Nene Valley or Oxfordshire kilns, whilst the later-3rd and early-4th centuries are represented by the flanged dishes and bowls. The possible Romano-Saxon vessel probably dates from the second half of the 4th century A.D.

Of a minimum of 262 vessels present only 14 (5%) appear to be true native products in contrast to the 60% and 58% at Eastwood and Calfstock Lane, respectively. Another 69 vessels (27%) are imported from abroad or distant British centres, whilst the great majority of 179 vessels (68%) are probably typical Romano-British products of semi-local kilns. It is to be hoped that one day detailed spectrographic analysis of all pottery from Romano-British sites, such as Darenth, will help form the basis for the identification of kiln sites and the distribution of their products.

(3) THE CABRIABANUS TILE FROM THE ROMAN AISLED BUILDING, DARENTH, 1969

A single fragment of a tile-voussoir (Nos. 456 and 457) was found just outside the east wall of the aisled building at Darenth, associated with pottery dating from about A.D. 200. It carries the name of Cabriabanus on two faces, applied by means of a roller-shaped die, probably made of wood. The roller was not positioned with any accuracy and the die can be estimated to have been about 7 in. in circumference and the roller about $2\frac{1}{4}$ in. in diameter.

The name Cabriabanus is known from only one other site and that is at Plaxtol, also in Kent. Several fragments of tile with his name on them were recovered from a Roman building at Allan's Farm, Plaxtol in 1857 (Ref. 248). Of these several fragments are now in Maidstone Museum where examination in 1973 suggested that they too were probably parts of tile-voussoirs. The letters in all cases are identical and it seems certain that the Plaxtol and the Darenth tiles were marked with the same die.

The composite reconstruction of the Plaxtol tiles (Ref. 249 and 250) had suggested three lines of text reading respectively, from top to bottom, PARIETALEM, CABRIABANVS and FABRICAVI, meaning 'I Cabriabanus made this wall-tile'. One side (No. 456) of the Darenth tile, however, has the name Cabriabanus rolled twice, the second central impression clearly removed the upper part of the first. This understood, it now seems likely that the incomplete third line at Plaxtol is an initial application partially removed by a subsequent sweep in an identical manner. The top line of the Plaxtol tile may be the upper half of the Cabriabanus die, but of this there is no trace on the Darenth tile, where the corresponding line is unintelligible.

Both Darenth and Plaxtol are situated in West Kent and the two sites are only about 12 miles apart. The number of Cabriabanus tiles at Plaxtol suggests that either they were made on the site or that a large batch was imported. It must be significant that only one marked tile has been found at Darenth where the site has been extensively excavated. It may also be significant that Cabriabanus tiles are not yet known from any other excavated villa site in Kent though no doubt one day others will be found. It may be that Cabriabanus was in fact making large numbers of voussoir and other tiles for sale over a wide area, but that few of his products were marked. On the present slender evidence it seems likely that he was working at Plaxtol close to where today there are extensive brickworks.

(4) THE MAMMALIAN BONES FROM THE ROMAN AISLED BUILDING, DARENTH, 1969

By Mary Harman

All the bones from this site were examined. Most were identifiable and in a good state of preservation. Only stratified bones have been considered. The minimum number of animals present is estimated from the most frequently occurring bones of each species, considering also differences in age. The age of the animals at death is based on evidence of the dentition, using figures given by Silver (Ref. 251). Goats may be represented among the sheep, but it has not been possible to distinguish them.

About 200 bones were found in direct association with the Roman aisled building. Of these, five came from the South Ditch and were associated with pottery of about A.D. 200–240. These consisted of the scapula and femur of an ox; the radius of a sheep and parts of the left and right frontals of a red deer, with antlers attached, one sawn off, just above the brow tine, one partly sawn through and then broken off.

The remainder of the bones were from deposits of the later-3rd and early-4th centuries. Table D shows the number of different bones of each species present and the minimum number of the common domestic species. Table E shows the age of the animals at death.

Since the sample is extremely small, it would be unwise to draw conclusions from the relative proportions of the animals, though cattle, pigs and sheep were obviously the most important of the domestic animals. It is likely that red deer were hunted in the surrounding area, since there are bones, as well as the antler fragments, which include utilised pieces.

The skeleton of a human infant, virtually complete, was found buried in the upper part of the filling of the Deep Pit. The left part of the mandible was present, with unerupted deciduous incisor crowns. The infant was probably recently born or foetal at death.

	Cattle		Sheep		Pig	
	L	R	L	R	L	R
Skull						2
Maxilla					2	
Mandible	1	3	3	1	5	1
Scapula	1	3	2	1		1
Humerus		1				
Radius	1	1			2	1
Metacarpal		2	1	1		
Pelvis		2				
Femur	1		1		1	
Tibia		3	1	1	1	1
Metatarsal	2	2	1	1		
Phalanx 1		1				
Totals	25		14		18	
Minimum number of animals	4		4		6	

and Horse:	Mandibular fragment	
	Left and right scapulae	
Dog:	Skull	
	Right mandible	
Red deer:	6 antler fragments	
	Left mandible M 1, 2, 3 in wear	
	Metatarsal shaft fragment	

TABLE D

Frequency of bones from each species present in the 3rd and 4th century deposits and minimum number of animals from those deposits, Darenth, 1969

		Modern figures	Old figures	No. of examples
Cattle	Dm 1, 2, 3, M1 (2 unerupted)	*c.* 1 year	*c.* 1½ years	1
	M1, 2, 3 in wear	Over 2½ years	Over 4½ years	4
Sheep	Dm 1, 2, 3, (M1 erupting)	*c.* 3 m.	*c.* 6 m.	1
	Dm 1, 2, 3, M1, 2	*c.* 1 years	*c.* 1½ years	1
	Pm 2, 3, 4, M1, 2, 3 worn	Over 2 years	Over 4 years	2
Pig	Dm 1, 2, 3	*c.* 3 m.		1
	Dm 1, 2, 3, M1, (2 unerupted)	*c.* 6 m.	*c.* 1 year	1
	Pm 4, M1, 2, (3 unerupted)	*c.* 16 m.	*c.* 2½ years	1
	Pm 1, 2, 3, 4, M1, 2, (3 erupting)	*c.* 18 m.	*c.* 3 years	1
	Pm 1, 2, 3, 4, M1, 2, 3 worn	Over 2 years	Over 3 years	3
	Pm 1, 2, 3, 4 worn, broken	Over 18 m.	Over 2 years	2

TABLE E

Age of animals at death. Tooth eruption and wear. Darenth, 1969

(5) THE HUMAN SKELETON FROM THE ROMAN AISLED BUILDING, DARENTH, 1969

By Mrs. Carole Keepax

This skeleton was found buried in a wooden coffin on the east side of the aisled building (SDV-200). It represents the virtually complete skeleton of an adult female, lacking some bones of the hands and feet and the ends of some long bones. The skull is complete, with hardly any distortion. There is an unusual vascular groove on the right side of the frontal bone. No wormian bones are present. There is a very slight maxillary torus and mandibular torus. The dental formula is:

$$
\begin{array}{ccccccccc|ccccccccc}
 & & \text{OC} & & & & & & & & & & & & \text{OC} & & & \\
8 & 7 & 6 & 5 & 4 & 3 & 2 & 1 & | & 1 & 2 & 3 & 4 & 5 & 6 & 7 & 8 \\
\hline
8 & 7 & 6 & 5 & 4 & \text{/} & \text{/} & \text{/} & | & 1 & 2 & 3 & 4 & 5 & 6 & 7 & 8 \\
\end{array}
$$

/ = post-mortem tooth loss.

Both upper second molars have mild occlusal caries. There are slight calculus deposits associated with **very** slight alveolar recession. There is slight rotation of 1|. Tooth wear is slight, indicating an age between 17 and 25 years. However, some vertebrae (in the middle thoracic region) display a medium degree of osteo-arthritic lipping (mainly on the neural arches). Some of the ribs are also affected. This indicates that an age assessment of about 20–30 years is possibly more realistic.

An interesting anomaly of the sacrum was noted. The first sacral vertebra is unfused on the dorsal side. The neural arch thus formed consists of two parts, which touch but do not join, just to the left of the midline.

The following skull measurements were taken:

Max. length (L)	180 mm.	Palate length (G'1)	43·8 mm.
Max. parietal breadth (B)	132	Zygomatic breadth (J)	125
Min. frontal breadth (B')	93·7	Breadth of rt. orbit (o1')	40·7 (?)
Basio-bregmatic height (H')	130	Ht. of rt. orbit (o2)	34·9
Basion-nasion (LB)	100	Foraminal length (FL)	34·6
Frontal arc (S1)	129	Foraminal breadth (FB)	30·4
Parietal arc (S2)	118	Nasal breadth (NB)	23·5

Occipital arc (S₃)	113	mm.	Nasal height (NH')	49·5 mm.

Occipital arc (S$_3$)	113 mm.	Nasal height (NH')	49·5 mm.
Frontal chord (S'$_1$)	110·2	Simotic chord (SC)	7·9
Parietal chord (S'$_2$)	107·8	Bi-dacryonic chord (DC)	20·5 (?)
Occipital chord (S'$_3$)	96·0	Bi-condylar width (W$_1$)	97(?)
Biasterionic breadth (BiB)	112·5	Least ramus breadth (RB')	30·5
Nasion-alveolar point (G'H)	68·1	Sagittal ht. of mandible (H$_1$)	26·2
Basion-alveolar point (GL)	89·5	Ht. at 2nd molar (M$_2$H)	25·0
Facial breadth (GB)	88·0	Condyle length (CYL)	17·7
Palate breadth (G$_2$)	35·9	Coronoid height (CH)	55·3

(6) THE OTHER FINDS

Antler

Four tools made out of red deer antler were recovered during the 1969 excavations. All came from deposits above the floors of the Period IV aisled building, one each in Rooms 8 and 9 and one each in Rooms 5 and 11. The first two were found in association with 3rd and 4th century pottery in that part of the building abandoned in Period V and the last two were found in association with 4th century material. A fifth antler tool was found during the 1894-5 excavations (Ref. 280).

Of these tools two are hammer-rake heads (Nos. 453 and 455) originally fitted with wooden handles. Almost identical tools have been found at South Shields (Ref. 252) in Roman military contexts and similar antler tools are known from other Roman sites in Britain (Ref. 253). A third antler tool is a small hammer-head (No. 454) originally fitted with a wooden handle and the fourth is probably a handle which still contains part of an iron tang (not illustrated).

Millstones and quernstones

Parts of seven millstones and quernstones were found during the 1969 excavations and of these stones 1–3 were left *in situ*.

Stone 1. Five fragments of a Millstone Grit millstone, or quernstone, were found built into the buttress added to the south-east corner of the Period IV aisled building. It seems likely that a largely complete stone is represented. It is 2–3 in. thick and probably had a diameter of about 2 ft. 6 in. A single fragment of an almost identical stone was found in Room 6.

Stone 2. A single fragment of another Millstone Grit, mill or quernstone, had been built into the south-west corner of the Period IV building. This was about 2·5 in. thick, but of unknown diameter.

Stone 3. Two fragments of a pink sandstone, mill or quernstone, had also been built into the south-west corner of the Period IV building. These represented a stone about 4 in. thick and about 3 ft. in diameter. Another small fragment of a similar stone was found in Room 1.

Stone 4. A large fragment of another Millstone Grit, millstone or quernstone, about 1·5 to 2 in. thick and about 2 ft. 3 in. in diameter, has a central hole about 2 in. wide. The working surface has 15 concentric rings and the other side is roughly tooled. This fragment weighs about 10 lb. 9 oz. and when complete it probably weighed about 35 lb. From Room 9 in association with pottery of the 3rd and 4th centuries (SDV-58).

Stone 5. A fragment of a calcareous sandstone quernstone, perhaps a small lowerstone, is about 1·4 in. thick and about 5·5 in. wide. This piece weighs about 2 lb. 12 oz. and when complete probably weighed about 4 to 6 lb. From the same deposit as No. 4 (SDV-58).

Stone 6. A fragment of a coarse-grained gritstone, probably Millstone Grit, either a millstone or quernstone, is 2 to 2·5 in. thick and at least 1 ft. 10 in. in diameter. It weighs about 14 lb. and when complete it probably weighed between 80 and 100 lb. From an unstratified deposit above the aisled building (SDV-56).

Stone 7. A large piece of a coarse-grained gritstone, again perhaps Millstone Grit, either a millstone or quern-stone, is 2·2 to 2·5 in. thick and has a diameter of at least 2 ft. 5 in. It has a central hole of uncertain width and at least 17 concentric rings on the working surface, the other side being only roughly tooled. This fragment weighs 29 lb. and when complete it probably weighed about 120 lb. From the same deposit as Nos. 4 and 5 (SDV-58).

Bone pins

Only four bone pins were recovered during the 1969 excavations. The broken end of a polished, headless pin at least 2·3 in. in length was found in the filling of the South Ditch. The broken end of an unpolished bone pin with a cone-shaped head at least 1·9 in. long was found in Room 8 in association with 3rd and 4th century pottery. A complete, lightly polished pin with a small oval head and a total length of 3·4 in. was found in Room 9 also in association with 3rd and 4th century pottery. A fourth pin with a finely tapered head and separate collar at least 1·2 in. long was found on the floor at the north end of Room 1.

Iron

About 150 corroded iron objects were recovered from the 1969 excavations. The great majority appear to be iron nails of square section, between 2 and 5 in. in length. Of the rest a single clamp-nail for a box-flue tile, a key and a small hinge, can be identified. None of the ironwork has been treated and none is illustrated.

Glass

Only ten small pieces of Roman glass were found in the 1969 excavations and of these two represent blue-green bottles of rectangular form, but uncertain size. One was unstratified and the other came from the South Ditch. The remaining eight pieces are window-glass. These are either blue-green, pale green or milky-white and represent a maximum of seven window panes. Of these three came from unstratified contexts, three came from outside the aisled building and one was found enclosed in the chalk forming the floor of Room 1. These few fragments are not enough to establish that any of the structures had glass windows.

Bronze Spoon

A small bronze spoon, slightly bent and with a damaged bowl, was found in the filling of the ditch running under the east side of the bath-building. The handle is circular in section, tapered and 3·9 in. long. The bowl is circular, cupped and 0·9 in. in diameter. There are traces of silvering on both sides of the bowl and on the adjacent part of the handle (SDV-11).

Catalogue of the Illustrated Finds from the Roman Aisled Building Darenth, 1969 (Figs. 42–46)

From Beneath Period III Ramp (SDV-118)

No. 312. Cooking-pot with bead rim of sandy ware. Grey paste and orange-brown surface. 2nd century.

No. 313. Dish with bead rim of sandy ware. Grey paste and surface. Chamfered base and traces of burnishing. This is one of a range of vessels introduced early in the 2nd century, but tending to become coarse, thicker and with much more pronounced rims at the end of the century. Often regarded as Antonine, but found at Reculver (Ref. 254) and Faversham (Ref. 255) in contexts of the early-3rd century. In Northern Britain vessels of this type are dated A.D. 190–240 (Ref. 256). Gillam Type 313.

From Fill of South Ditch (SDV-110 and 111)

No. 314. Cooking-pot with cavetto rim of sandy ware. Grey paste and surface.

No. 315. Dish with bead rim of sandy ware. Grey-brown paste and grey-black surface. Burnished all over. Probably A.D. 200–240.

No. 316. Cooking-pot with everted rim of sandy ware. Grey-brown paste and surface. This type of rim was found in direct association with the bead rim dishes (No. 313 above) at both Reculver and Faversham, both dated to the early-3rd century. In Northern Britain they occur in deposits dated A.D. 160–280 (Gillam Type 143/144).

No. 317. Dish with bead rim of sandy ware. Grey-brown paste and grey surface. Burnished all over and decorated with burnished diagonal lines. Probably A.D. 200–240, but here the faint curve in the wall is unusual.

No. 318. Beaker with outcurved rim of Castor ware. White paste and black-brown surface. Probably 3rd century.

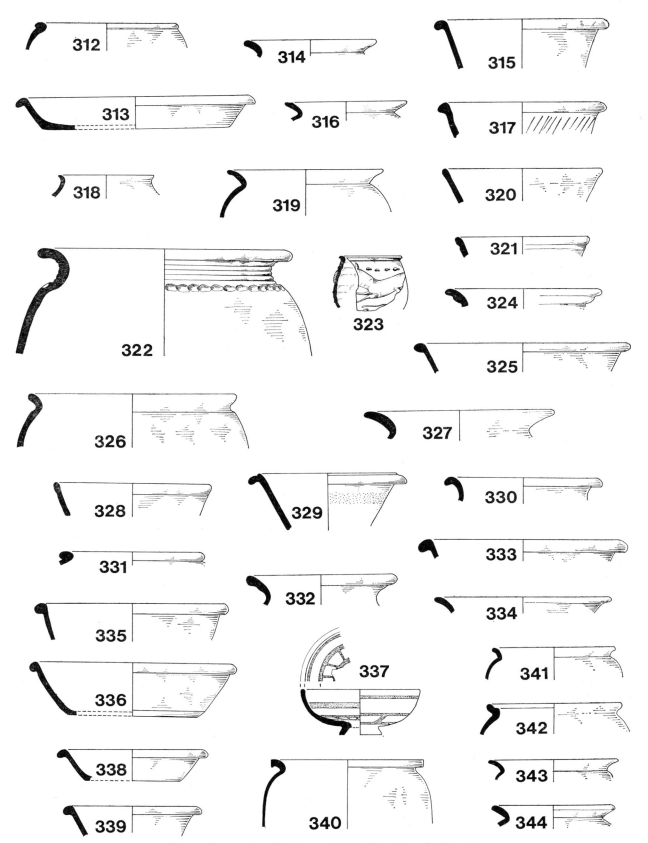

Fig. 42. *Coarse pottery* (¼), *Roman aisled building, Darenth (Site 21)*.

No. 319. Cooking-pot with everted rim of sandy ware. Grey paste and grey-black surface. Burnished on shoulder and inside rim. Again mostly a late-2nd, or early-3rd, century type.

No. 320. Dish with straight side and upright rim of sandy ware. Grey paste and surface. Slight trace of burnishing. These straight-sided dishes occur frequently in association with both the bead rim dish (as No. 313) and the everted rim cooking-pots (as No. 316), as at both Reculver and Faversham. At Brixworth (Ref. 257) they occur in Antonine contexts and in Northern Britain (Gillam Type 328) they are dated A.D. 150–200. The 2nd and early-3rd century examples are generally well-fired, finer and usually much thinner than the later 3rd-century types which developed from this form.

No. 321. Dish with straight side and upright rim of sandy ware. Grey paste and surface. Small groove below rim and traces of white slip. Probably late-2nd, or early-3rd, century.

No. 322. Storage jar with outcurved rim of Patch Grove ware. Mottled grey-black paste and orange-buff surface. Three faint cordons on neck and stabbing on shoulder. The somewhat flattened profile of this vessel suggests that it is late in the Patch Grove series and probably dates to the second half of the 2nd century A.D.

From Beneath Floor of Room 1 (SDV-107)

No. 323. Hunt-cup with cornice rim of Castor ware. Cream paste with brown surface. Applied decoration depicting running animal framed between rows of studs. Probably late-2nd, or early-3rd, century (Gillam Type 85).

From Beneath Floor of Room 2 (SDV-113)

No. 324. Cooking-pot with everted, thickened rim of sandy ware. Grey paste and surface.
No. 325. Dish with bead rim of sandy ware. Grey paste and grey-brown surface. Similar to No. 315, probably A.D. 200–240.

From Floor of Room 8 (SDV-33)

No. 326. Cooking-pot with outcurved rim of sandy ware. Grey paste and surface. Burnished rim and shoulder.
No. 327. Cooking-pot with everted rim of sandy ware. Grey paste and grey-brown surface. A more developed version of No. 316 and probably dating to the first half of the 3rd century. At Leicester (Ref. 258) this type of vessel seems to have appeared at about A.D. 200.
No. 328. Dish with straight side and upright rim of sandy ware. Grey paste and surface. Faint external groove. Probably late-2nd, or early-3rd, century.
No. 329. Dish with flanged rim of sandy ware. Grey paste and grey-black surface. Burnished exterior except for band below rim. This vessel may be the prototype of the common flanged dishes of the late-3rd and 4th centuries. Here the vessel is well-fired and thin-walled, in contrast to many of the later versions, whilst the flange springs virtually from the rim. Although sometimes described as Antonine vessels of this particular type are not common in Antonine deposits at Dover and Reculver, where they seem to have superceded the bead-rim dish by the middle of the 3rd century. Probably A.D. 200–250.
No. 330. Cooking-pot with slightly outcurved angular rim of sandy ware. Grey-brown paste and surface. Burnished neck and rim.
No. 331. Cooking-pot with bead rim of sandy ware. Grey paste and surface. A 2nd century type probably a rubbish survival.
No. 332. Cooking-pot with slightly thickened cavetto rim of sandy ware. Grey paste and surface. Burnished neck and rim.
No. 333. Dish with bead rim of sandy ware. Grey paste and surface. Again probably A.D. 200–240.
No. 334. Cooking-pot with everted rim of sandy ware. Grey paste and surface.

From Debris in Room 9 (SDV-36, 56 and 62)

No. 335. Dish with bead rim of sandy ware. Grey paste and grey-black surface. Traces of burnishing all over. Probably A.D. 200–240.
No. 336. Dish with bead rim of sandy ware. Grey-brown paste and surface. Chamfered base and burnished all over. Probably the same date as No. 335.
No. 337. Bowl with upright rim of hard smooth ware. White paste and surface with orange-brown slip decoration inside and out. Not common and perhaps a product of the Nene Valley potteries of the 3rd, or 4th, century.
No. 338. Dish with bead rim of sandy ware. Black-brown paste and black surface. Chamfered base and curved wall. Probably A.D. 200–240.
No. 339. Dish with bead rim of sandy ware. Grey paste and grey-brown surface.
No. 340. Cooking-pot with outcurved, squared rim of sandy ware. Grey paste and grey-brown surface. This is a common type frequently occurring in direct association with the bead rim (as No. 313) and straight-sided dishes and the everted rim cooking-pots (as No. 316) as found at Faversham and in the early-3rd century fort-construction period at Reculver. It also occurs in late-2nd century deposits at Verulamium (Ref. 259) and in pottery kilns Nos. 27 and 28 at Colchester (Ref. 260).
No. 341. Jar or cooking-pot with outcurved rim of sandy ware. Grey-brown paste and surface.
No. 342. Jar or cooking-pot with recessed rim of sandy ware. Grey-brown paste with grey-black surface. In Northern Britain in deposits dated A.D. 140–260 (Gillam Types 150/151).
No. 343. Jar or small cooking-pot with everted rim of sandy ware. Grey-brown paste and surface. Similar to No. 316.
No. 344. Jar or small cooking-pot with everted rim of sandy ware. Grey paste and surface. A thicker version of No. 343.
No. 345. Mortarium with downturned flange of sandy ware. White paste and surface and coarse black and white grit. Two faint incised lines on flange. Late-2nd century (Gillam Type 265 and Colchester Form 497).

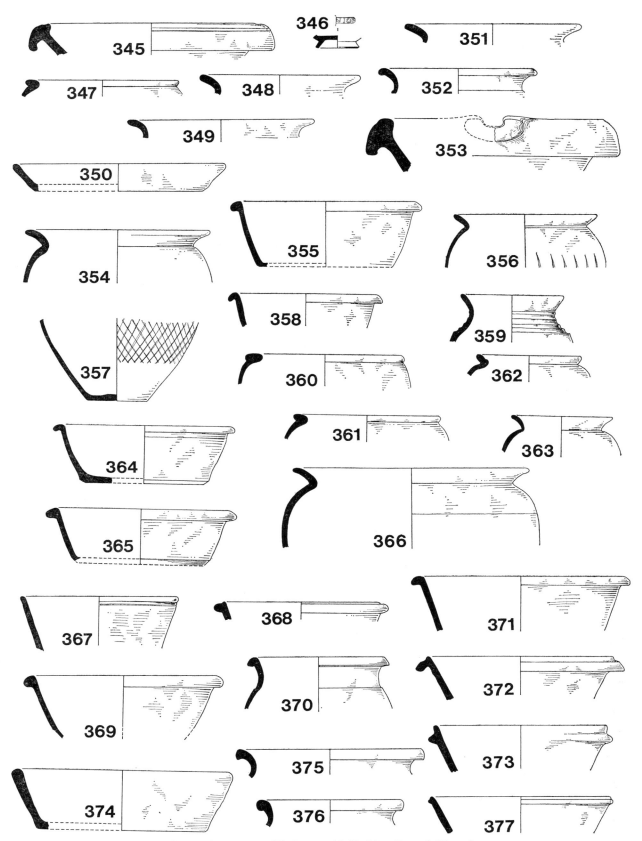

Fig. 43. *Coarse pottery* ($\frac{1}{4}$), *Roman aisled building, Darenth (Site 21).*

No. 346. Base of cup of samian ware (perhaps Form 33). Stamped JANI OF. Probably mid-2nd century.

No. 347. Cooking-pot with bead rim of sandy ware. Grey paste and surface. 2nd century.

No. 348. Cooking-pot with cavetto rim of sandy ware. Grey paste and surface.

No. 349. Cooking-pot with cavetto rim of sandy ware. Grey paste and surface.

No. 350. Dish with straight side and upright rim of sandy ware. Grey paste and surface. Probably early-3rd century.

From Black Loam Under East Drain (SDV-44)

No. 351. Cooking-pot with cavetto rim of sandy ware. Grey-brown paste, black-brown surface and exterior burnishing. Late-2nd, or early-3rd, century.

No. 352. Jar with outcurved thickened rim of sandy ware. Grey-brown paste and black surface. Burnished exterior.

No. 353. Mortarium with downturned flange of fine, soft ware. Cream paste and surface. Part of spout, grit uncertain. Late-2nd, or 3rd, century (Colchester Forms 498 and 499).

No. 354. Cooking-pot with everted rim of sandy ware. Grey-brown paste and surface. Burnished exterior. Similar to Nos. 319 and 327. Probably late-2nd, or early-3rd, century.

No. 355. Dish with bead rim of sandy ware. Grey paste and grey-brown surface. Chamfered base and burnished all over. Probably A.D. 200-240.

No. 356. Cooking-pot with everted rim of sandy ware. Grey-brown paste and surface. Burnished exterior, inside rim and vertical lines.

No. 357. Cooking-pot of sandy ware. Grey paste and surface. Burnished acute lattice pattern.

No. 358. Dish with downturned rim of sandy ware. Grey-brown paste and grey-black surface. A variant of the bead rim dish and probably of 3rd century date.

No. 359. Small jar with narrow outcurved rim of Patch Grove ware. Mottled grey-black paste and buff-black surface. Series of faint cordons on neck. Probably 2nd century.

No. 360. Cooking-pot with bead rim of sandy ware. Grey-brown paste and surface. 2nd century.

No. 361. Cooking-pot with bead rim of sandy ware. Grey-brown paste and surface. 2nd century.

No. 362. Jar or cooking-pot with recessed rim of sandy ware. Grey-brown paste and brown surface. A smaller version of No. 342. In Northern Britain dated to A.D. 140-260.

No. 363. Jar with everted rim of sandy ware. Grey-brown paste and grey surface. Traces of burnishing. Similar to No. 343.

No. 364. Dish with flanged rim of sandy ware. Grey-brown paste and grey-black surface. Chamfered base and black slip below rim.

No. 365. Dish with large bead rim. Grey-brown paste and surface. Probably A.D. 200-240.

No. 366. Cooking-pot with everted rim of sandy ware. Grey-brown paste and surface. Similar to No. 327. Probably first half of 3rd century.

From Black Loam Over East Drain (SDV-105)

No. 367. Dish with straight side and upright rim of sandy ware. Black-brown paste and surface. Burnished all over and faint incised grooves beneath rim. A slightly thinner and finer version of No. 328. Probably late-2nd, or early-3rd, century.

No. 368. Dish with rounded flanged rim of sandy ware. Grey paste and grey-brown surface. Burnished all over. This vessel appears to be the transitional type between the bead rim dish (as No. 313) and the more normal, thinner flanged dish (as No. 329).

No. 369. Dish with bead rim of sandy ware. Grey-brown paste and yellow-brown surface. Burnished all over. Probably A.D. 200-240.

From Primary Filling of Deep Pit (SDV-78)

No. 370. Jar with slightly outcurved, angular rim of sandy ware. Grey-brown paste and surface.

From Upper Filling of Deep Pit (SDV-79)

No. 371. Dish with bead rim of sandy ware. Grey-brown paste and black-brown surface. Burnished all over. Probably A.D. 200-240.

No. 372. Dish with downturned flanged rim of sandy ware. Grey-brown paste and grey surface. Traces of burnishing all over. This is an example of the fully developed flanged dish common in the later-3rd and 4th centuries, probably evolving from the earlier bead rim dish. The downturned, somewhat flattened flanged rim is similar to others from Leicester (Ref. 261) in late-3rd and 4th century contexts and at Brixworth (Ref. 262) also in late-3rd and the first half of the 4th century deposits.

No. 373. Dish with tapered flanged rim of sandy ware. Grey paste and grey-black surface. Traces of burnishing all over. A coarser version of No. 372, but with a lower more angular flange. Common 4th century type.

No. 374. Dish with thickened upright rim of calcite-gritted ware. Black paste and orange-brown surface. A much coarser version of the straight-sided dish of the late-2nd and early-3rd centuries. Similar vessels occur in Northern Britain in the contexts of the mid 4th century (Gillam Types 330 and 333).

No. 375. Cooking-pot with cavetto thickened rim of sandy ware. Grey paste and surface.

No. 376. Cooking-pot with outcurved thickened rim of sandy ware. Grey paste and surface. Slight trace of burnishing.

No. 377. Dish with token flanged rim of sandy ware. Grey paste and surface. Not common, probably 4th century.

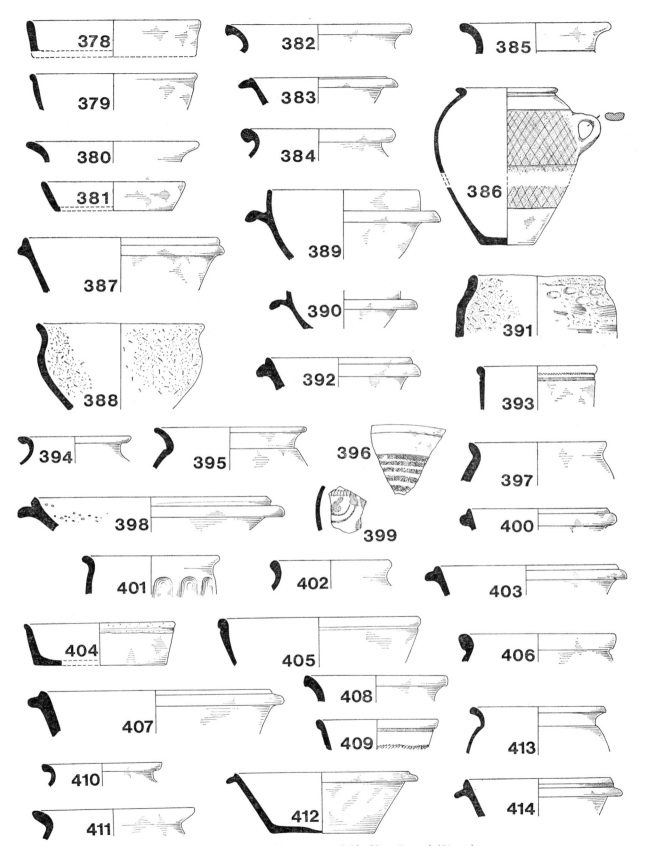

Fig. 44. *Coarse pottery* (¼), *Roman aisled building, Darenth (Site 21).*

From Floor of Room 11 (SDV-90)

No. 378. Dish with straight side and upright rim of colour-coated ware. Orange-grey paste and orange-black surface. A faint projection on the inside could be the beginning of the wall returning at an angle which would suggest that this was in fact a bowl with a vertical wall in imitation of samian Form 45. Fourth century as at Richborough (Ref. 263).

No. 379. Dish or bowl with slightly beaded rim of colour-coated ware. Orange paste and surface.

No. 380. Cooking-pot with everted rim of sandy ware. Grey paste and grey-brown surface. Burnished externally and inside rim.

No. 381. Shallow dish with straight side and upright rim of sandy ware. Grey paste and grey-black surface. Burnished all over. A later version of the straight-sided dish of the late-2nd and early-3rd centuries.

No. 382. Cooking-pot with outcurved, squared rim of sandy ware. Grey paste and surface. A more developed version of No. 340, frequently occurring with the bead rim and straight-sided dishes of the late-2nd and early-3rd centuries.

No. 383. Dish with flanged rim of sandy ware. Grey paste and surface. Burnished all over. Another example of the common flanged dish of all late-3rd and 4th centuries as at Colchester (Form 305) and Brixworth (Nos. 41 to 45).

No. 384 Jar with thickened, rolled rim of sandy ware. Grey-brown paste and grey surface. A common type with a wide date-range. Early-2nd to 4th centuries.

From Floor of Room 1, Southern Area (SDV 77 and 84)

No. 385. Cooking-pot with cavetto rim of sandy ware. Grey paste and orange-grey surface.

No. 386. Jar with small beaded rim of sandy ware. Grey paste and grey-black surface. Burnished base, rim and shoulder and zones of burnished, acute lattice pattern and slightly countersunk handle. This vessel seems to be out of context with most of the rest of the pottery from this site. Its near parallels at Brixworth (No. 173) and in Northern Britain (Gillam Types 118 and 126) are all dated to the first half of the 2nd century.

No. 387. Dish with tapered flanged rim of sandy ware. Grey paste and grey surface. Similar to No. 373 dated to the late-3rd and 4th centuries.

No. 388. Hand-made cooking-pot with slightly outcurved rim of sandy ware. Grey-black paste and black surface. Traces of external burnishing. Probably late-4th century.

No. 389. Bowl with upright rim and downturned flange of colour-coated ware. Orange-grey paste and orange surface coated with an orange-red slip. In imitation of samian Form 38 and dated to the second half of the 4th century in Northern Britain (Gillam Types 204–206) and Colchester (Form 316).

No. 390. Bowl with downturned flange of colour-coated ware, slightly smaller than No. 389. Second half of 4th century.

No. 391. Hand-made cooking-pot with irregular, thickened rim of sandy ware. Grey-black paste and grey-brown surface. Broadly similar to No. 388 and probably dating to the second half of the 4th century. If these vessels had not been found in association with Roman pottery they might have been regarded as Anglo-Saxon and of 5th century date.

From Floor of Room 2 (SDV-92 and 98)

No. 392. Bowl with beaded flanged rim of sandy ware. Buff paste and surface. Similar to No. 407. Probably 4th century.

No. 393. Bowl with small bead rim of colour-coated ware. Orange paste and surface with orange-red slip. Rouletting under rim and along groove below rim. Probably in imitation of samian Form 37 and of late-3rd, or 4th, century date.

No. 394. Jar with outcurved, slightly thickened rim of sandy ware. Grey-brown paste and surface.

No. 395. Cooking-pot with everted rim of sandy ware. Grey paste and grey-black surface. Burnished externally and inside rim. A common type in Northern Britain from A.D. 160–280 (Gillam Type 143–144).

No. 396. Bowl with upright beaded rim of colour-coated ware. Orange paste and surface with orange-red slip and geometric patterns. In imitation of samian Form 37. Found in Kent at Canterbury (Ref. 264) and Richborough (Refs. 265 and 266). Second half of 4th century. Argonne Ware.

No. 397. Hand-made cooking-pot with out-turned rim of calcite-gritted ware. Grey paste and grey-black surface.

No. 398. Mortarium with flanged rim of fine soft ware. Cream paste and surface and coarse red and white grits. A common 4th century form.

No. 399. Wall-sherd of beaker of colour-coated ware. Orange paste and black slip decorated with applied white decoration and band of rouletting. Similar vessels with this applied decoration occur in late-3rd century deposits at Reculver.

No. 400. Dish with beaded flanged rim of sandy ware. Grey paste and black surface with traces of burnishing. A slightly thickened version of No. 387 dated to the late-3rd and 4th centuries.

No. 401. Squat bowl with outcurved rim of colour-coated ware. Orange-grey paste and orange slip. Similar to the bowls at Richborough (Ref. 267, Forms 476 to 479) dated to the second half of the 4th century.

From Floor of Room 5 (SDV-91)

No. 402. Jar with outcurved, thickened rim of sandy ware. Grey-brown paste and grey surface with traces of external burnishing.

No. 403. Dish with flanged rim of sandy ware. Grey paste and surface with traces of burnishing. Late-3rd to 4th centuries.

No. 404. Dish with straight side and upright rim of sandy ware. Grey paste and grey-black burnished surface and burnished lines on base. This is the much later and coarser version of the straight sided dish as No. 320. Late-3rd, or 4th, century.

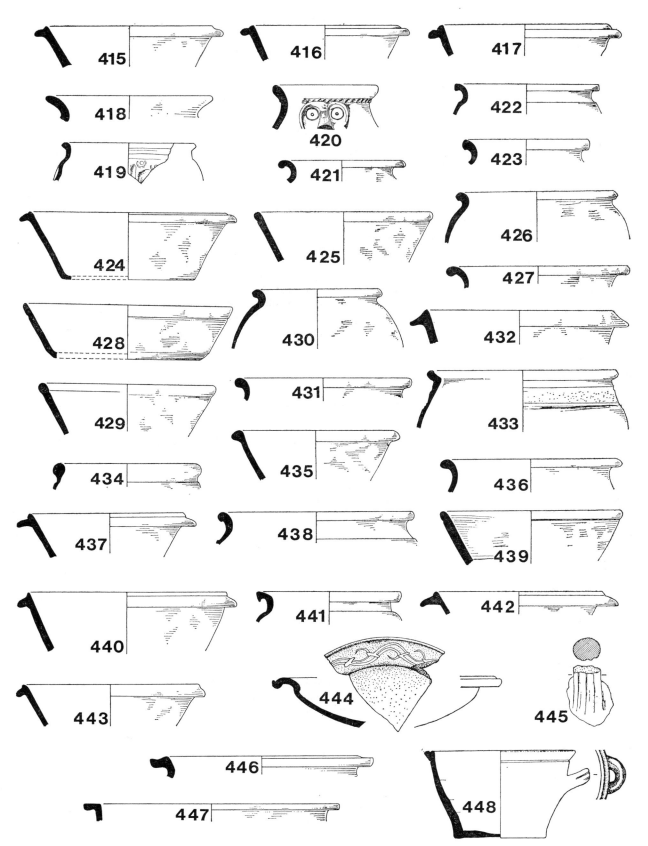

Fig. 45. Coarse pottery (¼), Roman aisled building, Darenth (Site 21).

No. 405. Bowl with slightly beaded rim of colour-coated ware. Orange-grey paste and surface coated with orange-red slip. Faint groove below rim. In imitation of samian Form 37 and broadly similar to No. 396, but not decorated. Second half of 4th century.

No. 406. Jar with ovoid rim of colour-coated ware. Orange paste and slip. Faint groove below rim.

No. 407. Dish with thickened flanged rim of sandy ware. Grey-brown paste, grey-black surface and burnished all over. Late-3rd, or 4th, century.

No. 408. Jar with outcurved squared rim of sandy ware. Grey paste and grey-brown surface.

No. 409. Bowl with upright, slightly beaded rim of colour-coated ware. Orange paste and surface with traces of red slip. Bands of rouletting below rim and on body. Similar to Nos. 379 and 393 in imitation of samian Form 37. Late-3rd, or 4th, century.

No. 410. Jar with outcurved thickened rim of sandy ware. Grey paste and surface.

No. 411. Jar with out-turned thickened rim of sandy ware. Orange-brown paste and surface.

From Floor of Room 6 (SDV-89)

No. 412. Dish with slightly downturned, flanged rim of sandy ware. Grey-brown paste and grey-black surface, burnished all over. Similar to No. 383. Second half of 3rd and 4th centuries.

No. 413. Cooking-pot with cavetto rim of sandy ware. Grey paste and surface with faint incision at junction of neck and shoulder. Similar to a vessel found at Corbridge (Gillam Type 142) dated A.D. 190–280.

No. 414. Dish with slightly downturned flanged rim of sandy ware. Grey paste and surface and burnished all over. A moderately finely finished vessel, probably dating to the late-3rd, or early-4th, century.

No. 415. Dish with flanged rim of sandy ware. Orange paste and surface with traces of burnishing all over.

No. 416. Dish with flanged rim of sandy ware. Orange paste and surface with traces of burnishing all over.

From Floor of Room 1, Northern Area (SDV-75)

No. 417. Dish with slightly downturned, flanged rim of sandy ware. Grey-brown paste and black surface and traces of burnishing. Late-3rd, or 4th, century.

No. 418. Cooking-pot with outcurved rim of calcite-gritted or shell-loaded ware. Grey-brown paste and black-brown surface with traces of burnishing.

No. 419. Bowl with outcurved, thickened rim of sandy ware. Grey-brown paste and burnished black surface. Side indented, grooved and decorated with circular impressions. Similar to those vessels described (Ref. 268) as Romano-Saxon of the second half of the 4th century.

From Filling of West Drain (SDV 31, 59, 65 and 67)

No. 420. Face-urn with outcurved rim of sandy ware. Grey-orange paste and orange surface. Face applied to neck and indented decoration under rim. Very similar vessels were being produced in kilns at Colchester during the 2nd and perhaps the 3rd centuries (Ref. 269).

No. 421. Cooking-pot with rolled rim of sandy ware. Grey-brown paste and grey-black surface with traces of burnishing.

No. 422. Cooking-pot with outcurved, squared rim of sandy ware. Grey-brown paste and grey surface. Similar to No. 340. Late-2nd, or early-3rd, century.

No. 423. Cooking-pot with thickened, cavetto rim of sandy ware. Grey paste and surface.

No. 424. Dish with slightly downturned flanged rim of sandy ware. Grey-brown paste, grey-black surface and burnished all over. Similar to Nos. 383 and 412. Second half of 3rd and 4th centuries.

No. 425. Dish with straight side and upright rim of sandy ware. Grey-brown paste and black surface, burnished all over. Very similar to No. 367 and probably late-2nd, or early-3rd, century.

No. 426. Cooking-pot with outcurved, thickened rim of sandy ware. Grey-brown paste and surface with traces of external burnishing.

No. 427. Cooking-pot with outcurved, thickened rim of sandy ware. Grey-brown paste with brown surface.

Nos. 428 and 429. Dishes with straight sides and upright rims of sandy ware. Grey-brown paste and grey surface. Faint grooves on each side of rim and the former burnished. Probably early-3rd century.

No. 430. As 426.

No. 431. Cooking-pot with outcurved, thickened rim of sandy ware. Grey paste and surface with traces of burnishing.

No. 432. Dish with downturned, tapered flanged rim of sandy ware. Grey paste with grey-brown surface. Traces of burnishing. An unusual variant of the normal flanged bowl, similar to one found at Leicester (Ref. 270) and there dated to the early-3rd century.

No. 433. Cooking-pot with upturned, recessed rim of sandy ware. Grey paste and surface. Burnished bands on exterior. A finely finished vessel belonging to the range of recessed rim cooking-pots of the 2nd and 3rd centuries.

No. 434. Cooking-pot with rounded rim of sandy ware. Grey-brown paste with grey-black surface. Burnished rim. Similar to No. 402.

No. 435. Dish with beaded rim of sandy ware. Grey-brown paste and grey surface with traces of burnishing. Probably A.D. 200–240.

Plate XB. *The successive floors in the central part of the aisled building, with the rod marking the Period III floor. Darenth Roman Villa, Darenth (Site 21)*

Plate XA. *The east side of the hall of the Period IV aisled building showing the brick piers and two of the bays (one subsequently blocked). Darenth Roman Villa, Darenth (Site 21)*

Plate XIB. *The large corn-drying oven in Room 3 of the aisled building. Darenth Roman Villa, Darenth (Site 21)*

Plate XIA. *The foundation of the south wall of the Period III structure partially buried by the tiled floor of the Period IV eastern aisle (Room 5). Darenth Roman Villa, Darenth (Site 21)*

Plate XIIB. *The East Drain just outside the east wall of the aisled building showing the wooden trough-shaped lining. Darenth Roman Villa, Darenth (Site 21)*

Plate XIIA. *The east aisle (Room 5) of the Period IV aisled building showing the tiled floor sealing the Period III foundation (nearest rod), sealing the South Ditch (under second rod) with the Period V cross-wall in the foreground. Darenth Roman Villa, Darenth (Site 21)*

No. 436. Cooking-pot with outcurved, thickened rim of sandy ware. Grey-brown paste and grey surface with traces of burnishing. Similar to No. 431.

No. 437. Dish with wide flanged rim of sandy ware. Grey paste and surface and burnished all over. Similar to Nos. 414 and 383. Second half of the 3rd, or 4th, century.

No. 438. Cooking-pot with outcurved, thickened rim of sandy ware. Grey paste and surface. Burnished externally and on inside rim, with faint cordon on shoulder. Similar to Nos. 431 and 436.

No. 439. Dish with straight side and upright rim of sandy ware. Grey paste, grey-brown surface and burnished all over. Small groove below rim. Similar to Nos. 428 and 429. Probably 3rd century.

Nos. 440, 442 and 443. Dishes with flanged rims of sandy ware. Grey paste, grey or grey-brown surfaces, burnished all over. Late-3rd, or 4th, century.

No. 441. Cooking-pot with squared rim of sandy ware. Grey-brown paste and grey surface. Similar to Nos. 340 and 422. Late-2nd, or early-3rd, century.

From Room 2 (SDV-98)
No. 444. Bowl with outcurved flanged rim of colour-coated ware. Grey paste, orange surface with orange-red slip and white slip scroll decoration on flange. In imitation of samian Form 36. Similar to vessels at Richborough (Ref. 271) where they are dated to the late-3rd, or 4th, century.

Unstratified (SDV-29)
No. 445. Rod-handle of large jug of sandy ware. Grey paste and buff surface with patchy green and yellow glaze. Medieval, late-13th, or 14th, century.

From Medieval Layers in Area North of Grave (SDV-52)
No. 446. Cooking-pot with horizontal rim of shell-loaded ware. Grey paste and grey surface. Medieval, 14th century (Ref. 272).

Unstratified from Villa Site (SDV-49)
No. 447. Cooking-pot with horizontal rim of shell-loaded ware. Grey-brown paste and black surface. Medieval, 13th century (Ref. 273).

From Pit B in Room 8 (SDV-60)
No. 448. Handled dish with upright, thickened reeded rim of sandy ware. Orange paste, mottled surface with traces of brown glaze. Top of rim and interior completely glazed. Late-17th, or early-18th, century (Ref. 274).

No. 451. Double-sided bone comb with teeth of varying thickness. Central part probably made in several pieces held by a lateral bone strip on each side and secured by five iron rivets. There is a simple incised pattern on both sides and a pair of functional notches at each end. Similar double-sided combs occur frequently on Roman and early-Saxon sites. From the rubble inside the Roman bath-building (SDV-6). Probably 3rd century.

No. 452. Fragment of a tile-voussoir decorated by means of a roller-die. Compass and chevron design as Lowther Group 4 (Ref. 250). The compass pattern is slightly oval and either too much pressure was applied to the roller or the pattern distorted in firing. From black loam and flints in Room 7 (SDV-48).

No. 453. Antler tool forming combined hammer and rake, made from the base of a red deer antler. The main stem has been sawn to create the hammer-head and a rectangular hole chiselled out to take a wooden handle. Both the rake tines and the hammer-head are polished through use. From Room 9 in direct association with material of the late-3rd and 4th centuries (SDV-58).

No. 454. Antler tool forming a two-sided hammer-head, probably from another red deer antler. A rectangular socket has been chiselled out to take a wooden handle, in turn fixed by a lateral pin pushed through small circular holes. Each end damaged by use. From the floor of Room 5 (SDV-91). Found in association with 4th century pottery and a coin.

No. 455. Antler two-pronged, rake made from the base of a red deer antler. A rectangular socket has been chiselled out to take a wooden handle and both tines cut at about 45°. Damaged and slightly worn. From floor of Room 11 (SDV-93). Probably 4th century A.D.

Nos. 456 and 457. Two joining sides of a tile-voussoir 6·4 in. wide at the tapered end. The name CABRIABANVS has been applied to both external faces by means of a cylindrical die. One side (No. 456) has the name applied twice, the lower line being partly erased by the second sweep and it is clear that the same roller was used in each case. On the second side (No. 457) the upper line and the letters along the bottom are illegible, but the same bold CABRIABA has been rolled across the centre (see separate report above). Found in black loam deposit just east of the aisled building with pottery dating to about A.D. 200. Unworn, no trace of mortar on any surface and perhaps never used in a building (SDV-43).

No. 458. Graffito on small pot-base, probably a domestic cooking-pot, of sandy grey paste and buff-brown surface. Examined by Mr. R. P. Wright who suggests that it reads VITIA X and that this is likely to read 'Vitia, her mark'. From floor of Room 2 (SDV-98). Found in association with 4th century coins.

No. 459. Damaged, lower part of a pottery candle-stick of coarse grey-black ware with black-brown surface. From West Drain (SDV-59). Associated with 3rd and 4th century pottery.

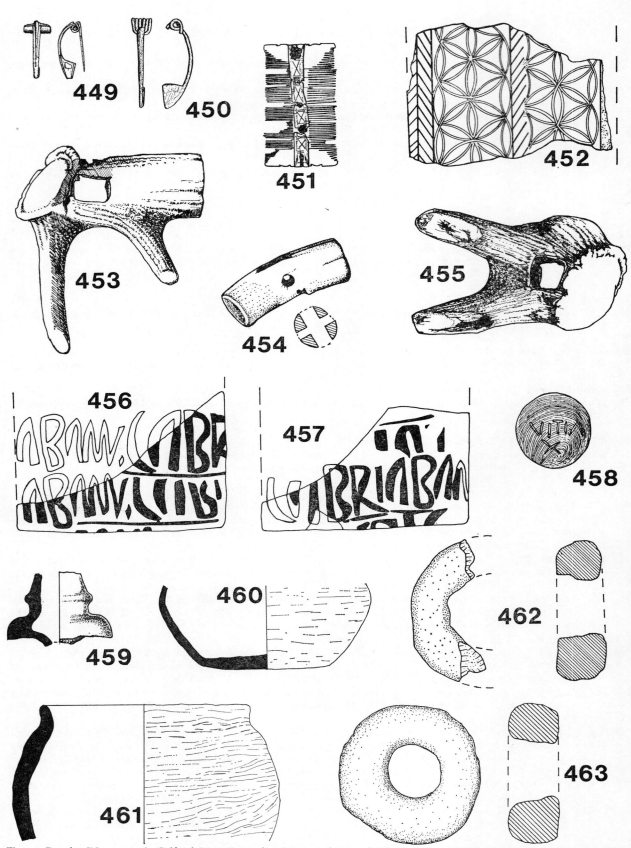

Fig. 46. Brooches (Nos. 449–50), Calfstock Lane, Farningham (Site 19); bone comb (No. 451), flue-tiles (Nos. 452, 456–7), antler tools (Nos. 453–5) and pottery (Nos. 458–9), Roman aisled building, Darenth (Site 21); pottery (Nos. 460–1) and loom-weights (Nos. 462–3) (⅓), Saxon occupation-site, Darenth (Site 22).

SITE 22. An Anglo-Saxon Occupation-site at Darenth, Kent

This site (N.G.R. TQ.5634.7064) lies within the limits of the well-known Roman villa (Ref. 275) in the parish of Darenth, Kent about ½ a mile south of the parish church and on the east bank of the River Darent (O.S. parcel 3368). It was discovered by the Group on 13th April, 1969 during the excavation of a small trial-hole aimed at checking the relationship of the Roman bath-building (Ref. 276), then under excavation (Site 21), with those structures found by George Payne in 1894–5. The trial-hole located, as planned, the north-east corner of the long building (termed 'Room 65') at the south-west corner of the villa complex uncovered by George Payne (Fig. 36). A small group of unstratified objects was recovered immediately to the north-east of this point which, on examination, proved to contain both Roman and Saxon material. Grateful thanks are due to Mr. W. F. Jeffries for drawing the illustrated finds from this site (Fig. 46).

The Saxon finds include parts of two pots (Nos. 460–1) and parts of at least two loom-weights (Nos. 462–3), one very fragmentary. The pots are coarse, hand-made vessels with grass tempering and have at least partially rounded bases. The larger one is broadly similar to several found in the Anglo-Saxon cemetery at Orpington (Ref. 277), only six miles to the south-west, which are either 5th or 6th century. Unfortunately, neither vessel is decorated nor has very distinctive characteristics, but Dr. J. N. L. Myres has kindly examined some of the sherds and tentatively suggested a 6th century date. He has also added that the sherds could possibly represent three different vessels.

The loom-weights are the typical quoit-shaped ones commonly found on early Saxon sites. A *grubenhaus* at Upton, Northants (Ref. 278) produced more than 60, where they were dated to the late-6th, or early-7th, century. A hut at Mucking, Essex (Ref. 279) contained clay loom-weights of similar form and these have been dated to the 6th or 7th centuries.

The evidence, though slight, is quite positive and suggests beyond all reasonable doubt that the Roman villa site at Darenth was occupied for at least part of the pagan-Saxon period. This is confirmed by some of the material from the original excavation now in Rochester Museum, kindly made available by Mr. I. M. Moad. Of particular interest is a fine antler needle (Ref. 280) almost identical to needles from the Saxon *grubenhaus* at Lower Warbank, Keston (Site 23) and another from a site at Dartford (Ref. 281), both probably 6th century in date. Final confirmation of Saxon settlement on the villa site was recovered during the rescue-excavations by the CIB Archaeological Rescue Corps in 1972 (report in preparation). No attempt is made here to consider the implications of this site, nor its relationship with other early Saxon sites in the county, as this is being done elsewhere.

Catalogue of the Illustrated Finds from the Saxon site at Darenth (Fig. 46)

No. 460. Cooking-pot of coarse grass-tempered ware with black paste, buff-brown surface and slightly sagging base. From the villa site (SDV-26). Probably 6th century.

No. 461. Cooking-pot of coarse grass-tempered ware with black paste, smooth buff-brown surface and simple upright rim. From the villa site (SDV-26). Probably 6th century.

No. 462. About half of a baked-clay loom-weight with a black paste and buff surface. Sub-circular in section, about 5 in. in overall diameter and weighs about 6 oz. From the villa site (SDV-26). Found in association with Nos. 460 and 461 and a common Saxon type, probably 6th century.

No. 463. A complete baked-clay loom-weight with red-brown surface, similar to No. 462. Circular, with a diameter of 4·5 in., central perforation 1·7 to 2 in. and weighs about 13 oz. From the villa site (SDV-26). Found in association with Nos. 460–2, probably 6th century.

SITE 23. An Anglo-Saxon Hut at Lower Warbank, Keston, Kent

This site (N.G.R. TQ.4142.6322) lies in Lower Warbank Field (O.S. parcel 4518) on Keston Court Farm, about a ¼ of a mile north-west of the parish church. It lies in an open field about 200 ft. from the north hedge and about 130 ft. from the west hedge (Fig. 47). The site is on a broad south-facing slope on Upper Chalk at about 425 ft. O.D.

The site was discovered in June, 1970 during the seasonal training-excavation on the Roman villa and Iron Age sites in the same field due to be destroyed by Ringway 3. The training scheme, which started in 1968, is run jointly by the West Kent Group and the London Borough of Bromley. The nearby Roman cemetery, contain-

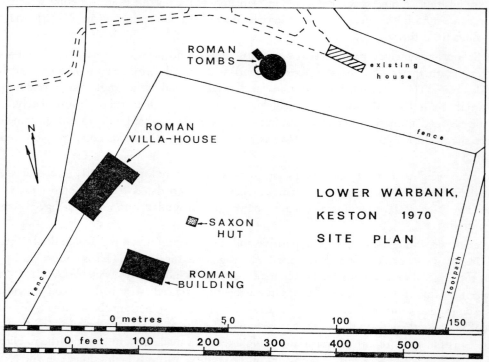

Fig. 47. *Plan showing site of Saxon hut and Roman structures, Lower Warbank, Keston (Site 23).*

ing monumental tombs and excavated by the Group in 1967–8 (Ref. 282) lies about 250 ft. to the north. The discovery of the Saxon hut (Ref. 283), at the extreme edge of the training-site was the first positive archaeological evidence of Saxon settlement found in the parish of Keston. Other Saxon huts may await discovery nearby. The Group gratefully acknowledges the help and interest of Mr. A. G. Lockley Cook; Miss M. Harman for her report on the skeletal material and Dr. J. N. L. Myres who has reported on the decorated potsherds. The plan is the work of Mr. R. Tedbury and the drawings of the finds are by various members of the Group.

THE EXCAVATION (Fig. 48)

The hut was first detected as a large rectangular pit cut into the underlying chalk. In detail it measured 13 ft. 3 in. east-west and 11 ft. 8 in. north-south with its longer axis following the contour of the slope. The sides had been cut almost vertical and the corners at about 90°. The base had been cut horizontally so that on the uphill (north) side it lay 1 ft. 4 in. beneath the surface of the solid chalk, whilst on the downhill side it was only about 8 in. (see north-south section). It seems that originally it had been dug to a depth of about 1½ to 2 ft.

Within the hut were three large post-holes (see east-west section) and a series of 29 small stake-holes all cut into the hard chalk floor. Externally, on the east side, was a rough arc of smaller holes which must have held small posts, but not necessarily connected with the hut. The large post-holes on the east and west sides (A and B) were each 1 ft. 8 in. in diameter, 1 ft. 8 in. deep and had steep or vertical sides. Both were filled with compact chalk rubble which had been packed around a large upright post. No trace of the actual posts survived, but circular columns of black-brown loam, 9 in. in diameter, clearly indicated the positions of the wooden uprights. Post-hole C

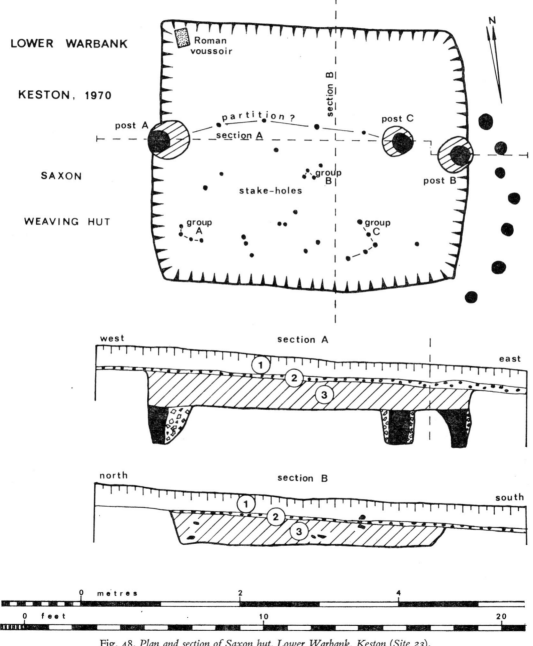

Fig. 48. *Plan and section of Saxon hut, Lower Warbank, Keston (Site 23).*

was broadly similar, but was only 1 ft. 5 in. in diameter and 1 ft. 6 in. deep. It, too, had contained a wooden post, 9½ in. in diameter packed around with chalk, but here the post appeared to lean slightly to the east.

The stake-holes in the floor were confined largely to the southern half of the hut. These were mostly circular, about 1-3 in. in diameter and between 2-9 in. deep and may have been drilled with a metal tool. Four were rectangular in shape, about 2 by 2 in. and probably held posts driven into the floor. No comprehensive pattern emerges, but there are several possible alignments across the hut, though these may be fortuitous. Much more significant are three groups of stake-holes (marked A, B and C on the plan) which appear to form near right-angles and which suggest light structures. Group A in the south-west corner seems unrelated to the other two, but it is quite possible that groups B and C relate to the same structure which had a length of about 4 ft. 6 in. There is some evidence to suggest that this structure was an upright wooden loom (see discussion below). Many of the other stake-holes could also relate to other looms constructed at different times.

In addition to the possible loom an arc of four more stake-holes more or less evenly spaced was found between Post A and Post C. This appears to divide the hut into two unequal parts. The smaller area thus formed north of the arc is devoid of stake-holes which are accordingly confined to the larger, southern area. It is possible, though not proven, that the arc of stakes represents a thin barrier, or partition, separating the suggested weaving-area from the north area, perhaps used for some other purpose, such as sleeping-quarters or storage.

The filling of the hut consisted of an even black-brown loam, partially disturbed by burrowing animals. There was no trace of any prepared floors, or of debris from collapsed walls or roof, or of a hearth. A total of about 360 potsherds was recovered from the filling of which about 230 were Saxon, about 125 Roman and at least four were Iron Age. There were 90 pieces of Roman tile and about 380 bones. Of the Saxon pottery at least twelve vessels can be identified, of which only three were decorated (Nos. 467, 471-2) and all found within 6 in. of the hut floor. The fragmentary nature of all these vessels suggests they were deposited as domestic rubbish.

The primary layer also produced a number of other interesting objects. These included two bone pins (No. 473), weaving needles of antler and bone (Nos. 475-6), a bone comb (No. 477), a pair of bronze tweezers (No. 479) and a lead loom-weight (No. 480). Several of these items relate to a weaving process, probably carried out in the immediate vicinity or more probably in the hut itself. A Roman bronze coin of Tetricus I (c. A.D. 270) was found 10 in. above the hut floor and this may have been washed into the hut sometime after it was abandoned.

DATING AND DISCUSSION

It is at once clear that this hut belongs to the Anglo-Saxon *grubenhaus* class as noted at more than a dozen British sites, mostly of the 5th-7th centuries (Ref. 284) having originated in Northern Europe. Its size, shape and depth are typical of *grubenhäuser* elsewhere, the major British parallels being at Mucking, Essex (Ref. 285), Sutton Courtenay, Berkshire (Ref. 286) and West Stowe, Suffolk (Ref. 287). The posts set partly into the sides on the long axis are characteristic features of many of these huts and must have supported a ridged roof. The middle post is not a constant feature in these huts, but it certainly occurs in huts at Sutton Courtenay though at Keston it may have been inserted at a later date, at an angle to help support the roof or the east post.

It seems clear that this hut is the very first of this type to be found in rural Kent though Saxon huts found at Canterbury seem to have had sunken floors (Ref. 288). It seems likely that the hut was used for weaving. The bone pins, weaving needles, lead weight and bone comb all provide some evidence for this and indeed many of the sunken-huts at Mucking and West Stowe have been identified as weaving-huts. The various groups of stake-holes in the Keston hut suggest light wooden structures of vertical form which may have been looms. In particular two groups appear to relate to a single structure with a length of about 4 ft. 6 in. This corresponds very well with a Saxon loom identified at Sutton Courtenay (Ref. 289) which had a length of 4 ft. 6 in. Another similar cluster of four stake-holes found in a Saxon sunken-hut at Bishopstone, Sussex (Ref. 290) in 1968 could also represent the frame of a loom.

Much of the domestic rubbish in the hut appears to have been dumped into it probably after the hut had gone out of use. The large proportion of Roman material, nearly 50% of the datable objects, must represent residual debris from the nearby Roman buildings. The animal meat-bones include those of pigs, cattle, sheep, red and roe deer, with a considerable preference for the former, though here again a large element of Roman residual material may be present. If the bones do reflect fairly the Saxon occupation of the site then a pastoral form of farming may be indicated with sheep providing both meat for eating and wool for weaving.

The provision of a precise date for this hut, based upon the material in it, is at this early stage somewhat difficult and a complete discussion will be published at a later date. Some of the more significant pieces of pottery have, however, been examined by Dr. J. N. L. Myres who has suggested that these may date from the 6th century A.D. Dr. Myres has also remarked that the stamped pieces look like 6th century Saxon pottery, rather than anything specifically Kentish, resembling material from Saxon sites along the Thames estuary.

Several of the other vessels appear to parallel pots recovered from 5th century huts at Mucking. The bone comb is noted on other early Saxon sites, including a 5th century hut at West Stowe.

As regards the lead ring, perhaps a loom-weight, somewhat similar ones have been found in Saxon huts of the 5th–7th centuries at Mucking (Ref. 291). Some had already been found in the adjacent Linford quarry excavation by Mr. K. J. Barton in 1955. Mrs. M. U. Jones has kindly supplied drawings of some of those found at Mucking and remarked that they were found with 5th century pottery and melted lead in one hut. Mrs. Jones has also noted that lead rings have been found at Hanwell, Middlesex (Ref. 292) and at Ezinge terp, Holland (Groningen Museum).

It seems from the available evidence that the material found in the hut at Keston is both 5th and 6th century in date and this may well represent rubbish, as the fragmentary nature suggests, discarded over a period of time. In view of the comparative small number of finds it is perhaps wiser, at this stage, to offer a tentative date of c. A.D. 450–550 for the Saxon hut at Keston.

The implications of this important new discovery are not without significance or interest. It adds another name to the short list of known early Anglo-Saxon habitation sites south of the Thames. In East Kent it is clear that Canterbury (Ref. 293) and much of its hinterland were in Anglo-Saxon hands by about the middle of the 5th century and perhaps much earlier. It is probable that Germanic troops were in much of that area, perhaps introduced as mercenaries in the Hengist tradition. Certainly the presence of Germanic mercenaries in the early years of the 5th century is now attested at Richborough, Kent (Ref. 294), Dorchester, Oxfordshire (Ref. 295), Winchester, Hampshire (Ref. 296) and Shakenoak, Oxfordshire (Ref. 297) where tangible archaeological evidence has been recovered. So far there is no evidence of either mercenaries or fixed habitation sites in West Kent prior to the middle of the 5th century and it has been suggested that the River Medway provided a useful boundary.

The new evidence from Keston and to a lesser extent from Darenth (Site 22) does, however, help substantiate Anglo-Saxon settlement in North-West Kent during A.D. 450–550. This is clearly supported by the large inhumation-cremation cemetery at Orpington (Ref. 298) roughly mid-way between the two sites and dated A.D. 450–550. So too, is the dating endorsed by the correspondingly early burials at Cliffe, Higham, Northfleet and Horton Kirby (Ref. 299) all within twelve miles of Darenth.

Significantly, the battle of Crayford (traditionally dated A.D. 457, but probably earlier), when 'The Britons then forsook the land of Kent and in great consternation fled to London' (Ref. 300) may mark the end of the sub-Roman phase and the expansion into West Kent of Anglo-Saxon domination. Significantly, the Saxon pottery from West Kent is more akin to that of the Thames Saxons than that of East Kent and it seems likely that the new elements represented entered the area via the Thames and its tributaries. Crayford lies only 10 miles from London, Keston 11 and Darenth just 15 miles.

Of special interest is the occurrence of the Keston and Darenth Anglo-Saxon occupation-sites within the limits of large upstanding Roman villas. So too the cemetery at Orpington was astride a large Roman settlement of uncertain form and in East Kent the Saxon huts at Canterbury were within the Roman town, whilst at nearby Wingham, Germanic pottery has been recovered from the villa (Ref. 301). Prof. Frere has suggested that Canterbury was never deserted, but that late-Roman and Saxon occupation were both contemporary and continuous. What is more difficult to know is if this also happened in the countryside. It seems most unlikely that all the villa-estates were totally abandoned during the first half of the 5th century and the likelihood is that at least some continued their essential farming functions, if on a much reduced scale. It may be that early mercenaries were deliberately settled on the Wingham estate whilst it was still a viable unit and that in West Kent the later expansion was equally a process of both replacement and reoccupation of abandoned sites. As always the comparative lack of datable evidence of the first half of the 5th century bedevils the issue, but more work at Keston may supply some of the answers. Elsewhere there is an increasing amount of evidence, as at Porchester, Hampshire (Ref. 302) and Shakenoak, Oxfordshire (Ref. 297), of Saxon deposits following close upon Romano-British features.

THE FINDS

(I) THE MAMMALIAN BONES FROM THE SAXON HUT AT KESTON

By Mary Harman

A total of 380 bone fragments was recovered from the floor of the Saxon hut in association with more than 200 sherds of pottery of the 6th century A.D. Since the hut also contained more than 220 pieces of Romano-British pottery and tile it is likely that the bone sample is similarly contaminated. All the bones from the hut were examined. Most were identifiable and in a good state of preservation. The minimum number of animals present is estimated from the most frequently occurring bone of each species, considering also differences in age. The age of the animals at death is based on the evidence of the dentition, using figures given by Silver (Ref. 251). Goats may be represented among the sheep, but it has not been possible to distinguish them.

Table A shows the number of each bone present from each species represented on the site and the minimum number of animals present. Table B shows the age of the animals at death.

	Cattle		Sheep		Pig	
	L	R	L	R	L	R
Horn core	I			I		
Skull		2				2
Maxilla					3	I
Mandible		I	I	2	2	3
Scapula		I	I	I	2	I
Humerus	I			I	3	4
Radius			2		4	I
Metacarpal	I	I				
Pelvis			2	2	I	2
Femur					I	I
Tibia	I	I		I	4	
Astragalus			I		3	2
Calcaneum					2	2
Metatarsal		I	I	I		
Phalanx 1						
2					5	
3	I				I	
Totals	13		17		50	
Minimum number of animals	2		2		8	

plus   Roe deer: Left mandible
                         Left innominate
        Red deer: Right humerus
                         Right radius

TABLE A

Frequency of bones from each species on the site and minimum number of animals represented, Saxon Hut, Keston

Tooth eruption sequence and wear	Modern figures	Old figures	No. of examples
Sheep			
(Pm 2, unerupted . . . 4 erupting)			
M1, 2 (3 erupting)	c. 2 y.	c. 3½ y.	1
Pm 2, 3, 4. M1, 2, 3 in wear	Over 2 y.	Over 4 y.	1
Pig			
Dm 1, 2, little wear	c. 3 m.		1
Dm 1, 2, 3, 4, M1 in wear, 2 unerupted	c. 6 m.	c. 15 m.	1
Dm 1, 2, 3, M1 in wear (2 erupting)	c. 1 y.	c. 2 y.	2
C erupting Pm 1, Dm 2, 3, 4, worn	c. 1 y.		1
Pm 4 M1, 2 (3 partially worn)	c. 21 m.	c. 3 y.	3

TABLE B
Age of animals at death, Saxon Hut, Keston

Although the sample is a small one it is clear that on this site pigs were of greater importance than either cattle or sheep. All the pig jaws found were from animals which had died at the earliest age at which they would have supplied the maximum amount of meat, or younger. Of the two oxen represented, one at least was under two years old. One of the sheep represented had lived for several years.

Domestic animals, particularly pigs, obviously were involved in the economy of the community using the site. The deer bones found suggest that hunting may have provided a minor part of the food supply.

I am grateful to Mr. Raymond Chaplin for help with the identification of the deer bones.

Catalogue of the Illustrated Finds from the Saxon Hut, Keston (Fig. 49)

No. 464. Plain shouldered urn of hard, dense ware with black paste and black-brown surface (LWB-N24-32). Similar to one found at Lackford, Suffolk (Ref. 303) dated to about A.D. 500 (Myres Type 914).

No. 465. Small pot of hard, dense ware with a mottled black-brown paste, smooth brown surface and slightly everted rim (LWB-N23-2).

No. 466. Wide-mouthed pot of hard, dense ware with light-brown paste and rough, uneven black-brown surface (LWB-M23-5). Broadly similar vessels have been found in a 5th century Saxon *grubenhaus* at Mucking, Essex (Ref. 304, Hut 26, No. 416e).

No. 467. Small pot of hard, dense ware with mottled brown paste and smooth, black surface. Narrow mouth, bulbous body and stamped rosette pattern on shoulder (LWB-N24-38). Probably 6th century.

No. 468. Wide bowl, or dish, of grass-tempered ware with black paste and surface (LWB-N24-3). Similar to vessels from a 5th century hut at Mucking (Hut 26, No. 414a), from Laceby, Lincs. and Northfleet, Kent (Myres Types 481 and 1948, respectively).

No. 469. Wide bowl, or dish, of grass-tempered ware with black paste and black-brown surface (LWB-N24-3). Broadly similar to No. 468.

No. 470. Wide-mouthed pot of hard, dense ware with brown core and rough, uneven orange-black surface (LWB-N24-14).

No. 471. Shoulder fragment of hard, dense ware with grey-black paste and smooth, black surface. Vertical lines of stamped rosettes between pairs of incised lines, probably on a broad boss (LWB-M24-4). Similar decoration occurs on a sub-biconical vessel from Long Wittenham, Berks (Myres Type 1993). Probably 6th century.

No. 472. Lower part of a hard, dense ware pot with grey-black paste and smooth, brown surface. Incised chevron pattern and row of circular indentations above incised horizontal groove (LWB-M23-4). Similar decoration occurs on a wide-mouthed biconical vessel from Little Weldon, Northants (Myres Type 810), probably of 6th century date.

No. 473. One of two similar carved bone or antler needles with both ends sharpened to a point. Some signs of wear (LWB-N24-56).

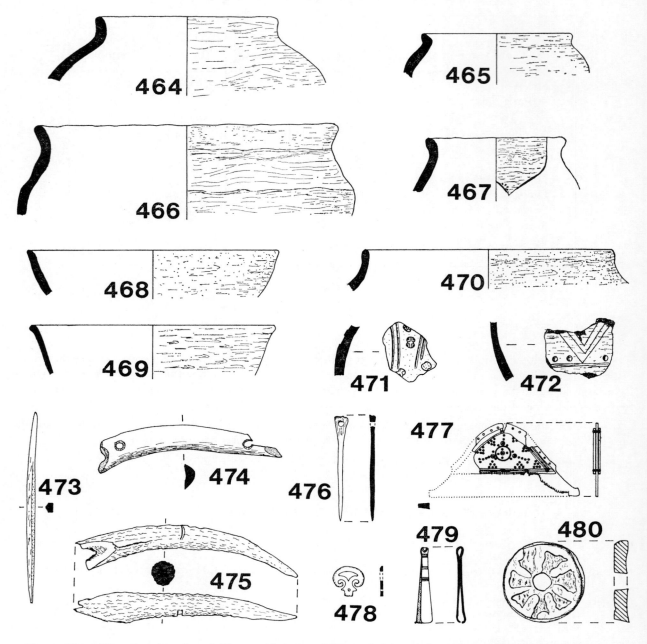

Fig. 49. *Pottery (Nos. 464–72), antler tools (Nos. 473–6), bone comb (No. 477) and metal objects (Nos. 478–80) ($\frac{1}{3}$), Saxon hut, Lower Warbank, Keston (Site 23).*

No. 474. Bone or antler object, perhaps a handle or even a broad needle, made from a split long-bone and semicircular in section. Two circular perforations, one slightly iron-stained, suggest that this object was fixed with iron rivets. Each end is chopped at about 45° (LWB-N23-6).

No. 475. Antler tool, perhaps a needle, with broad end cut away on two sides. Small transverse cut across centre (LWB-M24-12).

No. 476. Polished bone or antler needle, with sharp point and broad, perforated end (LWB-N24-37). An almost identical needle was recovered in association with Saxon pottery, probably of 6th century date, at Dartford (Ref. 305) about 11 miles to the north-east. Similar needles have been found in unstratified contexts at Darenth (Ref. 306), where early Saxon material has been recorded (Site 22) and at Leicester (Ref. 307).

No. 477. Single-sided bone comb, probably used for weaving, consisting of six parts and secured by eight iron rivets. All the teeth and one arm are missing. Multiple compass-drawn patterns within incised lines on both sides. The comb was made in three layers held together by the rivets. The middle section consists of the two side arms and two central rectangular plates each about 0·8 in. wide. The two outer sections are single elements on which the external decoration was applied. An arc of small perforations along the outer edge may have been either decorative or functional (LWB-N24). This is one of a fairly uncommon type of Saxon comb quite distinct from the normal double or single edged combs of rectangular form. Probably no more than about twenty such combs are so far known and of those published one from Colchester (Ref. 308), found in association with Saxon pottery but not properly stratified, is perhaps the nearest. Two more from Richborough, not stratified, are broadly similar (Refs. 309 and 310). Several have been found in the recently excavated Anglo-Saxon village at West Stowe, Suffolk (Ref. 287), from *grubenhäuser* and also in association with early-5th century pottery.

No. 478. Bronze openwork mount, perhaps for a belt or harness (LWB-M23-7). This appears to be a variant of the common Roman fitting, both with and without openwork, found on military sites. At Richborough (Ref. 311) they occur in varying contexts, but one at least is dated to about A.D. 400.

No. 479. Pair of bronze tweezers with three bands of incised lines and grooved end (LWB-M24-3). Tweezers of this type, with varying decoration, occur frequently in Saxon graves. A plain example of simple form was found at Orpington (Ref. 312) and may date between A.D. 450 and 550; two more were found at Winterbourne Gunner, Wiltshire (Ref. 313), in graves of the 6th century; another from a 6th century grave at Petersfinger, Wiltshire (Ref. 314); one from a Saxon grave at Sarre, Kent (Ref. 315) and a close parallel was found in a Saxon grave at Barrington, Cambridgeshire (Ref. 316).

No. 480. Flat, circular lead weight, probably a loom-weight, with central perforation. Tapered edge and upper surface decorated with simple radial pattern (LWB-N24-61). These weights are not common, but broadly similar examples have been found in Saxon huts of the 5th and 6th centuries at Mucking.

Site 24. The Anglo-Saxon Cemetery at Polhill, Dunton Green, Kent

SUMMARY

The Anglo-Saxon cemetery at Polhill appears to have been in use during the second half of the 7th and first half of the 8th centuries A.D. It occupied a high prominence on the scarp slope of the North Downs and flanked the Pilgrim's Way. Although its setting is typical of many pagan Saxon sites it is likely that the burials, all inhumations, were nominally Christian. The cemetery covered an area of about 2 acres in which 107 graves were recorded, but allowing for those destroyed by roadworks the original number was probably greater than 150. Taking into account the multiple burials it is likely that about 200 people were buried here. From this it is clear that Polhill is the largest Anglo-Saxon cemetery so far discovered in West Kent and this tends to imply a nearby community of corresponding size and importance. The most likely settlement-site is Otford, about a mile to the east, where the North Downs Ridgeway descends into the valley to cross the River Darent. Otford is first mentioned by name in A.D. 776 as the site of an important battle.

Almost certainly every grave was aligned roughly east-west with the foot towards the east. The graves were normally rectangular with adult graves generally 6–7 ft. long by 2–3 ft. wide and originally 2–3 ft. deep and all cut into solid chalk. There was a high number of multiple graves with one containing three skeletons and 16 containing two, of which four had been inserted at a later date. These appear to be family graves and it seems likely that all graves were probably marked in some way. Six small ditched barrows, 13–17 ft. in diameter with eastern causeways, were found at the north-west end of the cemetery. Five were in a line, at least two had memorial-posts and one contained two graves.

The skeletons mostly lay on their backs and at least ten were in wooden coffins. Of 125 known skeletons at least 86 were adult and 30 were children under 15 years. Of 43 adults identified 31 were male and 12 female. Of the people represented by the skeletons about 24% had died by the age of 16 years; another 26% had died by the age of 25 years; another 28% died before the age of 50 and only about 3% survived more than 50 years. Twenty-three were not identifiable. Infant mortality was not represented and the average life expectancy was about 24 years, suggesting that over an hundred-year period the cemetery may represent a community of 50 people. The adult males were generally 5 ft. 6 in. to 6 ft. 2 in. and the females 5 ft. 2 in. to 5 ft. 6 in. Two skeletons showed signs of osteoarthritis.

A total of 69 graves produced grave-goods and at least seventeen others did not. Twelve men were buried with spears and only four with seaxes. Many of the women were buried with beads, rings, brooches or other personal possessions. The majority of men, women and children were buried with small iron knives. The high proportion of unfurnished or semi-furnished graves reflects the decline in the practice of depositing grave goods with the dead in later Saxon cemeteries. Some of the earlier graves appear on the lower slope and many of the later graves were rather higher. The richer seax graves and the barrows imply that the more important members of the community were buried at the west end. The grave goods are neither rich nor socially distinguished and it seems that the leaders of the community buried at Polhill did not come from the higher classes of Anglo-Saxon society.

A small sub-rectangular structure, about 14 by 8 ft. was found at the north-west corner of the cemetery and this may represent a Saxon funerary hut.

INTRODUCTION

The site (N.G.R. TQ.5504.1590) of this extensive Anglo-Saxon cemetery lies within the parish of Dunton Green, about 3 miles north-west of the centre of Sevenoaks, Kent (Fig. 50). It occupies a bold prominence (O.S. parcel 2800) at the junction of the Darent Valley with the west side of the North Downs scarp and there are extensive views through an arc of about 250 degrees. The site occupies a one-in-six slope and is framed between the 390 and 420 ft. contours on the north side of the Pilgrim's Way. The bed-rock is hard Upper Chalk.

It seems highly probable that the cemetery was discovered about 1839 when the Sevenoaks Turnpike

Road was diverted (Ref. 317) to the line of what is now the A21 trunk-road. No details of such early discoveries were recorded though the oral tradition of skeletons and weapons survived and was noted by Gordon Ward in 1931 (Ref. 318). These were all too readily associated with the well-known battle of Otford in A.D. 776 (Ref. 319) fought between the Mercians and the Men of Kent.

In 1956 more graves were encountered when the A21 was improved at its junction with the Pilgrim's Way. Another 13 graves (Area A: Graves 1–13) were then recorded (Ref. 320). Subsequently, in 1956 and 1958, the Otford Historical Society carried out an area-excavation (Area B) on the west side of the A21 in an attempt to locate further graves. None was encountered and it is now clear that this excavation just missed the southern edge of the cemetery (Ref. 321). At least three more skeletons (Area C: Graves 14–16) were, however, revealed in August 1959 when more of the bank on the west side was mechanically excavated under another road-improvement. Two more skeletons (Graves 17 and 18) were uncovered in November, 1959 and January, 1960 by schoolboys digging in the exposed face of the chalk. Some information on these graves was collected by members of the Otford Historical Society, the details of which were readily made available by Mr. R. D. Clarke. In about 1963 workmen putting in a small reservoir 180 ft. west of the 1956 discoveries encountered at least one more grave (Grave 19), but no details were recorded.

In October, 1964 work began on the construction of the Sevenoaks Bypass starting from Polhill. A 40 ft. wide strip of ground was then removed on the west side of the A21 by mechanical means. Another grave was revealed and others may have been destroyed without trace. The contractor reported the matter to the Kent County Council, who in turn reported to the local police. Finally, Maidstone Museum contacted the writer. An immediate inspection revealed more graves in the area and resulted in a rapid six-day emergency excavation, the first to be carried out under the new Kent Archaeological Research Groups' Council (now C.K.A.) emergency scheme. Fourteen graves (Area D: Graves 20–32, 35) were fully excavated and recorded and two more (Graves 33 and 34) located in a pipe-trench dug about 200 ft. further west (Ref. 322).

From this work it was clear that the cemetery extended much further to the west than previously supposed. In spite of warnings to all concerned another strip of ground (Area E) was then removed without notice and it must be that several more graves were destroyed without record. In November, 1966 a large area (Area F) was removed by mechanical means on the east side of the A21 and a close watch revealed only one more grave (Grave 36). In the same month another pipe-trench, again leading to the reservoir, cut through three more graves (Graves 37–39).

The situation was clearly getting out of hand and as the whole area was scheduled for yet another major road-development some really positive and urgent action was needed. Constant pleas to the Ministry of Public Building and Works eventually led to the launching of a large-scale emergency excavation on its behalf, by the West Kent Border Archaeological Group. This was done with the support of the Council for Kentish Archaeology emergency scheme and the help of many Kent groups. Three weeks intensive work in late-March and early-April, 1967 resulted in the discovery of another 63 graves (Graves 40–102); another two weeks work in July and August, 1967 located five more graves (Graves 103–107) and a small hut (Ref. 323). It seems likely that the south and west limits of the cemetery were reached in 1967 and it is known that the area to the north has been quarried for chalk. Even so it is still possible that stray graves may remain in small peripheral areas not available for excavation.

This Report deals mainly with the 1964 and 1967 excavations, but details of the earlier graves have been included in the inventory of graves. The total cost of the excavation was about £320, some £41 less than estimated. The finds are housed in the Group's Centre at Bromley awaiting suitable museum display-facilities in the Borough.

ACKNOWLEDGEMENTS

The satisfactory completion of the excavations at Polhill was the result of hard work and ready co-operation by many people in a variety of ways. Thanks are due first to the site-contractors Dick Hampton (Earth Moving) Ltd., and to the Kent County Council engineers for sharing the site with the Group during the October, 1964 excavation. Subsequently, to Mr. A. G. Lavers of Jessup's (Lime Production) Ltd., for his ready consent to the 1967 excavations and to Mr. R. S. Pearson for his interest and support. The help of the Army authorities, under Major B. A. Lipscombe, R.E., who kindly supplied plant for the Easter 1967 work is gratefully acknowledged, so too is the help of Lenfield Engineering Ltd. of Maidstone who, on the advice of Mr. A. Farrell, kindly supplied a Massey-Ferguson excavator free of charge for the work in July, 1967.

Of the more than 90 volunteers who assisted with the various excavations special thanks are due to members of the Gravesend, Fawkham, Lewisham, London Field Club, Lower Medway, Otford, Reculver, Sittingbourne and West Kent groups who collectively formed the back-bone of the operation. Particular mention must be made of Misses M. Harman, M. Last, A. McGary, E. Mynott (now Mrs. Philp) and J. Teulon; and Messrs. A. Appleby, R. Gierth, C. Jones, J. Parsons, A. Thomas, P. Tombs and J.Willson for their hard work for extended periods.

Considerable help with the preparation of this report for publication has been given by members of the West Kent Group working in their Centre at Bromley. In particular thanks are due to Mrs. J. Lock for completing the overall site-plan; to Mr. J. A. Willson for drawing some of the more specialised small-finds and also the grave-plans; to Miss P. George for mounting the individual drawings the remainder of which were completed in the Ancient Monuments drawing-office.

Of specialist help Mrs. Sonia Hawkes has very kindly written at length on the dating and social significance of the cemetery and Mrs. A. Gibson has readily prepared a detailed catalogue of the illustrated finds. Professor R. J. Harrison and Professor A. E. W. Miles have both kindly reported on groups of skeletal material and Mrs. C. Keepax has kindly commented on the five graves located after the main excavation. Miss Elisabeth Crowfoot has provided a short report on the textiles; Dr. A. R. Cox on two of the iron knives and the Ancient Monuments laboratory has identified wood-samples from the sockets of several spearheads. To all concerned the writer extends his own personal thanks.

THE EXCAVATIONS (Fig. 50)

THE CEMETERY (Plate XIVB)

The site was generally covered by between 10 and 20 in. of topsoil and this was removed by mechanical means during the large-scale excavations of 1967 to expose the underlying natural chalk. An area of about 2 acres was cleared and this established the west and south limits of the cemetery. The north limit was masked by huge mounds of quarry-debris and the east limit was probably reached by the road-works in 1956. It is clear from this that the cemetery had an overall east-west length of about 500 ft. and a minimum north-south width of about 200 ft. and thus covered an area of about 2 acres. The graves appeared as faint discolourations in the chalk where the fillings contained a mixture of topsoil and chalk rubble. The cemetery was excavated systematically from east to west, each grave being numbered on location and allocated to a volunteer who was responsible for its excavation and a measured drawing. Each grave was then photographed, recorded, plotted and the contents lifted. The skeletal material from each grave was then bagged and boxed separately and transported like this to the London Hospital Medical College for study. The spacing between the graves varied considerably and there was a particular concentration at the south-west corner. A total of 107 graves has been recorded and plotted on the plan and it is certain that many others were destroyed at different times without record. No cremation burial has been recorded anywhere on the site and it seems certain that this was exclusively an inhumation cemetery.

THE SINGLE AND MULTIPLE GRAVES (Plates XVA-XVIII)

Of the 107 graves listed only 86 were recorded under satisfactory conditions. All of these were aligned broadly east-west and of the others only one, found in 1956, appears to have been aligned north-south. The axes varied from 020° to 120° though the great majority of graves were between 050° and 080°. Seven graves were enclosed within six small barrows (see below). Each grave had been dug into solid chalk to a depth of between 3 and 24 in. and allowing for a 10 in. layer of topsoil it is probable that most of the graves were originally 2 or 3 ft. deep. The great majority was rectangular with well-cut corners and there was some evidence to suggest that at least ten contained wooden coffins. The adult graves were generally between 6 and 7 ft. 6 in. in length and between 2 and 3 ft. in width. The longest grave was 8 ft. 6 in. (Grave 30) and the widest single grave 3 ft. 10 in. (Grave 45). The majority of children's graves was between 3 ft. 6 in. and 5 ft. in length and about 2 ft. 6 in. in width. The smallest grave was 3 ft. 4 in. in length (Grave 78).

The skeletal remains varied considerably, some graves containing nearly complete skeletons and others no bones at all. Generally child bones and the smaller adult bones had not survived. The great majority of the skeletons

found lay on their backs, face upwards and arms and legs at their sides. In every recorded instance the skeleton faced east with the head at the west end of the grave.

Of special interest were the multiple graves. One grave (Grave 99) contained three adult skeletons and another 16 graves contained two, of which at least seven contained adult and child. Of the double graves four produced evidence that one of the bodies had been inserted sometime after the original grave had been filled. In one, (Grave 60) the upper skeleton was separated from the lower by a clear 4 in. of soil and lay on a different alignment. In another (Grave 52) the original body had been partly removed when the second was inserted and the disturbed bones replaced on one side. Here the later grave-digger had detoured to the midriff of the earlier body, perhaps in search of valuable grave-goods. Finally, in a double grave containing an adult and child (Grave 86) the adult's grave could be seen to form an extension on the south side of the original cut. Of the other double graves it seems from the position of the bodies that in at least eleven cases each pair must have been buried at the same time. It seems probable than in each instance members of the same family were buried together. It is interesting to note in three cases an adult male was buried with a child and in four cases a female with a child. Exactly how members of the same family died at the same time is a matter for conjecture! The suggestion that these were family graves is supported by the four cases where deliberate attempts were made to insert additional bodies into pre-existing graves. It follows from this that most or all of the graves must have been marked on the surface in some way and that some at least could be identified. That the graves were marked is supported by the fact that no two graves were accidentally superimposed and indeed this conclusion was reached of the graves in the Holborough cemetery (Ref. 324). That the 'inserted' burials sometimes partially overlapped the sides of earlier graves was accidental and largely unavoidable.

The triple grave contained the skeletons of a male and two females (Fig. 51). Both females appear to have been tucked into the sides of the grave and the male then dragged backwards to rest partly between and across the others. The rather unorthodox position of the male and the irregular outline of the grave may indicate a hurried burial.

GRAVE-GOODS (discussion on page 186)

Of the 107 graves recorded 69 contained grave-goods, 17 contained none and 21 other graves were recorded in unsatisfactory conditions. It is also clear that many other graves containing grave-goods were discovered at Polhill in the 19th century. In each case the objects had been placed deliberately in the grave, presumably to be used by the deceased in the journey through the after-life. This custom was prevalent throughout most of the 5th, 6th, 7th and early-8th centuries A.D., a wide range of objects being deposited.

At Polhill no grave contained evidence of a shield and only four graves, Grave 9 and a group (Graves 83–85) on the extreme west side of the cemetery, contained seaxes. There were 13 spearheads, distributed in 12 graves, normally placed alongside the body with the point to the west. More than 50 graves contained small iron knives, normally placed at the centre or left waist in graves of men, women and children. About 20 graves contained either iron or bronze buckles often found at the waist and probably forming part of a belt. In one case (Grave 75) a series of iron fittings encircling the waist of a skeleton must have formed part of such a belt. Only 13 graves contained beads, ten produced rings and only two contained brooches. In addition there were many other objects of iron and bronze such as latch-lifters, purse-mounts, keys and similar items. Of special interest was a complete pot (Grave 94), a bone comb (Grave 53) and a fine cylindrical bronze work-box (Grave 43). Glass vessels were totally absent.

So far as the identification of skeletons allows all the seaxes and spears were buried with men and necklaces, beads, brooches and rings generally with women. Most graves contained only one, two or three objects, but several produced five or more items.

THE BARROWS (Plates XIXA and B)

At the north-west corner of the cemetery was a group of six barrows, five of which contained single graves and one which contained two graves. Five of the barrows were roughly in a north-east by south-west line covering a distance of about 120 ft. The sixth lay about 30 ft. further west. The single graves were enclosed centrally by shallow, flat-bottomed V-shaped ditches 1 ft. to 1 ft. 6 in. in width as surviving and from about 5 to 11 in. deep. Four had internal diameters of 11 ft. and a fifth of 13 ft. 9 in. The external diameters were between 13 ft. and

16 ft. 9 in. In at least four cases a deliberate eastern causeway, either 2 ft. 6 in. or 4 ft. wide had been left, but in only two cases did this line up with the axis of the grave. The larger barrow containing the two graves (Graves 94 and 95) had been at least partially enclosed by a shallow ditch, 1 ft. 3 in. wide, of which only traces survived on the east and west sides. Its internal width was 12 ft. and it seems likely that its overall north-south length would have been about 17 ft. The two graves appeared to rest symmetrically within the barrow-ditch.

The shallow ditches were filled with light-brown loam containing small pieces of chalk rubble. It seems probable that the soil originally dug from these ditches would have been placed over the graves to form a low, central mound. At one site in Wiltshire, however, the filling of the barrow-ditch suggested an external bank (Ref. 325), but at Polhill it was impossible to tell the direction of the infilling.

Two of the barrows (Graves 59 and 106) contained single post-holes, one circular the other rectangular, close to both the open causeway and to the foot of the grave. It seems probable that these held upright wooden memorial-posts as noted on other Saxon cemetery sites (Ref. 326). The barrows contained adults and children, the majority buried with grave-goods and at least four buried in wooden coffins. The small grave (Grave 94) within the largest barrow produced no skeletal remains, but contained the only pot buried on the site and a silver ring. The associated grave (Grave 95) contained an adult female, a child and several possessions (Fig. 51).

Small barrows are known in other cemeteries in Britain though rarely in any number. In Kent they can still be seen on Barham Down (Ref. 327) and others are known at Finglesham (Ref. 328) and at Chartham Down (Ref. 329). The five barrows forming an alignment on the west side of the cemetery at Polhill probably represent later burials of the more important families. A similar barrow-alignment seems to be reflected in the Anglo-Saxon cemetery at Finglesham (publication pending).

THE SKELETAL MATERIAL

The bulk of the skeletal remains from Graves 20–35 was examined by Professor R. J. Harrison of the Anatomy School, University of Cambridge, who kindly prepared a detailed report in which he aged and sexed most of the skeletons. The bulk of the skeletal remains from Graves 40–102 was examined by Professor A. E. W. Miles of the Dental School, University of London assisted by Mr. D. H. Haines. Professor Miles has also submitted a detailed report in which about half of the skeletons were aged and sexed. Lack of space prevents detailed publication here of these excellent reports, but the conclusions have been incorporated in the inventory of graves and are discussed below.

Allowing for the multiple burials the 107 recorded graves had contained at least 125 skeletons. Of these 86 were of adults, 30 were of children under the age of 15 years and 9 were indeterminate. No infant-burials were found nor any trace of very small graves which may have contained them and it seems that infant mortality, probably high in Saxon times, cannot be assessed from the Polhill evidence. Of the adults 31 were male, 12 female and with 43 indeterminate skeletons these particular figures can have little value. Only 72 of the adult skeletons were aged, but with the children the grave and skeletal measurements allow a much easier estimate and most can be aged in this way. Table A (P. 169) gives the estimated ages of the skeletons from Polhill.

Whilst acknowledging the limitations of a study of these figures, particularly with regard to the high number of unassigned skeletons, several broad trends appear. It seems that about 24% of the population had died by the age of 15 and about half by the age of 25. Most of the remainder had expired before the age of 50. The greatest mortality seems to have been in the 15–25 age-group. In many respects these statistics reflect the provisional figures for the Saxon cemetery at Winnall II, Hampshire (Ref. 330) though that is based on a total of only 45 skeletons.

From the Polhill skeletons which have been aged it seems that the life expectancy at birth was about 24 years, as compared with more than 70 years in 1970 (Ref. 331). The Polhill figures agree with those already published for the site by Professor Miles (Ref. 332), but based on only those skeletons submitted to him. His histogram suggested an average age of 24 years which he compared with 31 years at the Saxon cemetery at Breedon-on-the-Hill, Leicestershire (8th century); 30 years in Ancient Greece and 35 years in 13th century medieval England (Ref. 333). Professor Miles has remarked that the low average age at Polhill could reflect an unusually high number of child-burials.

As regards stature the reports of both Professor Harrison and Professor Miles record the identifiable males as between 5 ft. 6 in. and 6 ft. 2 in. and the females as between 5 ft. 2 in. and 5 ft. 6 in. Many of the teeth showed considerable signs of attrition and in two cases (Graves 20 and 27) some bones showed signs of osteoarthritis.

Plate XIIIB. *Room 11 of Period V showing the tiled floor of the Period IV aisled building. Darenth Roman Villa, Darenth (Site 21)*

Plate XIIIA. *The Deep Pit showing the wood-lined drain, the wooden beams and the Period V wall of the aisled building constructed over the filling. Darenth Roman Villa, Darenth (Site 21)*

Plate XIVA. *The Roman burial found east of the aisled building. Darenth Roman Villa, Darenth (Site 21)*

Plate XIVB. *The south-west corner of the Anglo-Saxon cemetery under excavation. Polhill, Dunton Green (Site 24)*

Plate XVB. *Grave 85, Anglo-Saxon cemetery, Polhill, Dunton Green (Site 24)*

Plate XVA. *Grave 45, Anglo-Saxon cemetery, Polhill, Dunton Green (Site 24)*

Plate XVIB. *Grave 43, Anglo-Saxon cemetery, Polhill, Dunton Green (Site 24)*

Plate XVIA. *Grave 42, Anglo-Saxon cemetery, Polhill, Dunton Green (Site 24)*

	Ages		Numbers	Totals	%
Children	1–5 years		16		
	6–15 years		12		
	Not aged		2		
				30	24
Adults	15–25 years		33		26
	26–35 years		20		16
	36–50 years		15		12
	51 and over		4		3
	Not aged		14		12
				86	
Indeterminate			9	9	7
				125	100

TABLE A
Numbers of aged skeletons found at Polhill

THE HUT (Fig. 52).

A series of 16 large post-holes was found at the north-west corner of the cemetery and seems to represent the site of a small hut (Plate XXA). The holes were generally circular, with flat bottoms and vertical sides, being generally filled with brown loam and chalk rubble. The following table gives the basic information on each hole:

Post-hole	Shape	Size	Depth	Filling
1	Circular	Diam. 7 in.	11 in.	Black loam (upper); brown loam and chalk rubble (lower)
2	Circular	Diam. 7 in.	10 in.	Brown loam and chalk rubble
3	Circular	Diam. 11 in.	19 in.	Brown loam, chalk rubble and potsherd
4	D-shaped	11 × 8 in.	12 in.	Brown loam and chalk rubble
5	Circular	Diam. 11 in.	7 in.	Black loam and potsherds
6	Circular	Diam. 9 in.	14 in.	Black loam and potsherd
7	Circular	Diam. 12 in.	19 in.	Brown loam, chalk rubble, hone and potsherds
8	Sub-rectangular	12 × 8 in.	14 in.	Black loam and potsherds
9	Circular	Diam. 11 in.	13 in.	Brown loam and chalk rubble
10	Circular	Diam. 10 in.	18 in.	Black loam, bone and potsherd
11	Circular	Diam. 9 in.	13 in.	Chalk rubble and potsherds
12	Circular	Diam. 10 in.	3 in.	Brown loam and chalk rubble
13	Rectangular	17 × 10 in.	6 in.	Brown loam and chalk rubble
14	Circular	Diam. 13 in.	14 in.	Black-brown loam and potsherd
15	Oval	14 × 10 in.	6 in.	Grey-black loam, potsherds and carbon
16	Oval	16 × 10 in.	10 in.	Brown loam and chalk rubble

TABLE B
Details of the post-holes, Saxon hut, Polhill

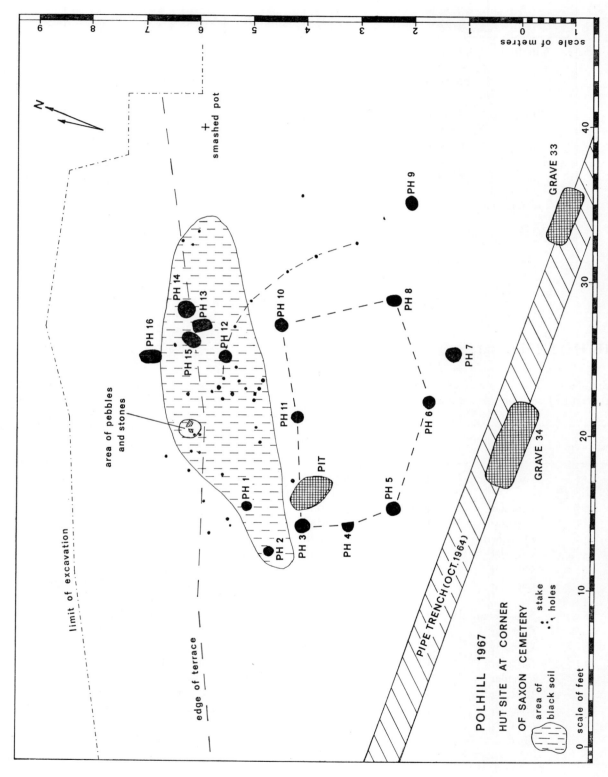

Fig. 52. *Plan of Hut at north–west corner of Anglo–Saxon cemetery, Polhill, Dunton Green (Site 24).*

It seems clear that most must have held a substantial wooden post between 6 and 10 in. in diameter. The outline produced by these 16 post-holes is irregular, but by selecting seven (Post-holes Nos. 3–6, 8, 10 and 11) a broadly rectangular plan about 14 ft. by 8 ft. can be produced. It is probable that this structure was a hut and that the other posts did not form part of the main frame. It stood on a narrow platform, or terrace, cut into the chalk and was covered by between 1 and 2 ft. of light-brown loam, probably representing hillwash or the result of later ploughing.

In the north-west corner of the suggested outline was an ovoid pit, 3 ft. by 2 ft. with steep sides, a flat base and just 4 in. deep. Its filling of black-brown loam contained a single potsherd and ten animal bones of indeterminate character. In addition a series of 37 stake-holes was found outside the hut on the north and east sides. All but one were circular, being vertical-sided, 1 to 4 in. in diameter and 3 to 9 in. deep. Most were in small groups or alignments, but an arc (dashed on the plan, Fig. 52) of at least six appears to flank the probable hut on its north-east side. It is likely that these stake-holes represent some slight structures, perhaps built for a process such as weaving or drying. Similar stake-holes occur within the Saxon *grubenhaus* at Lower Warbank, Keston (Site 23) and these may represent weaving-looms.

In the same general area as the stake-holes and seeming to delimit the hut on its north side was an extensive deposit of black loam covering an area of about 23 by 6 ft. It contained 167 potsherds, bones, flint flakes and a small group of pebbles and irregular sandstone blocks. It covered most of the stake-holes and several of the post-holes and it appears to represent domestic rubbish discarded behind the hut. In addition to this material 1,032 potsherds and other objects were found unstratified from the immediate area of the hut or from the post-holes. The fillings of graves produced another 95 potsherds and other objects and another 41 were found elsewhere about the cemetery (all of these are shown in Table C).

The flint material consists almost entirely of waste flakes of varying size. The majority has a single strike-scar and cortex. Most are patinated white, show no trace of re-touch and are largely lacking in diagnostic characteristics. They occur in large numbers in the area of the probable hut, but not elsewhere on the site and they were found in direct association with the other domestic rubbish.

The few bones from the hut area include those of sheep, the canine tooth of a pig and a single horn-core of a sheep or goat. About half of the bones had been burned. The sandstone is similar to the ferruginous sandstone which occurs in the Lower Greensand. Each piece was irregular in shape and unworked though at least three pieces appear to have been polished. The pebbles are small, water-rolled and were probably obtained from a river or from gravel deposits in the area. The 'pot-boilers' are simply fire-cracked flints. Only two other finds came from the

	From the cemetery area		From the hut area				
	Filling of graves	Un-stratified	Filling post-holes	Black loam	Pit	Un-stratified	Totals
Flint material	5	4	3	29	—	522	563
Bone	1	1	2	38	10	22	74
Sandstone	—	—	1	13	—	1	15
Pebbles	—	—	3	34	—	5	42
'Pot-boilers'	1	—	—	8	—	24	33
Shell-loaded pottery	12	4	10	8	—	310	344
Iron objects	1	1	—	1	—	—	3
Other pottery	75	31	11	36	1	118	272
Totals	95	41	30	167	11	1,002	1,346

TABLE C

Material recovered, other than grave-goods and human skeletal remains, from the Polhill site

hut area. One was a small piece of corroded iron and the other was the broken end of a circular sandstone hone, about 1·3 in. in diameter, which was found in Post-hole 7.

Of the pottery about 60 sherds can be identified as Romano-British and these came either from the fillings of the graves or from unstratified contexts, none being found in the hut area. These included a sherd of samian Form 27 (1st century A.D.), a sherd of a Gallo-Belgic vessel (mid-1st century A.D.) and native Patch Grove ware (second half of 1st, or 2nd, century A.D.). The pottery also included eleven medieval potsherds (probably 13th century) found unstratified near the north-west corner of the site.

The remaining 500 or so potsherds can be divided into two distinct groups, the great majority of both coming from the hut area or from the fillings of adjacent graves. One group consists of a very coarse, thick black ware containing a high proportion of crushed shell and with an orange-brown surface. Larger pieces found together east of the hut may represent a single pot though reconstruction is not possible. Although represented here by 344 sherds only one simple, outcurved rim is present and it is very difficult to suggest complete profiles. No obvious parallels of Saxon date come to mind, but it is worth noting that the only pot to come from the Polhill cemetery (Grave 94) was lightly shell-loaded though of rather different character.

The second group of pottery is much finer, though again hand-made and undecorated. The paste is mostly grey-black with occasional particles of fine grit and the surfaces mostly black-brown, though several orange-brown surfaces occur. Although the sherds are very small it seems likely that as many as ten vessels are represented, some being burnished. It is likely that these are mostly from small and medium-sized cooking-pots and there appears to be one fragment of a rounded base. One sherd is part of a vessel with an out-curved rim and another part of a smal carinated pot. The pottery is, however, similar to sherds of dense-black ware found by the Group in the Anglo-Saxon *grubenhaus* at Keston only 6 miles to the north-west. It is also similar to pottery recovered by the CIB Archaeological Rescue Corps from Saxon huts at Darenth in 1972 (publication pending), only 8 miles north-east of Polhill. Both of these sites are likely to be 5th or 6th century in date and significantly, perhaps, shell-loaded wares are absent at each.

As regards the pottery it is likely that the Romano-British sherds are derived from a nearby (unknown) site, whereas the small amount of medieval pottery all came from an unstratified context away from the hut. The bulk of the shell-loaded and dense-black wares was found in direct association with the hut and it seems reasonable, therefore, to describe the hut as Saxon. This is to a large extent confirmed by the relative positions of the hut and the adjacent graves. Although the graves flank the hut on two sides none cuts it, nor does the hut override any grave and it seems that they respect each other. If this is not just an unusual coincidence then either the hut was standing when nearby graves were dug or the hut was erected to avoid pre-existing graves which were clearly marked. The former is much more likely as some of the sherds associated with the hut had found their way into the grave fillings and suggest that it pre-dates at least some of them. On balance it is likely that the cemetery and huts are roughly contemporary in date.

Exactly what function this hut served is far from clear, if indeed it was a hut. Its form and size reflect the huts of the 5th–7th centuries, but in no sense can it be regarded as a *grubenhaus*. Such domestic huts are anyway not normally placed directly on cemetery sites and clearly this structure stands apart from the norm. A rectangular structure was recorded at Bishopstone, Sussex (Ref. 334) within the limits of a large Anglo-Saxon cemetery and this may represent a useful parallel. Perhaps both were built for some ceremonial purpose connected with the burials, or perhaps even housed someone either guarding the site or perhaps performing some ritualistic function. It may be significant that the hut at Polhill was at the extreme corner of the site where the later burials tended to be and it is possible that when built it stood apart from the earliest graves. So too, it should be noted, did the barrows and important seax graves cluster at that end of the cemetery.

DISCUSSION

Only some of the more general aspects of the site are discussed here as the dating and social significance of the cemetery are dealt with below by Mrs. Sonia Hawkes.

The county of Kent is particularly rich in Anglo-Saxon cemeteries and so far more than 150, of varying size, have been recorded (Ref. 335). In West Kent large cemeteries occur at Horton Kirby, which contained 114 burials (Ref. 336); at Orpington, which had 71 burials (Ref. 337) and at Holborough which contained more than 40 burials (Ref. 324). All of these sites are within twelve miles of Polhill. In addition to the 107 known graves at

Polhill allowance must be made for those destroyed by road-works at different times. Looking at the gaps in the plan, but accepting the possibility of an uneven distribution, it seems highly likely that the original number of graves must have been in excess of 150. The cemetery is thus the largest so far recorded in West Kent.

The large size of the cemetery tends to imply a community of corresponding size in the close vicinity. The focal point of the immediate area is Otford, about a mile to the east of the cemetery, which seems the most likely settlement-site though nearer sites are possible. The cemetery does anyway stand on a crest dominating the whole region and it can be seen clearly from the centre of Otford. The village occupies a strategic position at the point where the North Downs Ridgeway (Ref. 179) descends into the valley and crosses the River Darent, more or less on the line of the present-day Pilgrim's Way. Otford was certainly important in Roman times with at least two substantial buildings, farmsteads and an extensive cremation-cemetery (Ref. 338). A single 6th century cremation-burial near the village may indicate a very early Anglo-Saxon community though the first mention of Otford is in A.D. 776 (Ref. 339). Some land in the area passed to the archbishops of Canterbury in late-Saxon times, whose lordship is recorded in the Domesday Survey and whose medieval manor was replaced by a Tudor palace in the 16th century (Ref. 340). Clearly, Otford has been a place of unusual importance for more than a thousand years and if the Polhill cemetery does reflect settlement there then the community must have been comparatively large in the 7th and 8th centuries A.D.

It is interesting to consider the possible numbers of the community represented by the cemetery. Allowing for the multiple graves and those destroyed the original number of people buried must have been about 200. As the dating evidence suggests that the cemetery was in use for about 100 years the average number of burials seems to have been about two per year. With a life expectancy of about 24 years it seems, therefore, that this cemetery represents a community of about 50 people. It must be stressed that this does not take into account infant mortality, apparently not represented on the site, nor other factors or circumstances not known to us. It does, however, provide a very broad basis for the purpose of future study and even if the figures are largely unrepresentative they do seem to preclude a community of several hundreds. Whatever the figures the evidence suggests a local community larger than any other so far known in West Kent between A.D. 650–750.

As regards the burials themselves the multiple graves are of special interest. Double burials do occur in other large cemeteries, but seldom in any number. Of at least twelve Kent cemeteries containing double burials only one of those published had more than three doubles and that was the very large Kingston cemetery (13 double burials) which contained a total of more than 300 burials (Ref. 341). With 16 double burials, out of a known total of 107, it is clear that Polhill had an unusually high number. Triple burials are again rare and in Kent only two or three other examples appear to have been recorded, though five skeletons were found in a grave at Bifrons (Ref. 342) and six in a grave at Stowting (Ref. 343).

INVENTORY OF GRAVES

1. Found during roadworks, June 1956. Miss M. Blumstein.

Grave 1
Adult male. No details or finds recorded.

Grave 2
Child. No details or finds recorded.

Grave 3
Adult female, aged 20–25 years. No details or finds recorded.

Grave 4
Axis about 060°. Adult female, aged about 40–50 years. Supine, right hand on pelvis, left arm by side. No grave-goods.

Grave 5
Axis about 060°. Adult female, aged 40–50 years. Supine, arms at sides. No grave-goods.

Grave 6
Axis about 060°. Young male aged 15–16 years. Supine, with left arm across pelvis and right arm by side. No grave-goods.

Grave 7
Axis about 060°. Adult male, aged 50–60 years. Supine, arms at sides. No grave-goods.

Grave 8
Axis about 060°. Adult male, aged 27–28 years. Supine, extended hands folded in lap.
(a) Small iron knife (11 cm.), by right side (disturbed).
(b) Iron buckle, under the body (disturbed).

Grave 9
Axis about 060°. Young male, aged 15–16 years. Supine.
(a) Iron seax (29·5 cm.), perhaps from beneath legs.

Grave 10
Axis about 060°. Adult male, aged about 45 years. Supine, arms by sides. No grave-goods recorded.

Grave 11
Axis about 355–005°, facing north. Male. Supine.
(a) Iron knife (19·5 cm.) resting on sacrum.
(b) Iron knife (incomplete) under sacrum, point towards head.

Grave 12
Axis about 060°. Male. Supine.
(a) Small knife on sacrum.

Grave 13
No details recorded. Perhaps female.
(a) Two iron latch-lifters with single hook ends.

2. Chance discoveries 1959-1963. Noted by Otford Historical Society.

Grave 14
Found during roadworks. Good condition, adult male, about 25 years of age and 5 ft. 7 in. in height. No other details.

Graves 15 and 16
Found during roadworks. No details or finds recorded.

Graves 17 and 18
Discovered by school-boys digging into the exposed chalk face. No details or finds recorded.

Grave 19
Discovered by workmen excavating base of reservoir on west side of site. No details or finds recorded.

3. Emergency-excavation October, 1964 during construction of Sevenoaks By-pass. West Kent Border Archaeological Group, assisted by other Kent groups under the Council for Kentish Archaeology emergency-scheme.

Grave 20
Axis 105°. Rectangular. 7 ft. 5 in. by 2 ft. 2 in. and 1 ft. 5 in. deep. Complete adult male, aged over 40 years and 5 ft. 8 in. in height. Supine, arms straight, left arm by side with hand on pelvis, right arm bent across chest. Chalk rubble packing on three sides suggests outline of wooden coffin at least 5 ft. 10 in. long and 1 ft. 3 in. wide.
(a) Iron knife, point towards head, under left pelvis (No. 560).

Grave 21
Axis 100°. Rectangular. At least 6 ft. 7 in. (east end damaged by bulldozer) by 2 ft. 1 in. and 10 in. deep. Fragmentary skeleton of adult, probably male, aged 40 years and at least 5 ft. 2 in. in height. Supine, legs and right arm straight.
(a) Iron knife, point towards feet, at left waist (No. 561).

Grave 22

Axis 105°. Rectangular. 6 ft. 10 in. by 2 ft. 1 in. and 1 ft. 3 in. deep. Partially complete skeleton of adult, probably male, aged 22–25 years and at least 5 ft. 4 in. in height. On back, head to left, arms and legs straight.

(a) Iron knife, point towards head, at left waist (No. 562).

Grave 23

Axis 110°. Rectangular. 8 ft. by 2 ft. 4 in. and 1 ft. 4 in. deep. Partially complete skeleton of adult male, aged 35–45 years and 5 ft. 7 in. in height. Chalk rubble packing on two sides suggests outline of wooden coffin about 6 ft. 2 in. by 1 ft. 4 in. Supine, legs straight, left arm across pelvis.

(a) Iron knife, point towards head, at left waist (No. 563).

(b) Group of six small iron objects on left waist, perhaps belt fittings (badly corroded).

Grave 24

Axis 95°. Rectangular. 4 ft. 10 in. by 2 ft. and 11 in. deep. Trace of child's skull, less than 5 years of age. No grave-goods.

Grave 25

Axis 020°. Rectangular. Damaged by bulldozer. At least 6 ft. 3 in. by 1 ft. 10 in. and 3 in. deep. Damaged skeleton, of adult at least 5 ft. 2 in. in height. Supine, left arm by side, right arm across waist, legs slightly bent to left. Originally excavated and photographed by Mr. Gordon Ankcorn.

(a) Iron knife, point towards head, at left waist (No. 564).

Grave 26

Axis 040°. Rectangular. 6 ft. 6 in. by 4 ft. 10 in. and 10 in. deep. Partially complete skeleton of adult male, 46–55 years of age, at least 5 ft. 3 in. in height, probably nearer 6 ft. On back, head to right, arms slightly bent and away from body, left leg straight, right leg slightly bent.

(a) Iron knife, vertical, at left waist (No. 565).

(b) Bronze buckle at centre waist (No. 491).

Grave 27

Axis 070°. Rectangular. 6 ft. 11 in. by 2 ft. 6 in. and 6 in. deep. Partially complete skeleton of adult male, aged 40–45 years and 5 ft. 7 in. in height. On back, head left, legs bent at 90° to left, right arm bent across body, left arm straight with hand on thigh. Signs of osteoarthritis.

(a) Iron spearhead on right shoulder with blade by right ear (No. 602).

(b) Iron knife, point towards head, on left pelvis and probably held in right hand (No. 566).

(c) Iron buckle at centre waist.

(d) Bronze stud at centre waist, perhaps belt-fitting.

Grave 28

Axis 055°. Rectangular. Damaged by bulldozer. 6 ft. 8 in. by 2 ft. 4 in. and 2 ft. deep. Incomplete skeleton of adult male, aged about 45 years and at least 5 ft. 6 in. in height. Head to right, legs straight.

(a) Iron knife, point towards feet, at left waist (No. 567).

(b) Two bronze buckles and strap-tags on right ankle (Nos. 492, 494 and 506).

(c) Bronze buckle at centre waist (No. 493).

(d) Iron objects on chest (corroded).

Grave 29

Axis 060°. Sub-rectangular. 5 ft. 5 in. by 2 ft. 5 in. and 10 in. deep. Largely complete skeleton of adult, probably female, aged 17–25 years and 5 ft. 6 in. in height, contracted to fit grave. On back, head to right, left arm and legs straight, right arm across pelvis.

(a) Iron knife, point to north-west, on chest (No. 568).

(b) Red bead on chest (No. 516).

Grave 30

Axis 070°. Sub-rectangular. 8 ft. 6 in. by 3 ft. 3 in. and 2 ft. deep. Partial skeleton of adult male, aged 25–30 years and 5 ft. 7 in. in height. On back, head to left, legs straight. Chalk rubble packing on two sides suggests wooden coffin.

(a) Iron knife, point to south-east, on left thigh (No. 569).

(b) Bronze lace-tag, below feet (No. 507).

Grave 31

Axis 045°. Sub-rectangular, cupped base. 6 ft. 8 in. by 1 ft. 8 in. and 4 in. deep. Fragmented skeleton of adult, probably male, 17–25 years and at least 5 ft. 3 in. in height. On back, head to right, legs together curving slightly to left, right arm bent double with hand on neck, left arm bent double with hand by head.
(a) Iron knife, point to north-east, at about right waist (No. 570).
(b) Iron object, probably a spearhead-socket (broken), along skull (No. 536).

Grave 32

Axis 070°. Sub-rectangular. 6 ft. 5 in. (foot destroyed by machine) by 1 ft. 8 in. and 8 in. deep. Largely complete skeleton of an adult male, 20–25 years of age, height more than 5 ft. 7 in. Supine, legs and right arm straight, left arm along waist. Packing on one side.
(a) Iron knife, resting at 45°, fallen inside left pelvis (No. 571).

Grave 33

Axis 075°. Rectangular, cut by pipe-trench. 3 ft. 9 in. by about 2 ft. and 5 in. deep. No bones or finds recovered. Probably grave of a child, aged 1–5 years.

Grave 34

Axis 085°. Sub-rectangular, cut by pipe-trench. 5 ft. 9 in. by about 2 ft. and 10 in. deep. Fragments of skull only. Child, perhaps 5–10 years. No grave-goods.

Grave 35

Axis 100°. Rectangular. 6 ft. 11 in. by 2 ft. 2 in. and 10 in. deep. Complete skeleton of adult male, 40–45 years and 6 ft. 2 in. in height. Supine, legs straight, right arm along waist, left arm by side with hand on thigh. Chalk rubble packing on both sides suggests presence of wooden coffin. No grave-goods.

4. Chance discoveries 1966. Recorded by B. J. Philp.

Grave 36

Axis 035°. Partly destroyed by machine. At least 4 ft. 2 in. by 1 ft. 8 in. and 6 in. deep. Partial skeleton, head, arms and feet missing. On left side, with knees bent at 90°. Adult, age about 25 years. No grave-goods recovered. Trace of black soil on base of grave.

Grave 37

Axis 065°. Sub-rectangular. West end destroyed by pipe-trench. At least 4 ft. 8 in. by 3 ft. and 8 in. deep. No skeletal remains. Probably adult female.
(a) Circular bronze disc brooch at about left thigh (No. 486).
(b) Iron knife, point to south-east, at about centre waist.
(c) Group of 12 beads at about chest level (Nos. 517–518).
(d) Bronze pendant, next to beads (No. 508).
(e) Two bronze rings, next to beads and pendant.

Grave 38

Axis 065°. Rectangular with rounded corners. 7 ft. 3 in. by 4 ft. and 1 ft. 5 in. deep. Centre cut through by pipe-trench. Partial skeleton of adult, probably female, aged about 23 years and at least 4 ft. 10 in. in height. Supine, arms slightly bent, legs probably straight.
(a) An iron knife and sharpening-tool(?) points towards feet, to right of lower right arm (Nos. 572–573).
(b) Two silver finger-rings on chest (No. 531).
(c) One bead, next to rings (No. 519).
(d) A bronze pin, next to rings and bead (No. 509).

Grave 39

Axis 065°. Rectangular, west end cut by pipe-trench. At least 5 ft. 2 in. by 2 ft. 11 in. and 10 in. deep. Partial skeleton of adult, probably female, aged 20–25 years and about 5 ft. in height. On back, legs and arms straight, right hand on pelvis.
(a) Group of iron objects between knees (Nos. 537–538), perhaps part of a chatelaine.

5. Rescue excavation March–April and July–August, 1967 by West Kent Border Archaeological Group, assisted by other Kent groups under the Council for Kentish Archaeology emergency-scheme.

Grave 40
Axis 065°. Rectangular. 6 ft. 7 in. by 3 ft. 4 in. and 1 ft. 1 in. deep. Largely complete adult male skeleton, aged about 20 years, 5 ft. 10 in. in height. Supine, arms and legs straight.
(a) Iron spearhead to left of head (No. 603).
(b) Bronze buckle between waist and left arm.
(c) Iron knife(?), parallel to body, next to buckle.
Bronze strip (No. 510) found in filling.

Grave 41
Axis 070°. Rectangular. 7 ft. 6 in. by 3 ft. 10 in. and 1 ft. 4 in. deep. Fragmentary skeleton of adult, aged about 26 years, but height greater than 5 ft. Grave-goods suggest female burial. Supine, legs straight, arms slightly bent outwards.
(a) Nine beads on right shoulder or by head (Nos. 520–521).
(b) Two finger-rings, one bronze and one silver, on right shoulder next to beads (No. 532).
(c) Group of iron objects between pelvis and left arm (Nos. 539–542).

Grave 42 (double). Plate XVIA
Axis 055°. Sub-rectangular, base tapered. 5 ft. 9 in. by 2 ft. 11 in. and 8 in. deep. Two skeletons in reasonable condition.
South: Adult, at least 4 ft. tall. On right side with right leg straight and left leg bent across it and arms under body. Clearly laid on side of grave to accommodate second body.
North: Adult, aged about 25 years, height at least 4 ft. 6 in. Supine, hands clasped on chest, left leg bent at about 100°, right leg slightly bent. Right side lies over and touches south skeleton.
(a) Bronze ring in back-fill, probably connected with south skeleton.
(b) Iron buckle on right pelvis of north skeleton (No. 495).

Grave 43 (double). Fig. 51 and Plate XVIB
Axis 060°. Sub-rectangular. 6 ft. by 2 ft. 11 in. and 10 in. deep. Two adult skeletons, one placed on side along south edge of grave with arm resting across the other. Probably buried together.
South: On left side, legs straight and right hip fallen forward. Left arm bent double to touch head, right arm bent outwards across north skeleton. Not aged and at least 5 ft. in height.
North: On back, head to right, arms and legs straight. Aged about 30 years and at least 5 ft. in height, probably female judging by finds.
Group of objects partly on and below left pelvis of north skeleton, perhaps on a chatelaine.
(a) Bronze work-box containing threads and chain (Nos. 488–489).
(b) Circular bone disc with perforations for attaching objects (No. 490). Green and iron stains suggest work-box and other items were once attached to this.
(c) Iron key (No. 543), knife and other iron objects of uncertain function (Nos. 544–545).

Grave 44
Axis 065°. Rectangular, sloping sides. 6 ft. 5 in. by 4 ft. 2 in. and 1 ft. 2 in. deep. Partial skeleton, adult, aged about 35 years, but height greater than 5 ft. On back, head to left, legs and right arm straight, left arm bent at 45° with hand on pelvis.
(a) Iron knife, point towards head, on left pelvis (No. 574).
Traces of carbonised wood standing vertically at each end 5 ft. 6 in. apart suggesting length of coffin.

Grave 45. Plate XVA
Axis 070°. Rectangular, with rounded corners. 7 ft. by 3 ft. 10 in. and 1 ft. 7 in. deep. Good condition, probably adult male, at least 5 ft. 6 in. in height, aged about 60 years. Supine with legs and arms straight.
(a) Iron spearhead, parallel to body on right side, shaft probably across right forearm (No. 604).
(b) Bronze buckle at centre waist (No. 496).
(c) Iron knife, point towards head between ribs and left arm (No. 575).
(d) Group of small iron nail-like objects by right hand.

Grave 46

Axis 065°. Rectangular. 6 ft. 3 in. by 3 ft. 2 in. and 10 in. deep. Incomplete skeleton of adult male, aged 20–30 years and at least 4 ft. 10 in. in height. Supine, legs and left arm straight, right arm across hip. No grave-goods. Two small potsherds in filling.

Grave 47

Axis 065°. Rectangular. 6 ft. by 3 ft. 8 in. and 1 ft. 1 in. deep. Complete skeleton of adult male, aged 25 years and 5 ft. 8 in. in height. On back, head to right, legs and right arm straight, left arm slightly bent. No grave-goods. Small area of black loam on chest, perhaps remnant of coffin.

Grave 48

Axis 045°. Rectangular, with rounded corners. 4 ft. 2 in. by 2 ft. 3 in. and 9 in. deep. Fragmentary skeleton of child, about 3 ft. in height and perhaps 3–5 years old. On right side, head to right, knees bent at 45° and left arm to side. No grave-goods.

Grave 49

Axis 035°. Sub-rectangular. 4 ft. 6 in. by 3 ft. and 1 ft. 3 in. deep. Slight trace of child's skeleton, at least 3 ft. in height and perhaps 5–10 years old. No grave-goods.

Grave 50

Axis 070°. Faint rectangular outline. About 4 ft. by 3 ft. and only 6 in. deep at centre. Slight trace of child's skeleton, perhaps about 3 ft. in height and 3–5 years old. No grave-goods.

Grave 51

Axis 070°. Faint rectangular outline. 3 ft. 6 in. by 2 ft. 6 in. and 4 in. deep. Child's grave, faint trace of bone. Probably aged 2–5 years by size of grave.

Group of objects found near centre of grave may have been enclosed within a container.

(a) Two bronze discs or pendants (Nos. 511–512).
(b) Three bronze rings.
(c) Two yellow beads (No. 522).
(d) An iron object.

Grave 52 (double). Fig. 51 and Plate XVIIA

Two graves, one partly superimposed across the other. It seems that the grave-digger of the north grave made a slight detour into the centre of the original grave, perhaps to recover valuable grave-goods. Four of the long-bones disturbed in this operation were placed on the south side of the second grave.

South: Axis 070°. Rectangular. 6 ft. 6 in. by about 2 ft. 6 in. and 7 in. deep. Partial adult skeleton, aged about 23 years and height at least 5 ft. 4 in. Supine, right arm slightly bent and right leg straight.

North: Axis 065°. Sub-rectangular. 7 ft. 1 in. by about 2 ft. 6 in. and 9 in. deep. Largely complete skeleton of an adult female, aged about 33 years and at least 5 ft. 4 in. in height. On back, head to left, legs straight, right arm straight resting along pelvis, left arm bent across pelvis and waist.

(a) Iron buckle at waist of south skeleton.
(b) Iron knife in back-filling of second grave, probably disturbed from original grave (No. 576).

Grave 53. Fig. 51

Axis 055°. Irregular outline. 6 ft. by 3 ft. and 1 ft. 3 in. deep. Damaged skeleton of adult, aged about 50 years, but at least 5 ft. 2 in. in height. Grave-goods suggest female. On back, head to right, right arm and legs nearly straight, left arm slightly bent across pelvis and hand on right pelvis.

(a) Bone comb across right arm (No. 487).
(b) Iron ferrule with attached iron ring under left thigh, perhaps a trinket-bag (No. 546).
(c) Bronze brooch touching iron ring below left thigh (No. 513).
(d) Bronze finger-ring on left hand (No. 533).
(e) Iron knife in grave-filling (No. 577).

Grave 54

Axis 065°. Rectangular. 3 ft. 10 in. by 2 ft. 1 in. and only 2 in. deep. Slight traces of child's skeleton. Height greater than 1 ft. 9 in., probably 1–5 years old. On right side, legs probably bent. No grave-goods.

Grave 55

Outline not certain. Probably child's grave about 2 ft. by 2 ft. and only 2 in. deep. Small patch of crushed bone. Age, probably 1–5 years.

(a) Group of objects near centre, perhaps placed in a container, consisting of a bronze ring, a bronze disc, a pair of small pear-shaped glass objects set in thin bronze mounts and two beads.

Grave 56

Axis 055°. Sub-rectangular. 6 ft. 7 in. by 3 ft. 3 in. and 7 in. deep. Adult in reasonable condition, aged about 15 years, height at least 4 ft. 6 in. Supine, arms straight, legs slightly bent to right. Charcoal fragments in filling.

(a) Iron tool for sharpening (?) lying parallel to body, point towards head, between waist and left arm (No. 578).

Grave 57

Axis 055°. Sub-rectangular. 4 ft. 6 in. by 2 ft. 2 in. and 5 in. deep. Child, in poor condition, probably 10–15 years and height at least 3 ft. 9 in. Supine, arms and legs straight.

(a) Iron knife, resting diagonally with point towards north-west, by left waist.

Grave 58

Axis 055°. Sub-rectangular. 4 ft. by 2 ft. 2 in. and 8 in. deep. No bones survived. Child's grave, probably aged 3–5 years.

(a) Iron knife, lying east-west, near centre.

Grave 59 (barrow)

Axis 110°. Rectangular. 6 ft. 8 in. by 2 ft. 8 in. and 1 ft. 7 in. deep. Only fragmentary bones, probably of a child about 10 years. No grave-goods. Compact chalk rubble packing on north side suggests wooden coffin with maximum width of 1 ft. 5 in.

Grave enclosed centrally by a shallow V-shaped ditch, about 1 ft. 6 in. wide as surviving, with damaged eastern causeway not wider than 4 ft. Barrow-ditch diameters, 13 ft. 9 in. internally and about 16 ft. 3 in. externally. Circular post-hole, diameter 10 in. and 5 in. deep on south side, probably for memorial-post.

Grave 60 (double). Fig. 51

Two graves, one very largely superimposed over the other. 2–4 in. of soil between skeletons.

Upper: Axis 070°. Sub-rectangular. 7 ft. 2 in. by about 3 ft. and 1 ft. 4 in. deep. Complete skeleton of adult female, aged about 50 years and height 5 ft. 3 in. On back, head to right, legs and arms straight, with right hand on pelvis.

Lower: Axis 050°. Rectangular. About 5 ft. 6 in. by 3 ft. Partial skeleton of young adult, height about 4 ft. and age probably 15 years. Supine, legs straight, right arm at angle to body.

(a) Iron knife, point towards head, at about left waist of lower skeleton (No. 579).

Grave 61

Axis 065°. Sub-rectangular. 5 ft. 11 in. (east end of grave removed by pipe-trench) by 2 ft. 9 in. and 6 in. deep. Adult, fragmentary condition, aged about 35 years, 5 ft. 8 in.–5 ft. 10 in. in height. Supine, arms straight, legs bent outwards. Small area of carbon, 5 in. by 3 in., between lower legs.

(a) Iron knife, point to north-west on left waist (No. 580).

Grave 62

Axis 055°. Rectangular, with rounded corners. 7 ft. 2 in. by 3 ft. 7 in. and 1 ft. 5 in. deep. Complete male skeleton, aged about 45 years and 6 ft. 1 in.–6 ft. 3 in. in height. On back, head rolled to right. Arms and legs straight, with left hand on left thigh.

(a) Iron knife, parallel to body with point towards head, between waist and left arm.

(b) Iron buckle(?) at centre waist.

Grave 63 (double)

Axis 060°. Sub-rectangular. 6 ft. 7 in. (bottom of grave destroyed) by 3 ft. 6 in. and 5 in. deep. Two incomplete skeletons, both probably adults, one largely superimposed over the other.

Lower: Probably supine, with arms and legs straight and height greater than 4 ft. Largely removed when upper body placed in same grave, but skull replaced between legs of upper skeleton.

Upper: On back, head rolled to left, arms and legs straight. Lower legs destroyed, aged about 34 years and height greater than 4 ft. No grave-goods.

Grave 64 (double)

Axis 055°. Outline destroyed. About 6 ft. 8 in. by 4 ft. 7 in. and 6 in. deep. Two skeletons in fragmentary condition, side by side with arms just touching. Both at least young adults.

South: Supine, arms by sides slightly bent outwards, legs missing. Aged about 28 years.

North: Supine, arms by sides slightly bent outwards, left leg straight, right leg bent to touch left. At least 5 ft. in height, probably female.

(a) Iron knife, point north-west, against lower right arm of north skeleton.

(b) Iron latch-lifter between waist and right hand of north skeleton (No. 547).

(c) Silver finger-ring, on end, by left jaw of south skeleton (No. 534).

Grave 65

Axis 060°. Rectangular, with rounded corners. 7 ft. 1 in. by 3 ft. 5 in. and 7 in. deep. Partially complete skeleton of an adult male, aged about 26 years and about 5 ft. 6 in. in height. Supine, legs straight, both arms slightly bent outwards at elbows.

(a) Iron spearhead 9 in. to left of skull, laid parallel with body (No. 605).

(b) Bead and bronze buckle on top of skull (No. 523).

(c) Bronze buckle, centre pelvis (No. 484).

(d) Iron stud (?) on right pelvis.

(e) Circular bronze wheel-ornament, 3 in. left of left elbow (No. 530).

(f) Iron knife, point towards head, between thigh and left arm (No. 581).

Grave 66

Axis 070°. Sub-rectangular. 4 ft. 8 in. (east end missing) by 3 ft. and 1 ft. 1 in. deep. Partially complete skeleton of adult, age not determined, but height greater than 4 ft., probably female. On back, head to left, arms straight, legs slightly bent and angled to left.

(a) Group of nine iron objects, found beneath left femur. These include a key, a knife, a sharpening tool, an iron ring and a purse-mount. Some of these items may have been attached to the ring (Nos. 548–550 and 582–583).

Grave 67

Axis 055°. Perfectly rectangular, with well-cut corners. 6 ft. 8 in. by 2 ft. 9 in. and 1 ft. deep. Partial skeleton in poor condition. Probably adult, aged about 25 years, height about 5 ft. On back, head to right, legs and arms straight. No grave-goods.

Grave 68 (double). Fig. 51

Two skeletons laid side by side, arms just touching. Probably buried at the same time. Axis 055°. Rectangular, with well-cut corners. 6 ft. 8 in. by 4 ft. and 1 ft. deep.

South: Partial skeleton, aged about 15 years. On back, head to left, legs and arms straight. Height about 5 ft.

North: Partial skeleton of adult male, aged about 30 years, 5 ft. 9 in. in height. Supine, legs straight, left arm across pelvis.

(a) Two spearheads, to left of head of north skeleton (Nos. 606–607).

(b) Iron knife, point to north-east, on pelvis and under left arm of north skeleton (No. 584).

(c) Iron buckle, to left of waist of north skeleton (No. 497).

(d) Iron knife, point towards feet, at left waist of south skeleton (No. 585).

(e) Iron purse-mount on right arm of south skeleton (No. 551).

Both spearheads were found at a higher level than the skeletal remains and may have been inserted whilst the grave was being filled.

Grave 69 (double). Fig. 51

Two skeletons, adult and child, placed in single grave probably at the same time. Axis 060°. Rectangular, with well-cut corners. 7 ft. 3 in. by 3 ft. 7 in. and 10 in. deep.

South: Partially complete skeleton of an adult, aged about 45 years, height about 5 ft. 8 in. Probably male. Supine, legs and left arm straight, right arm slightly bent.

North: Incomplete skeleton of child about 3 ft. in height and about 5 years old. On right side facing adult, one leg straight, the other slightly bent.

(a) Iron knife, point east, by right waist of child (No. 586).

(b) Iron spearhead, north of adult skull, perhaps between the two skeletons (No. 608).

(c) Iron knife, point towards head, at left waist of adult (No. 587).

(d) Stain of bronze at waist of adult probably marks position of a buckle, not found.

Grave 70

Axis 075°. Rectangular, with well-cut corners (east end damaged). 4 ft. 7 in. by 2 ft. and 5 in. deep. Fragmentary skeleton of child, at least 2 ft. 6 in. in height, probably 5–10 years old. No grave-goods.

Grave 71

Axis 050°. Rectangular, with well-cut corners. 5 ft. 7 in. by 3 ft. 2 in. and 8 in. deep. Slight traces of skeleton, aged about 15 years, at least 4 ft. 2 in. in height and probably an adult female. Supine, legs straight.
(a) Group of 7 beads at about left shoulder (No. 524).
(b) Iron object at about left elbow (No. 552).

Grave 72

Axis 060°. Rectangular, with well-cut corners. 4 ft. 5 in. by 1 ft. 11 in. and 7 in. deep. Single long-bone of child, perhaps 5–10 years old.
(a) Iron knife, point towards head, at about left waist.

Grave 73. Fig. 51

Axis 060°. Rectangular, well-cut corners. 7 ft. 4 in. by 3 ft. 2 in. and 1 ft. deep. Largely complete skeleton of adult male aged about 25–30 years and about 5 ft. 8 in. in height. Supine, legs and arms straight.
(a) Iron spearhead to north of left shoulder (No. 609).
(b) Iron knife, point towards head, at right waist (No. 588).

Grave 74

Axis 065°. Rectangular, with well-cut corners. 7 ft. 2 in. by 3 ft. 2 in. and 8 in. deep. Left arm and knee joints only. Adult.
(a) Iron knife, point to south-west, at about left shoulder (No. 589).

Grave 75 (double). Fig. 51

Two skeletons, adult and child laid adjacent, but at angles to each other. Probably buried together.
Axis 065°. Rectangular. 7 ft. 3 in. by 4 ft. and 11 in. deep.
South: Largely complete adult skeleton, probably female, aged 25–30 years and 5 ft. 6 in. in height. Supine, legs straight, arms bent slightly outwards.
North: Fragmentary skeleton of a child, about 2 ft. 9 in. in height and probably 5 years old. On back, legs straight.
(a) Iron knife, point towards head, at left waist of child.
(b) Iron knife and chatelaine-link(?) at left waist of adult (No. 554).
(c) Series of small iron bars encircling waist of adult.
(d) Group of corroded iron objects to north of adult, perhaps fittings from a wooden box (No. 553).

Grave 76

Axis 050°. Rectangular, with slightly rounded corners. 6 ft. by 2 ft. 10 in. and 1 ft. 4 in. deep. Largely complete skeleton of adult aged about 21 years, a female and height of 5 ft. 5 in. On back, head to right. Legs straight, arms across waist with hands together. No grave-goods.
Two patches of carbon, one between lower legs and the other at foot of grave, may represent traces of a wooden coffin.

Grave 77

Axis 055°. Sub-rectangular. 6 ft. 8 in. by 4 ft. and 1 ft. 6 in. deep. Adult male skeleton in good condition, age 26–35 years, height 6 ft. 2 in. On back, head rolled forward onto right chest, legs straight, right hand on right thigh, left lower arm across pelvis. Probably contained within a wooden coffin.
(a) Iron knife, point to south-east, on left waist (No. 590).
(b) Iron buckle at right waist (No. 498).

Grave 78

Axis 065°. Rectangular, with rounded corners. 3 ft. 4 in. by 2 ft. 1 in. and 6 in. deep. No bones left, probably child aged 2–5 years.
(a) Green bead, at about chest position.

Grave 79

Axis 080°. Rectangular, with rounded corners. 7 ft. by 2 ft. 8 in. and 1 ft. 3 in. deep. Traces of long-bones and teeth. Probably an adult. Compact chalk packing on all sides suggests possible wooden coffin, corresponding with trace of black substance, perhaps 5 ft. 9 in. by 1 ft. 10 in.

(a) Iron knife, point towards feet, at about left waist (No. 591).

(b) Iron buckle with bronze plate at about right waist.

Grave 80

Axis 045°. Rectangular, with sloping sides. 3 ft. 10 in. by 2 ft. and 1 ft. 2 in. deep. Skull and leg of child, probably aged 2–5 years. No grave-goods.

Grave 81 (double). Fig. 51

Two adult skeletons laid side by side, the left arm of one just crossing the right arm of the other. Probably buried together. Axis 060°. Rectangular, with well-cut corners. 6 ft. 8 in. by 3 ft. 4 in. and 10 in. deep.

South: Partially complete skeleton, adult, age not determined, but height about 5 ft. 6 in. and probably male. On back, head to right, legs and right arm straight, left arm bent across arm of north skeleton.

North: Fragmentary skeleton of young adult male, height about 4 ft. 3 in. Supine, legs and arms straight.

(a) Iron spearhead to right of skull of south skeleton (No. 610).

(b) Iron knife, point towards head, at left waist of south skeleton (No. 592).

(c) Iron object under right pelvis of south skeleton.

Grave 82 (double)

Axis 060°. Rectangular with well-cut corners. 6 ft. 6 in. (east end cut by pipe-trench) by 3 ft. 6 in. and 1 ft. 2 in. deep. Two incomplete skeletons, adult and child, side by side.

South: Partially complete skeleton of adult female, aged 18–25 years, height greater than 5 ft. On back, head to left, arms slightly bent and legs straight.

North: Partially complete skeleton of child, age not determined, height about 4 ft. On back, head to right, legs straight and arms slightly bent with right arm overlapping the left arm of the adult skeleton.

(a) Iron knife at left waist of north skeleton with point to south (No. 593).

Grave 83 (double)

Two skeletons in a single grave. Arrangement of bodies not known as grave almost completely disturbed. Bones mixed together in backfilling. An adult, probably male, aged about 25 years and a child aged about 2 years. Axis 070°. Rectangular, with well-cut corners. 7 ft. 5 in. by 2 ft. 11 in. and 1 ft. 4 in. deep.

(a) Bronze scabbard-chape found in backfill (No. 515). This suggests the presence of a seax and implies an important grave with several grave-goods.

(b) Iron object in backfill.

Grave 84. Fig. 51

Axis 050°. Rectangular, with well-cut corners at top tapering towards base. 7 ft. by 2 ft. 10 in. and 11 in. deep. Largely complete skeleton of adult male, aged 18–22 years and 5 ft. 8 in. in height. Supine, legs straight with ankles crossed, arms slightly bent with hands on thighs.

(a) Iron spearhead to right of skull (No. 611).

(b) Iron seax beneath right arm, point towards feet, handle by shoulder (No. 483).

(c) Iron ring at waist, perhaps for belt.

(d) Group of iron objects by right arm.

(e) Iron knife and an iron purse-mount between waist and left arm (No. 555).

Grave 85. Fig. 51 and Plate XVB

Axis 050°. Rectangular. 6 ft. 10 in. by 2 ft. 8 in. and 1 ft. deep. Almost complete skeleton of adult male, aged 30–35 years, height between 5 ft 8 in. and 5 ft. 10 in. Supine, legs and right arm straight, left arm bent with hand on thigh.

(a) Iron spearhead to left of head (No. 612).

(b) Iron seax, point to north-east, across right thigh with handle by right elbow (No. 482).

(c) Iron knife, point to north, by left hand (No. 594).

(d) Iron belt-buckle(?) on pelvis (No. 500).

(e) Bronze buckle over black patch (leather?) to north of left arm (No. 499).

(f) Two bronze purse-fittings (No. 514) and an iron purse-mount (No. 556) over black patch (leather?).

Grave 86 (double)

Axis 080°. Rectangular, with well-cut corners. 6 ft. 10 in. by 2 ft. 8 in. and 1 ft. 2 in. deep. Two skeletons in fragmentary condition, one an adult undisturbed and occupying the main central part of the grave. The other, a child, only represented by scattered bones and occupying a recess on the north side of the grave (axis 075°). It seems probable that the child was buried first and the adult (perhaps the mother) inserted immediately adjacent at a subsequent time.

South: Supine, legs and arms straight with hands just resting on thighs. Adult, aged about 50 years, 5 ft. 4 in. in height.

North: Child. Only three scattered long-bones.

(a) Yellow bead, 4 in. north of left ankle of south skeleton.

(b) Two more beads, 3 in. north of skull of south skeleton (No. 525).

Grave 87

Axis 060°. Rectangular, with slightly rounded corners. 4 ft. 6 in. by 2 ft. 6 in. and 10 in. deep. Partial skeleton of child at least 3 ft. in height, probably 5–10 years old. No grave-goods. Single coarse potsherd in filling.

Grave 88

Axis 040°. Rectangular, with well-cut corners. 5 ft. 2 in. by 2 ft. 8 in. and 1 ft. deep. Largely complete skeleton of young male 12–16 years and 5 ft. 4 in. in height. On back, head rolled forward onto chest. Legs straight, but angled to left. Right arm straight and lower left arm sticking up above pelvis. Position of arm and skull suggests burial within a wooden coffin, but no positive trace found.

(a) Iron knife, parallel with body, under right waist (No. 595).

Grave 89

Axis 055°. Rectangular, with well-cut corners. 6 ft. 5 in. by 3 ft. 3 in. and 1 ft. 2 in. deep. Partially complete adult male, aged 18–25, 5 ft. 6 in. in height. On back, head rolled to left, arms and legs straight, right hand on right thigh.

(a) Iron knife, point to north-east, at left waist (No. 596).

(b) Bronze buckle on right pelvis (No. 501).

Grave 90

Axis 070°. Sub-rectangular. 6 ft. 3 in. by 3 ft. and 1 ft. 1 in. deep. Complete female skeleton, aged about 25 years and at least 5 ft. 3 in. in height. On back, head to right, arms and legs straight and right hand across right thigh.

(a) Iron knife, point south-west, at centre waist.

(b) Bone object with six iron rivets, between ribs and right arm, very fragmentary, perhaps a comb.

Grave 91 (barrow). Plate XIXA

Axis 105°. Rectangular, with rounded corners. 7 ft. 3 in. by 2 ft. 7 in. and 1 ft. 7 in. deep. Complete skeleton of adult male, aged about 30 years and height 5 ft. 8 in. On back, head rolled to left. Legs straight, both lower arms on pelvis. Compact chalk rubble packing on all sides revealed outline of wooden coffin 6 ft. by 1 ft. 5 in.

(a) Iron knife, parallel with body, under left elbow.

Grave enclosed centrally by shallow ditch about 1 ft. wide in damaged state with eastern causeway 2 ft. 6 in. wide. Barrow-ditch diameters, 11 ft. internally and 13 ft. externally.

Grave 92

Axis 130°. Rectangular, with rounded corners. 7 ft. by 2 ft. 7 in. and 1 ft. 7 in. deep. Almost complete skeleton of an adult female, aged 35 years and 5 ft. 2 in. in height. On back, head to right, arms straight by sides, right leg slightly bent and left leg bent 90° with knee across right femur. Evidence of quite bad osteoarthritis. Packing on all sides revealed the outline of a coffin 5 ft. 8 in. by 1 ft. 5 in. No grave-goods.

Grave 93 (barrow)

Axis 100°. Rectangular, with rounded corners. 7 ft. 6 in. by 2 ft. 9 in. and 1 ft. 8 in. deep. Partial skeleton of adult, age not determined, but height about 5 ft. Supine, legs and left arm straight, but right arm crossed above waist.

(a) Iron knife, parallel with body and point towards head, placed by left thigh (No. 597).

Grave enclosed centrally by shallow V-shaped ditch, about 1 ft. 4 in. wide as surviving. Possible eastern causeway removed by reservoir. Barrow-ditch diameters, 11 ft. internally and 13 ft. 8 in. externally.

Grave 94 (barrow) Plate XIXB

Axis 055°. Rectangular, with well-cut corners. 4 ft. by 2 ft. 1 in. and 8 in. deep. No bones. Probably grave of child 1–5 years.

(a) Silver ring near west end.

(b) Complete hand-made pot at north-east corner (No. 481).

Grave 95 (double within a barrow). Fig. 51 and Plates XVIII and XIXB

Two skeletons in a single grave, adult and child probably buried together.

Axis 060°. Rectangular. 7 ft. 3 in. by 3 ft. and 1 ft. 6 in. deep.

South: Complete skeleton of an adult, female, aged about 20–25 years and 5 ft. 5 in. in height. On back, head to left, legs straight, right arm bent across waist, left arm bent to side with hand on left pelvis.

North: Fragmentary skeleton of a child, about 3 ft. 6 in. in height and probably 5–10 years old. On back, legs slightly bent, right arm straight and left arm across waist.

(a) Iron buckle on pelvis of child (No. 502).

(b) Iron knife(?) at right waist of adult.

(c) Iron latch-lifter by right thigh of adult (No. 557).

(d) Four beads by left collar-bone of adult (No. 526).

Both graves 94 and 95 were enclosed symmetrically within a single shallow ditch 1 ft. 1 in. wide as surviving, but missing on the south and north sides. No trace of an eastern causeway. East-west internal width 12 ft. and north-south internal length about 15 ft.

Grave 96

Axis 050°. Rectangular, with well-cut corners. 3 ft. 9 in. by 2 ft. 2 in. and 1 ft. 2 in. deep. Slight trace of small skull, probably of a child 1–5 years. No grave-goods.

Two sherds of pottery found in the filling, one indeterminate and the other Roman samian ware (Form 27) of 1st century A.D. date.

Grave 97

Axis 060°. Sub-rectangular. 5 ft. 4 in. by 3 ft. 2 in. and 11 in. deep. Aged about 15 years and height between 4 and 5 ft. Probably male. Incomplete skeleton. Head to left, legs bent slightly to right.

(a) Iron spearhead to north of skull, shaft over left arm (No. 613).

(b) Iron knife, point to north-east, on left waist.

(c) Iron pin (?), point to east, by right waist.

(d) Bronze buckle-plate(?) by right waist.

Grave 98 (barrow). Fig. 51 and Plate XIXB

Axis 100°. Rectangular, with rounded corners. 7 ft. 8 in. by 2 ft. 8 in. and 1 ft. 11 in. deep. Packing on all sides suggests outline of coffin 6 ft. 5 in. by 1 ft. 5 in. Complete skeleton of person at least 50 years of age, probably male, at least 5 ft. in height. Supine, legs and arms straight with hands on thighs.

(a) Iron knife, point towards head, left of chest.

Grave enclosed centrally by shallow ditch about 1 ft. 6 in. wide in damaged state with eastern causeway 2 ft. 6 in. wide in line with grave. Barrow-ditch diameters, 11 ft. internally and 14 ft. externally.

Grave 99 (treble). Fig. 51 and Plate XVIIB

Three adult skeletons in a single grave of unusual size and shape. The larger, central skeleton partially overlaps the others and was clearly placed in the grave last.

Axis 060°. Sub-circular. 6 ft. by 5 ft. 2 in. and 1 ft. 7 in. deep.

South: Largely complete skeleton of an adult, age not determined, but about 5 ft. 3 in. in height. On left side with legs bent to left and right arm bent double on side. Head touching the shoulder of central skeleton.

Centre: Complete skeleton of adult male, at least 50 years old and about 5 ft. 8 in. in height. Supine, right arm by side over south skeleton, left arm straight by side, legs bent double splayed out on each other.

North: Complete skeleton of adult female, 18–26 years of age, 5 ft. 6 in. in height. On right side with head resting on hands, legs slightly bent to right.

(a) Iron knife, point to north, at right waist of centre skeleton (No. 598).

(b) Bronze buckle on lower left arm of centre skeleton (No. 503).

Plate XVIIB. Grave 99, Anglo-Saxon cemetery, Polhill, Dunton Green (Site 24)

Plate XVIIA. Grave 52, Anglo-Saxon cemetery, Polhill, Dunton Green (Site 24)

Plate XVIII. *Grave 95, Anglo-Saxon cemetery, Polhill, Dunton Green (Site 24)*

Grave 100

Axis 110°. Rectangular, with rounded corners. 4 ft. 4 in. (east end under north-west corner of reservoir compound) by 2 ft. and 1 ft. 10 in. deep. Partial skeleton of child, height about 3 ft. 3 in. probably 5–10 years old. Supine, arms and legs straight. No grave-goods.

Grave 101

Axis 050°. Rectangular, with well-cut corners. 6 ft. 3 in. by 3 ft. 5 in. and 9 in. deep. Largely complete skeleton of an adult, aged about 35 years. Supine, legs and left arm straight, right arm bent with hand on waist. No grave-goods.

Grave 102 (double). Fig. 51

Axis 050°. Rectangular, 7 ft. 3 in. (east end not found), by 5 ft. 1 in. and 1 ft. 5 in. deep. Two incomplete skeletons, probably male and female adults, lying together. Probably buried at the same time.

South: Probably female, aged about 20 years, height 5 ft. 10 in. On back, head rolled to right, right arm straight, left arm across waist of male, legs bent slightly to left.

North: Male, age not determined, height about 5 ft. 6 in. Laid on left side with back to female. Right arm bent at 90° to right, left arm under body, legs slightly bent to left.

(a) Iron spearhead, on skull with shaft along body, north skeleton (No. 614).

(b) Iron knife and sharpening tool (?) points north and south, north of waist of north skeleton (Nos. 599–600).

(c) Group of iron corner-brackets and iron handle, probably from wooden box about 12 in. by 8 in., at feet of north skeleton.

(d) A total of 13 beads (Nos. 527–528) was found in the grave. Ten of these were found beneath the chin of the south skeleton; two were found 4 in. north of the lower legs of the north skeleton and one was found to the south of the upper arm of the south skeleton.

(e) A group of five silver rings (No. 535), beneath the chin of the south skeleton, next to the ten beads.

(f) Iron knife, point to south, at left waist under left elbow of south skeleton.

Grave 103 (double)

Two adult skeletons buried in single grave side by side, heads only an inch apart and upper arm of south skeleton across upper arm of north skeleton. Probably buried together. Axis 065°. Probably rectangular. 5 ft. 1 in. (east end cut by bulldozer) by 3 ft. 5 in. and 3 in. deep. Badly disturbed.

South: Fragmentary skeleton of adult, possibly female, aged 17–25 years and at least 4 ft. 6 in. in height. Supine, left leg straight, right leg bent at 90°.

North: Fragmentary skeleton of adult, probably female, aged 17–25 years and at least 4 ft. 9 in. in height. On back, head right, legs bent slightly outwards, arms straight.

(a) Bronze buckle at right waist of south skeleton (No. 485).

(b) Iron knife between waist and left arm of north skeleton (No. 601).

(c) Iron buckle on left pelvis of north skeleton (No. 504).

Grave 104

Axis 080°. Rectangular, with rounded corners. 6 ft. 2 in. by 2 ft. 5 in. and 10 in. deep. No bones survived. Child, about 7 years.

(a) Iron latch-lifter (No. 558).

(b) Iron knife(?).

(c) Iron hook(?).

All these grave-goods were at about the left waist position.

Grave 105

Axis 065°. Rectangular, with rounded corners. 6 ft. 1 in. by 2 ft. 6 in. and 11 in. deep. Disjointed skeleton, adult, possibly female, age more than 45 years and height about 5 ft. 10 in. On back, head rolled to left, right lower arm bent across waist, left arm straight. Right leg bent double to left, left leg folded and disjointed under right leg. Skeleton bunched and well away from west end of grave. Arrangement suggests body had slipped to east end of a wooden coffin during burial. No grave-goods.

Grave 106 (barrow)

Axis 120°. Rectangular, with rounded corners. 6 ft. by 2 ft. 10 in. and 1 ft. 1 in. deep. Partially complete skeleton of a child about 8 years old. Height probably about 4 ft. On back, head to left, arms and legs straight.

Chalk rubble packing on all sides gave clear outline of wooden coffin, 4 ft. 7 in. by 1 ft. wide.

(a) Iron knife, point towards head, at left of waist.

(b) Iron buckle on left hip (No. 505).

Grave enclosed centrally by shallow V-shaped ditch, about 1 ft. 6 in. wide as surviving. Eastern causeway 4 ft. wide. Barrow-ditch diameters, 11 ft. internally and 14 ft. externally. Just inside the causeway on the north-east side of the grave was a rectangular pit 2 ft. 4 in. by 1 ft. 1 in. and 1 ft. 2 in. deep. The sides were vertical and the base uneven. It seems probable that this held a memorial-post.

Grave 107

Axis 095°. Rectangular, with rounded corners. 3 ft. 10 in. by 2 ft. 2 in. and 1 ft. deep. No bones survived, but clearly a child's grave, probably aged 2–5 years. No grave-goods. Single coarse potsherd in filling.

THE DATING AND SOCIAL SIGNIFICANCE OF THE BURIALS IN THE POLHILL CEMETERY

By Sonia Chadwick Hawkes, M.A., F.S.A.

INTRODUCTION

The thirteen graves salvaged in 1956, the first in the cemetery of which we have any details recorded, were rightly judged to date from the end of the 'pagan' period (Ref. 320). Subsequent rescue work on the site, which has brought the total of graves recorded to 107 and provided a useful and it is to be hoped representative series of finds for assessment, has not fundamentally altered the chronological position. As we shall see from consideration of their grave-goods, the earliest burials in the cemetery must date from the first half of the 7th century and the last from perhaps a century later. What we have at Polhill, therefore, is yet another addition to the increasing series of Anglo-Saxon burial-grounds, which, mainly coming into use after the Conversion, may be regarded as nominally Christian, proto-Christian, or at least only semi-pagan. Known examples of these cemeteries are now quite numerous and geographically widely scattered. At Winnall (Ref. 330), as at Leighton Buzzard (Ref. 344), a pagan cemetery appears to have been abandoned for a Christian one; an event dated on both archaeological and historical grounds to the middle of the 7th century. Like most other late cemeteries, including Polhill, however, Winnall II—the Christian cemetery—occupied a typically 'pagan' position on high ground well away from any likely site of settlement. In discussing the situation at Winnall and using both coin and documentary evidence, I suggested that use of such burial-sites may have continued, with graves largely unfurnished after the end of the 7th century, down to about the middle of the 8th, by which time regular Christian grave-yards were being created, along with churches, in the towns and villages themselves.

Village grave-yards of the later Saxon period are at present little known, but they are beginning to be recognised. A large example is currently under excavation at Elstow, Beds. and this, characterised by 'strict-orientation with the heads at the west and in nearly all instances the absence of grave-goods', is well dated by stratification and association to 'the stage beyond the intermediate phase represented by the Leighton Buzzard (Chamberlain's Barn) cemetery', namely to the later-8th century and after (Ref. 345). Another, seemingly of this same period, is beginning to appear in the village of Eynsford, W. Kent (Ref. 346), only 4 miles down the river Darent from the Polhill (Dunton Green) cemetery under discussion here.

Whether a pagan cemetery of the 5th and 6th centuries and a Christian burial-ground of the later Saxon period will ever turn up elsewhere in the parish of Dunton Green remains to be seen, but meanwhile the intermediate phase is well and typically represented by the cemetery on Polhill.

THE GRAVE-GOODS

Weapons

By far the most numerous type of weapon found in Anglo-Saxon graves of the 5th to 7th centuries is the spear, which seems to have been the customary weapon of the ordinary member of the warrior class. There was nothing haphazard about the ownership of weapons: it was a matter of legal right and obligation. Thus the spear seems to have been carried, in death as in life, by all freemen and, perhaps, certain privileged members of the semi-servile classes of Germanic society, who were entitled to bear arms. High-ranking freemen will have carried in addition the prestigious and expensive two-edged long-sword. In the 7th century in particular some men carried the single-edged seax, a slashing weapon which was simpler and therefore cheaper to make than the sword. There has been much debate about the social status of these seaxmen, but it is arguable that they ranked lower than the swordsmen and higher than the simple spearmen. Men of the lowest social classes, the slaves and the majority of the half-free, went unarmed (Refs. 347, 348).

At Polhill, in the well-recorded western side of the cemetery, we find (unless there was originally one in the robbed Grave 83) no sword. Twelve men and one boy were buried with spears, the man in Grave 68 having two with heads of different sizes. Two men, in Graves 84 and 85, had seaxes in addition to spears; the man in Grave 83 had had at least a seax; and another seax was found, apparently by itself, in Grave 9 down in the south-eastern part of the burial ground. The destruction of so many graves and the poor state of so much of the skeletal material makes it impossible to tell how many adult males there were in the cemetery. Moreover, as we shall see, there are grounds for supposing that at least one generation was buried after the Church had stamped out the practice of weapon-burial. It is thus impossible to make any accurate estimate of the number of freemen in this community, though such indications as we have suggest it was under 50% of the male total.

It is noteworthy that not one of the weapon-graves contained a shield and this is a point of chronological significance. In the 6th century the spear-bearing Anglo-Saxon male, however ill-provided with other goods, was very frequently buried with his shield. But in 7th century cemeteries, with very few exceptions, e.g. Holborough, W. Kent (Ref. 324) and Horndean, Hants. (Ref. 349), there is a marked falling off in the incidence of shield-burial. This is well illustrated by the situation at Finglesham, E. Kent (Ref. 350); here, whereas out of seven 6th century graves no less than five were provided with shields, there was none in any of the twenty-two spear-graves of the 7th century. The provision of arms in Anglo-Saxon graves is a subject needing detailed research, but at present it looks as though, after the first decades of the 7th century, it came about that only the richest and perhaps least Christian of males were interred with their shields. The majority seem to have been equipped only with the offensive weapons, i.e. sword, seax and spear, which were their essential symbols of status. The lack of shields at Polhill is as strong an indication of the cemetery's late date, therefore, as are the types of weapons that actually were placed with the dead.

1. THE SPEARS

In the present state of research it is not possible to give an exact date for most Anglo-Saxon spearheads: far more well-dated associations are needed and many of the types seem anyway to have been long-lived. A very considerable advance on our knowledge of the subject is shortly forthcoming, however, from Michael Swanton and I am much indebted to him for allowing me pre-publication use of his work to assist with this consideration of the Polhill spears.

The spearheads from Graves 27 and 69 (Fig. 59, Nos. 602 and 608) have long, tapering, straight-sided blades of lozengiform section, that make a high obtuse-angled junction with the piece of solid shank separating the blade from its lengthy cleft socket. They belong to Swanton's series F.2, which he places mainly in the 7th century. The associations of the two examples from Polhill are not helpful and the most that can be said is that the knife from Grave 69 (Fig. 58, No. 587) is of a type common in the 7th century. Elsewhere, no series F.2 spear has been found securely dated within the 6th century, but several associations with low-cone shield-bosses suggest that the type was well in favour by the early-7th century. At Strood, W. Kent (Ref. 351) for example, one was found in company with an imported Frankish pottery bottle, a low-cone boss and an angon (Swanton series A.2) similar to those found with the royal burial in the Sutton Hoo, Suffolk, ship-grave and with the princely burial under the barrow at Taplow, Bucks., both of which may now be dated c. 625. A close parallel to the Polhill Grave 69 spear occurs with a low-cone boss in a grave at Narford, Norfolk (Ref. 352, Fig. 13, f and g). Very close also is one of two spears from Grave 16 at Alton, Hants. (Ref. 352, figs. 19, c–j, 20, a–m), where the associated objects included a sword with cocked-hat pommel and an early-7th century Kentish silver buckle with triangular plate decorated by Style II gold filigree work. The buckle had been badly damaged and repaired in antiquity and the shield-boss is of the taller conical variety, so in this case the probable date is around the middle of the century. Spears of the F.2 series were popular in E. Kent and at Finglesham examples were found, together with narrow seaxes and typically 7th century buckles, in Graves 107 and 198: the horizontal stratigraphy of the cemetery suggests that these graves were dug early in the century. The 7th century cemeteries on Sibertswold and Kingston Down yielded others (Ref. 353, pl. xiv, nos. 3, 12, 16 and 19), but unfortunately their grave-attributions and associations are too uncertain to be helpful for close dating. It is notable that as yet no F.2 spear has been found with a shield-boss of the very tall conical (or sugar-loaf) series which are generally dated to the second half of the 7th century and this may mean that the type flourished mainly during the first half of the century.

The badly damaged spear from Grave 73 (Fig. 59, No. 609), which has lost its blade-tip and the whole of its socket, has had a very long, unusually light, almost straight-sided blade that makes a low obtuse-angled junction with the short solid neck of the missing socket. It is difficult to classify and may be either one of Swanton's angular series E.3, or its lighter variant E.4, or else one of the rarer, slender leaf-shaped forms of series C.3: all have cleft sockets which are short in proportion to the whole. Swanton sees all these long-bladed types, which are most numerous in the prosperous and iron-rich kingdom of E. Kent, as a 6th century development which found established favour in the 7th. Their associations, which include several sugar-loaf shield-bosses, suggest that they remained in favour up to at least the end of the 7th century. The only object associated with the Polhill specimen is a knife (Fig. 58, No. 588) which appears to have the angled back that is characteristic of the 7th century, but in an unexaggerated form that possibly indicates a relatively early date.

The spearheads from Graves 45 and 68 (Figs. 59, Nos. 604 and 607) have slender leaf-shaped blades with proportionately long sockets cleft up their entire length. That from Grave 45 is very lightly made. They belong to Swanton's not very numerous series D.1, which has a date-range extending from the 5th to the end of the 7th century. In Kent, where they are quite common, datable associations suggest they were most in favour during the first half of the 7th century. At Polhill the associated knives, buckles and strike-a-light (Figs. 57 and 58, Nos. 575 and 584-5; Fig. 54, Nos. 496-7; Fig. 56, No. 551) are all 7th century types.

The spearheads from Graves 65, 81, 85, 97, 102 and perhaps also the fragmentary specimen from Grave 68 (Fig. 59, Nos. 605, 610, 612, 613, 614 and 606) belong to Swanton's series C.2. They have proportionately long leaf-shaped blades which are separated from their cleft sockets by lengths of solid shank. Most of the blades are slender, that from Grave 102 being exceptionally light and attenuated. According to Swanton the development of this series began in the earliest days of the Anglo-Saxon settlement, but, from their frequent association with low-cone or sugar-loaf shield-bosses, the majority of examples date from the 7th century, as is clearly the case at Polhill. Published examples include one from a rich grave of the first half of the 7th century at Coombe Bissett, Wilts., and others from later 7th century graves at Loddington, Northants., and Lowbury Hill, Berks. (Ref. 352, Figs. 15 and 16; 25, a–e; 27 and 28, a–c).

The spearheads from Graves 40 and 84 (Figs. 59, Nos. 603 and 611) belong to Swanton's series C.5. They differ from the C.2 series by the stouter lozengiform section of their attenuated leaf-shaped blades and by the lack of any clear junction with their sockets, which are cleft up only a part of their length. The series has a mainly Kentish distribution, but probably has some affinity to the series B.1 of socketed spikes. There is a 7th century socketed spike from Kingston Down, Grave 173, associated with a buckle cast in one piece with an openwork rectangular plate (Ref. 353, 1856, p. 73 with fig. pl. xiv, 8), and there are several hybrids similar to the Polhill Grave 84 specimen from 7th-century graves at Finglesham. The interesting point here is that all seem to be late graves, and one, Grave 144, contained an openwork buckle similar to that from Kingston and virtually identical with that from Grave L at Broadstairs, E. Kent, which was coin-dated by sceattas to c. 690–700 (Ref. 354, p. 18 ff., figs. 11 and 12; and Ref. 355). While there is nothing conclusive about this, it does raise the possibility that Grave 84 may have been one of the latest weapon-graves in the Polhill cemetery. As we shall see, the associated finds—seax and strike-a-light (Figs. 53 and 56, Nos. 483 and 555)—do not contradict such an idea, and the finds from the adjacent Grave 85—seax and pouch-fittings as well as spear (Figs. 53 and 54, Nos. 482, 499, 514 etc.) tend to support it. Close parallels to the stocky spear from Grave 40 occur, in association with late insular varieties of the narrow seax, in Grave 36 at Shudy Camps (Ref. 356, Figs. 3,4 and 7,1) and, in the grave with the famous Winchester hanging bowl, at Oliver's Battery, Compton, Hants. (Ref. 357), both of which are datable to the middle or latter part of the 7th century.

2. THE SEAXES

Single-edged weapons resembling an enlarged knife have been found in three graves at Polhill, while a grave robbed in antiquity yielded the scabbard-chape of a fourth. English writers have been accustomed to use the term 'scramasax' for this weapon, but a good case has been made for preferring 'seax', the Old English word for 'knife' (Ref. 358). It has the additional merit of bringing our terminology into line with that currently used on the

Continent, in German archaeological literature, i.e. 'Sax'. It seems sensible to adopt it, more especially since it admits of easier use in such compounds as 'narrow seax' or 'seax-grave'.

The seax from Grave 9 at Polhill (Ref. 320) has a total length of 29·5 cm., a proportionately short tang which makes a weak angle with the back and a sharper angle with the cutting edge of the blade, and a blade 22·5 cm. long, 2·5 cm. wide, with a flat back c. 0·7 cm. thick. Both back and cutting edge appear to curve as the blade narrows to its point. This seax corresponds closely to Continental narrow seaxes of the 6th century (Ref. 359), but all things considered it would be surprising if it were as early. In this country seaxes are rarely found in 6th century contexts, and their absence from such rich male assemblages as those containing ring-swords (Ref. 360) makes it clear that they were not a regular feature of aristocratic male armament at this time. The earliest example known to me comes from Grave 49 at Kingsworthy, Hants. (excavated by the author in 1961, but as yet unpublished), where it was associated with an angular fullered spearhead, its socket inlaid with bronze wire bands, of Swanton's series J, a low convex carinated shield-boss with long grip, a bucket and tweezers. The date is late-5th or early-6th century. This seax has a blade, just over 21 cm. long and 2·5 cm. wide at its junction with the now broken tang, which differs from that of the Polhill specimen by virtue of its attenuated triangular form: the back, grooved on either side, is quite straight and meets the equally straight but tapered cutting edge without any curvature at the point. That this was the standard 6th century form is suggested by evidence from Gilton, E. Kent, which was one of the few cemeteries to produce seaxes of this date: they have survived, unhappily, only as drawings. In Grave 10, together with a sword, a spearhead, a shield-boss with silver-plated rivets and a heavy white metal shield-on-tongue buckle—the last two objects suggesting a date in the middle of the 6th century—there was a seax with a blade about 20 cm. long and 2 cm. wide at the junction with its short tang. The original sketches show the blade to have been remarkably similar, in its slender triangular form, to that of the Kingsworthy seax (Ref. 353, 7; and Ref. 361, II; 12, fig. 3 on 11 verso, and 46–7). Also very like in form and date, apparently, was the seax, 30·5 cm. long overall, from Gilton Grave 56 (Ref. 353, p. 21 and Ref. II, 361, p. 30 and 46–7). The associated objects in this case included buckles, a sword with spherical pommel, a large spearhead, another shield-boss with silver-plated rivets and a silver-gilt cocked-hat pommel which may well have belonged to the seax. Slight and small though it is, the seax from Polhill Grave 9 has not this tapered 6th century blade-form, but more nearly resembles early-7th century seaxes from Finglesham Grave 33 and Kingsworthy Grave 32, which, though slightly broader, have similar parallel sided blades with curvature at the tip of both back and cutting edges.

The seax from Grave 85 at Polhill (Fig. 53, No. 482) has a total length of 38 cm. The blade, 26 cm. long, 2·5 wide and 0·5 thick at the back, is not unlike that from Grave 9, but the tang is much longer in proportion and makes up nearly a third of the whole. This long two-handed grip occurs sometimes on the Continental narrow seax (Ref. 359, pl. xxv, 6), but is more frequent amongst the broad seaxes, as at Bülach in Switzerland, for example, where such forms have been dated to the second half of the 7th century (Ref. 362, p. 60). In this country, too, the long grip appears to be a late feature. Narrow seaxes exhibiting it, all larger than our Polhill specimen, are known from Sibertswold Grave 177, in association with a sugar-loaf shield-boss (Liverpool Museum, nos. M. 6305 and 6537; Ref. 353, p. 132 and Ref. 363); from Shudy Camps Grave 36 (Ref. 356, fig. 7,1); from another late cemetery at Milton, Berks. (Ref. 364) and from the late 'Winchester Bowl' Grave (Ref. 357). It also occurs on late broad seaxes (Refs. 358 and 365). Thus the case for attributing the Polhill Grave 85 seax to the second half of the 7th century is quite a strong one.

The seax from Grave 84 (Fig. 53, No. 483), with damaged point and tang-tip, has a surviving length of 53·5 cm. The blade was originally about 40 cm. long and 3·6 wide, with a straight, flat back 0·8 cm. thick, which slopes in at an obtuse angle towards the point: unless much has been lost, the tang seems to have been relatively short. This seax has the proportions and form of some Continental narrow seaxes (Ref. 366, p. 28, pl. xxx, 6), but is longer, heavier and certainly much later in date. In England it has no close parallels, though there is a rather smaller example, length 42·5 cm. and width 3·2, with much the same form and proportion, from Chadlington, Oxon. (Ref. 367, p. 26 f., pl. vii, C,6), a cemetery which appears not to have come into use before the second half of the 7th century. English seaxes equal in overall length to the Polhill specimen are mostly either of the long-grip variety, which have shorter blades, or else are amongst those rare Continental-type broad seaxes, listed above, which have stouter blades between 4 and 6 cm. in width. Thus the seax from Polhill Grave 84 seems an unusual piece, and it may well be that its lengthy blade represents an insular weapon-smith's attempt at a long seax. There is only one other long seax from an Anglo-Saxon grave, the classic example from Kidlington, Oxon (Ref. 435). Though the Kidlington seax is much longer and heavier, some of the Continental long seaxes are not much larger than the Polhill example. If it is to be regarded as an early long seax, it can scarcely be dated before the very end of the 7th century and might even belong in the early-8th.

The triangular sheet-bronze scabbard-chape, which is all that is left of the seax in the robbed Grave 83 (Fig. 54, No. 515), is a simple version of a type of fitment represented most opulently in this country by the silver chape on the seax from the late-7th century burial at Ford, Wilts. (Ref. 365, p. 106 and 114 f., figs. 5, h and 6, h5). There are two closely similar bronze chapes on narrow seaxes from Shudy Camps Grave 36 (Ref. 356, fig. 7,1) and Marina Drive, Dunstable, Grave D2 (Ref. 368, fig. 2,2). In all three cases the scabbard had had other fittings for suspension, reinforcement or decoration, so probably the Polhill scabbard had been quite elaborate too. Continental and English parallels suggest a date late in the 7th century.

Dress-fasteners and Ornaments

Since the pagan custom of burying the dead fully clothed and wearing their personal ornaments seems to have continued throughout the 7th and possibly into the 8th century, at Polhill, as in other cemeteries of its period, a good many graves yielded objects which had fastened or adorned the dress of the time. We shall see that this differed in many respects from what had been fashionable in the 6th century.

1. BROOCHES

During the 6th century, for example, brooches were almost universally worn by women and presumably had a practical as well as an ornamental function in fastening the clothing. They were generally worn in pairs, but in some regions, including Kent, a rich woman might have as many as five. In the 7th century the fashion changed and the type of dress worn seems not to have required brooches as an essential feature. Aside from rare occurrences of pairs of miniature safety-pin or annular brooches, which were presumably still worn occasionally on the under-dress, the chief 7th century brooch-type, found only in the richer graves, was a large jewelled disc, or more rarely annular, brooch, which was worn alone probably to fasten a cloak or other outer garment.

The only Anglo-Saxon brooch from the Polhill cemetery is the large disc, diam. 5·5 cm., found with the female skeleton in Grave 37 (Fig. 53, No. 486). This is a one-piece casting in bronze, with tinning on its back and gilding on its decorated face. Its rounded rim bears the so-called 'light-and-shade' pattern of alternating plain and beaded sections; the raised border inside this is decorated with punched annulets; at the centre is a large circular cell set with a translucent pale green glass bead, which is secured to the backplate by a bronze rivet; and radiating from this are three wedge-shaped cells alternating with smaller round cells. One of the wedge-cells is inlaid with a flat piece of translucent pale amber glass, the other two with badly fitting curved pieces of dulled pale green glass, originally translucent, which are likely to have been salvaged from a broken glass vessel; the small circular cells have studs of brighter pale blue-green translucent glass, with slightly domed upper surfaces. None of the settings had any gold foil backing. Between the cells, the surfaces of the brooch are entirely covered with cast 'chip-carving' ornament in the so-called Style II manner; it consists of three pairs of confronted animals, each with large pear-shaped hip and clawed foot, a double- or triple-strand body that is back-bent and interlaced with another stranded loop. Heads have been omitted, perhaps for reasons of space, and this extra loop may be a residual feature representing the animal's jaw biting its own back. For a clearer and better-executed version of this design one must look to the similar but finer gilt-bronze disc-brooch from Faversham (British Museum, No. 1068–70 and Ref. 369, pl. ii, 9), on which the heads and biting jaws are fully shown. Related animals, arranged processionally between four wedge-cells, occur on a smaller, silver, disc-brooch from Faversham, now in the Ashmolean Museum at Oxford (Ref. 370. Fig. 196; and Ref. 371, pl. xxxii, 10), and on its close parallel from Guston (Leeds City Museum (Ref. 372), likewise in E. Kent. (For information about and a photograph of this brooch I am indebted to Mr. George Speake.) More decrepit animal ornament of this type is to be seen on several other such brooches from the Faversham cemetery, but elsewhere in Kent cast disc-brooches with developed zoomorphic ornament are rare. In basic design and detail —'light and shade' rim, border of circlets, arrangement of cell-work—the Polhill brooch looks to be a typical product of the E. Kent workshops, and thus a new addition to the series of cast disc-brooches, called by Kendrick Style B (Ref. 369, p. 432) and by Leeds Class I (Ref. 371, p. 115 f.), produced there during the late-6th and early-7th centuries. The finest examples were made in silver, but examples made of gilt-bronze with tinned backs are not uncommon at Faversham, and since, as we have just seen, this is the site which has yielded the most numerous parallels to the animal ornament, it is tempting to suggest that our Polhill brooch may have been the product of an East Kentish jeweller who had worked for the community at Faversham. There are differences to be explained, however. At Faversham, even bronze disc-brooches of inferior workmanship are expensively inlaid with imported garnets, and where the odd setting of green or amber glass occurs it seems usually to have been the result of repair-work. Big and basically handsome as it is, the Polhill brooch is rendered crude and almost grotesque by its cheap glass inlays. If it were the product of an E. Kent workshop, we virtually have to accept the notion that it reached its burial-place in W. Kent only after a local craftsman had attempted to make good, with local materials, its lack or loss of the more exotic jewels proper to it. Alternatively, it may have been made in W. Kent by an itinerant jeweller who had no supply of, or was working for a customer who could not afford, the foreign garnet and shell which were so much more readily available amongst the richer communities across the Medway. Dating the brooch is not easy, but its developed animal ornament and its large size bring it into some typological relation with the larger and mainly later bronze disc-brooches from non-Kentish areas, such as one with Kentish affinities from Grave 21 at Winnall II (Ref. 330, p. 35 f., fig. 11, pl. ii), which suggests that it may have been amongst the latest of the Kentish cast disc-brooches. In all probability it was made during the first decades of the 7th century, but it was kept in use long enough to be buried in fairly battered condition. Rim, surface gilding and glass settings are all very worn; it was buried without a pin, and even the lug for attaching the pin shows wear after breakage in antiquity. A rough perforation just inside the rim-border indicates that the brooch may have been adapted for secondary use as a pendant. Since it was found lying in the grave by the woman's left thigh, and there are iron stains on the rim and the imprint of an iron rod—clearly not the brooch's pin—across the back, it may well have been attached to a chatelaine hanging from the waist. Another possibility is that it was buried, along with iron objects, in a bag at the hip. Thus all the circumstances point to a date of burial some time after the brooch was first made, and Grave 37 is unlikely to have been dug before the second quarter or middle of the 7th century.

The brooch from Grave 53 (Fig. 54, No. 513) was likewise found by the left thigh, in a pinless and decrepit state which again suggests the presence of a containing bag. Probably the small iron ring (Fig. 56, No. 546) found with the brooch had functioned, together with draw-strings, to close the bag's mouth. This brooch is not of Anglo-Saxon make, but is a lineal descendant of a British type of the 1st century A.D., known as the 'Colchester' brooch. It belongs to a class of cast two-piece variants of Camulodunum type IV (Ref. 373). The spring-coil of the pin—both missing on this imperfect specimen—was protected by short semi-cylindrical side-wings and attached by an axial bar passed along the coil through a pierced lug projecting from the head of the bow; the hook, which retained the external chord of the spring mechanism, is here cast solid with the bow, so that the functional upper part has become simply a pierced extension of the lug, and the elongated end of the hook merely a vestigial mould-ing on the bow; the broken catchplate originally had a single decorative piercing. This type of brooch was in use at Camulodunum during the period c. A.D. 50–65, on other sites it survived a little later, but after the end of the 1st century any appearances it makes are residual, as of course is the case here. The Anglo-Saxon woman in Grave 53 had probably picked it up, already in damaged condition, from some nearby Roman site and had kept it in her purse as a curiosity or even as a lucky charm. There is nothing unusual in this: Anglo-Saxon women seem to have been avid collectors of outworn trinkets of Roman and even pre-Roman make and one woman at Kingsworthy, Hants., was buried with no less than two Roman brooches, a strap-tag, a knife-handle, several coins and pieces of glass, all seemingly useless but to her clearly worth treasuring.

2. PIN

Pins occur in Anglo-Saxon graves of all periods, and were used both on the dress and on the hair or head-veil. The only example from Polhill is the small, slender, specimen from Grave 38 (Fig. 54, No. 509), which is 3·5 cm. long. The round-sectioned shaft is hammered at the top to produce a neat round head; is faintly grooved 2 cm. below the head, and from here is square-sectioned as it tapers to the point. The latter feature is typical of the 7th century, and may be seen on numerous pins from late graves in Kent and elsewhere (Ref. 353, pl. xii, nos. 18, 20, 22, 24, and 25; and Ref. 356, fig. 4,A). There is a particularly close parallel to the Polhill pin from Grave 5 at Camerton, Somerset (Ref. 371, pl. xxxi), for which the associated pendants and glass stud suggest a date very late in the 7th century (Ref. 330, p. 48 f.).

3. NECKLACES

The earlier fashion for great strings of amber and multi-coloured glass beads gave way in the 7th century to necklets composed of comparatively small numbers of mainly monochrome glass beads, often threaded together with silver or bronze wire rings and, in richer graves, with pendants. Though not very rich or impressive, the Polhill assemblages are typical of the new mode.

Seven women were buried with some sort of neck ornament. The female in Grave 102S had eleven beads and five silver rings, which had evidently been strung together in an arrangement best illustrated at Leighton

Buzzard. In this cemetery, by great good fortune, several necklets had their strings partly preserved, thus enabling us to see how the rings were knotted edge-to-edge and the beads suspended between them (Ref. 344, p. 198 f., figs. 8, 9, 13 and 17). At Finglesham, where necklace-strings had not survived, it was nevertheless possible, by careful excavation and planning, to recover the arrangement of several such 7th century necklets, with very similar results. The woman in Grave 37 had twelve beads, a pendant and two rings, the one in Grave 41 nine beads and two rings and in these cases it is possible that the rings had been sewn to the dress with the rest of the necklet in a festoon between them (Ref. 374, p. 76). Of the other women's graves, 71 had seven beads, 86S three beads, 38 one bead and two rings, and 64S just a single ring at the throat. Four children, probably girls, had neck-ornaments: in Grave 51 there were two beads, three rings and two pendants; in Grave 55 were two beads, two objects described by the excavators as 'ear-lobes', a bronze 'disc' (perhaps a pendant) and a bronze ring; in 78 there was just a single bead, and in 94 a single ring. Beads were associated with two skeletons identified as adult males. Except in the case of large sword-knot beads (Ref. 360) such occurrences are rare and often accidental. Thus the small single bead found on the skull in Grave 65 may well have been an accidental inclusion at the time of burial. The two beads by the feet of the man in the double burial 102 may have been in the box, the fittings of which lay nearby. These wooden caskets were usually buried with women and as the other person in the grave was a woman, the beads are likely to have belonged to her.

4. PENDANTS

Nothing can profitably be said about the pendants and discs from Graves 51 (Fig. 54, Nos. 511 and 512) and 55. That from Grave 37, of bronze, diam. 2 cm., and with an outer border and inner circle of punched dots (Fig. 54, No. 508), is more interesting. It is a very simple example of a class of pendant, made of bronze or silver and usually with a central boss, which sometimes occurs in 6th century graves, mainly in the Anglian areas, as at Holywell Row, Suffolk, Grave 11 (Ref. 374, fig. 2,4) and is often to be found in 7th century contexts over a wide geographical area (e.g. Ref. 353, pl. xi, 24; Ref. 374, fig. 23,1; Ref. 356, fig. 4, F, 1 and G, 1–2; Ref. 344, fig. 13, b; Ref. 368, fig. 3, 10). On the Polhill example the perforation is probably a secondary suspension device, the original loop having broken away.

5. RINGS

The necklace-rings from Graves 38, 41, 53, 102 (Fig. 55, Nos. 531–3, 535), as also those from Grave 37, are all made from pieces of silver or bronze wire with their tapered ends twisted into the so-called 'sliding knot' fastening. The loose and untidy twists on one example from Grave 41 suggest that it may have been a survival from the 6th century, but the remainder have the neat, tight, twists characteristic of 7th century examples (Ref. 330, p. 37 f.). The band-shaped ring from Grave 64 (Fig. 55, No. 534), though found by the jaw, must originally have been a finger-ring. It is not closely datable.

6. BEADS

The most interesting single bead from the cemetery is the broken half of a very large amethyst from Grave 37, original length perhaps as much as 4 cm. (Fig. 55, No. 518). As is normal with such beads, it has been ground and polished and the thread-hole drilled through from either end. Amethyst beads were not made in this country, of course, but were imported: they were made either in Italy or the Middle East and came here by way of the same long-distance trade, from the Byzantine orient via Italy and the Rhineland, that furnished other exotic goods —Coptic bowls and porphyry from Egypt, cowrie shells from the Red Sea—which can be found in the richer Anglo-Saxon graves of the 7th century. During the course of this century amethysts found their way to the most distant parts of Anglo-Saxon England, but it is in E. Kent that they are most common and best dated. In Grave 41 at Gilton, Ash (Ref. 353, p. 15 f.), the associations, which include a Kentish jewelled disc-brooch of simple type, a Mediterranean-style openwork zoomorphic belt-mount, silver rings and beads, and a Visigothic gold tremissis in mint condition (Ref. 375, p. 103, fig. 1, L2), put the earliest known date for the burial of an amethyst bead before the end of the 6th century. The great majority of graves with amethysts are later than this, however. The latest coin-dated burial-context is Sibertswold Grave 172 (Ref. 353, p. 130 and Ref. 375, p. 111, fig. 3), which falls in the third quarter of the 7th century, but in some places amethysts may have survived in use longer still. Thus in Polhill Grave 37 it is the disc-brooch which dates the bead rather than *vice versa*.

The large barrel-bead of orange frit from Grave 38 (Fig. 55, No. 519) is another distinctive type mainly of the 7th century (Ref. 359, p. 76). They were apparently imported along with the amethysts, with which they are so often found together here and abroad (Ref. 376, p. 142, pl. iii). In the rich woman's grave found in 1860 at

Sarre, E. Kent (Ref. 377, p. 55–6, fig. 60), which contained a Coptic bronze bowl and a composite gold disc-brooch, beads of orange frit and amethyst occur on the famous necklace of Provençal gold solidi, which cannot have been assembled in this country before *c*. 615 or been buried before the second quarter of the century (Ref. 375, p. 107; Ref. 378, p. 7, n. 19 and 16). Other insular occurrences are not so well dated at present, but north German evidence (Ref. 379, pl. B) shows the orange beads in use as late as the 8th century.

Of the remaining glass beads from Polhill, some, like the translucent Prussian-blue ring from Grave 102 and the long cylinder from Grave 41, or the opaque red cylinder with marvered decoration of opaque white festoons and yellow spots from Grave 86 (Fig. 55, Nos. 528, 521 and 525) are probably survivals from the 6th century, but the other beads found with them are of types which predominated in the 7th. Amongst the opaque glass mono-chrome beads, white barrels (Grave 41) and short cylinders (Graves 37 and 71), red barrels (Graves 37, 41, 86, 102), and yellow rings (Grave 95), are not unknown in 6th century contexts (Ref. 359, p. 74 ff.) but are much more common in the 7th: yellow bicones (Graves 37, 51 and 55) and green bicones and short cylinders (Graves 37, 55, 78, 86 and 102), on the other hand, seem to occur only in 7th century graves. The same goes for the various forms— bicones, short cylinders, fluted rings and spiral segmented—made of semi-translucent deep turquoise glass (Graves 37, 41, 71 and 95), and also for the discoidal beads of similar glass metal which are decorated by marvered trails of opaque white glass (Graves 95, 102 and post-hole 21). The latter are very distinctive and can be paralleled in 7th century graves at Leighton Buzzard (Ref. 344, fig. 12 Grave 32), at Finglesham and Kingsworthy.

7. WHEEL-ORNAMENT

The openwork roundel found by the left side of the spear-bearing male in Grave 65 (Fig. 55, No. 530) is something of a problem piece. In the first place, dress-ornaments other than belt- or strap-fasteners are very rare in men's graves; in the second, it has no exact parallels even in Anglo-Saxon women's graves. In fact this cast-bronze wheel-model, diam. 2·8 cm., its rim and four spokes round-sectioned, its central hub flat, finds its closest parallels in the late pre-Roman Iron Age. It bears a close resemblance to a votive wheel from the cult-site at Hounslow, Middx., which also yielded the better-known model boars (Ref. 380, p. 147, fig. 172); and it is similar also to a wheel-shaped harness-mount from the famous hoard at Stanwick, Yorks. (Ref. 381, p. 49, fig. 12, no. 93). On the rim of the Polhill wheel, flanking one of the spokes, are two bronze protuberances, about 1 cm. apart, which could be the worn-down stumps of a broken suspension loop, so, like the Stanwick wheel, it may originally have been a harness-mount. If it were a survival from at latest the middle of the 1st century A.D.—and from its heavily worn condition this is not impossible—it differs from the similarly antique brooch in Grave 53 in that its Anglo-Saxon owner went to the trouble and expense of having it embellished for re-use. Both the Hounslow and Stanwick wheels have central sockets for decorative studs now lost, and it is possible that something of the sort exists, obscured by corrosion, on the hub of our Polhill wheel. Any original stud must have been lost, however, for the present decoration is unmistakably Anglo-Saxon in craftsmanship and 7th century in date. On both sides of the discoidal hub are the remains of bronze or silver collars for the reception of decorative settings. One such remains and consists of a domed shell roundel enclosing a granule of translucent pale green glass. This use of glass, instead of the more usual cabochon garnet, recalls the similar economies practised on the brooch from Grave 37, and suggests that the same jeweller was responsible for both. The two graves were not far apart and the trinkets may have belonged to members of the same family. The use to which the man in Grave 65 put the renovated model wheel is not altogether clear, but the remains of thread around its rim in the area of the original suspension-loop suggests that it may have been tied to the belt. Since the wheel was one of the symbols of the ancient sky god—Thunor in the heathen Germanic pantheon—it is possible that the wearer regarded it as a pagan religious amulet. Alternatively, as such a simple four-spoke wheel resembles a cross, it may have been worn by a convert as a token of Christianity. This seems the more likely explanation, for objects of explicitly Christian symbolism are not uncommon, in male as well as female graves (Ref. 330, p. 54 f.), in the group of late cemeteries to which we now must add Polhill.

8. BELT-BUCKLES

The type of dress-fastener found most frequently at Polhill was the buckle which had clasped a belt worn around waist or hips. Examples (or traces) of them lay in the waist or pelvic region of twenty-one skeletons, and their sex-distribution is very interesting. Fourteen occurrences were certainly with men (Graves 26–28, 40, 45, 62, 65, 68N, 69S, 77, 85, 89, 97, 99C), while five were with adults (Graves 42N, 52S, 79, 103S, 103N) and two with children (Graves 95N and 106) whose sex could not be determined from their bones. That they too had been males seems likely from the fact that not a single buckle was found with any known female. During the 6th century in

Kent, buckles and belt-fittings had been as integral a part of female as of male dress, so their lack, or scarcity, in female assemblages of the 7th century, while not everywhere as striking as at Polhill, does seem to indicate a definite change of fashion: the buckled belt, though it might be retained as an optional extra, was clearly no longer a functional necessity to women.

The buckle from Grave 28 (Fig. 54, No. 493) stands apart from the rest by virtue of its hollow-backed loop and shield on tongue. Buckles with tongue-shield but no plate occur in Kent and the Frankish dominions mainly in graves of the middle and later 6th century. On most the shield has a rounded base, however, and the Polhill variant with straight-cut base has few parallels and, in this country, virtually no dated associations (Ref. 370, p. 117 ff., fig. 211,5 and Tab. V). But there is an example from Grave 2 at Minden, in the Trier district (Ref. 359, p. 182 f., pl. xxxvi, 4), which shows the type surviving well into the 7th century. The straight-cut base seems to have been evolved primarily to allow the tongue-shield to interlock with a type of cast rectangular plate with stepped ends. Bronze belt-sets with such buckles and plates were in use at Bifrons, E. Kent, in Graves 43 and 73 (Ref. 382 and Ref. 370, figs. 213 and 229, Tab. V), during the second half of the 6th century, but the forms certainly retained their popularity during the first decades of the 7th. This is clear from the number of examples made in precious metal with garnet-set cloisonné and gold filigree decoration (Ref. 370, figs. 223-5, 230-1), which includes the very fine specimen from the royal burial in the Sutton Hoo ship-grave (Ref. 383, pl. xix, g), now numismatically dated c. 625-30 (Ref. 384, p. 47 ff.). All things considered then, and not forgetting the probable date of the associated shoe-fittings, there can be no reason to doubt that the buckle from Grave 28 was buried, like the rest of the finds in the Polhill cemetery, during the 7th century, though probably during its first half.

The other bronze belt-buckles belong to a common type with oval loop, plain or only very simply decorated tongue and, where it survives, a doubled rectangular sheet-metal plate with two or three rivets at the base. The most decorative, from Graves 65 and 103S (Fig. 53, Nos. 484-5), are also the largest, being made for a belt about 1·8 cm. wide. Some of the others are very small indeed and were intended for mere straps down to 0·9 cm. wide. Buckles like these do not normally occur in graves of the 6th or early-7th centuries, for then the predominating fashion amongst men was for broader belts and correspondingly bigger and heavier buckles. It was only after the first decades of the 7th century, apparently, that narrow belts with this type of lightly constructed buckle became almost universal. They are well represented in our late cemeteries and a number of useful associations with middling to very tall sugar-loaf shield-bosses (Ref. 352, figs. 16-18, 29-30) make it clear that their vogue lasted at least until the end of the 7th century. The iron buckles are mostly similar, though they tend to be larger. One from Grave 42 (Fig. 54, No. 495) may have had a double tongue, an unusual feature which is paralleled in the late-7th century burial at Ford, Wilts. (Ref. 365, p. 106 f., pl. xxvii, b).

9. SHOE-FITTINGS

Already in the 6th century, the upper classes on the Continent and especially in the Frankish dominions, had begun to embellish their leather shoes and garter-straps with metal buckles and tags. But it was not till the 7th, when the fashion had spread down the social scale and become more universal (Ref. 385, p. 26 f.; Ref. 386, p. 66) that it was adopted amongst the English. Even then, though various kinds of bronze fittings for shoes, garters and leggings are known, from graves of both sexes, in several of our late cemeteries (Ref. 330, p. 39; Ref. 387, p. 69 f.), they are not particularly common. In fact it is really only in Kent, the region most subject to foreign influences, that complete sets of shoe-buckles and tags are found in any numbers.

At the feet of the man in Grave 28 at Polhill were two small bronze buckles with rectangular plates, similar to those discussed above (Fig. 54, Nos. 492 and 494), one at least with remains of leather adhering. With them were two small strap-tags (Fig. 54, No. 506), their bronze so corroded as nearly to disguise the animal-head decoration on their fronts. Clearly this was a set for fastening a pair of shoes. Similar sets, consisting of a pair of miniature buckles and two or more strap-tags, were found on and around the footbones of several 7th century burials at Finglesham, males in Graves 95 and 198, females in Graves 20 and 157. The tags in Grave 95, which were probably buried not later than the middle of the century, have animal-head decoration (Ref. 388, p. 22; fig. 4– drawn before cleaning and eyes omitted) not dissimilar to, though more stylish than, that on the examples from Polhill.

In most graves of the period, however, where there are shoe-fittings they consist only of lace-tags without buckles. In Burwell Grave 83 (Ref. 374, p. 65, fig. 31, B, no. 3) and Winnall Grave 10 (Ref. 330, p. 12, fig. 9), these tags are simple cylinders of sheet bronze with one end flattened and riveted to grip a narrow lace. Near the feet of the male skeleton in Grave 30 at Polhill, was a tiny terminal, length 2·5 cm., made of sheet bronze rolled into a neat cone, with the open end spanned by a rivet and the outer surface decorated by transverse grooves and cross-hatching (Fig. 54, No. 507). Similar hollow-cones, with or without rivets, are known from a number of 7th century women's graves in Kent: at Kingston Down, a pair found by the head in Grave 185 had perhaps been enclosed in a wooden casket, the position of another in Grave 211 is unrecorded (Ref. 353, p. 75 and 79; Ref. 361, III, 49 verso, fig. 2); at Finglesham, in Graves 68, 163 and 180, single examples were found by the feet. The function of these objects is not absolutely certain—Faussett considered them ferrules for bone pins—but, despite their tendency to occur singly, it seems possible that they tipped the ends of leather thongs or laces used on shoes or leggings.

Accessories, Utensils and Containers

10. PURSE-FITTINGS AND STRIKE-A-LIGHT MOUNTS

Purses, pouches, wallets or bags are known, or can be inferred, from a good many Anglo-Saxon graves, especially those of women, but as they seem to have been made of leather or cloth their presence is often detectable only when they have fittings or contents of an imperishable kind. Thus in Grave 53 at Polhill it is primarily the condition and position of the brooch which suggests that the woman had a trinket-bag.

Definite traces of a leather pouch were found at the left hip of the seaxman in Grave 85, where they were associated with bronze fittings consisting of two small buckles with rectangular plates and two tab-shaped sheet-metal plates with stout rivets which had been passed through a thickness (of leather?) of about 6 mm. (Fig. 54, Nos. 499 and 514). Pouches with such bronze fittings are relatively rare and the two best-recorded parallels both come from men's graves of the late-7th century. In Grave 36 at Shudy Camps, which contained the seax with two-handed grip already compared to that from Polhill Grave 85, there was a leather pouch with three silvered bronze plates riveted to it and a small buckle and strap-tag lying close by (Ref. 356, p. 14, figs. 7, no. 2, and 8). In Grave 145 at Finglesham, the jumbled remains of a purse on the left forearm included a pair of riveted plates virtually identical with those from Polhill and still with leather adhering, a pair of miniature buckles and two tiny lace-tags. It contained a small hoard of eight silver sceattas, which date the burial to c. 700 (Ref. 375, p. 116, pl. ii, F 3–10; Ref. 389, p. 1). Any reconstruction of these purses will be somewhat conjectural, but it seems likely that the plates were riveted to the body of the purse and the buckles and strap-tags either fastened the flap of the purse or served to attach it to the belt.

Unlike the Finglesham and Shudy Camps purses, that from Grave 85 at Polhill contained, or was associated with, an iron object of a type which, in this country, has usually been called a 'purse-mount' (Fig. 56, No. 556). The German term is 'Feuerstahl', which is best translated as 'strike-a-light'. There need be no conflict of ideas here, since, as Lethbridge has argued (Ref. 374, p. 86) these objects probably served a dual purpose, as part of the framework of the tinder-pouch and as the steel from which to strike the spark for fire-lighting. Three others were found in the Polhill cemetery; one at the left waist of the seaxman in Grave 84, one under the left thigh of the woman in Grave 66 and another on the right arm of the woman in Grave 68 (Fig. 56, Nos. 555, 550 and 551). All have a flat and markedly triangular striking surface and where they survive, elongated and incurved terminals: the complete specimens from Graves 66 and 84 measure 7·4 and 8·5 cm. respectively. In form they differ noticeably from the more slender versions in vogue during the 6th century and in this country the best parallels appear to come from graves of the middle and later part of the 7th century. There are published examples from Burwell, Graves 42, 83 and 90 (Ref. 374, p. 54 f., figs. 26 and 27; p. 63, fig. 31, p. 66, fig. 30), from Shudy Camps, Graves 34 and 57 (Ref. 356, pp. 13 and 19, fig. 1) and from Lowbury Hill, Berks., in a rich sword-grave with tall sugar-loaf shield-boss (Ref. 352, fig. 27, k). Similar forms occur on the Continent and in both South and North Germany close parallels to the Polhill examples were buried in graves as late as the first half of the 8th century (Ref. 390, pls. ii, 10 and 24, xi, 5, and xxxiv, 15—from Altessing, Graves 4 and 7, Hellmitzheim, Grave 20 and Pfullingen; Ref. 379, fig. 47 and pl. xi—from Tangendorf, Grave 3 and Maschen, Grave 200). An interesting difference is that on the Continent they occur only with men, whereas in England they are found with skeletons of either sex.

11. KEYS AND CHATELAINES

Anglo-Saxon women were frequently buried with one or more keys or latch-lifters. At Polhill, the large specimens in Graves 43, 64, 66, 95 and perhaps also the textile-swaddled fragment in Grave 104 (Fig. 56, Nos. 543, 547, 548, 557 and 558) are likely to have been door-keys, either for house or store-room. They must surely indicate that the women who carried them occupied a position of domestic responsibility in the community, and it is interesting to note that these were not the women buried with jewellery. It looks, therefore, as if the female grave-goods reflect some class distinction, and that the key-bearer was not the lady of the house but the housekeeper.

Keys were usually suspended from the girdle by means of a simple ring, as in Grave 66 (Fig. 56, No. 549), but sometimes, as in Grave 43, they seem to have been attached, along with other objects, to a chatelaine. The iron links of the chatelaine in Grave 41 (Fig. 56, Nos. 539–541) may have served to suspend a pair of iron shears (Fig. 56, No. 542). Objects resembling chatelaine-links were also found in Graves 39 and 75S (Fig. 56, Nos. 538 and 554) and suggest that the male sex-identity arrived at from the bones is incorrect. Many chatelaines of the period were elaborate compositions including openwork metal discs, metal or bone rings, metal links or chains and dependent objects of various kinds. The only example of this kind at Polhill was that in Grave 43, where not only a key but also a bone ring and a bronze thread-box with bronze and iron chains were somehow suspended together at the woman's left side.

12. BONE RING (Grave 43; Fig. 53, No. 490)

This flat bone ring, max. diam. 6·3 cm., was once quite ornate: one side bears heavily eroded traces of an all-over pattern of double-ring-and-dot punch-work. Spaced more or less evenly around its edge are four holes (one now broken) which are stained quite through with iron oxide, as if iron links or rings had once been attached and a fifth which is significantly without metal staining, as if on this side attachment had been by means of a thong or thread. Exactly how this object functioned in the chatelaine-complex cannot now be determined, but comparison should be made with a similarly decorated and pierced bone ring in Grave 83 at Burwell (Ref. 374, p. 62 ff., figs. 31, A and 33), which is thought to have hung from the chatelaine with toilet articles attached to it. There was another such ring associated with chatelaine-remains in Grave 76 at Burwell (Ref. 374, p. 61, fig. 32) and others in similar situations in several 7th century graves at Finglesham. One of these was in Grave 8, which contained a bronze thread-box. This will be discussed further below.

13. BRONZE THREAD-BOX (Grave 43; Fig. 53, No. 489)

This cylindrical bronze box, overall height 4·7 cm., max. diam. 4 cm., is made of four separate pieces of thick sheet bronze; two broad strips for the sides of body and lid, two discs for closing the ends. Both strips were rolled into cylinders, their ends being overlapped and riveted, and in calculating their diameters, allowance was made for the lid to fit snugly over the body-cylinder. In height the lid-cylinder is 2·1 cm. and the body 3·2, but the latter has a partly functional, partly decorative, stop-ridge hammered up in relief 2·1 cm. from the bottom. Thus, when the box is closed, the ridge is exactly in the middle and the exposed and decorated parts of lid and body are of equal dimensions. The decoration, entirely carried out by means of repoussé dots less than 1 mm. across and done before the strips were rolled and riveted, is identical on both halves of the box. It consists of a band of simple, curvaceous, two-strand interlace within single borders. The basal disc is flat, the upper slightly convex: both are decorated by repoussé dots forming three concentric circles quartered by a simple Latin cross and both bear traces under their edges of the solder which fixed them in place. The riveted sides of body and lid are perforated for the insertion of attachment loops, which have their twin shanks tapped over on the underside and may have been meant to swivel, as one now does. Associated with the box were four figure-of-eight links cast in bronze, two still with the remains of iron links adhering in either end, the others encrusted with iron rust. Since the loops on the box itself also have broken iron rings or links hooked through them, the likelihood is that the halves of the box were joined by a chain of alternating bronze and iron links, or two short chains suspended from a ring—perhaps a lost metal ring, perhaps the bone ring discussed above. The chain or chains must have been long enough to permit the removal of the lid to get at the contents of the box, which partly survived and consisted of threads.

Bronze thread-boxes, also known as work-boxes, occur with such frequency in Anglo-Saxon women's graves of the 7th century that they are one of the period's leading type-fossils (Ref. 371, p. 96 ff.; Ref. 391, p. 31). This example from Polhill brings the total of provenanced occurrences to at least thirty-five (Refs. 436–445). Kent boasts the highest total after Yorkshire. The Polhill box is the only example from the western part of the modern county, but E. Kent has produced specimens from Dover, Buckland, Grave 107 (British Museum; excavated V. I. Evison), Finglesham; Grave 8 (excavated S. C. Hawkes), Kingston Down; Graves, 96 and 222 and Sibertswold; Grave 60 (Liverpool Museum: Ref. 353, p. 58, 81 and 112, figs. 11, 7 and 8 on pl. xiii).

In a number of instances—Uncleby 29, Painsthorpe Wold, Barton 2, Hurdlow, Kempston (both), Dunstable (both), Kingston 96, Sibertswold 60, and of course, Polhill Grave 43—the boxes had remained sufficiently airtight for their contents to be preserved. All were found to contain organic materials, mostly hanks of different kinds of thread and little pieces of cloth and one or two may have contained needles. It is perhaps somewhat astonishing to find that these carefully-made and often elaborately-decorated objects had functioned merely as containers for sewing-kits, but such seems to have been the case in Scandinavia too. Well-preserved sewing-threads were found in a box, intricately decorated with engraved zoomorphic ornament in late Style II manner, from Grave 426 at Nørre Sandegaard, Bornholm (Ref. 376, p. 135 ff., 145 ff., figs. 9–11, 14–15) and a like use is to be presumed for the similar box from Grave 1 at Kyndby, Sjaelland (Ref. 392, p. 75, 129 ff., figs. 5–7). Both boxes are squatter than the majority of our insular series and have a different lid-construction. They are more akin to a numerous series of squat cylindrical boxes from 7th century East Frankish graves (Ref. 393, p. 44, figs. 20–21, list and map 4; Ref. 359, p. 124 f., pl. xxiii, 5–6), which were likewise worn at the girdle but which, as far as their contents are known, seem not to have been thread-boxes so much as containers for aromatic herbs and spices.

In the great majority of cases the lid was designed to be pulled off and like the body, was provided with its own attachment-loop to permit independent suspension from a chain. The Polhill box had side-fastening chains and this was the most usual mode of attachment, though, in Kingston Grave 222, the atypically tall and plain box has one chain affixed to the centre of its lid. Occasionally, as on the boxes from Sibertswold Grave 60 and Finglesham Grave 8, lid and body were joined by small hinges, but in general no obstacle was placed in the way of easy access to the interior. There is thus a major difference between the English and East Frankish boxes which must surely have been dictated by their different functions. Their aromatic and sometimes exotic contents have caused the major series of Continental boxes to be classed, along with a series of more lavishly decorated, hinged, spherical containers (Ref. 393, p. 38 ff., figs. 17–19, list and map 3, pl. xi, 1–4), as 'amulet-capsules' of a prophylactic or talismanic significance, which Professor Werner believes to have been Christian. As such they may well have been designed to be kept closed except on very rare occasions. The English boxes, by contrast, appear to have had a straightforward domestic use and easy removal of the lid must have been a matter of practical convenience.

Their origin is still somewhat obscure. There are no 6th century English prototypes and boxes analogous in form and use on the Continent are rare (Ref. 393 p. 46). One, buried not far from the Channel coast near Londinières, Seine Inférieure (Ref. 394, p. 310 f. and fig.), is so very like the English examples that it must surely have been an export. The clue is perhaps to be found in the other parallels cited by Werner. There is an undecorated example, with the remains of a centre-lid attachment as on the Kingston Grave 222 box, from late-6th or early-7th century Grave 87 in the Lombardic cemetery of Nocera Umbra in Italy (Ref. 395) and just across the Alps from Lombard Italy, two further examples are known from graves in Burgundy, at Arçon (Ref. 396) and with remains of threads at Lussy (Ref. 397, p. 187, fig. 129). Just possibly, then, the inspiration for the thread-boxes was amongst the many contributions that 7th century Anglo-Saxon culture received, by way of trade and the Roman Mission, from Italy. With few exceptions, however—notably the box from Kingston 222, which looks like an import from such a quarter—the great majority of our thread-boxes represent and illustrate a wholly insular development.

Just a few are plain; the famous piece from Burwell Grave 42 has developed Style II animal ornament and figural scenes executed in repoussé, but this is exceptional; the great majority are decorated, like the Polhill box, with simple geometric patterns composed of rows of tiny punched dots. The sides of the lid generally bear simple horizontal lines; the bodies combinations of horizontal, vertical and diagonal lines or chevrons. The unprovenanced box in the Ashmolean Museum bears a swag pattern, but curvilinear ornament is rare and I know of nothing comparable with the simple but smoothly sophisticated interlacing on the Polhill box. Technically and artistically this is a very superior example of its kind. Most thread-boxes have lids that are short in proportion to the decorated parts of their bodies and thus the symmetrical construction and lay-out of ornament on the Polhill specimen is unusual. The nearest constructional parallel is afforded by the box from Dover, which, though in other respects— oval section, enormous attachment-tab and undecorated sides—it differs markedly, likewise has lid and body of equal height. The concentric ring ornament on the lid and basal discs of the Polhill box is standard and its combination with a cross-pattern is frequent. Cross-motifs appear in one form or another on the lid and/or bases of thread-boxes from Uncleby Grave 29, Garton Grave 7, Barton Grave 2, Cransley, Burwell Grave 42, Northleigh, Ashmolean unprovenanced, Finglesham Grave 8, Kingston Grave 96 and Sibertswold Grave 60. This can scarcely have been coincidental and it seems that our thread-boxes, though not strictly amulet capsules, nevertheless very often bore overtly Christian symbolism.

This is not in the least surprising if we consider the dates of these boxes. That they are type-fossils of the 7th century has already been stated, but when one examines the dating evidence more closely it becomes clear that not one of these boxes need have been buried in a pre-Christian context. To take the Kentish situation first, it is noticeable that none has been found in any of the rich graves with jewelled disc-brooches of the late-6th and early-7th centuries. Where the boxes have datable associations they appear to be appreciably later: the cross-decorated gold pendant from Kingston Grave 96 (Ref. 353, pl. iv, 11) is unlikely to have been made before the middle third of the 7th century; and while there is nothing closely datable in Finglesham Grave 8 itself, it lay alongside and was presumably contemporary with Grave 7, in which a child had been furnished with coins that date her burial to *c*. 675 (Ref. 375, p. 115 f., pl. ii, F.1 and F.2). Grave 7 also contained silver 'bulla' pendants and biconical gold wire beads and thus helps to date, within the second half of the 7th century, necklets and associated finds from a whole series of important women's graves (Ref. 330, p. 47 f.). Amongst the objects so dated are a good many of our thread-boxes. The grave under Standlow contained a biconical silver bead. Silver bullae were found in one of the thread-box graves at Kempston (18.1.1864), in Burwell Grave 121 (Ref. 374, fig. 36, 3) and in Garton Grave 7, where there was a zoomorphic annular brooch of late type (Ref. 398, p. 248, pl. lxxv, No. 367). A comparable brooch was found in Uncleby Grave 3, along with two thread-boxes and a buckle (Ref. 371, pl. xxvii) of a type discussed earlier as datable to *c*. 690–700. Bidford Grave 100 contained a sapphire-headed pin of a type elsewhere found in association with 'bulla' pendants and biconical wire beads (Ref. 330, p. 47 f.). On the box from Burwell Grave 42, the Style II animal ornament and scenes of men fighting monsters must be seen as an inferior and later rendering of similar themes used on some of the finest jewellery from the Sutton Hoo Ship, now known to have been buried *c*. 625 (Refs. 399 and 407). The box had received heavy wear and was clearly many years old when it was finally buried, together with a pin of the type discussed above, late in the 7th century. The Northleigh box bears on its lid scratched interlace ornament of late-7th century type. Ornamented objects found in association with two other thread-boxes, the bronze die from Barton-on-Humber Grave 1 (Ref. 400, p. 71 ff., fig. 12, 1, 1a) and the chatelaine pendant from Painsthorpe Wold barrow 4 (Ref. 398, pl. xxv, fig. 281) are not so readily datable, but they are certainly not early-7th century pieces.

In conclusion, then, it seems that the thread-boxes were in use chiefly, if not exclusively, during the second half of the 7th century and that this is the context for Polhill Grave 43.

14. COMBS

A fragmentary bone comb was found in Grave 53 (Fig. 53, No. 487) and the bone object from Grave 90 may have been part of another. Both were graves of women. The most common type of comb used during the early Anglo-Saxon period was the parallel-sided, double-edged, form, with compositive toothed blades held together by a pair of riveted mid-ribs (Ref. 401, p. 75 f.), which was a survivor from Roman times. During the course of the 7th century, however, alike in England and on the Continent, there came into use alongside it a single-edged comb, with curved back-plate, which was ultimately to become the leading form of the Viking age (Ref. 402, p. 87 ff.). This is the type represented in Polhill Grave 53, where, unhappily, it has no significant associations. But 7th century occurrences in England are not so very infrequent and several similar combs have come from well-dated graves. Perhaps the earliest of them is the very richly furnished Grave 299 at Kingston Down (Ref. 353, p. 91 ff.) the contents of which included a damaged jewelled disc-brooch of Leed's Class 1b (Ref. 371, p. 115 ff.), of late-6th or very early-7th century date, which was with the comb in the box at the woman's feet and a typologically later composite form of disc, Leed's Class II, which she was wearing at her neck. This burial may have taken place during the second quarter of the 7th century and it is interesting that the comb, relatively small and simple, looks to be typologically an early specimen (Ref. 353, pl. xiii, 4). A longer and more lavishly decorated single comb from Kingston Grave 142 (Ref. 353, p. 66 f., pl. xiii, 2), another rich grave with a necklace of amethyst beads, silver crosses and garnet-set gold pendant, is likely to have been buried during the second half of the century. Of like date is the long comb from Burwell Grave 121 (Ref. 372, fig. 36, 5), associated with silver bulla-pendants and thread-box, perhaps also the more decorative comb from Grave 83 (Ref. 374, fig. 34) and certainly the elaborate comb from Garton Grave 12 (Ref. 398, p. 251, pl. lxxxvii, fig. 671) which was associated with objects including a gold-mounted lignite pendant, similar to those from a very late-7th century barrow-burial on Roundway Down, Wiltshire (Ref. 330, p. 47 ff., pl. v). Thus, though the subject deserves fuller research than it has received so far, present evidence suggests that the long hump-backed single comb was more prevalent after the middle of the century than before.

15. SHEARS

A small pair of iron shears, suitable for cutting cloth, thread and hair, was found with the woman in Grave 41 (Fig. 56, No. 542). These implements are found in both male and female graves, but for some reason seem to be more frequent in graves of the 7th century than earlier (Ref. 403).

16. KNIVES

Of the fifty-seven knives found in this cemetery (Figs. 57 and 58), twenty-nine came from graves of men, leaving only five (one anyway robbed in antiquity) without this essential cutting and eating tool; twelve came from graves of women, leaving as many as thirteen without; eight came from graves of unsexed adults, leaving ten without; and only eight came from graves of juveniles under fifteen years of age, leaving twenty-one without. The knives from Anglo-Saxon graves have not so far been afforded any systematic study, but general impressions suggest that they may be classed and dated according to the types distinguished by Böhner (Ref. 359, p. 214 f.) for the Trier region: Type A, with back and cutting edge both incurving to the point, which was used from the 5th to the 7th century; Type B, with straight back, which was the favourite type of the 5th and 6th centuries but went out of use in the 7th; Type C, with cutting edge virtually straight and back strongly angled or curved into the point, which was the leading type of the 7th century; and Type D, with cutting edge making a convex and the back a concave, with the curve to the point, which was a specialised type of the 7th century. The Polhill knives are in many cases too fragmentary for classification, but it will be seen from the illustrations that type A is represented in Graves 25, 66 and 68; Type B only in Grave 23; Type C in Graves 20, 21, 22, 27, 28, 31, 38, 45, 53, 60, 61, 69, 73, 77, 81, 85, 93, 99 and 102; and Type D in Grave 74. The overwhelming preponderance of the dominant 7th century Type C is fully in accord with the rest of the dating evidence from the cemetery. However, the extreme forms of Type C represented in Graves 20, 22, 61 and especially 99 should be noticed for in areas of the Continent where furnished burial continued into the 8th century, knives with this marked degree of angularity or curvature of the back are the standard form (Ref. 390, passim; Ref. 404, figs. 2 and 3). It is possible, therefore, that some of the knives from Polhill are likewise of the 8th century.

17. TOOLS

Parallel-sided, blunt-edged, blunt-ended iron tools, with tang for attaching a wooden handle, occur very frequently in 7th century graves (Ref. 330, p. 44). At Polhill they were buried with the females in Graves 38 and 66, the male in Grave 102 and the unsexed adult in Grave 56 (Fig. 57, Nos. 573, 578; Fig. 58, Nos. 583, 599). In all cases they were found at the waist and in three in close association with a knife. This is usually the case in other cemeteries too and they are presumed to have been some form of steel or sharpening tool.

18. CASKETS

In the Frankish dominions, the richer women of the 6th century were sometimes buried with caskets in which they had stored trinkets and treasured personal possessions, but in Anglo-Saxon England such caskets are unknown before the 7th century, when they became all the rage. Their iron or bronze handles, angle-pieces, hinges and locks are amongst the most frequently recurring finds in our late, proto-Christian cemeteries: Faussett's Kentish cemeteries and also Finglesham yielded numerous examples, Lethbridge found several in his Cambridgeshire cemeteries and they appear more sporadically elsewhere (Ref. 344, p. 196). The Roman form of the locks, reappearing here after a lapse of two centuries, suggests that these caskets may have been another introduction from the world of the Mediterranean. With very few exceptions indeed, they were buried with women and contained such things as combs, tools, spinning and weaving equipment, amulets such as cowrie shells and bits and pieces of jewellery. At Polhill possible box-fittings were found by the feet of the adult in Grave 75, who, though identified on anthropological grounds as male, was probably a female. An iron handle and corner pieces of a box were found in Grave 102. Though placed by the feet of the man, it had probably belonged to the woman buried alongside him.

19. POTTERY

The cemetery's solitary pot, from the child's Grave 94 (Fig. 53, No. 481), with its markedly everted rim, globular body and round base, cannot readily be paralleled among the 7th century forms normally present in our late cemeteries. But there are similarities between it and North German pottery of the 8th century (Ref. 404, fig. 2) and it is also possible to see in it a precursor of Kentish hand-made forms of the later Saxon period (Ref. 405, fig. 9, 1). The Polhill pot may well be of 8th century date.

GENERAL ANALYSIS

The eighty-eight graves excavated since 1964 contained the skeletons of one-hundred-and-six individuals, comprising seventy-seven adults and twenty-nine children, none of whom had been at all richly provided with grave-goods. Even the burials of the better-equipped and presumably socially superior members of the community had been furnished, in the case of women, just with a few dress-ornaments and domestic utensils and, in the case of men, with essential dress-fasteners, utensils and the weapons which they were legally entitled to carry in life and afterwards, before the Church finally stamped the practice out, to take with them into the grave. Only one burial, of a child, was provided with a container for a food-offering. Further, a total of thirty-six (34%) individuals, comprising twenty (26%) adults and sixteen (55%) children, were buried without any associated objects at all. Another twenty-six (24·5%), comprising seventeen (22%) adults and nine (31%) children, were buried with only a knife or other single utilitarian object, while another nine (12%) adults had only a knife and belt-buckle. Thus as many as seventy-one (67%) individuals in this community, comprising forty-six (60%) adults and twenty-five (86%) children, were buried either with nothing or merely with everyday essentials. This high proportion of unfurnished or semi-furnished burials, not typical in the full pagan period, is characteristic of late cemeteries everywhere. It seems to be symptomatic of a gradual decline, after the Conversion, in the practice of depositing grave-goods with the dead.

In this regard it is noticeable at Polhill, as in the unpublished cemeteries at Finglesham and St. Peter's in East Kent, that the burials surrounded by penannular ditches and originally under small barrows, which one would expect to have been of people socially superior to the majority, are in fact outstandingly ill-provided with grave-goods. That, despite their sparse furnishings, they had indeed been of relatively high-ranking personages is suggested, at Polhill, by the size and regular shape of the graves, their wooden coffins and by the way they cluster around the enigmatic group of post-holes in the upper western corner of the cemetery: post-holes which may have formed the ground plan of some religious structure or have fulfilled some ritual purpose. The answer at Polhill seems to be that the ditched barrow-graves were a late phenomenon, belonging to a time when grave-goods had been reduced to a minimum.

At present the latest securely datable graves in our proto-Christian cemeteries are those few with purse-hoards of silver sceattas (Refs. 355 and 389) ascribable to a period extending from the very end of the 7th century through the first decades of the 8th and none of them has yielded additional finds other than purse-fittings, belt-buckles, keys or knives. We have no coin-dated jewellery or weapons for the period after c. 675 and thus no certain proof that such things were being buried with the dead as late as the 8th century. The coin-graves, therefore, have only a limited use in establishing the absolute chronology of the later burials in such a cemetery as Polhill. But they do at least tell us that we can expect to find semi-furnished and unfurnished burial continuing in these proto-Christian cemeteries for some time after the end of the 7th century. At Polhill, amongst the sparse finds from the barrow-graves (Fig. 51), we have the pot from Grave 94, tentatively dated to the 8th century; we have the iron buckles from Graves 95 and 106, which, though of an undistinguished and long-lived type, can nonetheless be closely paralleled in Grave 145 at Finglesham, sceatta-dated to c. 700; and from Grave 99, adjacent to the barrow-group, we have a typologically late Type C knife, again paralleled in Finglesham Grave 145, which on the Continent could be dated in the 8th century. Therefore, though the evidence is slight, it seems quite possible that the barrow-graves and some of the adjacent flat-graves, in the upper westerly corner of the Polhill cemetery, may have been dug during the first half of the 8th century. And so too may the little group of ill-furnished male Graves, nos. 20–23, at least two of which contained late-looking knives, that lie to the N.N.E. along what appears to have been the upper limit of the cemetery.

On this east side of the site, road-works had caused the total destruction of the cemetery's original terrain, but on the better-preserved and fully-excavated western side it can be seen that the upper boundary lay roughly along the 420 ft., the lower along the 400 ft. contour-line, with the burials occupying the steep 1 : 6 slope in between. Reminding ourselves that the probable 8th century burials were all dug at the top of this slope, it is time now to consider the better-furnished and presumably earlier graves, lower down the hill.

Taking the men first and excluding for the moment those in the area incompletely excavated and partly destroyed by road-works, we have twelve weapon-graves. With only one exception, that of the child in Grave 97, all these armed males lie below the 410 ft. contour-line and thus lower than the barrow-graves. This example of what is known as 'horizontal stratigraphy' may have some chronological validity. It is perhaps not irrelevant to note that the two spears which I have tentatively dated, on independent archaeological grounds, early-to-middle 7th century, occur in Graves 73 and 69, which are down near the lower limit of the cemetery and that a spear with analogues datable middle-to-late 7th century occurs in Grave 40, which lies midway up the hill near the 410 ft. contour-line. But the simplistic view, that burial proceeded from the bottom to the top in strict chronological order, should be slightly modified by a critical look at the male assemblages and a comparison of it with that of the female, for together they make it clear that there must have been family burial-areas within the cemetery that

Plate XIXA. *Barrow containing Grave 91, Anglo–Saxon cemetery, Polhill, Dunton Green*
(Site 24)

Plate XIXB. *Barrows containing Graves 94, 95 and 98, Anglo–Saxon cemetery, Polhill,*
Dunton Green (Site 24)

Plate XXA. *Post-holes at the north-west corner of the Anglo-Saxon cemetery, probably representing a funerary structure or hut, Polhill, Dunton Green (Site 24)*

Plate XXB. *Medieval tile-kiln in Chapel Wood, Hartley (Site 28)*

contained more than one generation's dead. The most obvious of these groups is that of the three seaxmen, probably all members of the community's 'top family', who were buried midway between the 400 and 410 ft. contour-lines on the extreme western edge of the cemetery and whose weapons and other grave-goods have been considered in some detail. If I am correct in my dating of his seax and spear, the young man in Grave 84 may have been buried towards or even slightly after A.D. 700, perhaps a generation later than the older man in Grave 85 who lay immediately beside him on the uphill side. Had Grave 83 not been robbed, the relationship between these three men might have been further clarified, but the impression they give is of two rather than three full generations of one family.

Turning now to the datable women we find that the richest and earliest of them, the lady with the jewelled disc-brooch in Grave 37, was buried during the period second quarter to middle-7th century. She lies somewhat above the lower limit of the cemetery, quite close to the contemporary spearman in Grave 69 and she is in some way linked, through possession of ornaments set with green glass, to the spearman in Grave 65. He lies about 30 ft. downhill from her, on the lower edge of the cemetery. Immediately alongside and below her is the woman in Grave 38, who may have been her contemporary or a member of the next generation. Perhaps the latest datable woman is the one buried with the thread-box in Grave 43, who is likely to have been buried late in the 7th century and it is interesting to note how she lies, well above the 410 ft. contour-line, close to the barrow-group. Thus far the women's graves do not upset any notional horizontal stratigraphy. But now we must turn to the east side of the fully excavated area and note two further women's burials of the second half of the 7th century, the female with the hump-backed comb in Grave 53 and the lady with the bead- and wire-ring necklet in Grave 102. The latter of course dates the spearman buried with her. Both graves lie on the 400 ft. contour-line, but in fact they are not on the cemetery's lower limit because here there is an unexcavated area and then graves extending down to and below the 390 ft. contour-line. So much has gone unexcavated that it is profitless to speculate whether here too some of the lower burials were earlier. The plans suggest that the part of the cemetery largely destroyed by road-works was of greater extent than the western area we have been discussing hitherto. Analysis of this imperfectly explored part of the cemetery would be useless and it only remains to repeat that nothing salvaged from it suggests a date before the 7th century.

To sum up our conclusions about the western area of the Polhill cemetery, burial seems to have started not much before the middle of the 7th century and to have continued unbroken into the 8th. Analysis of the grave-goods has shown that there was a nucleus of early burials on and close to the 400 ft. contour-line and that later burials fanned out up and along the slope in a chronological sequence partly modified by family groupings. The 8th century burials were at the top of the cemetery, along the 420 ft. contour-line, with the barrow-burials in the westerly corner.

It is assumed that these people were from the start nominal Christians and objects of possible Christian significance have been noticed with one of the earlier burials, in Grave 65 and one of the later, in Grave 43.

Fascinating though it has been to examine the cemetery in depth and to attempt to distinguish social gradations in the people there buried, the fact remains that even for the 7th century the grave-goods are not rich or socially distinguished. The prestigious long-sword, indicative of high social rank, which has been found in 7th century graves in many parts of England, including West Kent, was found with none of the men at Polhill. The high-class jewellery of the period, likewise known from every part of England, including West Kent (Ref. 406) is conspicuously absent from the women's graves at Polhill. We may conclude, therefore, that unless the largely destroyed eastern side of the cemetery was much richer, the leaders of the community buried at Polhill did not come from the higher classes of Anglo-Saxon society, but were perhaps of the 'Ceorl' class; the freeman and smaller landholders who were the backbone of society in rural England.

A METALLURGICAL REPORT ON TWO IRON KNIVES FROM POLHILL

By Dr. A. R. Cox

In Anglo-Saxon times, iron swords and scramasaxes were made by forge-welding thin pieces of iron together. In some cases as many as forty-three separate pieces were used, but the resulting improvements in toughness and reliability were no doubt appreciated. In a report of the battle in Swanfirth against Snorri, Steinthor found 'the fair wrought sword bit not whenas it smote armour, and oft he must straighten it under his foot' (Ref. 408). For the two Polhill knives, however, radiography showed them to consist of only one piece, suggesting their purpose was essentially domestic.

The actual structure of one knife (from Grave 77) showed what is metallurgically termed equiaxial ferrite containing both elongated slag stringers and other inclusions, probably carbides. Compared with this a piece of the second knife (from Grave 90) showed considerable variation in the grain size, the outer ones being smaller than those at the centre, whilst in one area some acicular ferrite was evident.

In practical terms, the first knife (Grave 77) contained little carbon, $<0.05\%$ and both knives were forged at high temperatures. In the second instance (Grave 90) the temperature was less than 900 °C. and the iron was hammered manually. Some attempt to harden the knife by quenching in water is apparent, but since the carbon content is so low no increase in hardness is obtained. The hardness of the knives was about 150 V.P.N., which compares with a value of 330 V.P.N. from an ordinary present-day kitchen knife.

In conclusion, the knives appear similar to those previously found on Saxon sites and confirm the skill of the early smith.

REPORT ON WOOD-SPECIMENS FROM SAXON GRAVES AT POLHILL

(supplied by Ancient Monuments Laboratory)

Traces of wood were detected in a number of iron objects found in the graves at Polhill. Careful examination has shown that eight specimens can be identified, as follows:

Grave 27   Spearhead. Traces of hazel in socket.
Grave 31   Iron shaft, perhaps a spearhead. Traces of ash in socket.
Grave 65   Spearhead. Traces of hazel in socket.
Grave 68   Spearhead. Traces of oak in socket.
Grave 81   Spearhead. Traces of oak in socket.
Grave 84   Spearhead. Traces of oak in socket.
Grave 85   Spearhead. Traces of hazel in socket.
Grave 97   Spearhead. Traces of oak in socket.

TEXTILE FRAGMENTS FROM POLHILL

By Elisabeth Crowfoot

No. 1. Attached to a Bronze Buckle (Grave 28)

Inside chape, remains of leather belt; fibrous patch on underside also probably leather, from tongue of belt. Top side of chape, traces of replaced fine Z-spun threads from weave.

No. 2. Inside Bronze Work-box (Grave 43)

A lump of fibrous matter, measuring roughly 3·5 by 3·1 cm., with a splinter of wood in the middle. The fibres are brittle and deteriorated, but as far as can be seen form Z-spun threads, with perhaps some plyed fragments. Dr. M. L. Ryder describes the fibre as 'too degraded for a positive identification, although it looks like flax'. A few tiny plant fragments, probably a moss, were caught among the threads.

Unfortunately the textile matter is too far deteriorated to say if it was simply linen thread loosely wound round the wooden splinter, or if fragments of weave were present. These attractive work-boxes have elsewhere been found to contain not only spools and balls of yarn, but also little scraps of woven fabric and threads left over or unravelled from finished work. The most varied collection, in a box from Kempston, Bedfordshire, includes pieces from two linen textiles, plain weave and twill, scraps of wool twill with remains of coloured embroidery and a tangle of threads similar to those used in the pattern. A work-box from Sibertswold Down, Kent (Grave 60) contained a fragment of fine green and brown wool tablet-weave, a mass of plyed yarn, probably the unused warp-ends and unspun wool fibres; in one from Marina Drive, Dunstable (Grave E 1/2) were fragments of linen and wool plain weaves and linen thread wound round an iron pin. In this case, three of the linen fragments have a narrow hem on one side and one of those from the Kempston box has stitches possibly from an oversewn seam.

Obviously fine coloured threads were worth preserving, though the linen fragments do not seem so immediately re-usable. They might perhaps have had some significance for the owner of the box, but it seems most likely that Anglo-Saxons, like many modern needlewomen, but with perhaps more economic justification, made a habit of hoarding any little scraps that might come in useful.

Acknowledgements: Kempston, British Museum, 189.6.24.339,340; Sibertswold, to be published by Sonia Chadwick Hawkes for Liverpool City Museum; Marina Drive, Dunstable, report by Dr. A. B. Wildman, Wool Industries Research Association, by permission of Luton Museum.

No. 3. Attached to an Iron Purse-mount (Grave 68)

One surface, area 5·5 by 3·5 cm. overall, replaced textile lying in a curve or twist, long Z-spun threads c. 9 to 0·5 cm. Much of the surface is deteriorated, but where clearest the threads seem to interlace in long chevrons, suggesting a tablet-woven border or band; this must have been over 2 cm. wide and the length of the twists indicates a coarse weft and perhaps loosening of the weave before the warp-ends finish in a fringe; at one broken-off edge four bunches of 4-5 threads each lie slanting across each other, suggesting these ends were plaited. The type of tablet-weave may have been a 2-hole diagonal version (cf. very similar threads in a narrow border from Mucking, Grave 622); an area of short twists in one part perhaps indicates a pattern (see diagram for a 6th century braid from Snartomo, Norway, Ref. 409).

This fragment could have come from a braid used to fasten the purse to a belt, from the belt itself, or from the border on a garment; if this ended in a plaited fringe, it would most probably have decorated a cloak.

No. 4. Attached to a Bronze Buckle-plate (Grave 79)

Replaced textile, probably several folds, clearest area 0·9 by 0·4 cm. on broken fragment and on plate 1·3 by 0·5 cm. Z-spun both systems, probably plain weave, surface deteriorated. Impressions of insect pupae. Inside and under the plate, fragments probably leather from belt.

No. 5. Attached to a Bronze Scabbard-chape (Grave 83)

Replaced coarse fibres next to the bronze on the outer surface, probably fleece, or raised nap from a weave. Inside tip, layer of fibrous matter, probably leather; at end furthest from point, a coarse flax thread, Z-spun, probably 4-ply S, lies inside the bronze channel; a tuft of this thread protrudes from the leather by the rivet, suggesting it was used to fasten the leather covering to the scabbard before the bronze tip was riveted on.

Catalogue of the Illustrated Finds from Polhill, Dunton Green (Figs. 53–59)

By Audrey Gibson

(The finds not drawn, particularly some of the iron objects, were generally too fragmentary for adequate illustration)

Pottery

Only one complete pottery vessel was found in the whole cemetery and this came from the north-east corner of a child's grave within the largest barrow. It was filled with soil and there was no trace of cremated bone.

No. 481. (Grave 94). Coarse, hand-made pot without decoration, of black ware with an uneven black-brown surface. Slight traces of shell tempering. Probably 8th century.

Seaxes

Only three graves are known to have contained seaxes, but a bronze scabbard-chape in another grave (Grave 83) suggests the presence of a fourth. One seax was found in Grave 9 in the 1956 salvage excavation.

No. 482. (Grave 85). Short iron seax about 15 in. in overall length. Thin blade with flat back and tapered point. Round pommel 1·1 in. wide, on handle. Probably second half of 7th century.

No. 483. (Grave 84). Iron seax, probably originally about 1 ft. 9 in. in overall length, with pommel missing. Blade 0·3 in. thick, with flat back and tapered point. Probably late-7th, or early-8th, century.

Buckles (for discussion see page 193)

No. 484. (Grave 65). Bronze buckle with oval loop and slightly curved tongue. Faint incised transverse lines on loop and single incised line on tongue. Double-square plate folded around loop and held by three bronze rivets and decorated with 'E' shaped pattern of punched dots, probably middle to late-7th century.

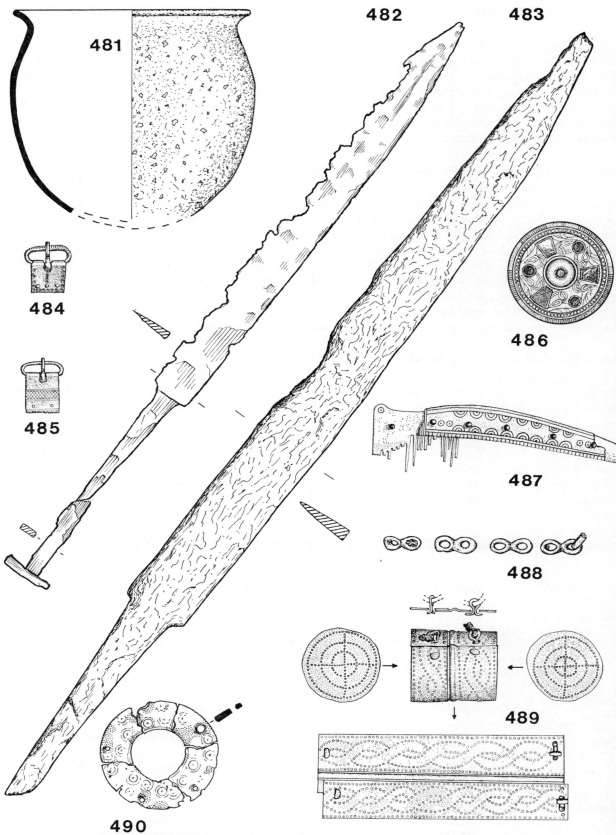

481 482 483

484

485

486

487

488

489

490

Fig. 53. *Iron seaxes and other finds from graves* (½), *Anglo-Saxon cemetery, Polhill, Dunton Green (Site 24).*

No. 485. (Graves 103S). Bronze buckle with plain, rather flattened oval loop and bent tongue. Double-oblong plate with serrated edge held by two bronze rivets, decorated with three bands of triple incised lines and a zone of incised cross-hatching.

Brooch (for discussion see page 190)
No. 486. A circular bronze disc-brooch with silvered back and highly ornamented front. First half of the 7th century.

Comb
This was the only complete comb found on the site.
No. 487. (Grave 53). Single-sided bone comb, in three parts held by at least six iron rivets. Deposited largely complete as the missing teeth were found with it and were probably broken by the pressure of the earth. Ring and dot pattern on both sides. Probably after the middle of the 7th century.

Work-Box, Chain and Bone Ring
These objects were found in close association in one grave (Grave 43) and it seems clear that they were at one time joined together. The bone ring had iron-stains by at least four of its perforations and it seems likely that small iron hooks had once been attached. Each of the four bronze links also had traces of iron in each loop and it seems that these had been joined to the iron hooks. The bronze work-box had a pair of loose bronze split-pins on one side which still had small pieces of iron through their looped heads. It seems clear that a short chain of bronze links and iron loops, or hoops, had once joined the box and the bone ring as noted at several other sites. A small group of iron objects, including a key, was found nearby and some of these may also have been attached to the bone ring.
No. 488. (Grave 43). A group of four bronze double-links with traces of attached iron hooks.
No. 489. (Grave 43). Cylindrical bronze work-box in two halves, one partly fitting inside the other in the form of a large lid. Both parts made from single strips of sheet bronze about 0·8 and 1·3 in. in width and each fixed by two bronze rivets. Both ends closed by separate circular sheets of thin bronze, probably soldered on. Richly decorated with punched-dot designs applied before the work-box was assembled. The box was found to contain threads as noted on other sites (see page 196). Probably second half of the 7th century.
No. 490. (Grave 43). Flat bone disc with five variable perforations, four showing iron staining caused by iron attachments. Faint traces of ring and dot decoration on one side, badly worn. 7th century.

Buckles
A total of 24 buckles was found at Polhill of which only 17 are here illustrated. Two of the most interesting bronze ones have already been described (see above) and of the other 15, eight are bronze and seven iron. Most have rectangular plates fixed with two or three rivets and oval or sub-rectangular loops. The tongues vary in width and are either straight or curved. Decoration is limited to occasional incised lines or in one case (No. 484) to punched decoration.
No. 491. (Grave 26). Bronze buckle with incised line on tongue.
No. 492. (Grave 28). Bronze buckle, badly corroded. 7th century.
No. 493. (Grave 28). Bronze buckle with oval loop of triangular section, except where reduced to take the hinge of the tongue. Base of tongue splayed and decorated with punched-dots. Probably first half of 7th century.
No. 494. (Grave 28). Bronze buckle, corroded. 7th century.
No. 495. (Grave 42). Large iron buckle. Late-7th century.
No. 496. (Grave 45). Bronze buckle, corroded. 7th century.
No. 497. (Grave 68). Large iron buckle, heavily corroded. 7th century.
No. 498. (Grave 77). Large iron buckle.
No. 499. (Grave 85). Small bronze buckle similar to No. 496. Late-7th century.
No. 500. (Grave 85). Large iron buckle, heavily corroded.
No. 501. (Grave 89). Buckle with bronze loop and iron tongue.
No. 502. (Grave 95). Iron buckle, corroded.
No. 503. (Grave 99). Small bronze buckle.
No. 504. (Grave 103N). Simple iron buckle.
No. 505. (Grave 106). Simple iron buckle.

Miscellaneous Bronze Objects
Of the various bronze objects recovered from different graves twelve are illustrated. Of these the brooch (No. 513) and the scabbard-chape (No. 515) are particularly interesting.
No. 506. (Grave 28). A pair of bronze strap-tags, badly corroded. 7th century.
No. 507. (Grave 30). A pointed lace-tag closed with a small bronze rivet. Made from a single sheet of bronze decorated with cross-hatched pattern. 7th century.
No. 508. (Grave 37). Flat, circular pendant of bronze, perforated for suspension with outer ring and central cluster of punched-dot decoration. Probably 7th century.
No. 509. (Grave 38). Long thin, round-headed bronze pin. Probably late-7th century.
No. 510. (Grave 40). Strip of bronze in U-shape profile. Uncertain purpose, probably part of a larger object.
No. 511. (Grave 51). Small flat, silvered bronze disc or pendant with attached bronze clip.

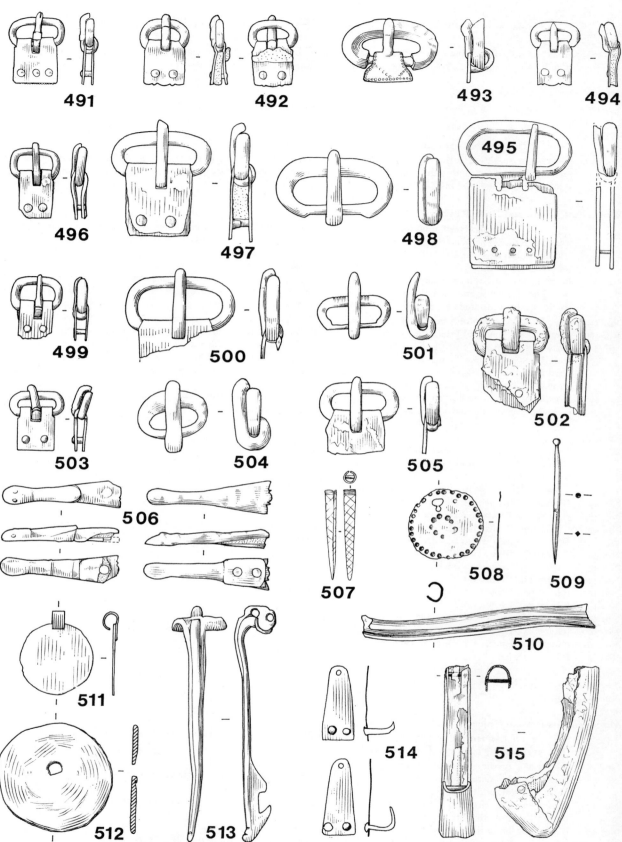

Fig. 54. *Buckles and bronze objects from graves* ($\frac{1}{1}$), *Anglo-Saxon cemetery, Polhill, Dunton Green (Site 24).*

No. 512. (Grave 51). Flat bronze disc or pendant with central hole punched for suspension.

No. 513. (Grave 53). Bronze long-brooch with pin and spring missing. Pierced for spring and catch-plate cut to receive bent pin. Incomplete and bent when buried. Judging by its condition and style this may have been a memento (for discussion see page 191). In use at Colchester A.D. 50–65.

No. 514. (Grave 85). A pair of bronze, pear-shaped purse-fittings each with three perforations to take bronze rivets. Found with purse-mount. Late-7th century.

No. 515. (Grave 83). Fragment of bronze scabbard-chape fixed by bronze rivets. Faint traces of thread-like material, perhaps part of the actual scabbard. Probably late-7th century.

Beads

Twelve graves were found to contain a total of 56 beads, occurring either singly or in groups and generally with female skeletons. In only five cases (Graves 37, 41, 71, 95 and 102) the close association of four or more beads, always on the upper part of the chest suggests necklets of simple type. The beads, of varying colours, were mostly either barrel-shaped or biconical. The majority were opaque and made of frit or glass, though one was made from a natural crystal.

No. 516. (Grave 29). A single barrel-shaped bead of red-brown opaque glass.

No. 517. (Grave 37). A group of eleven beads, roughly as found, probably from a necklace. Eight barrel-shaped (three green, two grey, two brown and one red-brown) and two biconical beads (green and yellow) of opaque glass and a larger melon-shaped bead of blue glass.

No. 518. (Grave 37). Fragment of a polished amethyst bead found in close association with the eleven smaller ones.

No. 519. (Grave 38). A single barrel-shaped bead of orange frit. This type mainly occurs in the 7th century.

No. 520. (Grave 41). A group of eight beads, as found, probably part of a necklace. Six barrel-shaped (two blue, two red-brown and two grey), a blue biconical, all of opaque glass and a spiral-shaped bead of blue glass.

No. 521. (Grave 41). A single cylindrical bead of blue glass, found in close association with the other eight beads from this grave. These predominated in the 7th century.

No. 522. (Grave 51). Two yellow beads, one barrel-shaped and one biconical, of opaque glass.

No. 523. (Grave 65). A poorly made quoit-shaped bead of multi-coloured glass.

No. 524. (Grave 71). A group of seven beads, six biconical dark blue and one barrel-shaped pale blue, all of opaque glass. Found in a group at about left shoulder and probably representing a necklet.

No. 525. (Grave 86). Two beads, one barrel-shaped red-brown and the other cylindrical with a red-brown body containing a continuous trail of white festoons and small yellow spots, both of opaque glass. These predominated in the 7th century.

No. 526. (Grave 95). A group of four beads, probably representing a necklet. Two barrel-shaped (yellow and red-brown), one biconical (dark blue) and a quoit-shaped blue bead with a white spiral inlay, all of opaque glass.

No. 527. (Grave 102). Group of eleven beads, ten of which were found at neck and probably represent a necklet. Nine barrel-shaped of normal size (four green, four red-brown and one a speckled yellow, green and brown) and a large barrel-shaped dark blue bead with a double row of red-brown spots, all of opaque glass. The eleventh bead was of dark blue glass with pearl-coloured surface.

No. 528. (Grave 102). Two beads, both quoit-shaped, one black and the other of dark blue with a clear white and faint red spiral inlay. These predominated in the 7th century.

No. 529. (Unstratified). A group of three beads, two barrel-shaped (brown and red-brown) and a green-blue quoit-shaped glass bead with a thin white spiral inlay.

Four other beads (not illustrated) were also found. Two biconical (green and yellow) beads were found in Grave 55, a single green biconical bead came from Grave 78 and a pale green bead was found in Grave 86.

Wheel-ornament (for discussion see p. 193).

No. 530. (Grave 65). Circular bronze ornament, with four arms joining central roundel on which was mounted a small bronze ring inset with a very small circular, pale green glass ball. Closest parallels are in the late pre-Roman Iron Age.

Rings

Only 18 small metal rings were recovered from nine graves in the cemetery, of which eight were bronze and the rest silver. In the five cases where two or more rings occur together, they formed part of a group of objects, usually on the upper chest, probably representing small necklets.

No. 531. (Grave 38). A pair of silver wire rings of circular section. 7th century.

No. 532. (Grave 41). Two wire rings, one silver the other bronze, of circular section. Probably survivals from the 6th century.

No. 533. (Grave 53). A single bronze wire ring of circular section. 7th century.

No. 534. (Grave 64). A silver ring, about 3–4 mm. wide, large enough to fit a male finger.

No. 535. (Grave 102). A group of five silver rings of varying sizes, all of circular section and one decorated with three zones of incised lines. 7th century.

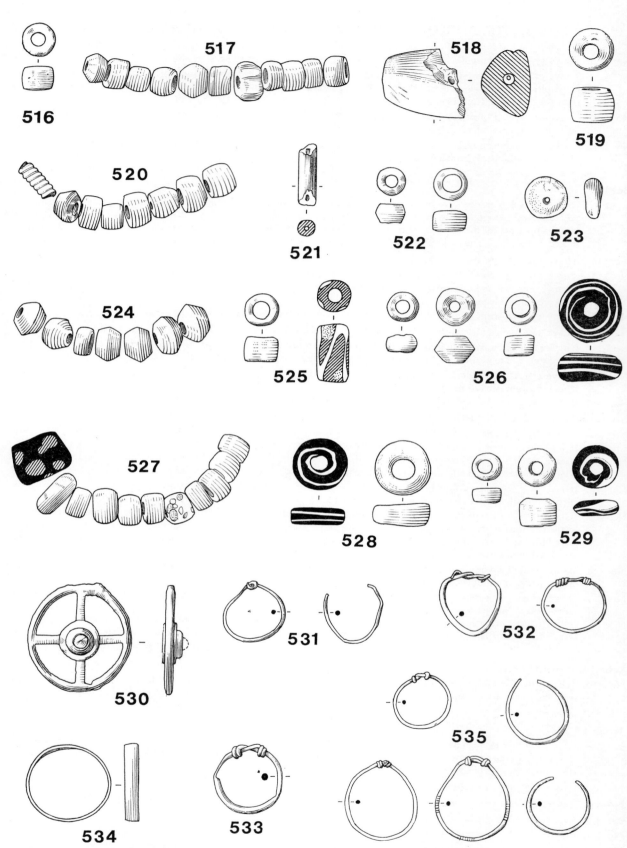

Fig. 55. *Beads, wheel ornament and finger-rings from graves* ($\frac{1}{1}$), *Anglo-Saxon cemetery, Polhill, Dunton Green (Site 24).*

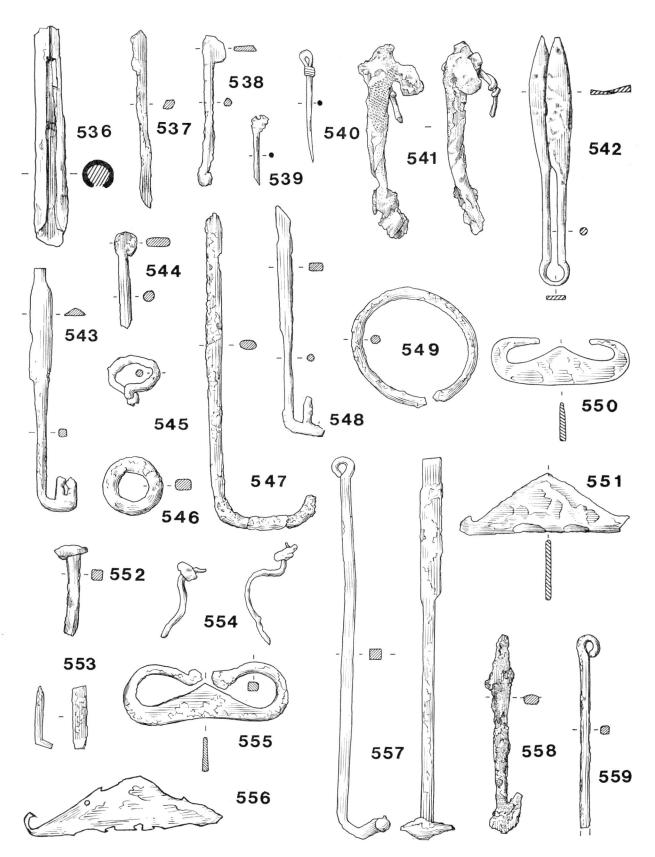

Fig. 56. *Iron objects from graves* ($\frac{1}{2}$), *Anglo-Saxon cemetery, Polhill, Dunton Green (Site 24).*

Iron Fittings

No. 536. (Grave 31). Iron object, circular in section, with socket for wooden shaft, probably part of a spearhead. Wood in socket identified as ash.

No. 537. (Grave 39). Thin rod-like object of iron, perhaps the arm of a broken key.

No. 538. (Grave 39). Iron object, probably attached to ring at lower end; perhaps part of shears or a key.

No. 539. (Grave 41). Small iron object, of uncertain purpose.

No. 540. (Grave 41). Pointed iron object with twisted loop for suspension.

No. 541. (Grave 41). A pair of badly corroded iron objects of uncertain purpose.

No. 542. (Grave 41). A pair of iron shears or clippers. Probably 7th century.

No. 543. (Grave 43). An iron key probably attached to the bone ring.

No. 544. (Grave 43). Iron object similar to No. 538 above.

No. 545. (Grave 43). Twisted iron loop, perhaps a handle.

No. 546. (Grave 53). Circular iron ring, part of a trinket-bag.

No. 547. (Grave 64). A long iron latch-lifter, incomplete.

No. 548. (Grave 66). An iron key.

No. 549. (Grave 66). Incomplete iron ring.

No. 550. (Grave 66). Ovoid iron purse-mount or clasp with inturned terminals. Middle-late-7th century.

No. 551. (Grave 68). Triangular iron purse-mount or clasp with broken terminals. Middle-late-7th century.

No. 552. (Grave 71). A flat-headed iron object, dowel-like in form and perhaps the handle of a knife.

No. 553. (Grave 75). Small angled iron object, perhaps fitting from wooden box.

No. 554. (Grave 75S). Twisted iron object, resembling a chatelaine-link.

No. 555. (Grave 84). Ovoid iron purse-mount with inturned terminals and traces of wood attached. Middle-late-7th century.

No. 556. (Grave 85). Triangular iron purse-mount or clasp with short inturned terminals. Middle-late-7th century.

No. 557. (Grave 95). Iron latch-lifter with loop for suspension.

No. 558. (Grave 104). Iron latch-lifter, traces of material attached.

No. 559. (Unstratified). Iron object with loop for suspension, function uncertain.

Iron Knives and Tools

A total of about 50 iron knives was recovered from the Polhill cemetery, these being the most common objects buried with the dead. The knives varied in size and shape, but all had blades which were triangular in section and narrow tangs suggesting wooden handles. Four small, handled tools, with parallel sides and generally rectangular in section, mostly accompanied knives and probably represent sharpening devices.

No. 560. (Grave 20). Knife with pointed blade, bow-shaped back and traces of wood on tang. Early-8th century. Böhner Type C.

No. 561. (Grave 21). Small knife with pointed blade.

No. 562. (Grave 22). Small knife with broad blade. Early-8th century. Böhner Type C.

No. 563. (Grave 23). Incomplete knife. 5th and 6th centuries. Böhner Type B.

No. 564. (Grave 25). Knife with tapered blade. 5th–7th centuries. Böhner Type A.

No. 565. (Grave 26). Knife with tapered blade.

No. 566. (Grave 27). Large knife blade with tang missing.

No. 567. (Grave 28). Small knife with bow-shaped back.

No. 568. (Grave 29). Knife with long thin blade.

No. 569. (Grave 30). Incomplete knife with broad blade.

No. 570. (Grave 31). Knife with thin tapered blade.

No. 571. (Grave 32). Small knife, incomplete.

No. 572. (Grave 38). Knife with tapered point.

No. 573. (Grave 38). Small iron tool with parallel sides, rectangular in section, perhaps for sharpening. Found frequently in 7th century graves.

No. 574. (Grave 44). Broken blade of knife.

No. 575. (Grave 45). Large knife, badly corroded. 7th century.

No. 576. (Grave 52). Incomplete knife.

No. 577. (In filling of Grave 53). Large knife with broad blade.

No. 578. (Grave 56). Small iron tool, with parallel sides, rectangular in section, perhaps for sharpening. Found frequently in 7th century graves.

No. 579. (Grave 60). Large knife with bow-shaped back.

No. 580. (Grave 61). Knife with broad blade and tapered point. Early-8th century. Böhner Type C.

No. 581. (Grave 65). Large knife, drawn after cleaning.

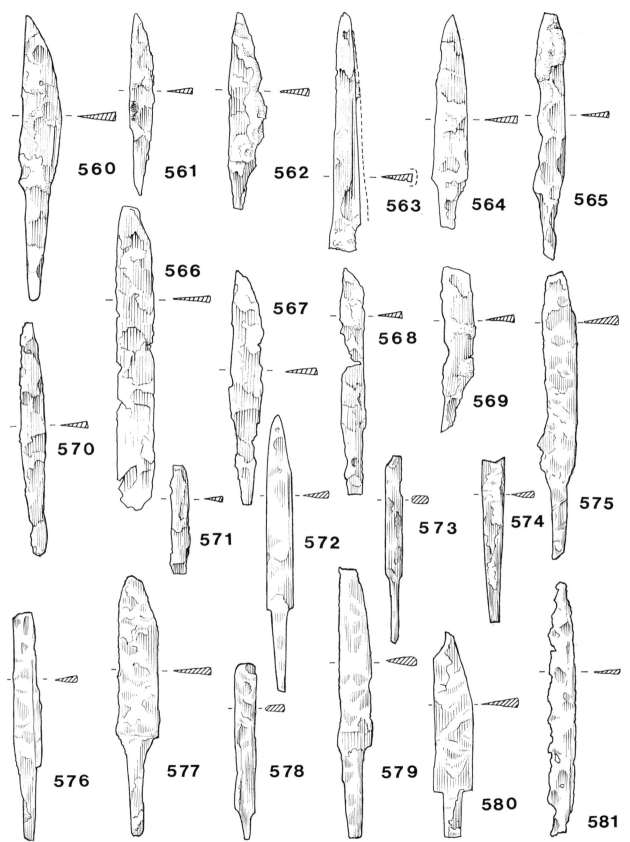

Fig. 57. Iron knives and tools (Nos. 573 and 578) from graves (½), Anglo-Saxon cemetery, Polhill, Dunton Green (Site 24).

No. 582.   (Grave 66). Small knife with tapered blade. 5th–7th centuries. Böhner Type A.
No. 583.   (Grave 66). Short tool with parallel sides, rectangular in section, perhaps for sharpening. Found frequently in 7th century graves.
No. 584.   (Grave 68). Knife with tapered point. 5th–7th centuries. Böhner Type A.
No. 585.   (Grave 68). Knife with tapered blade. 7th century.
No. 586.   (Grave 69). Knife with tapered point.
No. 587.   (Grave 69). Large knife, point missing. Common in the 7th century.
No. 588.   (Grave 73). Large knife with tapered point.
No. 589.   (Grave 74). Knife with slightly curved blade.
No. 590.   (Grave 77). Knife with bow-shaped back, drawn after cleaning.
No. 591.   (Grave 79). Knife with bow-shaped back.
No. 592.   (Grave 81). Large knife with tapered point.
No. 593.   (Grave 82). Knife with bow-shaped back.
No. 594.   (Grave 85). Knife with bow-shaped back.
No. 595.   (Grave 88). Blade of large knife, tang missing.
No. 596.   (Grave 89). Large knife, point missing.
No. 597.   (Grave 93). Small knife with bow-shaped back.
No. 598.   (Grave 99). Large knife with tapered point. Probably early-8th century. Böhner Type C.
No. 599.   (Grave 102). Small tool with parallel sides and rectangular section, perhaps for sharpening. Found frequently in 7th century graves.
No. 600.   (Grave 102). Knife with tapered point.
No. 601.   (Grave 103). Small knife with bent tang and point missing.

Iron Spearheads

A total of 13 spearheads came from 12 graves, in each identified case that of a male. All vary slightly in size and shape, but each had a socketed shaft and a broader blade tapering to a point. Eleven are broadly leaf-shaped and two are angular.

No. 602.   (Grave 27). Large spearhead with angular blade and long narrow shaft. Wood in socket identified as hazel. Normally a 7th century type. Swanton's series F.2.
No. 603.   (Grave 40). Small spearhead with wide blade and short shaft. Probably mid-late 7th century. Swanton's series C.5.
No. 604.   (Grave 45). Similar to No. 603 above. 5th-to-end of 7th centuries. Swanton's series D.1.
No. 605.   (Grave 65). Spearhead with medium blade. Wood in socket identified as hazel. 7th century. Swanton's series C.2.
No. 606.   (Grave 68). Small spearhead with narrow blade and broken shaft. Wood in socket identified as oak. 7th century. Perhaps Swanton's series C.2.
No. 607.   (Grave 68). Spearhead with broad blade and long, split shaft. 5th-to-end of 7th centuries.
No. 608.   (Grave 69). Large spearhead with angular blade and long thick shaft. Normally a 7th century type. Swanton's series F.2.
No. 609.   (Grave 73). Thin, broad-bladed spearhead (damaged) with narrow shaft. Early-to-middle-7th century. Swanton's series E.3, E.4. or C.3.
No. 610.   (Grave 81). Spearhead with broad blade and part of wood still in socket of shaft, identified as oak. 7th century. Swanton's series C.2.
No. 611.   (Grave 84). Large spearhead with broad blade and broken shaft. Wood in shaft identified as oak. Probably mid-late-7th century. Swanton's series C.5.
No. 612.   (Grave 85). Similar to No. 611 above. 7th century. Swanton's series C.2. Wood in shaft identified as hazel.
No. 613.   (Grave 97). Large spearhead with broad blade and wood still in socket, identified as oak. 7th century. Swanton's series C.2.
No. 614.   (Grave 102). Spearhead with narrow blade and thick shaft. 7th century. Swanton's series C.2.

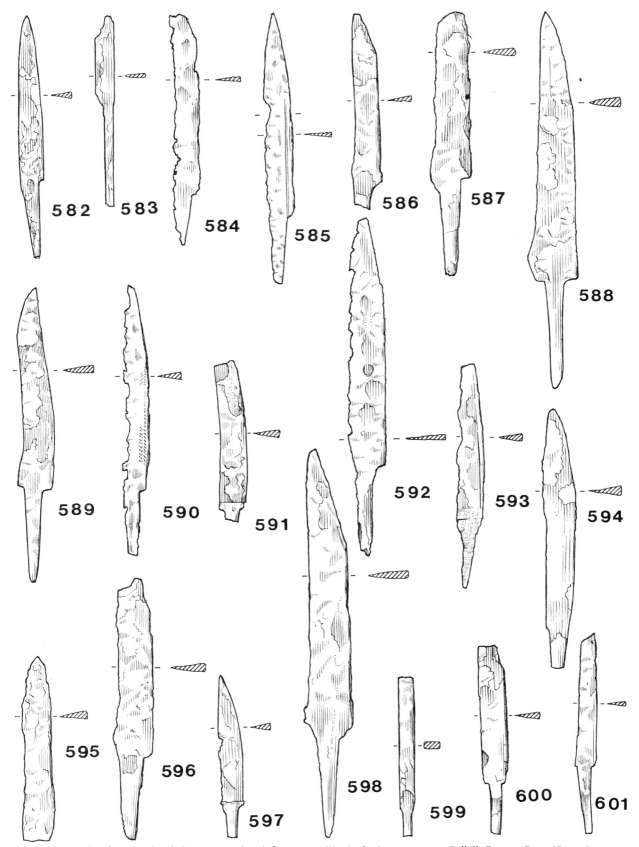

Fig. 58. Iron knives and tools (Nos. 583 and 599) from graves (½), Anglo-Saxon cemetery, Polhill, Dunton Green (Site 24).

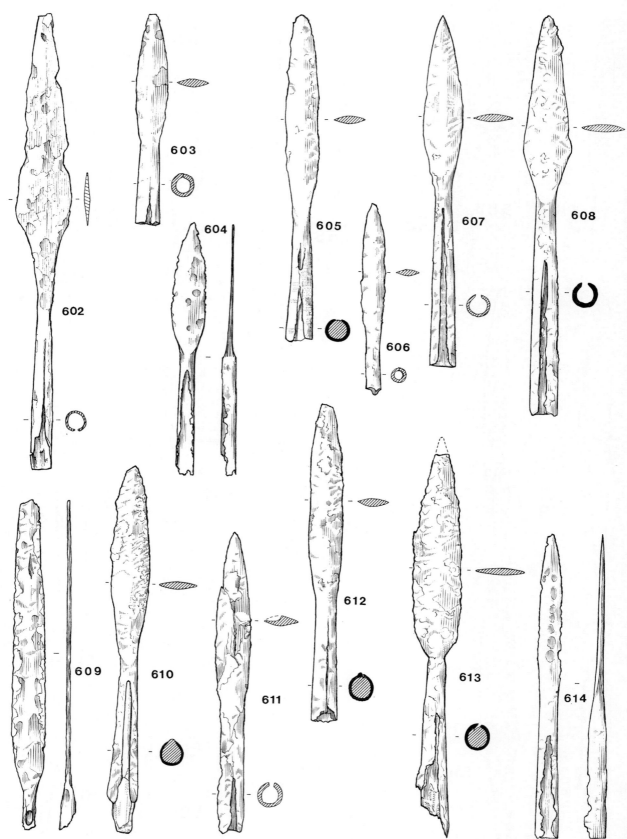

Fig. 59. *Iron spearheads from graves, Anglo-Saxon cemetery* (⅓), *Polhill, Dunton Green (Site 24).*

SITE 25. A Medieval Site at Little Farleigh Green, Farleigh, Surrey

This site (N.G.R. TQ.3790.6030) lies in a large open field (O.S. parcel 90) in the parish of Farleigh, Surrey about ½ a mile east of St. Mary's Church. It lies on level ground to the north of Little Farleigh Green Farm on Clay-with-flints at about 560 ft. O.D.

The site was found on 29th August, 1965 during 'Operation Gaspipe'. The pipe-trench cut roughly north-east to south-west across the field about 500 ft. north of the track outside the farm. This revealed nine features over a distance of about 630 ft.

Feature	Profile	Width	Depth	From East Hedge	Notes
1	V-shaped	17½ ft.	5 ft. plus	30 ft.	North-south ditch, pottery
2	U- ,,	2 ft.	2 ft.	125 ft.	Pit
3	U- ,,	2 ft.	2 ft.	162 ft.	Pit, north side
4	U- ,,	2 ft.	2 ft.	209 ft.	North-south ditch
5	U- ,,	3 ft.	3 ft.	235 ft.	North-south ditch
6	V- ,,	20 ft.	6 ft. plus	254 ft.	North-south ditch, carbon and chalk rubble
7	U- ,,	4 ft.	4 ft.	296 ft.	North-south ditch
8	U- ,,	3½ ft.	2 ft.	626 ft.	Pit, north side
9	V- ,,	14 ft.	6 ft. plus	662 ft.	North-south ditch, potsherd, chalk rubble

TABLE A

Details of features found on the Little Farleigh Green site

The number of features and the large area covered tends to suggest an extensive settlement on this site, but unfortunately finds were few. Only 25 potsherds, several struck flakes of flint and small pieces of thin roof-tile were recovered from unstratified contexts. One sherd came from the spoilheap adjacent to Feature 9 and all the others came from the contractor's spoil representing the fill of Feature 1, both being wide ditches marking the limits of the site. The bulk of the sherds appears to be hard, sandy Limpsfield ware probably of 13th, or 14th, century date (Nos. 615–619). At least six vessels seem to be represented, mostly cooking-pots with sagging bases and short, flattened rims.

If all nine features are of the same date then an extensive and highly interesting site may be indicated. The length was at least 630 ft. and the site probably covered several acres. The three wide ditches are similar in character and roughly parallel to each other and it seems likely that they may link together to the south and north to form one or more enclosures. The pottery discarded as domestic rubbish in the upper filling of the east ditch suggests occupation for at least the late-13th, or early-14th, century. The whole character of the site is at once reminiscent of that at Chapel Wood, Hartley, Kent (Site 28) and another deserted medieval village, or manor-site, may be indicated.

Catalogue of the Illustrated Pottery from Little Farleigh Green, Farleigh (Fig. 60)

No. 615. A wide bowl, or dish, with undercut, flanged rim of coarse sandy ware. Light grey paste and surface, probably from the Limpsfield kilns. From spoil by Feature 1 (GP-22-7).

No. 616. Cooking-pot with thickened rim of coarse sandy ware. Light grey paste and surface, probably from the Limpsfield kilns. From spoil by Feature 1 (GP-22-7).

No. 617. Cooking-pot with flanged rim of coarse sandy ware. Light grey paste and dark grey surface. From spoil by Feature 1 (GP-22-7).

No. 618. Cooking-pot almost identical to No. 616, probably from the Limpsfield kilns. From spoil by Feature 1 (GP-22-7).

No. 619. Jug with raised base of fine sandy ware. Light grey paste with pink surface and splashes of green glaze. From spoil by Feature 1 (GP-22-7). Probably late-13th, or early-14th, century. The cooking pots and bowl all lack shell-loading and their horizontal or thickened rims are generally considered to be of late-13th, or early-14th, century date on sites in Kent (Ref. 410).

SITE 26. A Medieval Site near Farleigh Court, Farleigh, Surrey

This site (N.G.R. TQ.3728.6004) lies in an open field (O.S. parcel 82A2) in the parish of Farleigh, Surrey only about 400 ft. south-east of St. Mary's Church. It lies on gently sloping ground on Clay-with-flints at about 550 ft. O.D. and slightly less than ½ a mile west of the medieval site at Little Farleigh Green (Site 25). Farleigh appears in the Domesday Survey of 1086 (Ref. 411) as Farlega, held by Robert de Watville.

The site was discovered on 11th September, 1965 during 'Operation Gaspipe'. The pipe-trench, cutting roughly north-east to south-west across the field, revealed a single ditch, or pit, 775 ft. east of the bridle-road and about 100 ft. from the north hedge.

The feature, which was bowl-shaped in section, about 6 ft. wide and 4 ft. deep, appeared to align north-west by south-east. Its filling of grey-brown loam over large flints contained about 30 potsherds. The great majority represents a cooking-pot and a dish (Nos. 620–1), probably of 13th or 14th century date. Two other indeterminate sherds have a soft, corky texture.

It seems probable that this pit, or ditch, related to the medieval settlement centred on the nearby church, a two-cell Norman structure which survives largely intact. The pottery may represent domestic rubbish discarded from a nearby building, no trace of which was found.

Catalogue of the Illustrated Pottery from Farleigh Court (Fig. 60)

No. 620. Cooking-pot with slightly thickened, outcurved rim of coarse sandy ware and probably with a slight, sagging base. Light grey paste and grey-brown surface. From the pit or ditch (GP-23-1). A form common on Kentish sites, as at Canterbury where it occurs in a pit dated to the second half of the 13th century (Ref. 412).

No. 621. Large dish with flanged pie-crust rim of coarse gritty ware. Dark grey paste and surface. From the pit or ditch (GP-23-1). Dishes of this type occur in late-13th and early-14th century contexts in Kent, again at Canterbury (Ref. 413).

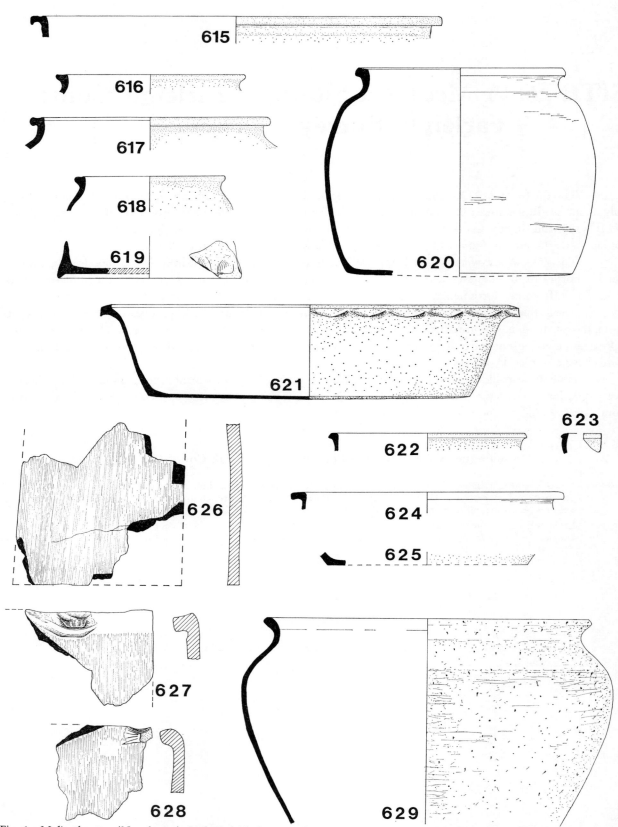

Fig. 60. *Medieval pottery (Nos. 615–19), Little Farleigh Green, Farleigh (Site 25); medieval pottery (Nos. 620–1), Farleigh Court, Farleigh (Site 26); medieval pottery (Nos. 622–5), Combe Bank, Sundridge (Site 27); medieval titles (Nos. 626–8), Chapel Wood, Hartley (Site 28) and medieval pot (No. 629), Eglantine Farm, Horton Kirby (Site 29). All at ¼.*

SITE 27. A Medieval Site at Combe Bank, Sundridge, Kent

This site (N.G.R. TQ.4735.5651) lies in a small open field (O.S. parcel 3365) in the parish of Sundridge, Kent about 1 mile north-west of the parish church and just to the north of Combe Bank Wood. It is situated on gently sloping ground roughly midway between the Pilgrim's Way and the River Darent. Here the river flows eastwards in the wide valley formed by the chalk scarp and the Greensand ridge. The site is on thick Gault Clay and the O.D. is about 375 ft. The centre of the site lies about 300 ft. from the east hedge and 200 ft. from the west hedge.

The site was discovered on 6th August, 1966 during 'Operation Gaspipe West'. The pipe-trench cut roughly east-west across the field and it was after the topsoil had been bulldozed that a number of potsherds, an iron knife and a flint foundation were revealed. The material was recovered from an area 120 ft. in length and about 30 ft. in width which may extend to both south and north. There was otherwise a general absence of roof-tile and building stone.

The flint foundation took the form of a mass of packed flints which gave the appearance of having been carefully laid and which contained a few small pieces of greensand. The flints were only found on each side of the bulldozed area and it is likely that it originally extended across the full width of 30 ft. Just 19 ft. survived along the south edge and only 17 ft. 6 in. along the north edge and it may be that the foundation represents a structure, or hard-standing, on an east-west axis. The presence of huge heaps of topsoil and of several long lengths of steel pipe prevented further investigation.

Just 100 potsherds were recovered from the site and these represent at least eight vessels (Nos. 622–5). Most are hard, sandy wares of the type produced at Limpsfield about five miles to the west and probably made during either the 13th or 14th centuries (Ref. 414).

Not much can be said about the extent and nature of this site. The flint foundation clearly forms part of it and the domestic pottery suggests occupation in the 13th or 14th centuries.

Catalogue of the Illustrated Pottery from Combe Bank, Sundridge (Fig. 60)

No. 622. Jar with small, thickened rim with upper bevel. Coarse sandy ware with light grey paste and surface, probably Limpsfield ware. Surface find (GPW-3).

No. 623. Small jar with beaded rim of coarse sandy ware. Light grey paste and buff surface. Surface find (GPW-3).

No. 624. Cooking-pot with flanged rim of smooth corky ware. Light grey paste and buff surface. Surface find (GPW-3). The rim form here is common on Kent sites where it is normally dated to the 13th century, as at Faversham (Ref. 415) and Pivington (Ref. 416).

No. 625. Base of cooking-pot of coarse sandy ware. Light grey paste with dark grey surface. Probably Limpsfield ware. Surface find (GPW-3).

SITE 28. A Medieval Tile-kiln at Chapel Wood, Hartley, Kent

SUMMARY

The excavation established that the structure uncovered in 1926 was not part of a Roman hypocaust, but a medieval tile-kiln of normal type. Similar structures elsewhere suggest that it may have been constructed in the 13th or 14th centuries. Presumably it was built to provide tiles for buildings within the adjacent earthwork. The latter certainly contains masonry structures and the small amount of domestic rubbish tends to confirm the date. It is likely that the complex represents a deserted medieval village to which early writers (Ref. 430) have applied the name Scotsgrove. The site is very extensive and only large-scale, properly conducted excavations under controlled conditions are likely to produce archaeologically significant results.

This site (N.G.R. TQ.6032.6639) lies within Chapel Wood (O.S. parcel 58C) in the parish of Hartley, Kent about 1,100 yards west-south-west of the parish church. It occupies fairly level ground on Clay-with-flints at an elevation of about 410 ft. O.D. The tile-kiln although within Chapel Wood is situated in the rear garden of Kenwood, Ash Road, Hartley being about 350 ft. west of the house and about 80 ft. south of a bank and ditch forming part of a medieval enclosure (Ref. 417).

In September, 1963 the owner of Kenwood, Mr. J. Ford, invited the writer to examine some overgrown foundations in his garden. An immediate inspection showed that these formed part of a medieval tile-kiln and suggested that limited excavation might recover useful details in spite of decades of weathering and damage. Accordingly, several members of the West Kent Group undertook a short excavation on the site from October to December, 1963 and also carried out a limited survey of the adjacent earthwork.

Research work showed that the site had been discovered originally by a Mr. A. Dennis in his garden at Hartley in about 1926. Excavations were then undertaken by the Rector of Hartley, the Rev. G. W. Bancks, who interpreted the foundations which he uncovered as a Roman hypocaust system, with unfortunate results. The *Journal of Roman Studies* for 1926 reports (Ref. 418), 'the hypocaust of a Roman villa was opened . . .', and the 1927 volume of *Archaeologia Cantiana* states (Ref. 419) 'that a fine Roman hypocaust has been brought to light'. The *Victoria County History*, published in 1932 (Ref. 420) more doubtfully records: 'Hartley. What may have been the hypocaust of a bath or house was opened . . .' The Rev. Bancks' own book on Hartley, published in 1927 (Ref. 421), not unnaturally contains references to the 'Roman hypocaust' which was quickly interpreted as 'the foundations of a large and important (Romano-British) mansion'. More important, he did include two very useful photographs which show features since destroyed and which also positively identify his foundations with those examined in 1963. One photograph (page 16), showing two gentlemen standing on the foundations suitably armed with garden spade and fork, will long remain an epic of Kentish archaeology. In 1940 Mr. R. F. Jessup suggested (Ref. 422) that the site could be that of a tile-kiln similar to one just found at Borough Green, which was certainly very much post-Roman in date. More than ten years later, however, the site was still being described (Ref. 423) as a 'Roman villa' and about then a nominal charge was being made to view the 'Roman' remains.

The Group wishes to acknowledge, first and foremost, the help of Mr. Ford for encouraging excavation on his land. Of the several volunteers who carried out the work special mention must be made of Miss E. Warman (now Mrs. E. Healey), Mr. C. Jones and Mr. G. Cramp for their sustained efforts on a difficult site. Mr. J. Willson readily agreed to prepare the plan of the tile-kiln and Mr. G. Clewley provided the drawings of the tiles. Mrs. E. Eames and Dr. J. Musty have both kindly examined samples of the nibbed tiles and discussed them at length and also suggested parallels for the kiln.[1]

---

[1] A detailed report on the excavation of this medieval tile-kiln was offered for publication in *Archaeologia Cantiana* in 1969. This was returned with the comment: 'My greatest misgiving is felt in regard to the dating of the kiln . . . medieval tiles do not have small projections and that this is accepted by architectural historians as a late development.' For discussion and dating of medieval nibbed roof-tiles see below.

1. THE TILE-KILN (Fig. 61 and Plate XXB)

The undergrowth and collapsed parts of the kiln were cleared and the excavation limited to determining the extent of the structure. This revealed a tile-kiln of the double-chambered type, oblong in shape and tapering slightly at the northern end. The overall length of the kiln was about 14 ft. and the width about 7 to 8 ft. The two parallel furnace chambers, each about 10 ft. by 2½ ft. were separated by a narrow spine wall about 1 ft. to 1 ft. 6 in. wide. The side and spine walls were constructed of roof-tile fragments laid flat and set in clay. From these sprang six pairs of flue-arches, each built of tile about 1 ft. wide and probably rising to about 1 ft. 6 in. above the base.

MEDIEVAL TILE KILN, HARTLEY, 1963

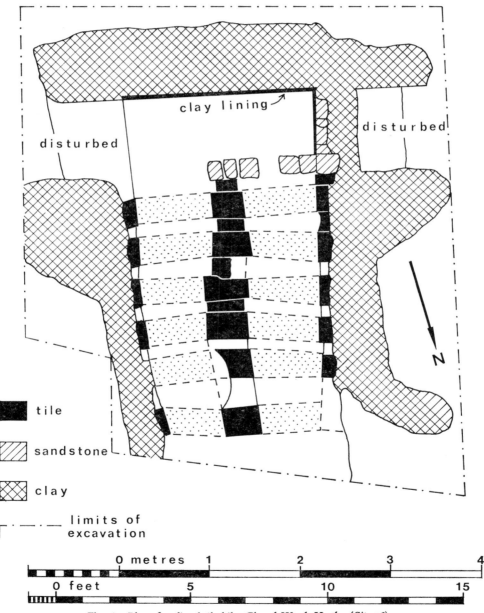

Fig. 61. *Plan of medieval tile-kiln, Chapel Wood, Hartley (Site 28).*

Only the bases of these arches had survived, but it is clear from the photographs taken during the original excavation that at least four survived intact in 1926.

At the south end of the kiln was another chamber 7 ft. long and 2½ ft. wide. This had a lining of sandstone blocks on two sides and traces of a heavily burnt clay rendering. Some of the blocks were squared and displayed diagonal tooling on the surfaces and it seems likely that they were originally intended for a masonry structure elsewhere. The south wall of the kiln was solidly constructed of small flints set in clay.

The kiln, constructed inside a large pit, had been packed round with clay and large flints, both as reinforcement and for insulation. A large depression on the north side of the kiln may represent the stoke-hole, but this was not tested by excavation. The base of the kiln was baked to a cinder-like texture and the clay bonding of the kiln had turned a bright orange. Many of the tiles had cracked and nearly all the exposed flints had shattered.

Fragments of tile taken from the structure showed that some of the tiles used were 7 in. wide, longer than 7 in. with a single nail-hole and a small flanged projection or nib, at one end. The total absence of pottery or other industrial residue, other than tile fragments, makes it virtually certain that the kiln was constructed for the manufacture of roof-tiles. The clay for the process was very probably obtained from the immediate area as would have been the wood used for fuel.

In plan the structure follows the pattern of medieval tile-kilns found elsewhere. In particular a floor-tile kiln found at Stoke, near Coventry in 1911 (Ref. 424) was constructed with a series of similar, parallel flue-arches over double-chambers. Another fine roof-tile kiln, also with double-chambers and a 9-in. spine wall, was excavated by Mrs. Eames at Beverley in Yorkshire in 1957-8 (Ref. 425) and dated by her to the 13th century. Mrs. Eames has pointed out the similarity of the internal lengths of the Beverley and Hartley kilns (8 ft. 10 in. and 10 ft. respectively) and suggests that the Hartley kiln should also be of medieval date. Dr. Musty has also confirmed that the overall construction of the Hartley kiln is very much in the medieval tradition. Part of another tile-kiln was excavated by the writer at Tyler Hill in 1967 (Ref. 426) adjacent to waster-heaps containing pottery of 13th or 14th century date. This, too, was rectangular in plan with double-chambers about 3 ft. wide, a central spine wall just 8 in. wide and arched flues similar to those at Hartley. In 1969 the University of Kent Archaeological Society, under the direction of Mr. G. Cramp, excavated two more tile-kilns near Tyler Hill (Ref. 427) which were dated to about A.D. 1300. One was sub-rectangular in plan, 12 by 9 ft. internally, but provided with two spine walls thereby forming three chambers.

As stated several of the tiles from the Hartley kiln had small, single projections, or nibs, at one end. These were formed by the addition of small lumps of clay pressed firmly into place before firing (Nos. 627-8). These nibs, still in use on many tiles today, helped fix the tile to the roof. Examples of early nibbed tiles have been found in 13th century deposits at Wharram Percy, Yorkshire (information kindly supplied by the excavator, Mr. J. G. Hurst). In addition Dr. Musty has pointed out that a medieval tile-kiln at Boston, Lincs., was actually producing nibbed tiles in the 14th century (Ref. 428). The kiln at Boston was rectangular, had treble-chambers and measured about 13 by 8 ft. overall. The nibbed tiles it produced were about 12 by 8 in., with a single square peg-hole and were thus slightly larger than those from Hartley. It is clear, therefore, that nibbed tiles were being produced during the 13th and 14th centuries over an area including Yorkshire, Lincolnshire and Kent.

2. THE MEDIEVAL EARTHWORK

The tile-kiln lay just to the south of a large rectangular medieval earthwork, the bank and ditch of which can be traced along most of its north, west and south sides. It seems likely that the present Ash Road may mark its eastern boundary. It covers an area roughly 800 ft. east-west by about 300 ft. north-south and thus appears to enclose an area of about five acres. The ditch averages about 10–15 ft. in width and about 3 ft. in depth. The bank, on the inner side of the ditch and doubtless formed by the upcast from the ditch, averages about 10–15 ft. and is about 2 ft. high. Allowing for silting and erosion it must be that the ditch was originally several feet deeper and the bank somewhat higher.

Within the earthwork are a series of low banks shown on the plan published in 1967. A small trial-hole across one of these banks revealed a compact mass of unmortared flint, probably representing a collapsed wall about 2 ft. thick. A second trial-hole, to the west of the outline of a rectangular structure, produced oyster shells, roof tiles and four small potsherds. Of the latter one was from a shell-loaded cooking-pot and another was from a green-glazed jug. Both probably date to the 13th or 14th centuries and the deposit appears to represent domestic rubbish.

The rectangular structure was extant in the 18th century (Ref. 429) when it was described as a 'chapel' and from which the wood presumably took its name. It seems likely that this building is one of the principal domestic structures within the earthwork and that others survive nearby, though not all need be medieval.

Catalogue of the Illustrated Tiles from Chapel Wood, Hartley (Fig. 60)

No. 626. Flat, oblong roof tile, slightly tapered, with an orange-brown paste and surface. Well-fired clay containing occasional particles of grit. Striations on surface. From kiln structure (HAR).

No. 627. Flat roof tile with blue-grey paste and orange surface. Unevenly fired clay containing black specks. Crude thumb-pressed nib about 0·8 in. wide, probably at top centre. Striations on surface. From kiln structure (HAR).

No. 628. Flat roof tile similar to No. 627. Crude thumb-pressed nib about 0·7 in. wide. Striations on surface. From kiln structure (HAR).

SITE 29. A Medieval Site on Eglantine Farm, Horton Kirby, Kent

This site (N.G.R. TQ.5670.6638) lies in the parish of Horton Kirby, Kent on farmland about $1\frac{1}{4}$ miles east-south-east of the parish church of Farningham. It lies in an open field (O.S. parcel 0005) on the east side of a small valley overlooking the main Darent valley $\frac{1}{2}$ a mile to the west. The site is on Upper Chalk at an elevation of about 350–380 ft. The centre of the site lies about 260 ft. from the east hedge and 210 ft. from the south hedge.

The site was discovered on 3rd November, 1969 during 'Operation Gaspipe East'. The pipe-trench, running south-east to north-west, cut through a series of eight features in a length of 356 ft. Six were pits or small ditches, one was a rectangular slot and the other a wide hollow (see Table A below). All were cut into solid chalk and were filled largely with brown loam and chalk rubble.

Feature	Profile	Width	Depth	From E. hedge	Notes
1	V-shaped	5 ft.	4 ft.	163 ft.	Ditch or pit
2	Rectangular	$1\frac{1}{4}$ ft.	$2\frac{1}{2}$ ft.	313 ft.	Slot or post-hole
3	Wide–U	4 ft.	2 ft.	316 ft.	Hollow
4	Rectangular	3 ft.	2 ft.	394 ft.	Pit? Carbon; pottery
5	U-shaped	4 ft.	3 ft.	411 ft.	Ditch or pit
6	V-shaped	3 ft.	$2\frac{1}{2}$ ft.	421 ft.	Ditch or pit
7	V-shaped	$2\frac{1}{2}$ ft.	3 ft.	476 ft.	Ditch or pit
8	V-shaped	$6\frac{1}{2}$ ft.	4 ft.	519 ft.	Ditch or pit

TABLE A

Details of features found on the site at Eglantine Farm

Only one feature (Feature 4) contained any datable material. This consisted of five small sherds of thin shell-loaded pottery very similar to that recovered from the many 1st century Romano-British sites in the area. Five much larger pieces of similar pottery from the same area, probably even from the same feature, were subsequently handed in for examination by Mr. M. Drake of Hartley. These are clearly not Romano-British, but part of a medieval cooking-pot (No. 629) of 12th or 13th century date.

It is difficult to say much about the nature and extent of this site. It seems to represent an occupation-site which, if all the features are contemporary, should be of medieval date. At the very least a hitherto unrecorded site of 12th or 13th century date seems to have been found. The large feature found at the west end of the site (Feature 8) may be a section of a delimiting ditch enclosing all or part of the site.

Catalogue of the Illustrated Pottery from Eglantine Farm (Fig. 60)

No. 629.   Large cooking-pot with outcurved rim of corky, shell-loaded ware. Dark grey paste and buff surface with soot on belly. From Feature 4 (GPE-1-D2). The simple rim, rounded profile and shell-filling all tend to suggest a date no later than the middle of the 13th century.

Plate XXI. *Ravenscroft, Bromley, A.D. 1660 (Site 30)*

[*facing p. 225*

SITE 30. Ravenscroft, Bromley, Kent (A.D. 1660)

This house (N.G.R. TQ.4060.6848) flanked the south side of Masons Hill in the Borough of Bromley, Kent about ½ a mile south-east of the parish church. It occupied a west facing slope overlooking the River Ravensbourne on Woolwich and Blackheath pebble-beds at an elevation of about 180 ft. O.D.

Having been built in 1660, Ravenscroft (Plate XXI) was one of the oldest and best-preserved buildings of merit in the Bromley area. It had been listed by the Ministry of Housing as a Grade II building and it appeared in the Statutory List for Bromley Borough. It was in use as an hotel in 1964, but was acquired under a compulsory purchase order by the South East Metropolitan Regional Hospital Board for an extension to Bromley Hospital. It was soon delisted and in May, 1965 it was demolished. Notification of the proposed demolition was given to the Group by the Council for British Archaeology. In what little time was left members were able to record the elevation and the plan and to make a photographic record (Ref. 431).

DESCRIPTION OF THE HOUSE

The Statutory List records:

'Dated 1660. Painted brick. The centre portion has two storeys and attic; cornice and large elaborate shaped gable with attic window. On the ground floor is a model glass conservatory. On each side is a projecting wing of two storeys with rusticated quoins, cornice and gable ends with kneelers (not of matching size). Leaded casement windows with wooden mullions and transoms. Later additions behind.'

To this can be added further details. The house faced north-east with its front parallel to Masons Hill. The overall width of the façade was 49 ft. 6 in., of which the east wing occupied 12 ft., the central block about 22 ft. and the west wing about 16 ft. The maximum height of the central block was 36 ft. 6 in.; the east wing 26 ft. and the west wing 28 ft. It is clear from this that the wings, although basically similar, were not matching and probably constructed at different times. The smaller, east wing was clearly an integral part of the same structure as the central block which displayed the date 1660 and it seems that the west wing was added later, perhaps to replace the original wing. Several substantial additions had been made to the back of the house and most probably dated from the 19th century. Copies of the plan of Ravenscroft are held by the Group and by the Historic Buildings Section of the Greater London Council. It was not possible to examine the structure during its demolition.

The façade of the building was undoubtedly the most interesting and attractive aspect of the house. On its style and character Mr. A. J. Percival, of Faversham, has kindly commented:

'The original house, built of brick with a triple-gabled façade, showed signs of Dutch influence. The central gable, curvilinear in form and with a semi-circular relieving arch over its garret window, reflected Dutch motifs. A plaque near the apex bore the date 1660. Both wings had rusticated quoining and straight-sided gables and there was an ornamental wall-anchor (also a Dutch motif) on the original east wing. Buildings showing similar signs of Dutch influence are quite common in East Anglia and East Kent (e.g. Smith's Hospital, Canterbury (1657); Rushbourne Manor, Hoath (1659) and several houses in Deal and Ramsgate). In the present Greater London area such buildings are now rare, though there were once several examples (e.g. part of Sion College, London Wall (1669).'

No attempt is here made to study the history of this house in any detail, but it is interesting to note various recent references to it. In 1889 (Ref. 432) the house was described as 'situated on Masons Hill, and is the property of E. Soames, Esq. The front of the house bears the date 1660, which is probably the year of its erection. The north front is original work, but some parts of the house have been altered during the past 30 years'. In 1899 (Ref. 433) a note on Bromley states: 'Mr. John Pieters, a Fleming by descent, had the old house on Masons Hill with the date 1660 in front, which now belongs to Mr. Soames'. A history of Bromley, published in 1929 (Ref. 434), notes that an earlier house may have occupied the site, perhaps dating back to about 1500. It also lists several early owners and records that the house was used for a school for most of the 18th century.

REFERENCES

ABBREVIATIONS

Neo.	Neolithic	Bel.	Belgic	A.S.	Anglo-Saxon
B.A.	Bronze Age	Rom.	Roman	Med.	Medieval
I.A.	Iron Age	R.B.	Romano-British	Post-med.	Post-medieval

REF. NO.	SUBJECT	AUTHOR	PUBLICATION
1	Discovery, Baston Manor site	Philp, B. J.	*K.A.R.* (then Newsletter), No. 5 (1966), 12.
2	Discovery, Baston Manor site	Philp, B. J.	*K.A.R.*, No. 18 (1969), 30.
3	Greenstone axe, Keston	Kelly, D. B.	*Arch. Cant.*, LXXIX (1964), 224
4	Greenstone axe, Keston	Fox, N. P.	*Arch. Cant.*, LXVI (1953), 161.
5	Neo. sites, East Kent	Dunning, G. C.	*Antiq. J.*, XLVI (1966), 1–25.
6	Neo. pot., Wingham	Greenfield, E.	*Arch. Cant.*, LXXIV (1960), 60–68.
7	Neo. pot., Whitehawk, Sussex	Curwen, E. C.	*Sussex Archaeol. Collect.*, LXXVII (1936), 60–92, fig. 1: 3.
8	Neo. pot., Trundle, Sussex	Curwen, E. C.	*Sussex Archaeol. Collect.*, LXX (1929), 33–85, pl. X: 39, 55 etc.
9	Neo. pot.	Williamson, R. P. R.	*Sussex Archaeol. Collect.*, LXXI (1930), 57–96, pl. X: 32.
10	Neo. pot., Trundle, Sussex	Curwen, E. C.	*Sussex Archaeol. Collect.*, LXX (1929), pl. X: 49, 57.
11	Neo. pot.	Williamson, R. P. R.	*Sussex Archaeol. Collect.*, LXXI (1930), pl. XI: 46.
12	Neo. pot., Ebbsfleet	Burchall, J. P. T. Piggott, S.	*Antiq. J.*, XIX (1939), 405–420.
13	Radiocarbon dating	Barker, H. Mackey, J.	*Radiocarbon*, 5 (1963), 105.
14	Neo. pot., Weybridge, Surrey	Gardner, E.	*Antiq. J.*, V (1925), 431.
15	Neo. pot., Iver, Bucks.	Lacaille, A. D.	*Rec. Buckinghamshire*, XIII (1934–40), 287, pl. I: V.
16	Neo. pot., Stanton Harcourt, Oxon.	Leeds, E. T.	*Oxoniensia*, V (1940), 6–9, pl. II: C.
17	Neo. pot., Heathrow, Middx.	Grimes, W. F.	*Excavations on Defence Sites*, I (1960), 186–197, fig. 77.
18	Neo. pot., Peterborough, Northants.	Leeds, E. T.	*Antiq. J.*, II (1922), 220–236, figs. 8b, 9 and 12.
19	Neo. pot., Astrop, Northants.	Leeds, E. T.	*Oxford Archaeol. Soc. Report* (1912), 114–118, fig. II: 1–4, 6–7.
20	Neo. pot., Icklingham, Suffolk	Piggott, S.	*Archaeol. J.*, LXXXVIII (1931), 124–126, fig. 17: 5–7.
21	Neo. pot., Cam, Gloucs.	Smith, I. F. Roe, F. E. S. Westley, B.	*Trans. Bristol Gloucestershire Archaeol. Soc.*, LXXXVII (1968), 14–28, fig. 2: 1.
22	Neo. pot., Avebury, Wilts.	Smith, I. F.	*Windmill Hill and Avebury:* Excavations by Alexander Keiller, 1925–1939 (1965), fig. 79: 356.
23	Neo. pot., West Kennet, Wilts.	Piggott, S.	*The West Kennet Long Barrow:* Excavations 1955–56 (1962), 38.
24	Beaker pot	Clarke, D. L.	*Beaker Pottery of Great Britain and Ireland*, Vol. I (1970), 132–133.
25	Beaker pot., Jaywick, Essex	Smith, I. F.	*University of London Institute of Archaeology, Eleventh Annual Report* (1955), 30–32, fig. 1 and fig. 2: 1.
26	Radiocarbon dating	Barker, H. Mackey, J.	*Radiocarbon*, 10, Part 1 (1968), 3.
27	Beaker pot.	Clarke, D. L.	*Beaker Pottery of Great Britain and Ireland*, Vol. I (1970), 157.
28	Beaker pot.	Clarke, D. L.	*Beaker Pottery of Great Britain and Ireland*, Vol. 2 (1970), Appendix 7, Map 4.
29	Neo. pot., Heathrow, Middx.	Grimes, W. F.	*Excavations on Defence Sites*, I (1960), fig. 77: 12.
30	Beaker pot.	Clarke, D. L.	*Beaker Pottery of Great Britain and Ireland* (1970), Vol. 1, 215; Vol. 2, figs. 921, 923.

REF. NO.	SUBJECT	AUTHOR	PUBLICATION
31	Beaker pot., Castleshaw, Yorks.	Clarke, D. L.	*Beaker Pottery of Great Britain and Ireland*, Vol. 2 (1970), fig. 975.
32	Neo. pot., West Kennet, Wilts.	Cunnington, M. E.	*The Pottery from the Long Barrow at West Kennet, Wiltshire* (1927), p. XIII: 113.
33	Neo. pot., Luce Sands, Wigtownshire	McInnes, I. J.	*Proc. Soc. Antiq. Scot.*, XCVII (1963–64), 40–81, fig. 3:93.
34	B.A. pot., Wilsford, Wilts.	Annable, F. K. Simpson, D. D. A.	*Guide Catalogue of the Neolithic and Bronze Age Collections in Devizes Museum* (1964), No. 445.
35	Beaker pot., Stainsby, Lincs.	Clarke, D. L.	*Beaker Pottery of Great Britain and Ireland*, Vol. 1 (1970), 238.
36a	Neo. flint, Hurst Fen, Suffolk	Clark, J. G. D. Higgs, E. S. Longworth, I. H.	*Proc. Prehist. Soc.*, XXVI (1960), 202.
36b	Neo. flint, Durrington Walls, Wilts.	Wainwright, G. J. Longworth, I. H.	*Durrington Walls: Excavations 1966–68* (1971), 164.
37	Neo. flint, Arreton Down, Isle of Wight	Ozanne, P. C. Ozanne, A.	*Proc. Prehist. Soc.*, XXVI (1960), 263.
38	Neo. flint, West Kennet, Wilts.	Piggott, S.	*West Kennet Long Barrow, Excavations 1955–6* (1962), 46.
39	Neo. stone, Winterbourne Stoke, Wilts.	Annable, F. K. Simpson, D. D. A.	*Guide Catalogue of the Neolithic and Bronze Age Collections in Devizes Museum* (1964), 88, Nos. 54 and 55.
40	Discovery, Mill Hill Site	Woods, E. S.	*Arch. Cant.*, LX (1947), 122.
41	Mesolithic Tool, Surrey	Rankine, W. F.	*A Mesolithic Survey of the West Surrey Greensand* (after 1949), 21, fig. 8: 2.
42	Discovery, Hayes Common Site	Warman, E.	*K.A.R.*, No. 3 (1966), 49.
43	Permission for work	Minutes	*Bromley Borough Council, Minutes* (1959–60), 563.
44	Bronze Age Pits, Itford Hill, Sussex	Burstow, G. P. Holleyman, G. A.	*Proc. Prehist. Soc.*, XXIII (1957), 167.
45	Hut Circles, Hayes	Clinch, G.	*Antiquarian Jottings* (1889), 125.
46	Linear and Defensive Earthworks, Hayes	Hogg, A. H. A. O'Neil, B. H. St. J. Stevens, C. E.	*Arch. Cant.*, LIV (1941), 29.
47	Earthwork, Keston	O'Neil, B. H. St. J.	*Arch. Cant.*, XLV (1933), 124.
48	I.A. Hillfort, Keston	Fox, N. P.	*Arch. Cant.*, LXXXIV (1969), 185.
49	'Pit Dwellings', Hayes	Petrie, W. M.	*Arch. Cant.*, XIII (1880), 13.
50	Neo. 'Village', Hayes	Clinch, G.	*V.C.H. Kent*, I (1908), 315.
51	Excavation of 'Hut', Hayes	Fox, E. V.	*Arch. Cant.*, LXIV (1951), xlii.
52	Military camps, Sussex	Margary, I. D.	*Sussex Archaeol. Collect.*, 107 (1969), 135.
53	Excavation of field-bank, Hayes	Philp, B. J.	*Arch. Cant.*, LXXI (1957), 233.
54	Defensive earthwork, Hayes	Camden, W.	*Britannia* (1610), 326 (also *V.C.H. Kent* I (1908), 403).
55	Hayes Court, Hayes	Thompson, H. P.	*A History of Hayes* (1935), 54.
56	Hayes boundaries		*Hayes, Documents No. 40 and 41* (Bromley Central Library).
57	Land enclosure	Mingay, G. E.	*Enclosure and the Small Farmer in the Age of the Industrial Revolution* (1968), 18.
58	Neo. flint and pot.	Smith, I. F.	*Windmill Hill and Avebury; Excavations by Alexander Keiller, 1925–1939* (1965).
59	Neo. flint	Clark, J. G. D. Higgs, E. S. Longworth, I. H.	*Proc. Prehist. Soc.*, XXVI (1960), 202–245.
60	Neo. flint	Movius, H. L. *et al.*	*American School of Prehistoric Research, Harvard Bulletin No. 26* (1968).
61	Neo. flint	Semenov.	*Prehistoric Technology* (1964).

REF. NO.	SUBJECT	AUTHOR	PUBLICATION
62	Neo. flint	Alexander, J. Ozanne, P. C. Ozanne, A.	*Proc. Prehist. Soc.*, XXVI (1960), 263–302.
63	Neo. flint	Wilson, K. E. Longworth, I. H. Wainwright, G. J.	*Brit. Mus. Quart.*, XXXV, Nos. 1–4 (1971), 117–124.
64	Flints	Clark, J. G. D.	*Antiq. J.*, XIII (1933), 266–296.
65	Arrowheads	Clark, J. G. D.	*Archaeol. J.*, XCI (1934), 32–58.
66	Flint, etc. Itford Hill, Sussex	Burstow, G. P. Holleyman, G. A.	*Proc. Prehist. Soc.*, XXIII (1957), 167–212.
67	Flint, etc. Shearplace Hill, Dorset	Rhatz, P. Apsimon, A.	*Proc. Prehist. Soc.*, XXVIII (1962), 289–328.
68	Loom-weights, Park Brow, Sussex	Wolseley, G. R. Smith, R. A. Hawley, W.	*Archaeologia*, LXXVI (1927), 4–5 and fig. D.
69	Loom-weights, Staple Howe, Yorks.	Brewster, T. C. M.	*The Excavation of Staple Howe* (1963), 128–130, fig. 73.
70	Querns, Winnall, Hants.	Hawkes, S. C.	*Proc. Hampshire Fld. Club Archaeol. Soc.*, XXVI (1969), 6
71	Querns, Green Lane, Farnham, Surrey	Lowther, A. W. G.	*A Survey of the Prehistory of the Farnham District* (1939), 170.
72	Arrowheads, Whitehawk, Sussex	Curwen, E.	*Sussex Archaeol. Collect.*, LXXVII (1936), 60–92.
73	Pot., Hawk's Hill, Surrey	Hastings, F. A. Cunliffe, B.	*Surrey Archaeol. Collect.*, LXII (1965), 31.
74	Patch Grove pot., Ightham	Perkins, J. B. Ward	*Arch. Cant.*, LI (1939), 179.
75	Patch Grove pot., Fawkham	Philp, B. J.	*Arch. Cant.*, LXXVIII (1963), 64.
76	Patch Grove pot., Lullingstone	Birchenough, E. Greenfield, E. Meates, G. W.	*Arch. Cant.*, LXIII (1950), 14.
77	Patch Grove pot.	Perkins, J. B. Ward	*Archaeologia*, XC (1944), 150.
78	Patch Grove pot., Joyden's Wood	Tester, P. J.	*Arch. Cant.*, LXVIII (1954), 174.
79	Patch Grove pot., Otford	Young, A.	*K.A.R.*, No. 6 (1966), 13.
80	Patch Grove pot., Keston	Philp, B. J.	*Curr. Archaeol.*, No. 14 (1969), 73.
81	Rom. pot., Colchester, Essex	Hawkes, C. F. C. Hull, M. R.	*Camulodunum* (1947), 206.
82	Native wares, Fawkham	Philp, B. J.	*Arch. Cant.*, LXXVIII (1963), 64.
83	Mortarium stamp, Colchester, Essex	Hartley, K. F. Richards, E. E.	*Trans. Essex Archaeol. Soc.* (3rd Series), Vol. I, part 1, 16, No. 7.
84	Mortarium fabric	Hartley, K. F. Richards, E. E.	*Bulletin of the Institute of Archaeology*, No. 5 (1965), 41, No. 223.
85	Rom. rings, London	Wheeler, R. E. M.	*London in Roman Times* (1930), 100 and fig. 30, No. 16.
86	Rom. rings, Colchester, Essex	Marshall, F. H.	*Catalogue of the Finger Rings, Greek, Etruscan and Roman in the British Museum* (1907), No. 1460.
87	Rom. rings, Great Casterton, Rutland	Todd, M.	*The Roman Fort at Great Casterton, Rutland* (1968), 53, No. 18 and pl. iv.
88	Rom. rings, Nymegen, Netherlands	Henkel, F.	*Die Römischen Fingerringe der Rheinlande* (1913), No. 1461.
89	Roman Intaglio		*Oxford Classical Dictionary* (1970), Second Edition, 751.
90	Roman Intaglio	Boardman, J.	*Greek Gems and Finger-Rings* (1971), 295 and pl. 635; 300 and pl. 766.
91	Roman Intaglio	Vollenweider, M. L.	*Die Steinschneidekunst und Ihre Künstler in Spatrepublikanischer und Augusteischer Zeit* (1966), 42 and pl. 32, 3–5.

REF. NO.	SUBJECT	AUTHOR	PUBLICATION
92	Roman Intaglio	Walters, H.	*Catalogue of Engraved Gems, Greek, Etruscan and Roman in the British Museum* (1926), No. 1046, pl. xv and Nos. 3009, 3167 and 3168, pl. xxxi.
93	Roman Intaglio	Sena Chiesa, G.	*Gemme del Museo Nazionale di Aquileia* (1966), Nos. 487–90.
94	Roman Intaglio	Zwierleindiehl, E.	*Antike Gemmen in Deutschen Sammlungen*, ii, Staatliche Museen Preussisher Kulturbesitz Antikenabteilung, Berlin (1969), No. 473.
95	Roman Intaglio	Furtwängler, A.	*Beschreibung der Geschnittenen Steinne im Antiquarium* (1896), No. 3087, 3089–91 and 4212–27.
96	Roman Intaglio	Henkel, F.	*Beschreibung der Geschnittenen Steinne im Antiquarium* (1896), No. 1612, pl. lxxviii, 345.
97	Roman Intaglio	Henig, M.	*Britannia*, I (1970), 249.
98	Rom. 'pin-ups', Nymegen, Netherlands	Maaskant-Kleibrink, M.	*A Glass Gem from the Castra at Nymegen, Bulletin van de Vereeniging tot Bevordering der Kennis van de Antieke Beschaving te 'S-Gravenhage*, XLIII (1968), 70.
99	Bead rim pot. W. Kent, E. Surrey	Philp, B. J.	*Arch. Cant.*, LXXVIII (1963), 64.
100	Bead rim pot.	Hawkes, C. Dunning, G. C.	*Archaeol. J.*, Vol. LXXXVII (1930), 283.
101	Bead rim pot., West Kent	Perkins, J. B. Ward	*Archaeologia*, Vol. XC (1944), 150.
102	Bead rim pot., Joyden's Wood	Tester, P. J. Caiger, J. E. L.	*Arch. Cant.*, LXVIII (1954), 174.
103	Shouldered jar, Highgate Wood, Highgate	Brown, A. E. Sheldon, H. L.	*London Archaeol.*, 1, No. 7 (1970), 150.
104	Shouldered jar, Colchester, Essex	Hull, M. R.	*Roman Colchester* (1958), 127, fig. 56, No. 53.
105	Native imitation, Colchester, Essex	Hull, M. R.	*Roman Colchester* (1958), 126, fig. 55, No. 28.
106	R.B. pot., Brixworth, Northants.	Woods, P. J.	*Brixworth Excavations* (1971), 10, fig. 8, No. 12.
107	R.B. pot., Canterbury	Frere, S.	*Arch. Cant.*, LXVIII (1954), 121, fig. 11, No. 96.
108	R.B. pot., N. Britain	Gillam, J. P.	*Types of Roman Coarse Pottery Vessels in Northern Britain* (1970), Forms 214–215.
109	R.B. pot., Leicester	Kenyon, K. M.	*Jewry Wall Site, Leicester* (1948), 155, fig. 42, Nos. 1–5.
110	R.B. pot., Highgate Wood, Highgate	Brown, A. E. Sheldon, H. L.	*London Archaeol.*, 1, No. 7 (1970), 153, fig. 1, Nos. 11–16.
111	R.B. pot., Colchester, Essex	Hawkes, C. F. C. Hull, M. R.	*Camulodunum* (1947), 262, Form 225.
112	R.B. pot., Canterbury	Williams, A.	*Arch. Cant.*, LX (1947), 81, fig. 6, No. 3.
113	R.B. pot., Richborough	Cunliffe, B. W.	*Excavations of the Roman Fort at Richborough, Kent*, V (1968), 119, No. 535.
114	R.B. pot., Colchester, Essex	Hull, M. R.	*Roman Colchester* (1958), 281, fig. 118, No. 155.
115	R.B. pot., Leicester	Kenyon, K. M.	*Jewry Wall Site, Leicester* (1948), 110, fig. 28, No. 3.
116	R.B. pot., Brixworth, Northants.	Wood, P. J.	*Brixworth Excavations* (1971), 30, fig. 31, No. 230.
117	Discovery 1889, N. Pole Lane, West Wickham	Taylor, M. V. Jessup, R. F. Hawkes, C. F. C.	*V.C.H. Kent*, III (1932), 174.
118	Rom. farmsteads, W. Kent	Philp, B. J.	*Arch. Cant.*, LXXVIII (1963), 74.
119	Animal bones	Silver, I. A.	*The Ageing of Domestic Animals, in Science in Archaeology* (1963), 250.
120	Loom-weights, Keston	Mynott, E.	*K.A.R.*, No. 30 (1972), 292.
121	Loom-weights, Verulamium	Wheeler, R. E. M. Wheeler, T. V.	*Verulamium* (1936), 178
122	Native imitation, Colchester, Essex	Hawkes, C. F. C. Hull, M. R.	*Camulodunum* (1947), 229, Form 68.

REF. NO.	SUBJECT	AUTHOR	PUBLICATION
123	Bel. pot., Eastwood, Fawkham	Philp, B. J.	*Arch. Cant.*, LXXVIII (1963), 68, No. 18.
124	Bel. pot., Verulamium	Wheeler, R. E. M. Wheeler, T. V.	*Verulamium* (1936), 165, Nos. 46a and 51.
125	Bel. pot., Colchester, Essex	Hawkes, C. F. C. Hull, M. R.	*Camulodunum* (1947), 261, Form 220A.
126	Bel. pot., Swarling	Bushe-Fox, J. P.	*Excavation of the Late-Celtic Urnfield at Swarling, Kent* (1925), 13, No. 23.
127	Bel. pot., Verulamium	Wheeler, R. E. M. Wheeler, T. V.	*Verulamium* (1936), 160, No. 32.
128	Bel. pot., Colchester, Essex	Hawkes, C. F. C. Hull, M. R.	*Camulodunum* (1947), 269, Form 259.
129	Bel. pot., Verulamium	Wheeler, R. E. M. Wheeler, T. V.	*Verulamium* (1936), 165, No. 52.
130	Bel. pot., Canterbury	Frere, S. S.	*Arch. Cant.*, LXVIII (1954), 107, No. 14.
131	I.A. pot., Hawk's Hill, Surrey	Cunliffe, B.	*Surrey Archaeol. Col.*, LXII (1965), 22, No. 15.
132	I.A. pot., Colchester, Essex	Hawkes, C. F. C. Hull, M. R.	*Camulodunum* (1947), 267, Form 252.
133	I.A. pot., Colchester, Essex	Hawkes, C. F. C. Hull, M. R.	*Camulodunum* (1947), 238, Form 113.
134	Bel. pot., Colchester, Essex	Hawkes, C. F. C. Hull, M. R.	*Camulodunum* (1947), 261, Form 221.
135	Bel. pot., Verulamium	Wheeler, R. E. M. Wheeler, T. V.	*Verulamium* (1936), 169, Form 610 D–F.
136	Bel. pot., Canterbury	Frere, S. S.	*Arch. Cant.*, LXVIII (1954), 107, No. 10.
137	Highgate Hill, Highgate	Brown, A. E. Sheldon, H. L.	*London Archaeol.*, I, No. 7 (1970), 150.
138	Rom. road	Margary, I. D.	*Roman Ways in the Weald* (1965), 132.
139	Rom. roads	Margary, I. D.	*Roman Roads in Britain* (1967), 22.
140	R.B. quernstones, Eastwood, Fawkham	Philp, B. J.	*Arch. Cant.*, LXXVIII (1963), 72.
141	R.B. farmsteads, W. Kent	Philp, B. J.	*Arch. Cant.*, LXXVIII (1963), 74.
142	Bel. pot., Eastwood, Fawkham	Philp, B. J.	*Arch. Cant.*, LXXVIII (1963), 69, Nos. 20–21.
143	Bel. pot., Richborough	Bushe-Fox, J. P.	*Excavations of the Roman Fort at Richborough, Kent*, III (1932), 170, No. 226.
144	I.A. pot., Maiden Castle, Dorset	Wheeler, R. E. M. Wheeler, T. V.	*Maiden Castle, Dorset* (1943), 219, No. 97 and 224, No. 138.
145	Bel. pot., Verulamium	Wheeler, R. E. M. Wheeler, T. V.	*Verulamium* (1936), 166, Nos. 61–62.
146	Rediscovery, Baston Manor, Hayes	Warman, E.	*K.A.R.*, No. 2 (Reprint 1970), 19.
147	Discovery, Baston Manor, Hayes	Corner, G. R.	*Archaeologia*, XXXVI (1855), 124.
148	Bath building, Boughton Monchelsea	Taylor, M. V.	*V.C.H. Kent* III (1932), 105.
149	Bath building, North Cray	Parsons, J. A.	*J. Roman Stud.*, XLVII (1957), 223.
150	Bath building, Plaxtol	Luard, M.	*Arch. Cant.*, II (1859), 1.
151	Bath building, Little Chart	Eames, J.	*Arch. Cant.*, LXXI (1957), 130.
152	W. Kent survey	Philp, B. J.	*Arch. Cant.*, LXXVIII (1963), 74.
153	Mortarium fabric	Hartley, K. F. Richards, E. E.	*Bulletin of the Institute of Archaeology*, 5 (1965), 39–43.
154	Mortarium stamp	Frere, S. S.	*Verulamium Excavations*, I (1972), 371.
155	Quernstones, Eastwood, Fawkham	Philp, B. J.	*Arch. Cant.*, LXXVIII (1963), 72.
156	Bronze nail-cleaner	Hickson, M.	*K.A.R.*, No. 32 (1973), 43.
157	Rom. pot., Stoneyfield, Farnham, Surrey	Lowther, A. W. G.	*A Survey of the Prehistory of the Farnham District* (1939), 246, fig. 103, Nos. 74–76.

REF. NO.	SUBJECT	AUTHOR	PUBLICATION
158	Rom. pot., Eastwood, Fawkham	Philp, B. J.	*Arch. Cant.*, LXXVIII (1963), 67, fig. 5, Nos. 13, 14.
159	Samian form Curle 11	Oswald, F. Pryce, T. D.	*An Introduction to the Study of Terra Sigillata* (1920), 211.
160	Rom. pot., Highgate	Brown, A. E. Sheldon, H. L.	*London Archaeol.*, I (1970), No. 7. 153.
161	Rom. pot., Greenhithe	Detsicas, A. P.	*Arch. Cant.*, LXXXI (1966), 167, fig. 11, No. 147 and fig. 1, No. 2.
162	Rom. pot., Brixworth	Woods, P. J.	*Brixworth Excavations* (1971), 65.
163	Rom. pot., Colchester, Essex	Hull, M. R.	*Roman Colchester* (1958), 127, fig. 56, No. 46.
164	Rom. farmsteads, W. Kent	Philp, B. J.	*Arch. Cant.*, LXXVIII (1963), 74.
165	Bel. pot., Verulamium	Wheeler, R. E. M. Wheeler, T. V.	*Verulamium* (1936), 161, Nos. 35 and 38.
166	Bel. pot., Colchester, Essex	Hawkes, C. F. C. Hull, M. R.	*Camulodunum* (1947), 259, Form 212 A.
167	Bel. pot., Swarling	Bushe-Fox, J. P.	*Excavation of the Late-Celtic Urnfield at Swarling, Kent* (1925), 14, No. 32.
168	Bel. pot., Colchester, Essex	Hawkes, C. F. C. Hull, M. R.	*Camulodunum* (1947), 264, form 235.
169	Rom. pot., Colchester, Essex	Hull, M. R.	*Roman Colchester* (1958), 282, form 123.
170	Rom. pot., Eastwood, Fawkham	Philp, B. J.	*Arch. Cant.*, LXXVIII (1963), 69.
171	Rom. pot., Colchester, Essex	Hawkes, C. F. C. Hull, M. R.	*Camulodunum* (1947), 244, Form 140.
172	Rom. pot., Jewry Wall, Leicester	Kenyon, K. M.	*Excavations at the Jewry Wall Site, Leicester* (1948), 83, Nos. 21–23.
173	Rom. pot., Reculver	Philp, B. J.	*Arch. Cant.*, LXXIII (1959), 113, No. 5.
174	Rom. pot., Farnham, Surrey	Lowther, A. W. G.	*A Survey of the Prehistory of the Farnham District* (1939), 242, Nos. 71, 74, 76.
175	Rom. pot., Reculver	Philp, B. J.	*Arch. Cant.*, LXXIII (1959), 111, No. 3 and notes.
176	Rom. pot., Faversham	Philp, B. J.	*Excavations at Faversham 1965* (1968), 83, Nos. 261–267.
177	Funeral pyres	Toynbee, J. M. C.	*Death and Burial in the Roman World* (1971), 49.
178	Roman road	Margary, I. D.	*Roman Ways in the Weald* (1965), 133.
179	North Downs Ridgeway	Margary, I. D.	*Roman Ways in the Weald* (1965), 259.
180	1st cent. pot., Colchester, Essex	Hawkes, C. F. C. Hull, M. R.	*Camulodunum* (1947), 168–286.
181	2nd cent. pot., Leicester	Kenyon, K. M.	*Excavations at the Jewry Wall Site, Leicester* (1948), 106, fig. 27, Nos. 52–3.
182	2nd cent. pot., Leicester	Kenyon, K. M.	*Excavations at the Jewry Wall Site, Leicester* (1948), 82, fig. 19, No. 20.
183	2nd cent. pot., Reculver	Philp, B. J.	*Arch. Cant.*, LXXIII (1959), 111.
184	2nd cent. pot., Faversham	Philp, B. J.	*Excavations at Faversham, 1965* (1968), 83, fig. 26, Nos. 261–267.
185	2nd cent. pot., N. Britain	Gillam, J. P.	*Types of Roman Coarse Pottery Vessels in Northern Britain* (1970), 1–72.
186	1st cent. pot., Fawkham	Philp, B. J.	*Arch. Cant.*, LXXVIII (1963), 66, No. 7.
187	1st cent. pot., Charlton	Elliston-Erwood, F. C.	*J. Brit. Archaeol. Ass.*, XXII (1916), 125–91.
188	1st cent. pot., Hawk's Hill	Cunliffe, B.	*Surrey Archaeol. Col.*, LXII (1965), 24, Pit 7, No. 1, etc.
189	1st and 2nd cent. pot., Leicester	Kenyon, K. M.	*Excavations at the Jewry Wall Site, Leicester* (1948), 87, fig. 21, No. 6.
190	1st cent. pot., Maiden Castle, Dorset	Wheeler, R. E. M.	*Maiden Castle Dorset* (1943), 234, fig. 73, No. 199.
191	1st cent. pot., Canterbury	Frere, S. S.	*Arch. Cant.*, LXVIII (1954), 107, fig. 4, Nos. 10, 11 and 16.

REF. NO.	SUBJECT	AUTHOR	PUBLICATION
192	1st cent. pot., Wheathampstead	Wheeler, R. E. M. Wheeler, T. V.	*Verulamium* (1936), pl. XLIX, No. 2.
193	Farmstead, Eastwood	Philp, B. J.	*Arch. Cant.*, LXXVIII (1963), 55.
194	Chalkwells	Caiger, J. E. L.	*Arch. Cant.*, LXXIV (1960), 81.
195	Shaft, Keston	Fox, N. P.	*Arch. Cant.*, LXXXII (1967), 184.
196	Shaft, Lullingstone	Meates, G. W.	*Arch. Cant.*, LXXIX (1964), lviii.
197	Cellar, Burham	Payne, G.	*Proc. Soc. Ant.*, XVI (1897), 105.
198	Cellar, Chalk	Allen, A.	*Arch. Cant.*, LXVI (1961), lxix.
199	Cellar, Faversham	Philp, B. J.	*Excavations at Faversham 1965* (1968), 69.
200	Cellar, Lullingstone	Meates, G. W. Greenfield, E. Birchenough, E.	*Arch. Cant.*, LXV (1952), 28.
201	Cellar, Whitstable	Jenkins, F.	*J. Roman Stud.*, 52 (1962), 190.
202	Chalk-blocks, Lullingstone	Greenfield, E. Meates, G. W. Birchenough, E.	*Arch. Cant.*, LXV (1952), 29.
203	Chalk-blocks, Springhead	Penn, W. S.	*Arch. Cant.*, LXXX (1965), 107.
204	Chalk-blocks, Dover	Philp, B. J.	*K.A.R.*, No. 23 (1971), 81.
205	Belgic shafts	Pliny	*Lib.*, XVII (8).
206	Rom. cemeteries	Philp, B. J.	*Arch. Cant.*, LXXVIII (1963), 74.
207	Rom. branch road	Philp, B. J.	*K.A.R.*, No. 24 (1971), 113.
208	Land mollusca	Stratton, L. W.	*'ournal of Conchology* (1954), Vol. 23, 405–412.
209	Land mollusca	Boycott, A. E.	*Journal of Ecology* (1934), Vol. 22, 1–38.
210	Native flagons	Hawkes, C. F. C. Hull, M. R.	*Camulodunum* (1947), 241.
211	Storage jar, Charlton	Elliston-Erwood, F. C.	*J. Brit. Archaeol. Ass.*, XXII and XXIX; and *Arch. Cant.*, LXIV, (1951), 158.
212	Rom. building, Franks Hall	Ritson, J. V.	*Arch. Cant.*, LXXVIII (1963), lv.
213	Rom. building, Oliver Crescent	Priest, S.	*Trans. of the Dartford District Antiquarian Society*, No. 1 (Dec. 1931), 67.
214	Rom. building, Farningham Wood	Smith, R. C.	*Gent. Mag. Lib.*, I, Part I (1887), 146.
215	Rom. brooches, Colchester, Essex	Hawkes, C. F. C. Hull, M. R.	*Camulodunum* (1947), 312, Type VII.
216	Rom. brooches, Maiden Castle	Wheeler, R. E. M.	*Maiden Castle, Dorset* (1943), 251.
217	Rom. brooches, Colchester, Essex	Hawkes, C. F. C. Hull, M. R.	*Camulodunum* (1947), 310, Type IV.
218	Rom. brooches, Richborough	Bushe-Fox, J. P.	*Excavation of the Roman Fort at Richborough*, I (1926), 43.
219	R.B. site, Fawkham	Philp, B. J.	*Arch. Cant.*, LXXVIII (1963), 55.
220	Bel. pot., Canterbury	Frere, S. S.	*Arch. Cant.*, LXVIII (1954), 107, No. 18.
221	Bel. pot., Faversham	Philp, B. J.	*Excavations at Faversham, 1965* (1968), Nos. 216 and 231.
222	R.B. pot., Leicester	Kenyon, K. M.	*Excavations at the Jewry Wall Site, Leicester* (1948), fig. 36, Nos. 28–29.
223	Patch Grove pot., Ightham	Perkins, J. B. W.	*Arch. Cant.*, LI (1939), 179, fig. 17, Nos. 1–4.
224	Potin coin, Sutton-at-Hone	Allen, D. F.	*K.A.R.*, No. 22 (1970), 58.
225	Excavation 1894–5	Payne, G.	*Arch. Cant.*, XXII (1897), 49.
226	Protection of field monuments	H.M.S.O.	*Enquiry into the Arrangements for the Protection of Field Monuments 1966–68* (1969) (Chairman—Sir David Walsh).
227	Excavation 1969	Philp, B. J.	*K.A.R.*, No. 18 (1969), 18 and No. 19 (1970), 16.
228	Rescue-excavations, Faversham	Philp, B. J.	*Excavations at Faversham 1965* (1968), 64.

REF. NO.	SUBJECT	AUTHOR	PUBLICATIONS
229	Bath building, North Cray	Parsons, J.	*J. Roman Stud.*, XLVII (1957), 223.
230	Corn-drying ovens, Hambleden, Bucks.	Gowland, W. G.	*Archaeologia.*, LXXI (1921), 158.
231	Corn-drying ovens, Atworth, Wilts.	Goodchild, R. G.	*Antiq. J.*, XXIII (1943), 148.
232	Corn-drying ovens, Great Casterton, Rutland	Corder, P.	*The Roman Town and Villa at Great Casterton, Rutland* (1950–8), 22.
233	External wall-plaster, Eccles	Detsicas, A. P.	*Arch. Cant.*, LXXXIII (1968), 45.
234	Rom. villas	Richmond, I. A.	*Roman Britain* (1963), 109.
235	Rom. agriculture	Rivet, A. L. F.	*The Roman Villa in Britain* (1969), 173.
236	Rom. aisled villas	Smith, J. T.	*Archaeol. J.*, CXX (1963), 1.
237	Rom. villa, Norton Disney, Lincs.	Oswald, A.	*Antiq. J.*, XVII (1937), 138–78.
238	Rom. villa, Mansfield Woodhouse, Notts.	Rooke, H.	*Archaeologia*, VIII (1787), 367.
239	Rom. villa, Clanville, Hants.	Haverfield, F.	*V.C.H. (Hants)*, I (1900), 296.
240	Rom. villa, Brading, I.O.W.	Price, J. E. Price, F. G. H.	*Remains of Roman Morton, near Brading* (1881).
241	Central entrance, aisled villas	Richmond, I. A.	*The Roman Villa in Britain* (1969), 65.
242	Rom. villa, Stroud, Hants.	Williams, A. M.	*Archaeol. J.*, LXVI (1909), 33.
243	Rom. villa, North Wanborough, Hants.	Collingwood, R. G. Taylor, M. V.	*J. Roman Stud.*, XXI (1931), 242.
244	Rom. villa, Llantwit Major, Glam.	Nash-Williams, V. E.	*Archaeol. Cambrensis*, CII (1953), 89–163.
245	Rom. villa, Great Casterton, Rutland	Corder, P.	*The Roman Town and Villa at Great Casterton* (1951–1961).
246	Rom. villa, Ickleton, Cambs.	Neville, R. C.	*Archaeol. J.*, VI (1849), 17.
247	Social implications	Collingwood, R. G. Richmond, I. A.	*The Archaeology of Roman Britain* (1969), 147.
248	Rom. tile, Plaxtol	Luard, M.	*Arch. Cant.*, II (1859), 4, pl. VI.
249	Rom. tile, Plaxtol	Haverfield, F.	*Proc. Soc. Ant.*, XXIII (1910), 108 and *The Romanization of Roman Britain* (1912), 27.
250	Rom. patterned voussoir tiles	Lowther, A. W. G.	*A Study of the Patterns on Roman Flue-tiles and their Distribution* (about 1950), 12, group 4, No. 10.
251	Mammalian dentition	Silver, I. A.	*Science in Archaeology* (1963), 250.
252	Rom. antler tools	Smith, D. J.	*Archaeol. Aeliana*, XLVI (1968), 281, fig. 4.
253	Rom. antler tools	Bagshawe, T. W.	*Antiq. J.*, XXIX (1949), 86, plate XI.
254	Rom. pot., Reculver	Philp, B. J.	*Arch. Cant.*, LXXIII (1959), 112, fig. 4, No. 3.
255	Rom. pot., Faversham	Philp, B. J.	*Excavations at Faversham 1965* (1968), 83, Nos. 261–267.
256	Rom. pot., N. Britain	Gillam, J. P.	*Types of Roman Coarse Pottery in Northern Britain* (1970).
257	Rom. pot., Brixworth, Northants.	Woods, P. J.	*Brixworth Excavations* (1971), 57, fig. 9, Forms 24–25.
258	Rom. pot., Leicester	Kenyon, K. M.	*Excavations at the Jewry Wall Site, Leicester* (1948), 100, fig. 26, No. 17.
259	Rom. pot., Verulamium	Wheeler, R. E. M. Wheeler, T. V.	*Verulamium* (1936), 185, fig. 28, No. 17.
260	Rom. pot., Colchester, Essex	Hull, M. R.	*The Roman Potters' Kilns of Colchester* (1963), 183, Form 277.
261	Rom. pot., Leicester.	Kenyon, K. M.	*Excavations at the Jewry Wall Site, Leicester* (1948), 82, fig. 19, No. 31.
262	Rom. pot., Brixworth, Northants.	Woods, P. J.	*Brixworth Excavations* (1971), 59, fig. 11, No. 40.
263	Rom. pot., Richborough	Bushe-Fox, J. P.	*Excavations of the Roman Fort at Richborough, Kent*, I (1926), pl. XXVIII, No. 107.
264	Rom. pot., Canterbury	Jenkins, F.	*Arch. Cant.*, LXIII (1950), 95, fig. 6, No. 22.
265	Rom. pot., Richborough	Smith, R. C.	*The Antiquities of Richborough, Reculver and Lympne, in Kent* (1850), Pl. IV.

REF. NO.	SUBJECT	AUTHOR	PUBLICATION
266	Rom. pot., Richborough	Bushe-Fox, J. P.	*Excavations of the Roman Fort at Richborough, Kent*, I, (1926), 102, Type 95
267	Rom. pot., Richborough	Bushe-Fox, J. P.	*Excavations of the Roman Fort at Richborough, Kent*, IV (1949), 270, Types 476–479.
268	Rom.-A.S. pot.	Myres, J. N. L.	*Dark Age Britain* (1956), 27.
269	Rom. pot., Colchester, Essex	Hull, M. R.	*The Roman Potters' Kilns of Colchester* (1963), 128, fig. 71, No. 18.
270	Rom. pot., Leicester	Kenyon, K. M.	*Excavations at the Jewry Wall Site, Leicester* (1948), 90, fig. 22, No. 9.
271	Rom. pot., Richborough	Bushe-Fox, J. P.	*Excavations of the Roman Fort at Richborough, Kent*, II (1928), 103, Nos. 175–178.
272	Med. pot., Pivington	Rigold, S. E.	*Arch. Cant.*, LXXVII (1962), 39, fig. 4, No. IV.
273	Med. pot., Ashford	Grove, L. R. A. Warhurst, A.	*Arch. Cant.*, LXV (1952), 185, fig. 4, No. 8.
274	Post-med. pot., Waltham Abbey, Essex	Huggins, P. J.	*Post-Medieval Archaeol.*, III (1968), 85, fig. 30, No. 8.
275	Rom. villa, Darenth	Payne, G.	*Arch. Cant.*, XXII (1897), 49.
276	1969 Excavation, Darenth	Philp, B. J.	*K.A.R.*, No. 19 (1970), 16.
277	Saxon cemetery, Orpington	Tester, P. J.	*Arch. Cant.*, LXXXIII (1969), 133, Nos. 13 and 14a.
278	Saxon hut, Upton, Northants.	Jackson, D. A. Harding, D. W. Myres, J. N. L.	*Antiq. J.*, XLIX (1969), 210.
279	Saxon hut, Essex	Jones, M. U.	*Medieval Archaeol.*, XIII (1969), 231.
280	Saxon finds, Darenth	Philp, B. J.	*K.A.R.*, No. 32 (1973), 47.
281	Saxon finds, Dartford	Tester, P. J.	*Arch. Cant.*, LXX (1956), 259, fig. 3.
282	Roman Cemetery, Keston	Philp, B. J.	*K.A.R.*, No. 11 (1968), 10.
283	Discovery	Philp, B. J.	*K.A.R.*, No. 25 (1971), 131.
284	Grubenhäuser in Britain	Leeds, E. T.	*Early Anglo-Saxon Art and Archaeology* (1936), 21.
285	Saxon huts, Mucking, Essex	Jones, M. U.	*Antiq. J.*, XLVIII (1968), 210.
286	Saxon huts, Sutton Courtenay, Berks.	Leeds, E. T.	*Archaeologia*, XCII (1947), 79.
287	Saxon huts, West Stowe, Suffolk	West, S. E.	*Medieval Archaeol.*, XII (1968), 161.
288	Saxon huts, Canterbury	Frere, S. S.	*The Civitas Capitals of Roman Britain* (1966), 91.
289	Saxon weaving loom, Sutton Courtenay, Berks.	Leeds, E. T.	*Archaeologia*, LXXVI (1926), 75.
290	Saxon huts, Bishopstone, Sussex	Armstrong, J. R.	*Weald and Downland Open Air Museum* (1971), 26.
291	Saxon lead-weight	Jones, M. U.	*Antiq. J.*, XLVIII (1968), 210.
292	Saxon lead-weight	Wheeler, R. E. M.	*London Museum Catalogue, No. 6* (1935), 136.
293	Saxon huts, Canterbury	Hawkes, S. C.	*Archaeol. J.*, CXXVI (1969), 187.
294	Germanic mercenaries, Richborough	Hawkes, S. C. Dunning, G. C.	*Medieval Archaeol.*, V (1961), 17.
295	Saxon occupation, Dorchester, Oxon.	Leeds, E. T. Kirk, J. R.	*Oxoniensia*, XVII–XVIII (1952–3), 69.
296	Saxon occupation, Winchester, Hants.	Clarke, G.	*Antiq. J.*, L (1970), 292.
297	Saxon occupation, Shakenoak, Oxon.	Broadribb, A. C. C. Hands, A. R. Walker, D. R.	*Excavations at Shakenoak Farm, nr. Wilcote, Oxon.*, III (1972), 74.
298	Saxon cemetery, Orpington	Tester, P. J.	*Arch. Cant.*, LXXXIII (1968), 149.
299	Saxon cemeteries, Kent	Leeds, E. T.	*The Archaeology of the Anglo-Saxon Settlements* (1913), 100.
300	Battle of Crayford		*The Anglo-Saxon Chronicle*, A.D. 457.
301	Saxons, Wingham villa	Jenkins, F.	*Arch. Cant.*, LXXII (1967), lx.
302	Saxons, Porchester, Hants.	Cunliffe, B.	*Antiq. J.*, LII (1972), 70.

REF. NO.	SUBJECT	AUTHOR	PUBLICATION
303	Saxon pot., Lackford, Suffolk	Myres, J. N. L.	*Anglo-Saxon Pottery and the Settlement of England* (1969).
304	Saxon pot., Mucking, Essex	Jones, M. U.	*Saxon Pottery from a Hut at Mucking, Essex.* (Berichten van de Rijksdienst voor het Oudheidkundig Bodemonderzoek (1969), 145.)
305	Saxon needle, Dartford	Tester, P. J.	*Arch. Cant.*, LXX (1956), 259, fig. 3.
306	Saxon needle, Darenth	Philp, B. J.	*K.A.R.*, No. 32 (1973).
307	Saxon needle, Leicester	Kenyon, K. M.	*Excavations at the Jewry Wall Site, Leicester* (1948), 266, No. 8.
308	Saxon comb, Colchester, Essex	Hull, M. R.	*Roman Colchester* (1958), 79, fig. 35, No. 2.
309	Saxon comb, Richborough	Bushe-Fox, J. P.	*Excavations of the Roman Fort at Richborough, Kent*, II (1928), 47, No. 43.
310	Saxon comb, Richborough	Bushe-Fox, J. P.	*Excavations of the Roman Fort at Richborough, Kent*, IV (1949), 150, No. 265.
311	Rom. fitting, Richborough	Bushe-Fox, J. P.	*Excavations of the Roman Fort at Richborough, Kent*, IV (1949), 145, No. 192.
312	Saxon tweezers, Orpington	Tester, P. J.	*Arch. Cant.*, LXXXIII (1968), 140, No. 29c.
313	Saxon tweezers, Winterbourne Gunner, Wilts.	Musty, J. Statton, J. E. D.	*Wilts. Arch. Mag.*, LIX (1964), 90, fig. 5, No. C3 and V6.
314	Saxon tweezers, Petersfinger, Wilts.	Leeds, M. A. Shortt, H. de S.	*An Anglo-Saxon Cemetery at Petersfinger, near Salisbury, Wilts.* (1953), pl. VIII—3, 68, 78.
315	Saxon tweezers, Sarre	Payne, G.	*Catalogue of the K.A.S. Collections at Maidstone* (1892), 24, No. 397.
316	Saxon tweezers, Barrington, Cambs.	Smith, R. C.	*Collectanea Antiqua*, VI, Parts I and II (1868), 161 and pl. XXXIV, No. 5.
317	1839 road	Dunlop, J.	*The Pleasant Town of Sevenoaks* (1964), 154.
318	Oral tradition	Ward, G.	*Sevenoaks Essays* (1931), 97.
319	Battle A.D. 776		*Anglo-Saxon Chronicle.*
320	Excavation 1956	Blumstein, M.	*Arch. Cant.*, LXX (1956), 278.
321	Excavation 1956–8	Stoyel, A. D.	*Arch. Cant.*, LXXIII (1959), 225.
322	Excavation 1964	Philp, B. J.	*K.A.R.*, No. 1 (1965), 2.
323	Excavation 1967	Philp, B. J.	*K.A.R.*, No. 9 (1967), 2; No. 10 (1967), 2.
324	A.S. cemetery, Holborough	Evison, V. I.	*Arch. Cant.*, LXX (1956), 84.
325	Barrow, Laverstock, Wilts.	Musty, J.	*Archaeol. J.*, XLIX (1969), 98.
326	Memorial posts	Hawkes, S. C.	*Medieval Archaeol.*, Vol. X (1966), 171.
327	A.S. barrows, Barham Down	Jessup, R.	*Arch. Cant.*, LVI (1943), 69.
328	A.S. barrows, Finglesham	Stebbing, W. P. D.	*Arch. Cant.*, XLI (1929), 115–25.
329	A.S. barrows, Chartham Down	Smith, R. A.	*V.C.H., Kent*, Vol. I (1908), 369–70.
330	A.S. cemetery, Winnall, Hants.	Meaney, A. L. Hawkes, S. C.	*Two Anglo-Saxon Cemeteries at Winnall* (1970), 20.
331	Expectation of life	H.M.S.O.	*Statistical Review of England and Wales for 1970*, 10, table B2.
332	Skeletal material, Polhill	Miles, A. E. W.	*Proc. of the Roy. Soc. of Medicine*, Vol. 62 (December 1969), 1311
333	Longevity		*A Study of the Life Table* (1949).
334	A.S. hut, Bishopstone, Sussex	Thompson, D.	*Medieval Archaeol.*, XII (1967), 161.
335	A.S. cemeteries in Kent	Meaney, A.	*Gazetteer of Anglo-Saxon Burial Sites* (1964), 108 42.
336	A.S. cemetery, Horton Kirby	Priest, S.	*Trans. of the Dartford District Archaeol. Soc.*, Vol. VIII (1938), 14.
337	A.S. cemetery, Orpington	Tester, P. J.	*Arch. Cant.*, LXXXIV (1969), 39.
338	R.B. farmstead, Otford	Pyke, J.	*K.A.R.*, No. 18 (1969), 27.

REF. NO.	SUBJECT	AUTHOR	PUBLICATION
339	Place-name, Otford	Wallenberg, J. K.	*The Place-names of Kent* (1934), 58.
340	History of Otford	Clarke, R. D.	*An Outline History of Otford*, 1967.
341	A.S. cemetery, Kingston	Smith, R. A.	*V.C.H. Kent*, Vol. I (1908), 345–48.
342	A.S. cemetery, Bifrons	Godfrey-Fausett, T. G.	*Arch. Cant.*, XIII (1880), 552.
343	A.S. cemetery, Stowting	Smith, R. A.	*V.C.H. Kent*, Vol. I (1908), 365–67.
344	A.S. cemeteries, Leighton Buzzard, Beds.	Hyslop, M.	*Archaeol. J.*, CXX (1963), 161.
345	Excavations, Elstow Abbey, Beds.	Baker, D.	*Bedfordshire Archaeol. J.*, IV (1969), 27.
346	Burial ground, Eynsford	Harker, S.	*K.A.R.*, No. 26 (1971–2), 163.
347	Merovingian culture	Steuer, H.	*Nachrichten aus Niedersachsens Urgeschichte*, XXXVII (1968), 18.
348	Merovingian culture	Werner, J.	*Settimane di Studio del Centro Italiano di Studi sull'alto Medioevo*, XV (1968), 95.
349	A.S. cemetery, Horndean, Hants.	Knocker, G. M.	*Proc. Hampshire Fld. Club*, XIX (1958), 117.
350	A.S. cemetery, Finglesham	Chadwick, S.	*Medieval Archaeol.*, II (1958), 1.
351	A.S. grave, Strood	Smith, R. C.	*Collectanea Antiqua*, V (1861), 129, pl. xi.
352	Sugar-loaf shield-bosses	Evison, V. I.	*Antiq. J.*, XLIII (1963), 38.
353	A.S. cemeteries, Kent	Faussett, B.	*Inventorium Sepulchrale* (ed. C. Roach Smith) (1856).
354	A.S. cemetery, Broadstairs	Hurd, H.	*Some Notes on Recent Archaeological Discoveries at Broadstairs* (1913).
355	Sceattas	Rigold, S. E.	*Brit. Numis. J.*, XXX (1960), 6.
356	A.S. cemetery, Shudy Camps, Cambs.	Lethbridge, T. C.	*Cambridge Antiq. Soc.*, n.s. V, 1936.
357	A.S. burial, Compton, Hants.	Andrew, W. J. Smith, R. A.	*Antiq. J.*, XI (1931), 5, fig. 2.
358	A.S. burials, Northolt Manor, Middx.	Evison, V. I.	*Medieval Archaeol.*, V (1961), 226.
359	Frankish graves	Böhner, K.	*Die Fränkischen Altertümer des Trierer Landes* (Germanische Denkmäler der Völkerwanderungszeit, Serie B, Band 1) (1958).
360	Sword-rings and beads	Evison, V. I.	*Archaeologia*, CI (1967), 63.
361	A.S. cemeteries, Kent	Faussett, B.	The 6-volume 18th cent. original of *Inventorium Sepulchrale* in Liverpool City Museum.
362	Cemetery, Switzerland	Werner, J.	*Das Almannische Gräberfeld von Bülach* (Monographien zur Ur- und Frühgeschichte der Schweiz, Band IX), (1953).
363	Saxon weapons		*Soc. Antiqs.*, London, MS. 723; Fol. 26.
364	Saxon weapons		*Ashmolean Museum* (1836), 123, 59.
365	Barrow, Laverstock, Wilts.	Musty, J. Evison, V. I.	*Antiq. J.*, XLIX (1969), 98.
366	Cemetery, Germany	Neuffer Müller, C.	*Ein Reihengräberfeld in Sontheim an der Brenz*, **Kr.** Heidenheim (Veröffentlichungen des Staatl. Amtes für Denkmalpflege Stuttgart. Reihe A, Vor- und Frühgeschichte, Heft 11) (1966).
367	A.S. cemeteries, North Oxon.	Leeds, E. T.	*Oxoniensia*, V (1940), 21.
368	A.S. cemetery, Dunstable, Beds.	Matthews, C. L. Morris, J. Brothwell, D. R.	*Bedfordshire Archaeol. J.*, I (1962), 25.
369	Polychrome jewellery, Kent	Kendrick, T. D.	*Antiquity*, VII (1933), 429.
370	A.S. in England	Åberg, N.	*The Anglo-Saxons in England* (1926).
371	A.S. art and archaeology	Leeds, E. T.	*Early Anglo-Saxon Art and Archaeology* (1936).
372	A.S. brooch, Guston	King, C. W.	*Archaeol. J.*, XXI (1864), 101.
373	Rom. brooch	Hawkes, C. F. C. Hull, M. R.	*Camulodunum* (1947), 310, pl. xci, Nos. 36–46.

REF. NO.	SUBJECT	AUTHOR	PUBLICATION
374	A.S. cemeteries, Cambs. and Suffolk	Lethbridge, T. C.	*Recent Excavations in Anglo-Saxon Cemeteries in Cambridgeshire and Suffolk* (Cambridge Antiq. Soc., 4to publ., n.s. III) (1931).
375	X-ray of coins and jewellery	Hawkes, S. C. Merrick, J. M. Metcalf, D. M.	*Archaeometry*, IX (1966), 98.
376	7th cent. beads, Denmark	Becker, C. J.	*Acta Archaeologica*, XXIV (1953), 127.
377	7th cent. beads, Sarre	Smith, R.	*A Guide to the Anglo-Saxon and Foreign Teutonic Antiquities* (British Museum) (1923).
378	7th cent. jewellery and beads	Rigold, S. E. Webster, L. E.	*Arch. Cant.*, LXXXV (1970), 1.
379	8th cent. beads	Wegewitz, W.	*Reihengräberfriedhöfe und Funde aus spätsächsischer Zeit im Kreis Harburg* (Göttinger Schriften zur Vor- und Frühgeschichte, Band 10) (1968).
380	I.A. antiquities	Smith, R.	*A Guide to the Antiquities of the Early Iron Age* (British Museum) (1925).
381	I.A. hoard, Stanwick, N.R. Yorks	Macgregor, M.	*Proc. Prehist. Soc.* XXVIII (1962), 17.
382	A.S. belt-sets, Bifrons	Godfrey-Fausett, T. G.	*Arch. Cant.*, X (1876), 315.
383	Sutton Hoo ship burial	Bruce-Mitford, R. L. S.	*The Sutton Hoo Ship Burial:* a Provisional Guide (British Museum) (1947).
384	Sutton Hoo ship burial	Bruce-Mitford, R. L. S.	*The Sutton Hoo Ship Burial:* a Handbook (British Museum) (1968).
385	Shoe-fittings	Fingerlin, G.	*Grab einer adlingen Frau aus Güttingen, Ldkrs. Konstanz* (Badische Fundber. Sonderheft 4) (1964).
386	Shoe-fittings	Koch, U.	*Die Grabfunde der Merowinger zeit aus dem Donautal um Regensburg* (Germanische Denkmäler der Völkerwanderungszeit, Serie A, Band X) (1968)
387	A.S. strap-tag, Shakenoak	Hawkes, S. C.	*Excavations at Shakenoak III* (1972), 69.
388	The Finglesham Man	Hawkes, S. C. Davidson, H. R. E. Hawkes, C.	*Antiquity*, XXXIX (1965), 17.
389	Sceattas	Rigold, S. E.	*Brit. Numis. J.*, XXXV (1966), 1.
390	Purse-fittings	Stein, F.	*Adelsgräber des achten Jahrhunderts in Deutschland* (Germanische Denkmäler der Völkerwanderungszeit, Serie A. Band IX) (1967).
391	A.S. thread-boxes	Ozanne, A.	*Medieval Archaeol.*, VI–VII (1962–3), 15.
392	A.S. thread-boxes	Ørsnes-Christensen, M.	*Acta Archaeologica*, XXVI (1955), 69.
393	A.S. amulet-capsules	Werner, J.	*Das Alamannische Fürstengrab von Wittislingen* (Münchner Beiträge zur Vor- und Frühgeschichte, Band 2) (1950), 46.
394	Thread-box	Cochet, Abbé	*La Normandie Souterraine* (1855).
395	Thread-box	Pasqui, P.	*Monumenti Antichi*, XXV (1919), 286, fig. 151.
396	Thread-box	Paribeni, R.	*Revue Charlemagne*, I (1911), pl. 25, 1.
397	Thread-box	Besson, M.	*L'Art Barbare dans l'ancien Diocèse de Lausanne* (1909), 187, fig. 129.
398	A.S. graves	Mortimer, J. R.	*Forty Years' Researches in the British and Saxon Burial Mounds of East Yorkshire* (1905).
399	Merovingian coins	Kent, J. P. C.	*Cunobelin* (Yearbook British Assoc. Numis. Soc.) (1967).
400	Grave goods, Barton-on-Humber, Lincs.	Capelle, T. Vierck, H.	*Frühmittelalterliche Studien*, V (1971), 42.
401	A.S. Southampton, Hants.	Addyman, P. V. Hill, D. H.	*Proc. Hampshire Fld. Club*, XXVI (1969), 61.
402	A.S. to Med. finds, York	Waterman, D. M.	*Archaeologia*, XCVII (1959), 59.
403	A.S. burials, Standlake Down, Oxon.	Dickinson, T. M.	*Oxoniensia*, forthcoming.

REFERENCES

REF. NO.	SUBJECT	AUTHOR	PUBLICATION
404	Knives and pottery	Schmid, P.	*Neue Ausgrabungen und Forschungen in Niedersachsen*, V (1970), 40.
405	A.S. pottery	Dunning, G. C.	*Medieval Archaeol.*, III (1959), 31.
406	A.S. jewellery	Cumberland, A.	*Arch. Cant.*, LIII (1940), 142, pl. I.
407	Merovingian coins	Kent, J. P. C.	*Royal Numismatic Soc. Special Publ. No. 8* (1972), 69.
408	Iron forge-welding	Tylecote, R. F.	*Metallurgy in Archaeology* (1962).
409	6th cent. braids	Dedckam, H.	*Tekstilfund fra Folkevandringstiden, Bergens Museums Aarbok* (1924–25), fig. 21.
410	Med. pot., Pivington	Rigold, S. E.	*Arch. Cant.*, LXXVII (1962), 40.
411	Domesday name		*V.C.H. Surrey, Vol. I* (1902), 315.
412	Med. pot., Canterbury	Frere, S. S.	*Arch. Cant.*, LXVIII (1954), 132.
413	Med. pot., Canterbury	Frere, S. S. Williams, A.	*Arch. Cant.*, LXI (1948), 41.
414	Limpsfield ware	Turner, D. J.	*Surrey Archaeol. Col.*, LXVII (1970), 50.
415	Med. pot., Faversham	Philp, B. J.	*Excavations at Faversham 1965* (1968), 54, Nos. 111–112.
416	Med. pot., Pivington	Rigold, S. E.	*Arch. Cant.*, LXXVII (1962), 39.
417	Survey of Chapel Wood	Keen, J. A.	*Arch. Cant.*, LXXXII (1967), 285.
418	Discovery of Hypocaust	Taylor, M. V. Collingwood, R. G.	*J. Roman Stud.*, XVI (1926), 237.
419	Discovery of Hypocaust	Druce, G. C.	*Arch. Cant.*, XXXIX (1927), xlix.
420	Discovery of Hypocaust	Taylor, M. V. Jessup, R. F. Hawkes, C. F. C.	*V.C.H. Kent, Vol. III* (1932), 117.
421	Discovery of Hypocaust	Bancks, G. W.	*Hartley Through the Ages* (1927), 20.
422	Tile-kiln	Jessup, R. F.	*Arch. Cant.*, LIII (1940), 142.
423	Rom. site	B.M.C.	*County Road Map and Gazetteer, No. 11*, Kent, 32.
424	Med. tile-kiln, Coventry, Warks.	Chatwin, P. B.	*Birmingham Archaeol. Soc. Trans.* LX (1936), 2.
425	Med. tile-kiln, Beverley, Yorks.	Eames, E.	*Med. Archaeol.*, V (1961), 137.
426	Med. tile-kiln, Tyler Hill	Philp, B. J.	*K.A.R.*, No. 10 (1967), 15.
427	Med. tile-kilns, Canterbury	Cramp, G.	*K.A.R.*, No. 19 (1970), 26 and No. 21 (1970), 11.
428	Nibbed tiles, Boston, Lincs.	Mayes, P.	*J. Brit. Archaeol. Ass.*, XXVIII (1965), 86.
429	Chapel Wood	Thorpe, J.	*Costumale Roffense* (1778), 64.
430	Scotsgrove	Hasted, E.	*History and Topographical Survey of the County of Kent*, Vol. 1 (1778), 284.
431	Recording work	Philp, B. J.	*K.A.R.*, No. 8 (1967), 12.
432	History of the house	Clinch, G.	*Antiquarian Jottings* (1889), 90.
433	History of the house	Norman, P.	*Arch. Cant.*, XXIV (1900), 139
434	History of the house	Horsburgh, E. L. S.	*Bromley, Kent* (1929), 283 and 427.
435	A.S. art and archæology	Baldwin Brown, G.	*The Arts in Early England* (1915).
436	A.S. thread-boxes, Uncleby, Yorks.	Smith, R.	*Proc. Soc. Antiq.*, XXIV (1912), 146.
437	A.S. thread-boxes, Yorks.	Smith, R.	*V.C.H. Yorkshire, Vol. II* (1912), 96.
438	A.S. thread-boxes, Barton, Lincs.	Sheppard, T.	*Hull Museum Publ. No. 208* (1940), pp. 258 ff, 46 ff.
439	A.S. thread-box, Hurdlow, Derbys.	Bateman, T.	*Ten Years Diggings in the Celtic and Saxon Grave-Hills* (1861), 52 ff.
440	A..S. thread-box, Standlow.	Bateman, T.	*Vestiges of the Antiquities of Derbyshire* (1848), 74 ff.
441	A.S. thread-box, Cransley, Northants.	Smith, R.	*V.C.H. Northants., Vol. I* (1902), 240.
442	A.S. thread-box, Bidford-on-Avon, Warwicks.	Humphreys, J., et al.	*Archaeologia*, LXXIII (1923), 101, fig. 5.
443	A.S. thread-boxes, Kempston, Beds.	Fitch, E.	*Assoc. Archit. Soc. Repts. and Papers*, VII (1864), pp. 289, 291 f., pl. v, 3.
444	A.S. thread-boxes, St. Albans, Herts.	Stead, I.	*Antiquity*, XLIII (1969), 47.
445	A.S. thread-box, Standlake, Oxon.	Leeds, E. T.	*V.C.H. Oxfordshire, Vol. I* (1939), 362.

INDEX